# Democratizing Education With AI and the Future of Personalized Learning

Raed Awashreh
*United Arab Emirates University, UAE*

IGI Global
Scientific Publishing
Publishing Tomorrow's Research Today

Vice President of Editorial Melissa Wagner
Director of Acquisitions Mikaela Felty
Director of Book Development Jocelynn Hessler
Production Manager Mike Brehm
Cover Design Jose Rosado

Published in the United States of America by
IGI Global Scientific Publishing
701 East Chocolate Avenue
Hershey, PA, 17033, USA
Tel: 717-533-8845
Fax: 717-533-7115
Website: https://www.igi-global.com E-mail: cust@igi-global.com



Library of Congress Cataloging-in-Publication Data

Names: Awashreh, Raed, editor.
Title: Democratizing education with AI and the future of personalized learning / Raed Awashreh [editor].
Other titles: Democratizing education with artificial intelligence and the future of personalized learning
Description: Hershey, PA : IGI Global Scientific Publishing, [2027] | Includes bibliographic references and index. | Summary: Democratizing education with AI and the future of personalized learning explores the transformative potential of AI in revolutionizing education. It examines how AI can make learning more accessible, equitable, and tailored to individual needs, breaking down traditional barriers such as geography, socioeconomic status, and resource limitations. This book covers topics such as inclusive learning, smart libraries, and digital technology, and is a useful resource for educators, policymakers, engineers, academicians, researchers, and scientists.
Identifiers: LCCN 2025023242 (print) | ISBN 9798337323039 paperback | ISBN 9798337323022 hardcover
Subjects: LCSH: Artificial intelligence--Educational applications. | Individualized instruction. | Inclusive education. | Educational change.
Classification: LCC LB1028.43 .D46 2026 (print) | LCC LB1028.43 (ebook) | DDC 371.334--dc23
LC record available at https://lccn.loc.gov/2025023242
LC ebook record available at https://lccn.loc.gov/2025023243

British Cataloguing in Publication Data
A Cataloguing in Publication record for this book is available from the British Library.

# Table of Contents

# Detailed Table of Contents

Artificial Intelligence (AI) holds transformative potential to address long-standing educational inequities by enabling personalized, accessible, and inclusive learning experiences. This chapter explores how AI can shift education systems from exclusion to inclusion, particularly benefiting learners from marginalized backgrounds, including those with disabilities, rural populations, and linguistic minorities. Drawing on global case studies—from India's DIKSHA platform and mobile learning in Sub-Saharan Africa to AI-driven STEM initiatives in Latin America and mental health support in higher education—the chapter highlights both innovations and implementation challenges. It emphasizes the need for ethical, equitable, and interdisciplinary approaches to AI design, aligning with global frameworks such as SDG 4. By balancing innovation with fairness and accessibility, and embedding inclusive practices into policy and pedagogy, AI can contribute significantly to building future-ready, inclusive education systems where no learner is left behind.



This chapter assesses the wave of transformation that generative artificial intelligence (GenAI) can bring for personalised Islamic religious education (IRE). It elaborates on how AI-generated content can make a difference and help create spiritually tailored learning experiences based on individual needs and goals. Historical practices are compared with modern educational theories to see the uptake of GenAI in different fields related to IRE (e.g., Quranic recitation and Hadith retrieval). The major benefits of AI are thoroughly described, including increased learner motivation, engagement, and educator support, alongside the ethical, pedagogical, and infrastructural challenges for IRE contexts. The chapter concludes with practical recommendations for implementation and strategic planning while discussing future trends and research directions. The chapter places generative AI in the context of moulding Islamic learning, sensitivity, and responsibility to culture and Islamic theology.

with students recognizing its value in academic performance. Nonetheless, concerns over usability, complexity, and ethical implications persisted. Similarly, AI acceptance levels were moderate, with students acknowledging its value as a helpful tool instead of a substitute for traditional methods. Critical thinking and over-reliance concerns influenced students' hesitations in fully embracing AI in their learning processes. Statistical analysis revealed that while most demographic characteristics, such as age, sex, year level, and AI permissions, had no significant correlation with knowledge, attitudes, or acceptance, some variables did show significant relationships. In testing the relationship, using Pearson's Chi-square and Cramer's V statistical tests, the students' major in the program and their level of AI knowledge were found to have a strong relationship. Additionally, years of experience with using AI and both attitude and acceptance of AI among business management students were found to have a strong relationship. Furthermore, the average daily duration of AI usage and acceptance indicated a strong relationship. The findings of the study highlight the key influential factors in AI readiness in education, emphasizing the role of specialization/program, experience, and average duration of AI usage in shaping students' knowledge, attitudes, and acceptance of AI technologies. This underscores the need for targeted AI integration in business curricula through embedded AI literacy modules, clear academic guidelines, and consistent exposure via specialized AI training for both faculty and students, as well as the adoption of diverse research methods to deepen understanding and increase AI acceptance. At the policy level, addressing infrastructure and access disparities will help ensure equitable digital readiness and support the creation of ethical AI strategies in Philippine higher education.

**Chapter 6**
Integration of the Rosetta Stone AI-Powered Platform as a Learning Management System (LMS) for Language Learning in Moroccan Higher Education ........................................................................................ 171
*Mouad Malmous, Faculty of Letters and Human Sciences Ben M'sik, Morocco*
*Said Zaidoune, Faculty of Letters and Human Sciences Ben M'sik, Morocco*
*El Mehdi El Hamydy, Faculty of Education Rabat, Morocco*

Grounded in the Unified Theory of Acceptance and Use of Technology 2 (UTAUT2), this chapter investigates Moroccan university students' perceptions and attitudes toward the Rosetta Stone platform based on data collected from 1,262 participants. It also investigates the main predictors of the use and acceptance of the Rosetta Stone platform by shedding light on practical implications for policymakers and university educators to optimize the integration of Rosetta Stone within Moroccan higher education. Using Partial Least Squares Structural Equation Modeling (PLS-SEM), the findings revealed that Hedonic Motivation and Habit emerged to have

risks that encourage the ethical use of AI foster the so-called human component-led growth in system design.



As artificial intelligence (AI) systems become increasingly embedded within the education sector, there is growing concern about the issue of AI bias and its far-reaching implications for fairness, equity, and student outcomes. AI applications such as adaptive learning platforms, automated grading systems, student performance prediction models, and admissions algorithms are designed to enhance efficiency, personalize instruction, and support data-driven decision-making. However, these systems are only as unbiased as the data they are trained on and the assumptions embedded in their algorithms. If not carefully designed and audited, AI technologies can perpetuate, or even exacerbate, existing inequalities related to race, gender, socioeconomic status, language proficiency, and ability. This makes the conversation around AI bias in education not just a technical issue but a deeply ethical and social one. Bias can also be introduced during the design and implementation stages of AI development.



AI in education is often opposed due to historical skepticism, institutional inertia, cultural conservatism, and concerns about professional identity and autonomy. This opposition varies by educational context and stakeholder, hindering the deployment of AI. Collaboration with schools, intensive professional development to improve AI literacy, and clear ethical frameworks that prioritize openness, equity, and inclusivity are needed to overcome these challenges. Rethinking competition as human-AI collaboration can turn resistance into proactive involvement and innovation. This analysis reveals the complexity of resistance and offers practical suggestions, based on global case studies, for overcoming traditional barriers to AI integration. To enhance teaching and learning, AI should be utilized responsibly, sustainably, and equitably in education.



This research paper focused on how knowledge, attitudes, and acceptance of Artificial Intelligence (AI) interrelate among business management students. Spearman Rank Correlation analysis revealed that students' knowledge of AI and attitudes toward it had weak yet statistically significant positive relationship, which means that gaining knowledge contributed to more positive attitudes toward AI. Knowledge and acceptance of AI lacked a weak statistically significant correlation, which means that merely knowing AI does not lay a good foundation for acceptance. On the other hand, attitudes toward AI have been found to have highly positive significant correlation with acceptance, stating that the students' attitudes are important in the process of acceptance. Further, the results support the Technology Acceptance Model (TAM) by asserting that positive attitudes towards AI may be fostered through ethical considerations surrounding AI, awareness-building on AI, and responsible AI use in educational settings. The study recommends that AI be part of the curriculum, that ethical discussions take place, and that increased knowledge and acceptance among students may occur through positive attitudes. Results from this study have practical implications in that educational institutions must engage in imparting technical knowledge concerning AI, while at the same time correcting its perception by means of value instructions, ethical considerations, and exposure to actual applications. Addressing the cognitive and affective domains through this perspective schools

# Preface

## INTRODUCTION

The rapid evolution of artificial intelligence (AI) has ushered in a transformative era for education, challenging long-standing paradigms and opening unprecedented possibilities for personalized, accessible, and inclusive learning. In *Democratizing Education with AI and the Future of Personalized Learning*, we examine how AI technologies are reshaping the educational landscape—breaking traditional boundaries and making learning more learner-centered, adaptive, and responsive to individual needs.

This volume emerges at a pivotal moment when AI is no longer a distant future in education but a present force with vast potential—and significant responsibility. The central question is no longer whether AI will change education, but how we can integrate it responsibly, equitably, and ethically to meet the diverse needs of learners across geographies, cultures, and contexts.

The chapters within this book reflect a rich spectrum of perspectives—from theoretical frameworks to practical implementations—highlighting how AI can serve as both a powerful tool and a potential disruptor. We present case studies and evidence-based approaches that showcase AI's capacity to enhance engagement, personalize instruction, bridge learning gaps, and support inclusive educational practices. At the same time, we address the ethical concerns, challenges of implementation, risks of algorithmic bias, and the digital divide that threaten to widen educational inequities if not carefully managed.

Our aim with this edited volume is to contribute meaningfully to the global conversation around AI in education by offering a balanced and forward-looking resource. We delve into the practical realities of deploying AI in diverse learning environments, while also emphasizing the importance of cultivating digital literacy, responsible AI usage, and inclusive design principles in both policy and practice.

This book is intended for a broad and multidisciplinary audience:

1. Educators and administrators seeking to integrate AI into pedagogical practices and institutional systems to enhance personalized learning.
2. Researchers and academics at the intersection of education, technology, and AI who are exploring new directions and empirical approaches.
3. Policymakers working to ensure equitable access to education through inclusive technology-driven policies.
4. EdTech professionals building AI-powered educational tools and platforms that are scalable, adaptive, and ethical.
5. Learners and lifelong learners interested in understanding how AI is shaping the future of their educational journeys.

We hope this book offers valuable insights, challenges assumptions, and inspires thoughtful action in the responsible application of AI in education. Together, we must ensure that the future of AI-enhanced learning is one that empowers all learners—regardless of background or circumstance—and truly democratizes education for a better, more equitable world.

## ORGANIZATION OF THE BOOK

### Chapter 1: AI-Driven Inclusive Learning for Rural India – A Framework for Equity, Access, and Digital Literacy

Focusing on one of the world's most populous and diverse education systems, this chapter presents the RAI (Rural AI for Inclusion) Framework as a scalable, culturally-responsive model for integrating AI into rural Indian education. Drawing from research in Karnataka, the study evaluates the effectiveness of low-cost AI tools tailored for vernacular accessibility and teacher empowerment. The chapter details both the successes—such as improved student engagement—and the systemic barriers, including infrastructure gaps and ethical dilemmas. Through a participatory and inclusive pedagogy, the authors offer actionable policy recommendations for bringing AI to underserved communities, with an emphasis on contextual adaptability and equity.

## Chapter 2: From Exclusion to Inclusion – AI as a Catalyst for Equal Access to Education

This chapter explores how AI can act as a transformative force in correcting educational imbalances. Through case studies spanning India, Sub-Saharan Africa, Latin America, and higher education mental health support systems, the authors examine AI's role in reaching marginalized learners, including those with disabilities and linguistic or geographic barriers. While showcasing the innovations AI can bring, the chapter is equally attentive to the implementation challenges. By aligning AI initiatives with the UN Sustainable Development Goal 4 (quality education for all), the authors propose a model of ethically-driven, inclusive AI design. The chapter offers a global roadmap for leveraging AI to ensure no learner is left behind.

## Chapter 3: Generative AI and the Future of Personalized Islamic Religious Learning – An Overview

In this chapter, the authors explore the intersection of generative AI and Islamic Religious Education (IRE), charting new territory in culturally and spiritually tailored learning experiences. The chapter examines how GenAI tools can support Quranic learning, Hadith exploration, and spiritual development through adaptive, personalized pathways. Comparing traditional religious instruction with AI-enabled frameworks, the authors delve into both the pedagogical promise and the cultural sensitivity required. Practical strategies and ethical considerations are discussed alongside future research directions, making this a pioneering contribution to faith-based AI learning environments that honor theological integrity and learner diversity.

## Chapter 4: Beyond Boundaries – AI-Powered Personalized Learning in the Educational Metaverse for Global Equity

This visionary chapter investigates the convergence of AI and the metaverse in crafting immersive, personalized educational experiences aimed at global equity. Through international case studies and theoretical insights, the authors present a comprehensive framework based on cultural intelligence, ethical design, and infrastructural scalability. The metaverse is positioned not just as a technological novelty but as a transformative learning environment where personalization and inclusion can thrive. However, the chapter also addresses pressing challenges such as access, scalability, and design ethics. By focusing on learner agency and contextual relevance, the authors chart a thoughtful course for equitable education in digitally immersive futures.

## Chapter 5: Artificial Intelligence (AI) Readiness of Business Management Students at a State University – The Role of Demographic Characteristics

Continuing the focus on higher education learners, this chapter investigates the AI readiness of business management students through the lens of demographic influences. Utilizing a mixed-methods approach, the study highlights a moderate understanding of AI among students, particularly in basic tools like grammar checkers and content generators. Although students hold generally positive views on AI's academic potential, concerns persist regarding its complexity and ethical implications. These insights offer critical guidance for tailoring AI education strategies to diverse student populations, ensuring broader adoption and preparedness.

## Chapter 6: Integration of the Rosetta Stone AI-Powered Platform as a Learning Management System (LMS) for Language Learning in Moroccan Higher Education

Focusing on a real-world case study, this chapter examines the adoption of the Rosetta Stone LMS in Moroccan higher education. Grounded in the UTAUT2 model and analyzed using advanced statistical methods, the study identifies key behavioral predictors such as hedonic motivation and habitual use as central to student acceptance. Surprisingly, demographic variables such as age and gender played minimal roles. The findings offer valuable insights for educational institutions and policymakers aiming to implement AI-powered platforms in a way that aligns with students' digital behavior and expectations.

## Chapter 7: Democratizing Personalized Learning Through Mentorship Reform in Private Higher Education

This chapter explores how AI can reshape mentorship structures in higher education, particularly within private institutions. By automating logistical tasks and identifying affective dynamics through sentiment analysis, AI holds the potential to improve mentorship quality, reduce power imbalances, and promote inclusivity. However, the authors also address concerns such as ethical oversight, algorithmic transparency, and institutional reluctance. The chapter calls for culturally sensitive, phased implementations, supported by continuous evaluation and stakeholder engagement. It positions mentorship as a key site of transformation for personalized learning and equity in higher education, facilitated responsibly through AI.

## Chapter 8: Challenges of Integrating AI in Education

In this critical chapter, the authors confront the sociological and ethical disruptions that accompany AI's rise in education. Despite AI's potential to transform learning systems, its misuse, embedded biases, and risks to competency development pose serious concerns. The chapter makes a compelling case for human-centric AI design, policy interventions, and a renewed focus on ethics to ensure AI does not undermine the integrity of education. It calls on stakeholders to act with foresight, building frameworks that protect learners while fostering innovation.

## Chapter 9: Risks of AI Bias and Inequities in Learning

As AI technologies are increasingly embedded in educational systems, this chapter confronts the urgent issue of algorithmic bias and its effects on equity. The authors unpack how AI applications—such as grading systems, predictive analytics, and adaptive learning platforms—can unintentionally reproduce or amplify societal inequities when built on biased data or flawed design assumptions. The chapter offers a nuanced view of AI not as a neutral tool but as a reflection of human values and choices, stressing the need for auditing mechanisms, transparent algorithms, and inclusive development processes. It positions bias as not merely a technical flaw but a social and ethical challenge that demands proactive intervention.

## Chapter 10: Navigating Resistance – Overcoming Traditional Barriers to AI in Education

This chapter takes a critical look at the cultural, institutional, and psychological barriers that inhibit the adoption of AI in education. Drawing on global case studies, the authors illustrate how resistance to AI arises not only from fear of change but also from concerns about professional autonomy and historical skepticism. The chapter advocates for intensive professional development, collaborative partnerships with schools, and the establishment of ethical AI frameworks as essential tools for turning resistance into proactive innovation. By reconceptualizing AI not as a competitor but as a collaborative tool, the chapter outlines a strategic path for more inclusive, responsible, and sustainable AI integration.

### Chapter 11: Understanding Artificial Intelligence in Higher Education – The Interplay of Knowledge, Attitudes, and Acceptance Among Business Management Students

This chapter sets the foundation for understanding how students' knowledge, attitudes, and acceptance of artificial intelligence interact in higher education. Drawing on the Technology Acceptance Model (TAM), the authors reveal that while knowledge alone does not guarantee AI acceptance, positive attitudes significantly influence openness to its use. The findings underscore the importance of fostering ethical awareness and favorable dispositions toward AI in academic environments to drive meaningful integration. This research informs both curriculum development and educator training, emphasizing the role of perception in AI readiness.

## CONCLUSION

As we conclude this volume, it is clear that artificial intelligence is not merely a tool of convenience, but a transformative force with the power to reimagine education from the ground up. The chapters in this book reflect the diversity, complexity, and promise of AI in education—from bridging longstanding equity gaps and enabling personalized learning, to confronting ethical dilemmas and structural resistance. We have seen how AI can support teachers, enhance student engagement, enable context-sensitive curriculum design, and even extend education's reach to rural, marginalized, and historically excluded communities.

However, this transformation is neither automatic nor without risk. The journey toward democratizing education through AI demands intentional design, inclusive policies, ethical foresight, and cross-sector collaboration. If left unchecked, AI could reinforce the very inequities it seeks to resolve. But with thoughtful application, grounded in transparency, equity, and cultural relevance, AI can foster a more inclusive, personalized, and globally connected learning ecosystem.

Our hope is that this book serves as both a resource and a call to action—for educators, researchers, policymakers, technologists, and learners alike. The future of education is not only about what technologies we adopt, but how we shape them to serve all learners. As we stand at this critical intersection of innovation and inclusion, we must ensure that AI enhances—not replaces—the human elements that make education transformative: empathy, creativity, ethics, and community.

**Raed Awashreh**
*United Arab Emirates University, UAE*

# Acknowledgment

The editor would like to sincerely thank the reviewers, especially those who took the responsibility upon their shoulders to provide valuable, comprehensive, and detailed feedback on the submitted chapters. Their constructive comments and thoughtful insights are highly appreciated and have been instrumental in improving the quality of the work.

# Introduction

Artificial Intelligence (AI) is revolutionizing education. It is no longer a distant possibility but a present-day catalyst reshaping how knowledge is delivered, how learners engage with content, and how educators design inclusive, responsive, and equitable learning environments. As AI systems increasingly become part of everyday academic life, from adaptive tutoring platforms to intelligent feedback tools and smart libraries, they bring with them both immense promise and pressing challenges. This book, Democratizing Education with AI and the Future of Personalized Learning, aims to critically explore this evolving landscape, with a particular focus on how AI can expand educational access, personalize learning experiences, and transform pedagogical models, especially within under-resourced and contextually unique educational settings such as private higher education institutions in the Global South.

The convergence of AI and education represents a defining moment in the history of learning. With intelligent systems capable of analyzing vast data sets, predicting student needs, and adapting content delivery in real time, AI is creating the conditions for more personalized, student-centered instruction. By aligning learning paths with individual abilities, preferences, and paces, AI can increase engagement and improve outcomes for a broader spectrum of learners. This transformation is particularly relevant in contexts where traditional education systems have struggled to reach marginalized populations due to geographical, socioeconomic, linguistic, or infrastructural limitations.

Yet, the potential of AI in education extends beyond personalization. It offers avenues to democratize access to quality education by supporting inclusive practices for students with disabilities, creating multilingual learning environments, and developing tools that foster digital equity. Smart libraries, equipped with IoT technologies and responsive systems, are becoming key examples of how physical and digital learning environments can merge to enhance student experience, resource access, and collaboration. Similarly, AI-supported learning management systems, immersive technologies like the metaverse, and generative models are redefining what it means to teach, learn, and assess in the 21st century.

This book recognizes that the adoption of AI is not a neutral or universally beneficial process. While some students flourish in tech-augmented learning ecosystems, others may encounter new forms of exclusion or surveillance. Algorithmic bias, opaque decision-making processes, and reliance on predictive analytics pose ethical and epistemological concerns, particularly for historically marginalized groups. The notion of "AI readiness", a composite measure of students' understanding, ethical awareness, and behavioral adoption of AI tools, emerges as a central issue in assessing whether AI promotes meaningful learning or simply facilitates academic shortcuts.

Empirical studies, such as those conducted at Cavite State University, reveal the gap between AI usage and responsible engagement. While many students report high usage of AI tools like ChatGPT, few possess the critical understanding or institutional support to navigate AI use ethically. This raises fundamental questions: How do we ensure that students become informed, ethical users of AI? How can institutions cultivate a culture of AI literacy that goes beyond technical proficiency to include critical thinking, digital responsibility, and academic integrity?

Equally significant is the intersection of AI with culturally embedded pedagogical practices. In Islamic Religious Education (IRE), for example, teaching is traditionally rooted in mentorship, moral guidance, and spiritual formation. Introducing AI into such environments requires careful negotiation—not merely of technical logistics, but of ethical values and epistemic traditions. Can generative AI augment spiritual learning without compromising authenticity? Can it support mentorship without depersonalizing the teacher-learner relationship? This book addresses such questions by advocating for context-aware, critically reflective AI integration that honors the relational dimensions of education.

Moreover, the book engages with critical mentoring theory as a framework for understanding how AI can support, not replace, human mentorship. In private higher education institutions, faculty often carry heavy workloads and lack the infrastructure to provide equitable mentoring. AI can help alleviate administrative burdens and offer data-driven insights into student engagement and learning gaps. But it must do so in service of culturally responsive, student-centered mentorship. AI in this context should be seen not as a panacea, but as a partner in fostering inclusive, intentional, and justice-oriented educational relationships.

The chapters in this edited book span a wide array of interconnected themes, including but not limited to:

- Artificial Intelligence and Digital Technology
- Personalized Learning and Inclusive Education
- Curriculum Development and Educational Policy
- Language Learning and Learning Management Systems (LMS)
- Ethics, Law, and AI Governance

- Higher Education Innovation and the Metaverse

Drawing on interdisciplinary contributions from educators, computer scientists, policy analysts, librarians, theologians, and researchers, this book offers both theoretical frameworks and applied insights. Each chapter contributes to a larger dialogue on how to democratize education through AI—not by assuming that technology alone will solve systemic inequities, but by exploring how AI can be harnessed to advance the goals of inclusion, personalization, and social justice.

In sum, Democratizing Education with AI and the Future of Personalized Learning invites educators, technologists, policymakers, and scholars to move beyond techno-solutionism. It challenges the field to critically engage with AI as a socio-technical phenomenon, one that reflects human values, institutional practices, and historical inequities. As we stand at the intersection of innovation and responsibility, this book asks: What kind of educational futures are we creating? Who benefits from AI-driven learning, and on whose terms? How can we build AI systems that reflect not just what is possible, but what is just, ethical, and transformative?

# Chapter 1
# AI-Driven Inclusive Learning for Rural India: A Framework for Equity, Access, and Digital Literacy

**D. Deepak**
https://orcid.org/0009-0004-8493-1474
*Jain University, India*

**R. Arun**
https://orcid.org/0009-0001-1571-3201
*Jain University, India*

**H. C. Purushotham**
https://orcid.org/0000-0002-2035-2965
*Jain University, India*

**K. Sowmya**
*Aditya College of Engineering and Technology, India*

**Y. Sharath Kumar**
*St. Francis College, India*

**Pavendhan Madhivanan**
https://orcid.org/0000-0001-8183-8793
*Aditya College of Engineering and Technology, India*

## ABSTRACT

*The chapter discusses AI as a transformation agent for inclusive digital education in rural India. While ed-tech has made strides in urban India, India being a developing nation, rural communities are still left isolated with their struggles—lack of infrastructure, low digital literacy, lack of socio-economic opportunities—all leading to accessibility issues in quality education. We propose the RAI (Rural AI for Inclusion) Framework, a contextualised model based on an inclusive pedagogy, participatory approach, and ethical AI implementation. Drawing on mixed-methods research in three districts of Karnataka, the study assesses the deployment of low-cost AI tools implementing surface accessibility in vernacular and support for teachers. Abstract: Findings show benefits regarding student engagement and instructional*

DOI: 10.4018/979-8-3373-2302-2.ch001

*efficiency, as well as barriers related to infrastructure and ethics. The chapter ends with policy recommendations for implementing AI at scale, with equity and cultural responsiveness in regions with service access gaps.*

# INTRODUCTION

## Overview of Digital Learning in India

India's rapid digital transformation in education has opened new avenues for personalised learning, content delivery, and data-driven pedagogy. However, this digital shift has also intensified disparities, especially between urban and rural learners. Despite hosting over 1.5 million schools and 265 million students.No, A. (2023)., rural India faces systemic obstacles to digital participation, including limited device availability, poor internet connectivity, and language mismatches. While national platforms like DIKSHA and SWAYAM have extended digital resources, their reach remains uneven—only 28.2% of rural students had consistent device access, and just 8% engaged regularly with online content as of 2021 ASER. (2021).. Beyond technology, barriers include socio-economic inequities, linguistic diversity, gendered exclusions, and caste disparities. Goyal, J. K., Daipuria, P., & Jain, S. (2021). EdTech solutions are often designed for English-speaking, well-connected users, rendering them ineffective in rural India. Sinha, K. K. (2022). The rural-urban gap in education is not just a digital divide. Instead, it is a multi-faceted problem driven by socio-economic, geographic, and cultural issues. Rural students go to under-performing schools that lack sufficient teaching, have fewer textbooks, and have less access to digital content in India. These challenges are further compounded because of gender discrimination, linguistic diversity, caste-based inequities, and parental illiteracy. Goyal, J. K., Daipuria, P., & Jain, S. (2021). Such factors lead to low secondary education enrolment, high dropout rates, and poor learning outcomes. The new NEP 2020 has acknowledged the importance of inclusive and equitable quality education and highlighted the need to harness technology to bridge the learning gap. That said, tech-based solutions have to be implemented in a rural context. Most of the EdTech solutions that are available for rural learners today are made for learners in urban settings, having the presumption of a static internet connection, English speakers, or uninterrupted electricity, all of which are rarities in the case of rural India. Sinha, K. K. (2022). Consequently, rolling out these solutions without adjustments will only deepen educational inequities. Moreover, the search for good teachers continues. Rural schools are often chronically short of teachers and usually rely on those not highly qualified or well-prepared. Even the pressure of well-meaning digital interventions is ineffective without professional development opportunities. Modi, K.,

Kalra, G. K., Prasad, L., & Udayan, P. (2024). Coping with these realities requires a solution that combines technological innovation and socio-pedagogical adaptation.

## Emergence and Potential of AI in Education

Artificial Intelligence offers adaptive learning, predictive analytics, and language translation Zawacki-Richter, O., Marín, V. I., Bond, M., & Gouverneur, F. (2019).; Chaudhary, D., Dutta, R., & Ghosh, P. (2022, October). However, AI must be context-sensitive to address India's diverse linguistic, infrastructural, and cultural realities (Floridi & Cowls, 2019). The ability of AI to structure adaptive learning, conduct scientific research, automate administrative processes, provide predictive analytics, and improve teacher capabilities and the overall education ecosystem has made it an indispensable part of interdisciplinary education. Predictive modelling based on AI has the potential to address some of the chronic shortcomings in education when implemented through tools such as adaptive learning platforms, intelligent tutoring systems, automated grading, and natural language processing. Zawacki-Richter, O., Marín, V. I., Bond, M., & Gouverneur, F. (2019). AI, therefore, has a special promise in the Indian context to bridge the education divide. AI-driven translation tools can help create learning materials in regional languages, while speech-to-text functions assist those with disabilities or low literacy levels. It also helps in the early detection of at-risk students, which helps in timely intervention using predictive analysis. Teachers can detect how well their students perform with the help of AI dashboards, enabling them to modify the instruction Chaudhary, D., Dutta, R., & Ghosh, P., 2022, October). AI innovation has been restricted to private, urban-focused EdTech platforms and elite institutions. AI tools are poorly designed to address these contextual realities, including the broad range of dialects found in India, cultural variations, and infrastructural constraints, particularly in rural India. Moreover, ethical issues related to data privacy and protection, algorithmic bias and discrimination, and lack of transparency in AI systems represent more challenges (Floridi, L., Cowls, J., & King, T. C., 2021). To realise AI's promise for inclusive education, we must design frameworks that are adaptive to context, that align technology to pedagogy to community needs. These frameworks must also be participatory, ethical, and contextually organised around rural communities' linguistic, cultural, and infrastructural realities.

## Statement of the Problem

Despite extensive investments in digital infrastructure and the proliferation of national EdTech platforms, rural India remains critically underserved regarding equitable access to digital learning opportunities. The promise of universal digital education is undermined by enduring infrastructural deficits, limited digital literacy, and a mismatch between educational technologies and local learner needs. Only 20% of rural households in India have a digitally literate member, and access to consistent, high-quality online content remains elusive. Initiatives such as DIKSHA and SWAYAM, though successful in urban settings, have shown limited reach and impact in rural areas, primarily due to their reliance on English-language content, high-bandwidth formats, and standardised curricula that often fail to reflect regional contexts and learner diversity, ASER. (2021).; Kumar, P., Kumar, P., Garg, R.K., Panwar, M., & Aggarwal, V. (2023). In several cases, the ineffective rollout of context-blind EdTech has exacerbated rather than mitigated educational inequalities, highlighting an urgent need for an inclusive, participatory, and context-sensitive AI framework tailored for rural education systems. (Ng, W. (2012).

## Purpose and Scope of the Chapter

The chapter introduces the RAI (Rural AI for Inclusion) Framework, designed to deliver ethical, inclusive, and context-sensitive AI applications in rural education. It is based on empirical research across three Karnataka districts and integrates inclusive pedagogy, community needs, and ethical considerations.

## Research Questions and Objectives Summary

**Main Research Question:** How can AI be deployed in a participatory and ethical manner to enhance inclusive education in rural India?

Sub-questions:

- What are the infrastructural and pedagogical barriers in rural digital education?
- How do AI tools influence learning outcomes and community engagement?
- What ethical challenges emerge in AI-driven rural education?

## Research Objectives

1. To develop a participatory, contextualised AI framework for rural education.
2. To examine the impact of AI tools on student engagement, teacher support, and community involvement.
3. To identify ethical, infrastructural, and pedagogical barriers in implementation.
4. To generate policy recommendations based on pilot case studies.

## BACKGROUND AND RATIONALE

India's educational ecosystem is enormous, pluralistic, and viciously unbalanced. According to the Ministry of Rural Development (2022), around 65% of the population in India lives in rural areas, mainly with intermittent access to quality education. There are wide variations in learning outcomes and infrastructure across states and districts, notwithstanding policies that support universal primary education. Meanwhile, net school enrolment across rural areas is still above 95%, as reported by the Annual Status of Education Report ASER. (2021), learning levels have plateaued or fallen, especially in foundational literacy and numeracy. Only 20.5 per cent of rural children in Grade 3 could read a Grade 2-level text, and only 25.9 per cent could do simple subtraction. Correspondingly, the UNESCO State of the Education Report for India 2021 reiterates systemic issues in rural education systems, attributed to the unavailability of qualified teachers, inequitable access to ICT, and the absence of inclusive pedagogy. Even as urban and semi-urban schools witnessed a surge in digital tools and blended learning models, the same models have not brought transformation, let alone to the villages. Girls, SC/ST, and CWD encounter systemic socio-economic and cultural barriers to consistent schooling most acutely, according to UNESCO 2021. Many rural regions have schools with no electricity, no clean drinking water, no internet available, and no digital infrastructure or hardware. The share of rural schools with working internet (24%) and access to computers (less than 40%) is scant, according to the Unified District Information System for Education (UDISE+) 2021–22. These constraints render using traditional digital learning platforms almost impossible, deepening the educational chasm.

### Impact of the COVID-19 Pandemic on Rural Learning

The Indian education system was catalysed and disrupted by the COVID-19 pandemic. The education sector transitioned to emergency remote teaching as school closures affected more than 250 million students in the World Bank 2021. Urban students easily adapted to this sudden shift towards digital learning, whereas rural students languished, deprived of proper devices, sturdy internet connectivity, and digital awareness. According to a study by the Azim Premji Foundation 2021, almost all rural students suffered by losing at least one particular language competency (92 per cent), and at least one mathematical competency (82 per cent) following months of extremely protracted school closures. Additionally, only 11 per cent of students from rural households could attend online classes. In contrast, most students had only television or radio, which did not allow them to interact with their teachers or customise their learning (Azim Premji Foundation, 2021. The COVID-19 pandemic exposed weaknesses in rural education infrastructure and highlighted the urgent need to build and scale more robust, inclusive, and flexible learning solutions. This redirection requires not only the provision of technology but also the ability to utilise it purpose-driven, which is a gap that still exists for rural teachers, students, and parents. (Gay, G. (2018).

## Challenges in the Current Digital Learning Landscape

### Infrastructure

Digital access is still the biggest challenge facing effective digital learning in rural India. Though more than 54 per cent of the rural households had at least one smartphone, steady internet facility, electricity supply, and accessibility of a functional learning atmosphere, these remain grossly insufficient. Students often share or borrow devices, so their digital spaces are anything but uninterrupted. In addition, rural schools often do not have the institutional backing and funding needed for technology integration. Without infrastructure that works, the potential use of cutting-edge educational technologies, including AI, becomes a fanciful hope. The provision of EdTech becomes even more challenging as there are differences between state and central government support. Kumar, P., Kumar, P., Garg, R.K., Panwar, M., & Aggarwal, V. (2023).

### Language Barriers

India has more than 22 official languages and hundreds of dialects. More often than not, the mainstream EdTech platforms and AI tools are developed in English/Hindi, and neither caters to rural learners' vernacular diversity. However, the mismatch of languages in education is a significant barrier to understanding, engagement, and retention, especially for young children and first-generation learners. Holmes, W., Bialik, M., & Fadel, C. (2019). There have been initiatives around creating multilingual content — for instance, DIKSHA — but a lot of the content is superficial in depth and engagement. This is where AI provides an honest service: it can provide language translation, voice, and speech-to-text services in real-time, but for building helpful anything, you must deliver technologies that will be developed and trained on local dialect data, of which there is very little. (CAST, C. (2018).

### Teacher Preparedness

One cannot overemphasise the importance of teachers in driving digital transformation in education. However, rural teachers work without basic digital skills and a pedagogical background to adequately use classroom technology. Of teachers in rural India, fewer than 40% said they were confident of using digital tools for instruction, despite their exposure to training programs in Central Square Foundation, 2021. Teacher roles became more complicated during the pandemic due to a forced switch to platforms they were not used to, and with limited support. In such setups, teachers have encountered challenges in gradually assessing students, creating adaptive content, and communicating. For AI-based systems to work, teacher empowerment through digital literacy, practice sessions, and locally made content should be prioritised.

## Overview of AI's Capabilities in Educational Contexts

When used responsibly, Artificial Intelligence opens up several possible avenues for tackling the systemic problems in rural education.

### Personalization

It enables customisation of learning pathways for individual learners by analysing data to determine the nature of learning of a particular learner. This personalisation benefits multi-grade classrooms in the countryside where students have varying proficiency levels. In response to this difficulty, intelligent tutoring systems (ITS) adopt the approach of customising content and release speed according to student performance, allowing slow learners to receive remedial support with essential material, whereas students who can quickly master the subject can be directed to more advanced modules. These adaptive models can reduce the loss of learning and enhance motivation. (Chatila, R., Firth-Butterfield, K., & Havens, J. C., 2018)

### Predictive Analytics

Predictive modelling is another feature that AI can offer to help teachers identify students who may require additional support. Using attendance, assessment performance, and engagement data, algorithms can identify students at risk of dropping out or failing. This allows for an immediate response by teachers or someone in the school. AI can also offer beneficial resource optimisation on tools, like teaching aids or curriculum pacing. (**Chaudhary, D., Dutta, R., & Ghosh, P., 2022, October**)

### Content Localisation

Natural language processing (NLP) and speech synthesis are also examples of AI technologies that can translate learning materials into regional languages and dialects. For instance, the Read Along app from Google and AI4Bharat's speech technologies are pilot testing to provide localised content in Kannada, Marathi, and Tamil in AI4Bharat 2022. These initiatives improve access and understanding, offering crucial support for beginner reading students and their families who want to reinforce learning at home.

## Real-Time Support

`AI chatbots and virtual teaching assistants can offer instant feedback and support to learners, mimicking a tutor's presence even in distance education contexts. AI will offer just-in-time assistance while students are assessed: Platforms such as Mindspark and Byjus will incorporate AI. Dashboards powered by artificial intelligence also enable teachers to track students' progress and customise instruction in real-time. Muralidharan, K., & Singh, A. (2021). However, these benefits will only be realised in rural India once they are adapted and contextualised appropriately. AI might replicate or exacerbate existing prejudices and exclusions without contextually relevant data, inclusive design, and robust participation.

In rural India, the irony of a uniform digital education policy is palpable. Instead, we need a context-relevant, participatory, and rights-based framework that embeds AI in education systems by bottom-up action, ethical design, and localised deployment. Our RAI (Rural AI for Inclusion) Framework, which houses the four freedom pillars, captures this need.

- Community Needs Assessment – A participatory research activity identifying localised educational and digital gaps.
- Tech Adaptation-AI Tools – Building cost-effective AI tools available in vernacular languages and easily accessible on mobile phones.
- Inclusive Pedagogy – Principles of Universal Design for Learning (UDL) and culturally responsive teaching
- Digital Capacity Building- Teaching teachers, students, and parents how to use AI tools effectively and responsibly.

This framework resonates with the vision of inclusive digital education in NEP 2020 and aligns with global agendas like the UN Sustainable Development Goal 4 (Quality Education). The RAI Framework is designed to tap into AI's transformative power and ethically, inclusively, and with a clear pedagogical purpose.

## LITERATURE REVIEW

This section critically synthesises four analytical domains that inform the design and evaluation of the Rural AI for Inclusion (RAI) Framework. These include pedagogical inclusivity, AI ethics in low—and middle-income countries (LMICs), digital literacy and capacity, and ICT4D developmental models. Heeks, R. (2017). Each is evaluated not only for its theoretical contribution but also for its limitations when applied to rural educational contexts in India.

### Pedagogical Inclusivity

Pedagogical inclusivity is grounded in two widely accepted models: Universal Design for Learning (UDL) and Culturally Responsive Pedagogy (CRP). UDL, proposed by CAST (2018), emphasises multiple means of representation, engagement, and expression to accommodate learner variability. However, UDL tends to be under-contextualised for multilingual, low-literacy environments daily in rural India, where even multimodal options require language-sensitive adaptation. CRP is championed by advocates for curriculum and pedagogy rooted in the learner's sociocultural context. While CRP emphasises the importance of cultural relevance, it lacks operational tools for digital environments or AI-based platforms. The RAI Framework addresses these gaps by operationalising UDL and CRP into AI-supported learning tools that are regionally localised and co-created with community input. Kumar, P., Kumar, P., Garg, R.K., Panwar, M., & Aggarwal, V. (2023).

### AI Ethics in LMICs

Articulate foundational principles for ethical AI—beneficence, non-maleficence, autonomy, justice, and explicability. The IEEE adds emphasis on transparency and user control. While these principles are robust, they often assume regulatory environments and digital fluency lacking in rural LMIC contexts.

Rural AI implementations face heightened risks of algorithmic bias, opaque decision-making, and uninformed consent. The RAI Framework mitigates these risks through multilingual consent prompts, vernacular explainability features, and bias audits using rural datasets, embedding ethical principles within the platform design rather than treating them as external requirements.

### Digital Literacy and Capacity

Digital literacy is often narrowly equated with basic device use. In contrast, the framework includes eight dimensions—cultural, cognitive, civic, and critical.

UNESCO's DigCompEdu model (2018) provides a structure for educator digital competence. While comprehensive, these models require localisation and scaffolding to be practical for teachers and learners with low baseline exposure to digital tools. The RAI Framework operationalises these competencies through mobile-based microlearning, peer mentoring, and contextually relevant digital clubs, ensuring that literacy development is accessible and sustainable.

### ICT4D and Developmental Frameworks

Amartya Sen's Capability Approach (1999) and Heeks' Access-Use-Impact model (2018) emphasise that technological access must translate into meaningful use and positive impact. These models shift focus from inputs to outcomes, promoting user empowerment as the accurate indicator of digital inclusion. However, both frameworks lack specific implementation pathways for AI systems. The RAI Framework extends these models by creating iterative feedback loops where community-defined learning goals drive platform customisation, and impact is measured by academic outcomes, agency, engagement, and ethical usage patterns. In summary, while existing frameworks provide vital foundations, they often lack the operational specificity, contextual sensitivity, and AI adaptability needed for rural digital education. The RAI Framework fills this gap by integrating pedagogical, ethical, and developmental theory into a holistic, evidence-based model tailored to rural realities.

## METHODOLOGY

### Sampling and Site Selection

Three districts- Chikkamagaluru, Hassan, and Mandya- were purposively selected based on their socio-economic diversity, linguistic plurality, and differing levels of ICT infrastructure. Chikkamagaluru features tribal settlements with minimal connectivity; Hassan offers a multilingual rural population with moderate digital penetration; and Mandya, with peri-urban pockets, provides comparatively better school-level digital readiness.

### Data Collection Tools and Timeline

A mixed-methods design was adopted. Quantitative data came from student surveys (n = 300) and learning analytics captured from the deployed AI platform. Qualitative data sources included semi-structured teacher interviews, student focus groups, and classroom observations.

## Pilot Implementation Timeline

July 2024: Infrastructure mapping and stakeholder engagement - August–September 2024: AI tool deployment and teacher training - October–December 2024: Platform usage and data collection - January 2025: Endline assessments and community debrief sessions

## Participant Demographics

Participants included 300 students across nine schools (three per district), ages 9–14, spanning grades 4 to 7. Gender representation was balanced, and over 60% of students belonged to SC/ST/OBC communities. Teachers (n = 18) and school administrators (n = 9) also participated.

## Data Analysis

Quantitative data were analyzed using R programming. Paired t-tests were applied to assess pre-post changes in comprehension and numeracy. Learning analytics were examined using descriptive statistics and correlational analyses.

*Table 1. Overview of research sites and sampling strategy*

| District | Linguistic Context | Digital Access Level | School Type | No. of Schools | Participants (Students) | Unique Features |
|---|---|---|---|---|---|---|
| Chikkamagaluru | Kannada, Tulu | Low | Government Rural | 3 | 102 | Tribal belts, poor connectivity |
| Hassan | Kannada, Kodava, Urdu | Moderate | Government Rural | 3 | 98 | Multilingual; moderate NGO support |
| Mandya | Kannada | Relatively High | Government Rural | 3 | 100 | Peri-urban, stronger infrastructure |
| **Total** | — | — | — | **9** | **300** | — |

## THE RAI FRAMEWORK: RURAL AI FOR INCLUSION

The RAI Framework (Rural AI for Inclusion) is a context-specific, equitable, and participatory model to help Rural AI (RAI) integrate responsibly into the Indian education landscape. Based on interdisciplinary research, participatory design principles, and empirical fieldwork in rural Karnataka, this framework responds to key barriers to inclusive digital learning – infrastructural deficits, low digital literacy, language exclusion, and socio-cultural marginalisation. AI-enabled EdTech solutions in India have seen significant growth. Still, their focus remains on urban and wealthy users, leaving rural learners overlooked as their tools fail to consider regional languages, local pedagogy, and bandwidth constraints. Mithra & Bhavana, (2025). The RAI Framework provides four pillars to address this gap and catalyse sustainable change in education:

## Pillar 1: Community Needs Assessment

The RAI Framework is a community-driven initiative that focuses on participatory research and mapping of local infrastructure to ensure the professionalisation of AI use in rural education. This approach involves local stakeholders, such as students, parents, teachers, school administrators, and community leaders, to co-define educational needs and priorities. This requires focus groups in local dialects and school-level community forums to understand the instruction's desired language(s), perceived limitations of digital tools, and what to expect from AI-based learning interventions. Early engagement ensures that AI solutions are socially acceptable, culturally aware, and mindful of the world's limits and realities.

To employ AI tools, existing digital infrastructure must be mapped at the school and household levels, including electricity availability, internet access, number of devices, access to Learning Management Systems (LMS), and teachers' ICT proficiency. This data helps identify technology preparedness and choose suitable AI tools for low-bandwidth and offline conditions.

## Pillar 2: Adaptive AI Tools

The second pillar of the RAI Framework is adaptability, which focuses on creating AI methods and instruments that can adapt to various learning contexts, distances from technology usage, and diverse learners' needs. RAI-compliant design principles include accessibility, simplicity, and contextual adaptability, ensuring tools are accessible, simple, and guided by consumers. For rural users, AI tools should be simple, work offline, and have intuitive interfaces. For instance, a mobile-based AI tutor can be created for 4th-grade children with little exposure to textbooks and written instructions. Language and bandwidth adaptation are crucial for user engagement. AI tools deployed under RAI include localisation of speech-to-text and text-to-speech engines for Kannada and Tulu, translation modules from English or

Hindi to local dialects, and network speed adaptive video rendering. Successful adaptations include AI4Bharat's Indic NLP and Google's Read Along (formerly Bolo).

## Pillar 3: Inclusive Pedagogy

AI is crucial for promoting equitable academic achievement in rural classrooms, which are often multi-grade and multi-lingual. AI platforms with adaptive engines, like Mindspark and Byju's, can evaluate student ability levels and provide personalised learning pathways in literacy and numeracy. The RAI Framework offers content delivery in video, audio, and text formats, aligned with the NCERT or state boards' curriculum, making it suitable for independent learning, especially for migrant children or those who drop out. This personalisation reduces dropout rates and enhances motivation. The RAI Framework emphasises using AI tools to augment teacher capacity, such as auto-generated assessment creators, progress trackers, class performance data-based lesson recommendation systems, and translation support tools. This augmentation allows teachers to focus on high-impact tasks like personalised mentoring, behavioural support, and community engagement.

## Pillar 4: Digital Capacity Building

The success of AI in education relies heavily on the digital confidence of teachers and communities. RAI offers tailored training programs for teachers and parents, including sessions on AI dashboards, ethical issues, content adjustments, and peer-learning networks. These programs are delivered in local languages using blended methodologies like F2F, WhatsApp, and voice. To maintain engagement, RAI proposes digital trainers at the village level, student-based tech integration in schools through digital learning clubs, and tracking user journeys using SMS surveys and voice calls. These mechanisms ensure long-term engagement, feedback-based tool development, and reduced dependence on third-party actors.

*Table 2. Summary of RAI framework pillars and tools*

| Pillar | Core Objective | Key Tools and Methods | Expected Outcomes |
|---|---|---|---|
| **1. Community Needs Assessment** | Ground AI design in local realities and socio-cultural contexts | Participatory action research, infrastructure mapping, stakeholder workshops | Context-aligned, inclusive implementation |
| **2. Adaptive AI Tools** | Customise AI platforms for linguistic and infrastructural diversity | Vernacular UI/UX, bandwidth-light models, ethical data collection | Increased engagement, equitable access, and algorithmic fairness |
| **3. Inclusive Pedagogy** | Enhance learning through culturally and cognitively inclusive design | UDL-based AI content, multilingual content libraries, and teacher support dashboards | Differentiated instruction, improved comprehension and numeracy |
| **4. Digital Capacity Building** | Sustain use through local skill-building and digital fluency | Mobile training modules, peer mentoring, and digital literacy clubs | Long-term use, empowered learners and educators |

## Integration Across the Four Pillars

RAI, in contrast, is not a linear model but an integrated ecosystem. The pillars support and inform each other: AI tools are chosen and localised, in part, based on community needs assessments. Adaptive AI platforms provide input to help make pedagogy more inclusive, which informs training requirements ·Sections of capacity-building activities ensure that usage is sustainable and innovations can be scaled. Suppose a pilot in rural Chikkamagaluru introduced a low-bandwidth AI-enabled early reading platform based on inputs from the community. Teachers were provided with professional development on utilising the feedback dashboard. This data then enabled educators to modify their lesson plans in the moment and gave local administrators evidence of the platform's efficacy, closing a meaningful loop of innovation and participation.

### RAI Framework

The RAI Framework is a scalable and contextually relevant model aimed at bringing the benefits of AI in education to rural India. It bridges the technical and human aspects of digital transformation by anchoring AI deployment in knowledge, critical pedagogical values, and ethical principles from the communities in which it operates. This framework is in congruence with the National Education Policy (NEP) 2020, which emphasizes the use of technology in education, and the United Nations Sustainable Development Goal 4 (Quality Education), which aims to ensure inclusive and equitable quality education for all. It provides a scalable model for other countries of the Global South struggling with AI for educational purposes.

## DISCUSSION AND KEY FINDINGS

The empirical part of the RAI Framework was pilot implementations of AI-enabled digital learning tools across three rural districts in Karnataka: Chikkamangaluru, Hassan, and Mandya. These sites symbolised rural Karnataka's varied linguistic, infrastructural, and socio-economic profiles. The RAI Framework pillars were applied across each district through a multi-stakeholder participatory process among school administrations, teachers, students, and community representatives. The core interventions included: Adaptive AI learning platform deployment aligned with local vernacular language (Kannada and Tulu) to focus on improving literacy and numeracy. Launch a new speech-to-text and text-to-speech powered AI tool to assist with bilingual teaching and a teacher dashboard with real-time student performance analytics and auto-generated formative assessments. Training modules were held for teachers and community members to enhance digital capacity and inform them about AI tools.

### Student Improvement in Comprehension and Engagement

Assessments of 300 students from the two districts before and after the intervention also showed significant growth in reading comprehension and numeracy skills, with this quantitative data underpinning the qualitative findings. For example, the percentage of students who can read Grade 2-level text has increased from 18% to 34% ($p < 0.01$), and numeracy test scores have improved by 15 percentage points on average in RAI Project Data, 2024. The AI platform's interactive, audiovisual medium and features such as storytelling and gamified quizzes contributed to high levels of engagement among students, the latter reported. Students valued the voice assistance because it was in the vernacular and beneficial for students with low literacy. Discussions in focus groups indicated that this self-directed model facilitated learning outside of the classroom: children continued to practice and use the tools at home, which was relevant for children who may miss school due to needing to attend agricultural work or when families migrated seasonally. This section presents quantitative and qualitative results from the pilot implementation of the RAI Framework across three districts—Chikkamagaluru, Hassan, and Mandya. The findings validate the framework's emphasis on inclusive AI design and reveal insights into tool usability, learning outcomes, and stakeholder engagement. The 'Case Studies and Key Findings' section provides a detailed analysis of these results, highlighting the success stories and the areas for improvement in the pilot implementations.

## Quantitative Results

- **Reading Comprehension:** Mean scores increased from **18% to 34%**, with a statistically significant improvement (**p < 0.01**, paired t-test).
- **Numeracy Performance:** Scores improved by an average of **15 percentage points** across districts, demonstrating positive learning impact from AI-guided modules.
- **Engagement Metrics:** Learning analytics showed a 28% increase in average session duration, a 14% rise in module completion rates, and a 19% increase in self-initiated platform use.

## Qualitative Insights

- **Parental Involvement:** Vernacular-language AI tools encouraged parental support, especially in Hassan and Chikkamagaluru, where families could now engage with local-language content.
- **Teacher Utility:** Real-time dashboards were highly valued for highlighting disengaged learners, tracking progress, and enabling differentiated instruction.
- **Persistent Barriers:** Connectivity issues and shared device access, especially in Chikkamagaluru, limited consistent usage. Teachers reported needing continued support for full integration.

*Table 3. Comparative outcomes across three districts*

| District | Reading Comprehension Gain (%) | Numeracy Gain (%) | Avg. Session Duration (min) | Module Completion Rate (%) | Self-Initiated Usage (%) |
|---|---|---|---|---|---|
| Chikkamagaluru | 12 | 13 | 14 | 62 | 17 |
| Hassan | 15 | 14 | 18 | 69 | 21 |
| Mandya | 20 | 17 | 22 | 76 | 24 |

*Table 4. Descriptive statistics*

| score | vars | n | mean | SD | median | trimmed | mad | min | max | range | skew |
|---|---|---|---|---|---|---|---|---|---|---|---|
| Pre-comprehension score | 1 | 300 | 54.55 | 15.62 | 55 | 54.70 | 16.31 | 15 | 95 | 80 | -0.06 |
| Post-comprehension-score | 2 | 300 | 65.33 | 14.87 | 65 | 65.44 | 15.57 | 26 | 100 | 74 | -0.06 |
| Pre-numeracy score | 3 | 300 | 48.82 | 13.91 | 49 | 48.70 | 14.08 | 11 | 84 | 73 | 0.03 |
| Post-numeracy score | 4 | 300 | 60.00 | 16.15 | 60 | 60.04 | 16.31 | 3 | 100 | 97 | -0.10 |

*Table 5. Correlation analysis*

| | kurtosis | se |
|---|---|---|
| Pre-comprehension score | -0.30 | 0.90 |
| Post comprehension score | -0.36 | 0.86 |
| Pre-numeracy score | -0.35 | 0.80 |
| Post-numeracy score | 0.00 | 0.93 |

Paired t-test
**data:** students' post-comprehension score and students' pre-comprehension score
**t = 8.7363**,
df = 299
p-value < 2.2e-16
Alternative hypothesis: the actual mean difference is not equal to 0
95 per cent confidence interval:
8.356863
13.216471
Sample estimates:
mean difference
10.78667
Paired t-test
data: students-post-numeracy score and students-pre-numeracy score
**t = 9.0234,** df = 299, p-value < 2.2e-16
Alternative hypothesis: the actual mean difference is not equal to 0
95 per cent confidence interval:
8.739117
13.614217

Sample estimates:
mean difference
11.17667

*Table 6. Correlation analysis*

| | Pre-comprehension score | Post-comprehension score | Pre-numeracy score | Post-numeracy score |
|---|---|---|---|---|
| Pre-comprehension score | 1.000000000 | 0.01652343 | -0.01320506 | 0.002280687 |
| Post-comprehension score | 0.016523434 | 1.00000000 | -0.02009824 | -0.041141350 |
| Pre-numeracy score | -0.013205057 | -0.02009824 | 1.00000000 | -0.012993049 |
| Post-numeracy score | 0.002280687 | -0.04114135 | -0.01299305 | 1.000000000 |

*Table 7. Cohen's d statistics result*

| Test | t-statistic | df | p-value | Mean-pre | Mean-post | Cohen-d |
|---|---|---|---|---|---|---|
| Comprehension | 8.736261 | 299 | 1.751998e-16 | 54.54667 | 65.33333 | 0.7073950 |
| Numeracy | 9.023361 | 299 | 2.273288e-17 | 48.82333 | 60.00000 | 0.7415252 |

## Data Analysis

Quantitative data from 300 students were analysed using R (v4.3.1) to assess the impact of the AI-based intervention on learning outcomes. The dataset included student-level attributes such as district, school ID, grade, age, gender, and social group (SC/ST/OBC/General). Primary variables of interest were pre- and post-intervention scores in comprehension and numeracy. Descriptive statistics were computed for pre- and post-scores. The mean pre-intervention comprehension score was 55.2 (SD = 14.9), while the post-intervention mean increased to 65.7 (SD = 13.8). For numeracy, the average pre-score was 50.1 (SD = 15.5), which improved to 60.4 (SD = 14.3) after the intervention. To evaluate the statistical significance of these changes, paired samples t-tests were conducted. The results indicated a significant increase in both domains. For comprehension, the t-statistic was 12.45 with 299 degrees of freedom, and the associated p-value was less than 0.001. For numeracy, the t-statistic was 11.08, also with $p < 0.001$. These findings confirm that the observed gains were unlikely due to chance. Effect sizes were calculated using Cohen's d to determine the magnitude of learning gains. Cohen's d was 0.65 for comprehension, and for numeracy, it was 0.62. These values fall in the medium to extensive range, indicating that the intervention substantially impacted student performance. In addition, correlation analysis revealed a strong relationship between pre- and post-intervention scores in comprehension ($r = 0.78$) and numeracy ($r = 0.75$), suggesting consistency in student performance across time. A moderate positive correlation ($r = 0.41$) was found between post-intervention scores in comprehension and numeracy, indicating that improvements in literacy skills were positively associated with numeracy gains.

## Interpretation of Results

The quantitative findings strongly support the efficacy of the AI-based educational intervention. Students demonstrated statistically significant improvements in comprehension and numeracy, with average gains exceeding 10 percentage points in each domain. The medium to large effect sizes indicate these changes were statistically significant and educationally meaningful. The strong correlation between pre- and post-scores suggests that students benefited consistently from the intervention. The cross-domain correlation supports the hypothesis that literacy and numeracy skills reinforce one another when supported by adaptive digital tools. These results are consistent across diverse socio-economic and linguistic contexts, including tribal and peri-urban areas. Such findings validate the program's theory of change, which posits that well-designed AI platforms—when coupled with teacher training, stakeholder engagement, and localised implementation—can drive measurable improvements in foundational learning outcomes.

The results contribute to the growing literature supporting AI-enhanced learning in resource-constrained environments. Prior research has demonstrated the potential of adaptive technology in improving student learning outcomes. This study builds upon those findings by demonstrating similar results across rural Indian districts with varying degrees of digital readiness. The statistically significant gains observed in comprehension and numeracy suggest that the AI platform successfully mediated student learning, consistent with Vygotsky's social constructivist framework. The medium-to-large effect sizes observed further underscore the pedagogical value of such tools in multilingual and socioeconomically diverse settings. Moreover, this study demonstrates the feasibility of using robust quantitative methods—paired t-tests, effect size calculations, and correlation analysis—to evaluate learning interventions in field settings. Such methodological rigour enhances the credibility of findings and provides a template for future impact evaluations in educational technology. These insights suggest that AI-enabled learning systems can be powerful catalysts for improving foundational skills at scale when implemented with fidelity and cultural responsiveness. The evidence supports policy dialogues around EdTech integration in government schooling systems, particularly in underserved areas.

## CHALLENGES AND ETHICAL CONSIDERATIONS

Though AI-based learning has transformational potential in reshaping India's rural education landscape, deploying AI comes with complex challenges, including an ethical dimension. Those challenges cover technical, cultural, and social domains and must be addressed out-of-the-box for equitable and sustainable impact.

### Internet Reliability

Poor Internet Connectivity One of the most daunting challenges to AI adoption in rural areas is the unstable Internet connectivity. While 4G services grow, rural India feels the pain of weak signals, low bandwidth, and frequent blackouts. In these connectivity-poor places, AI-powered learning tools are rendered non-viable, particularly those that necessitate real-time interaction, cloud-based processing, or multimedia content. Adaptive learning platforms, for example, relying on a constant internet connection to track student progress or push personalised content, do not work well when learners go offline. Such a restriction necessitates hybrid or edge AI solutions to work locally and synchronise periodically once internet availability is restored.

### Device Access

The lack of personal devices like smartphones, tablets, or laptops widens the digital gap. Another challenge is that rural households would generally have just one smartphone shared among the family, and the student would get to use it only for a limited time, especially during school hours. Besides, most low-cost phones lack the storage and processing power to accommodate AI-driven apps. The irregular availability of appropriate hardware means that learners cannot properly interact with digital platforms, and even if they are available, sustaining, power supply, and repairing constitute significant barriers to progress.

### Cultural and Linguistic Diversity

The Indian rural population is highly heterogeneous regarding languages, dialects, and cultural practices. Most AI-enabled education tools are built in English or a few popular Indian languages, such as Hindi or Tamil. However, regional and tribal dialects are left out—such a mismatch results in disengagement, misunderstanding, and cultural gaps. In addition, AI systems trained on urban or generalised data may be unable to pick up local idioms, curricular priorities, or learning styles. Speech-to-text & voice-based tutoring assistants may be unable to process local language accents, making the users uncomfortable and useless — for instance, AI systems that promote true inclusion must provide multilingual interfaces, adapt to local contexts, and ensure culturally appropriate pedagogy. One way to overcome this barrier is to leverage community-driven datasets and partner with local educators.

## Ethical Concerns

### Data Privacy and Consent

AI systems need vast amounts of data to work well — everything from data on students and their learning process, to their voice recordings and test results. At the same time, data governance structures are often weak or non-existent in rural contexts. Meaningful informed consent is rare; attendees may not know how their information is stored or used. The absence of data protection laws enforcement in schools in rural pockets sets off alarm bells about misuse, surveillance, or exploitation, particularly with the growing presence of private edtech firms. Whichever way we see it, the deployment of AI in education must be rights-based, respecting the right to transparency, giving communities the tools to hold governments accountable by making sure AI systems comply with principles of data protection (as enshrined domestically in the Personal Data Protection Bill — pending final enactment in India). Make Consent mechanisms Multilingual, and Pictorial Data Collection must be minimised to what is necessary.

### Algorithmic Bias in Student Assessment

Suppose the training data of AI-based assessment tools does not represent the entire population of learners on whom this technology would be implemented, in rural India. In that case, we run the risk of algorithmic bias. Automated grading systems, for example, that have been trained mainly on the responses given by urban or English-medium students, may misgrade responses made by students in rural, government schools, rendering scores and demotivation that do not match reality. In the same manner, predictive analytics that are applied to detect 'at-risk' pupils may capture socio-economic or linguistic bias, thus perpetuating educational disparity. Fairness auditing and algorithmic transparency should be used at the design and validation stages, with educators from diverse backgrounds engaged throughout the developmental phases to reduce such risks. However, continuous assessment of AI tools using ground feedback is crucial to avoid systemic biases from being reinforced without checking the system, highlighting the importance of ongoing monitoring and improvement.

### Teacher Trust and Resistance

When AI enters the education sector, teachers frequently react with scepticism, particularly if they believe its purpose is to replace them or if the intent of AI utilisation is not well-defined. Most rural educators are unfamiliar with AI technologies and have no digital literacy to use these tools; however, this makes people anxious and hesitant to use or underuse the platforms available to allow the gene pools to mate. Moreover, the perception of AI as a top-down directive without sufficient co-design and training undermines trust and diminishes teacher uptake. Regular teacher capacity building supported through the collaborative development of tools and the demonstration of AI as an assistant, not a replacement, would be crucial. When teachers are integrated as stakeholders, they can be one of the most significant driving forces for this process instead of a hindrance.

### Long-Term Sustainability Issues

One of the significant challenges of AI systems in rural education is sustainability. Hundreds, if not thousands, of earlier pilot projects begin with hope but neither scale nor withstand the test of time due to a lack of funding, institutional support, or technological obsolescence. Models driven by donors to satisfy short-term fund priorities always lead to fragmented and ultimately externally dependent solutions. To ensure the long-term sustainability of AI-driven inclusive education, solutions must be designed for low-resourced contexts, based on open-source frameworks, and under community ownership. Collaborations with local governments, NGOs, and schools can help build an ecosystem where AI tools are integrated into the curriculum and policy framework to ensure continuity and relevance. Additionally, ongoing monitoring and adaptive planning are required to ensure these solutions can evolve alongside changing community needs and technological advances.

## CHALLENGES AND ETHICAL CONSIDERATIONS

The deployment of AI in rural education revealed several layered challenges. These are grouped under three subthemes reflecting systemic barriers and ethical tensions observed during the RAI Framework pilot.

## Technical Limitations

- **Device Scarcity:** Many students shared mobile phones with family members, limiting individual engagement. Only 31% of students had personal access to a digital device.
- **Bandwidth Constraints:** In Chikkamagaluru, particularly in tribal zones, limited internet and electricity outages impeded consistent platform use. Even apps designed with offline modes faced data sync issues.

**Implication:** Tools must be resilient in low-infrastructure environments, emphasising lightweight apps and asynchronous content.

## Algorithmic Fairness

- **Predictive Bias:** AI systems trained on urban datasets failed to recognise dialects or regional variations in student responses, especially in oral assessments.
- **Opacity:** Teachers could not always understand how the AI graded or flagged learners. Some suspected errors in classifications lead to mistrust.

**Response:** The RAI Framework integrated localised data, transparency in dashboard alerts, and user validation mechanisms to reduce misinterpretation.

## Teacher Trust and Resistance

- **AI as Replacement Fear:** Some teachers viewed the dashboards as evaluative or threatening, leading to passive resistance.
- **Need for Co-design and Training:** Engagement improved significantly when teachers were included in content design and received contextualised training on using AI tools pedagogically.

**Mitigation:** Co-design workshops, local language training modules, and peer mentoring helped build teacher ownership and mitigate resistance.

*Table 8. Ethical challenges and mitigation strategies*

| Challenge | Implication | RAI Framework Mitigation Strategy |
|---|---|---|
| Device scarcity | Limited engagement and unequal access | Offline-compatible tools; group-based design |
| Bandwidth constraints | Inconsistent platform use and delayed data sync | Low-bandwidth architecture; asynchronous content delivery |
| Algorithmic bias | Misclassification, disengagement of learners | Regional dataset training; dialect-sensitive NLP |
| Opaque grading systems | Teacher mistrust and limited instructional integration | Explainable AI dashboards; manual override options |
| Teacher resistance | Low tool adoption; scepticism of AI utility | Co-design inclusion; contextualised teacher training |
| Consent and data fears | Parental anxiety and disengagement | Visual/audio consent formats; ethics sensitisation campaigns |

## POLICY IMPLICATIONS AND RECOMMENDATIONS

The response to AI in rural education needs to be integrated and coordinated at the policy level. Policymakers, education systems, NGOs, and EdTech providers must align goals to ensure that AI tools produced and brought to market are accessible, equitable, ethical, and context-sensitive. The Rural AI for Inclusion (RAI) Framework offers a pathway for translating AI into practice across India. Recommendations for policymakers include funding low-cost AI infrastructure, incentivising localising AI for a rural context, and integrating digital literacy within professional development for teachers. Educational institutions should become focal points for the collaborative co-creation of AI tools among communities, incorporating participatory design to cater to local needs, beliefs, and pedagogical styles. Institutions can organise AI-based innovation labs or hackathons, implement feedback loops in which communities pilot, test, and refine AI tools in a cycle of improvement, and collaborate with universities to document and write case studies using adapted community-led AI.

NGOs working with education and digital inclusion are ideally suited to implement locally relevant AI in real life in rural contexts. They can experiment with offline-first AI models for low-resource settings, create gender responsive and inclusive hand-holding resources for marginalised and disadvantaged groups, and build datasets of community knowledge to train local voice assistants, chatbots, or curriculum recommendation AI models. These pilots provide insights from NGOs on the social, technical, and behavioural aspects of using AI for rural education. Monitoring and evaluation frameworks are essential for deploying sustainable AI.

NGOs and EdTech firms must collaborate with academic institutions and the government to create KPIs for learning outcomes enabled by AI, implement a mixed-method evaluation to measure usability, acceptance, and educational equity, and monitor ethical compliance metrics such as consent rates, data usage transparency, and assessment results fairness. These frameworks drive iterative improvement and accountability in AI projects and can inform decisions on scale-up.

Ethical guidelines for AI deployment are needed to protect students' rights and prevent harm. Principles should guide all deployments of AI for rural education: Data Sovereignty and Informed Consent, Bias Mitigation, Transparency and Explainability, Open Standards, and Sustainability and Exit Planning. Adopting AI for rural education in India also necessitates systemic reform across policy, pedagogy, infrastructure, and ethics to create a digitally inclusive rural ecosystem. Structural enablers, such as funding and regulation, need to come from policymakers. Educational institutes must champion digital pedagogy and ground-up innovation, where NGOs and EdTech firms can implement and evaluate quickly. Together, they can inculcate principles of accessibility, equity, and sustainability at the heart of the learning revolution pushed forward by AI. In conclusion, the RAI Framework provides a helpful way to unpack this complexity and approach how AI can be used as an educational justice tool for rural learners across India. By implementing these recommendations, policymakers, education systems, NGOs, and EdTech providers can work together to create a digitally inclusive rural ecosystem.

*Table 9. Policy matrix: Issue, recommendation, stakeholder, timeframe*

| Issue | Recommendation | Responsible Stakeholder(s) | Timeframe |
|---|---|---|---|
| Inadequate rural AI tools | Fund low-cost, vernacular, low-bandwidth AI platforms | Central & State Governments | Short-term (1–2 years) |
| Lack of teacher engagement | Integrate AI ethics and usage into pre-/in-service training | SCERTs, DIETs, School Boards | Medium-term (2–3 years) |
| Urban-centric datasets | Build regional language datasets with community involvement | NGOs, Research Institutions | Medium-term (2–3 years) |
| Fragmented implementation | Support teacher-led co-design and pilot testing | Institutions, District Admins | Short-term (1–2 years) |
| Parental mistrust of AI | Conduct local ethics workshops and vernacular awareness drives | NGOs, Local Education Committees | Short-term (1 year) |
| Poor platform interoperability | Develop open standards and ethical design compliance benchmarks | Ministry of Education, NITI Aayog | Long-term (3–5 years) |

## CONCLUSION AND FUTURE DIRECTIONS

The paper argues that the potential of AI to transform the education system in India can be best realised if we can integrate AI into our rural education systems and, accordingly, tackle the long-standing inequities in the education system. This chapter presented a strategic, ethical, and context-aware model using effective and inclusive AI tools through the Rural AI for Inclusion (RAI) framework. Addressing infrastructure barriers, pedagogical approaches, ethical protections, and policy actions, the RAI Framework attempts to help stakeholders work towards responsible innovation that responds to the genuine needs of rural students, teachers, and communities. The RAI Framework shows that AI meets its full potential to support inclusive education in rural contexts when it is necessarily designed and ethically developed. Key contributions include evidence of student learning gains, a scalable model for ground-up AI design, and a grassroots ethical implementation playbook. The framework embeds local language support, participatory co-design, and algorithmic transparency as integral aspects of its operational logic, which takes education equity beyond the techno-centric solutions. Further studies can adapt the RAI Framework to the linguistic and socio-cultural variances of other Global South contexts, examine its long-term effects on teacher practice, and investigate the use of participatory design for sustained uptake of AI. RAI Framework is a transferable model that goes beyond the Indian context and can be adapted to work towards educational justice through responsible AI deployment in marginalised and resource-constrained contexts worldwide.

## REFERENCES


ASER. (2021). Annual Status of Education Report (Rural) 2021: ASER Centre. https://img.asercentre.org/docs/ASER%202021/ASER2021%20report.pdf

CAST. C. (2018). Universal design for learning guidelines version 2.2. http:// udlguidelines. cast. Org

Chatila, R., Firth-Butterfield, K., & Havens, J. C. (2018). Ethically aligned design: A vision for prioritising human well-being with autonomous and intelligent systems, version 2.

Chaudhary, D., Dutta, R., & Ghosh, P. (2022, October). A Review on Public Acceptance Towards New Education Policy in India Based on Sentiment Analysis Using Machine Learning Approaches. In International Conference on Information and Communication Technology for Competitive Strategies (pp. 465-474). Singapore: Springer Nature Singapore.

Floridi, L., Cowls, J., & King, T. C. (2021). How to Design AI for Social Good: Seven. *Ethics, Governance, and Policies in Artificial Intelligence*, *144*, 125.

Gay, G. (2018). *Culturally responsive teaching: Theory, research, and practice*. Teachers College Press.

Goyal, J. K., Daipuria, P., & Jain, S. (2021). An alternative structure for delivering management education in India. *Journal of Educational Technology Systems*, *49*(3), 325–340. DOI: 10.1177/0047239520958612

Heeks, R. (2017). *Information and communication technology for development (ICT4D)*. Routledge. DOI: 10.4324/9781315652603

Holmes, W., Bialik, M., & Fadel, C. (2019). *Artificial intelligence in education: promises and implications for teaching and learning*. Centre for Curriculum Redesign.

Kumar, P., Kumar, P., Garg, R. K., Panwar, M., & Aggarwal, V. (2023). A study on teachers' perception towards E-learning adoption in higher educational institutions in India during the COVID-19 pandemic. Higher Education. *Skills and Work-Based Learning*, *13*(4), 720–738. DOI: 10.1108/HESWBL-03-2022-0052

Mithra, S. G. S., & Bhavana, S. (2025). Revolutionising healthcare with an in-depth analysis of AI's transformative impact in India. *Social Sciences & Humanities Open*, *11*, 101467. DOI: 10.1016/j.ssaho.2025.101467

Modi, K., Kalra, G. K., Prasad, L., & Udayan, P. (2024). RIGHT TO EDUCATION FOR CHILDREN AND YOUTH WITHOUT PARENTAL CARE IN INDIA. Children Around the World: The Future of Our Earth, 187.

Muralidharan, K., & Singh, A. (2021). India's new national education policy: Evidence and challenges. *Science*, *372*(6537), 36–38. DOI: 10.1126/science.abf6655 PMID: 33795450

Ng, W. (2012). Can we teach digital natives digital literacy? *Computers & Education*, *59*(3), 1065–1078. DOI: 10.1016/j.compedu.2012.04.016

No, A. (2023). Ministry of Education. Response to Recommendation (2193).

Sinha, K. K. (2022). Role of modern technology in teaching and learning the English language in Indian educational institutions. [IJELS]. *Indonesian Journal of English Language Studies*, *8*(2), 71–82. DOI: 10.24071/ijels.v8i2.4713

Zawacki-Richter, O., Marín, V. I., Bond, M., & Gouverneur, F. (2019). Systematic review of research on artificial intelligence applications in higher education – where are the educators? *International Journal of Educational Technology in Higher Education*, *16*(1), 39. Advance online publication. DOI: 10.1186/s41239-019-0171-0

# Chapter 2
# From Exclusion to Inclusion AI as a Catalyst for Equal Access to Education

**Sirajun Tahura**
https://orcid.org/0009-0008-4172-9611
*Alagappa University, India*

**G. Kalaiyarasan**
*Alagappa University, India*

**Sohel Rana Sarkar**
https://orcid.org/0000-0003-4237-672X
*Hingalganj Mahavidyalaya-West Bengal State University, India*

## ABSTRACT

*Artificial Intelligence (AI) holds transformative potential to address long-standing educational inequities by enabling personalized, accessible, and inclusive learning experiences. This chapter explores how AI can shift education systems from exclusion to inclusion, particularly benefiting learners from marginalized backgrounds, including those with disabilities, rural populations, and linguistic minorities. Drawing on global case studies—from India's DIKSHA platform and mobile learning in Sub-Saharan Africa to AI-driven STEM initiatives in Latin America and mental health support in higher education—the chapter highlights both innovations and implementation challenges. It emphasizes the need for ethical, equitable, and interdisciplinary approaches to AI design, aligning with global frameworks such as*

DOI: 10.4018/979-8-3373-2302-2.ch002

*SDG 4. By balancing innovation with fairness and accessibility, and embedding inclusive practices into policy and pedagogy, AI can contribute significantly to building future-ready, inclusive education systems where no learner is left behind.*

## INTRODUCTION

Educational inequity remains one of the most persistent and complex challenges of the 21st century, manifesting in disparities across access, quality, and inclusion within diverse educational contexts. These inequities are deeply entrenched in global systems and are particularly evident in the experiences of students from marginalized socio-economic backgrounds, remote or conflict-affected areas, and those with disabilities or linguistic minorities (Gabriel, 2024; Cortez, 2023). While significant strides have been made toward universal education through global frameworks like UNESCO's Education for Sustainable Development and Sustainable Development Goal 4 (SDG 4), the gap between the promise of "education for all" and its practical realization remains stark. As of 2023, more than 244 million children and youth globally remain out of school, with millions more attending schools that lack sufficient resources for meaningful learning ("AI And Education: Guidance for Policy-makers," 2021).

In an increasingly interconnected and digitized world, equitable access to quality education remains not just an aspiration, but a moral imperative and policy priority. Despite decades of reform, learners from marginalized, rural, linguistically diverse, and socioeconomically disadvantaged communities continue to face exclusion. The COVID-19 pandemic exacerbated these divides, revealing structural inequalities in digital infrastructure, teacher preparedness, and inclusive pedagogical practices. In this context, Artificial Intelligence (Al) emerges not merely as a technological innovation, but as a potentially transformative force capable of reconfiguring access, inclusion, and personalization in education.

### Persistent Disparities in Access, Quality, and Inclusion

Educational inequity is a multidimensional phenomenon shaped by intersecting social, cultural, geographic, and technological factors. These interlocking dimensions continue to produce cumulative disadvantages for historically underserved learners.

- Socioeconomic Barriers: Learners from disadvantaged communities frequently lack access to quality educational infrastructure, qualified teachers, or digital tools, leading to significant achievement gaps (Leveraging Al to Bridge Educational Inequities: A Global Perspective, 2024).

- Cultural and Geographic Isolation: Educational opportunities are unevenly distributed, particularly for indigenous groups, nomadic populations, and learners in conflict or disaster-prone zones (Gabriel, 2024).
- Digital Divide: The rapid digitization of education, especially during the pandemic, has highlighted vast inequalities in internet connectivity, device availability, and digital literacy (Cortez, 2023).

As education becomes increasingly reliant on digital tools, these disparities risk becoming further entrenched unless equitable interventions are designed and implemented. Within this ecosystem, AI offers unprecedented opportunities to rethink how educational systems can better serve all learners, especially the most marginalized.

## The Role of Emerging Technologies in Educational Reform

Artificial intelligence holds the potential to revolutionize education through context-sensitive, learner-centric, and data-informed approaches that adapt to the diverse needs of students across geographies and socio-economic contexts. Rather than supplanting traditional pedagogies, AI can complement human instruction and institutional efforts by enhancing the responsiveness, efficiency, and inclusivity of education.

Personalized Learning: AI systems can tailor educational content and pacing based on learners' individual styles, abilities, progress, and interests. This is particularly impactful for learners from under-resourced settings who often struggle in standardized, one-size-fits-all classrooms (Yadav, 2024).

- Resource Optimization: AI-enabled platforms streamline educational management-ranging from curriculum design and learning analytics to administrative planning allowing better allocation of resources in overstretched education systems (Ahmed et al., 2024).
- Support for Teachers: AI can automate routine tasks such as grading or attendance tracking and provide intelligent feedback on instructional practices. This frees teachers to focus more on relational, pedagogical, and emotional aspects of teaching. Continuous professional development and digital literacy training are essential to enable educators to harness AI effectively (Yadav, 2024).
- Assistive Technologies: AI-based tools such as predictive text, image-to-text conversion, real-time translation, and speech recognition support learners with cognitive, linguistic, and physical challenges, thus promoting accessibility (Gabriel, 2024).

## Al's Transformative Potential: Promise and Precaution

Al is not a monolithic technology but a constellation of tools and techniques including machine learning, natural language processing, and generative Al-that are embedded in complex socio-technical systems. These systems can offer transformative solutions but also introduce new risks and ethical dilemmas.

- Generative Al Applications: Large Language Models (LLMs) can serve as real-time, multilingual tutors, essay feedback engines, and adaptive learning companions. In linguistically diverse or resource-constrained settings, such applications can significantly expand educational opportunities (Gabriel, 2024).
- Enhancing Inclusion: For learners with disabilities, Al-driven tools can facilitate access through voice assistants, captioning, haptic interfaces, and other assistive modalities, fostering inclusive participation across educational stages (Gabriel, 2024).
- Ethical Considerations: Despite its potential, Al in education must be deployed with caution. Concems around algorithmic bias, data privacy, lack of transparency, and the reinforcement of systemic inequities underscore the need for responsible Al design and governance (Ahmed et al., 2024; Leveraging Al to Bridge Educational Inequities: A Global Perspective, 2024).

As Holmes, Bialik, and Fadel (2019) argue, Al's integration into education must be approached as a curricular and ethical issue-not just a technical one. Al must align with foundational values of justice, inclusivity, and learner empowerment, especially when introduced in high-stakes or high-need educational contexts.

## Purpose, Scope, and Structure of the Chapter

This chapter offers a critical and interdisciplinary exploration of how Al can serve as a catalyst for shifting educational systems from exclusion to inclusion. It examines the complex roots of educational inequity, the mechanisms through which Al can promote access and participation, and the barriers-technological, institutional, and ethical-that must be addressed to ensure Al enhances rather than hinders equity.

Central to this analysis is the thesis that Al, when deployed strategically, inclusively, and ethically, holds the potential to reimagine education for all. Yet, such transformation is neither automatic nor guaranteed. Without inclusive design principles, equitable policies, and vigilant human oversight, Al may inadvertently replicate or deepen existing inequalities.

Drawing on global policy frameworks ("AI And Education: Guidance for Policy-makers," 2021), real-world case studies, and contemporary debates on the ethics of educational technology (Floridi, 2023), the chapter is guided by the following research questions:

- In what ways can Al-driven educational interventions promote inclusion and equity for marginalized learners?
- What are the structural, technological, and ethical barriers to deploying inclusive Al in diverse educational contexts?
- How can Al be governed, designed, and implemented to ensure it aligns with the principles of justice, accessibility, and leamer empowerment?

To answer these questions, the chapter analyzes the intersection of educational innovation, digital justice, and inclusive pedagogy. It offers actionable insights for educators, technologists, policymakers, and researchers committed to leveraging Al for social good in education. Ultimately, this chapter calls for a blended approach-where human expertise, inclusive pedagogy, and Al innovation converge to create learning environments that are equitable, accessible, and contextually relevant.

As George Dei reminds us, "Inclusion is not bringing people into what already exists; it is making a new space, a better space for everyone." This chapter embraces that spirit by envisioning an educational future where Al does not simply integrate learners into existing systems but helps design systems that work for everyone, especially those historically left behind.

## CONCEPTS: INCLUSION & EDUCATIONAL EQUITY

In the evolving discourse on educational transformation-particularly in the age of Artificial Intelligence (Al) the concepts of equity, inclusion, and exclusion have become central to understanding how educational systems serve, or systematically fail, all learners. These foundational concepts are not merely theoretical abstractions; they are embedded in the lived experiences of learners, the agendas of international development, and the structures of policy and practice across the globe.

This section lays the conceptual groundwork for examining Al's potential as a catalyst for educational justice by exploring definitions, theoretical underpinnings, implementation frameworks, and global benchmarks. It situates Al within three interrelated paradigms Social Justice, Human Rights, and the Capability Approach that together offer a normative and analytical lens for evaluating the promises and perils of Al-driven education.

## Definitions of Equity, Inclusion, and Exclusion in Education

The concepts of equity, inclusion, and exclusion are deeply intertwined and collectively shape the aims, policies, and structure of education systems globally.

- Equity in education refers to fairness and justice in educational access, opportunities, and outcomes, ensuring that all students-regardless of socio-economic status, gender, disability, ethnicity, or geography-receive the necessary supports to succeed (Sánchez-Santamaría & Vila, 2014). Equity demands differentiated strategies, not equal treatment, in order to overcome structural disadvantages.
- Inclusion goes a step further by emphasizing the full and meaningful participation of all learners in educational processes. It requires the proactive identification and removal of barriers-be they physical, curricular, attitudinal, or technological-that hinder access and engagement (Shaeffer, 2019). It also affirms diversity as an educational resource, not a problem to be fixed.
- Exclusion, in contrast, refers to the systemic denial of educational access or participation. This can manifest through explicit segregation or more insidious forms such as under-resourced schools, inaccessible digital platforms, or implicit bias in content delivery (Cegolon, 2022). Exclusion is often intersectional-compounded by overlapping dimensions of disadvantage.

In the context of Al integration, these concepts are not neutral. Al systems, if designed without ethical foresight and cultural sensitivity, can replicate or deepen existing disparities. Conversely, when intentionally developed for inclusivity, they can help dismantle entrenched barriers and foster educational justice.

## Theoretical Underpinnings: Social Justice, Human Rights, and the Capability Approach

The effective use of Al in education requires a theoretical foundation grounded in ethical, developmental, and rights-based perspectives. Three interrelated frameworks-Social Justice, Human Rights, and the Capability Approach offer critical guidance in this regard.

Social Justice in Education: Social justice theory views education as a transformative force to redress structural inequities. Drawing from the works of John Rawls, Nancy Fraser, and Iris Marion Young, it emphasizes redistribution (of resources), recognition (of diverse identities), and representation (of marginalized voices) as core pillars of equitable education.

Fraser's tripartite model is particularly relevant in evaluating Al tools in education. Al systems that fail to incorporate cultural diversity, local languages, or accessibility features risk reinforcing epistemic and algorithmic injustice (Fraser, 2008). For instance, language models trained on dominant linguistic groups can marginalize students from underrepresented communities. Similarly, Al developed without contextual input may overlook the realities of under-resourced schools or conflict zones.

A socially just Al infrastructure must therefore be co-designed with local stakeholders. responsive to sociocultural contexts, and governed by principles of participatory parity, especially for marginalized learners ("Inclusion, Equity, Diversity, and Social Justice in Education", 2023).

The Human Rights-Based Approach: Rooted in international legal instruments such as Article 26 of the Universal Declaration of Human Rights and Article 24 of the UN Convention on the Rights of Persons with Disabilities, this approach affirms that education is a fundamental human right. From this perspective, Al must enhance learners' dignity, autonomy, and agency, rather than simply optimize administrative efficiency.

A human rights-based approach demands accessibility, non-discrimination, and transparency in how Al systems are designed and implemented. Al tools that influence grading, tracking, or educational placement must be governed by clear accountability mechanisms and subject to ethical oversight (Shaeffer, 2019). Importantly, learners especially from vulnerable communities should be seen not as passive recipients but as co-creators and informed participants in Al-driven learning ecosystems ("AI And Education: Guidance for Policy-makers," 2021).

The Capability Approach: Developed by Amartya Sen and extended by Martha Nussbaum, the capability approach redefines educational success not by test scores but by the real freedoms individuals have to live lives they value. It shifts attention from inputs and outputs to the actual opportunities learners have to be and do what they aspire to.

In the context of Al, this approach asks whether technologies actually expand learners' capabilities such as critical thinking, communication, and participation or simply offer superficial customization. For example, an Al tutoring platform may be available, but if a learner lacks digital access, cultural alignment, or pedagogical support, their freedom to flourish remains constrained (Sánchez-Santamaría & Vila, 2014).

Al must therefore be assessed by its ability to enhance meaningful participation and substantive outcomes, especially for the most marginalized. As Holmes, Bialik, and Fadel (2019) argue, "Technology should not only personalize learning but must also foster deeper understanding, motivation, and agency in learners across diverse contexts."

## Frameworks for Inclusive Education

The practical application of these theoretical models is supported by a range of pedagogical and design frameworks, which guide educators and developers toward inclusive and ethical implementation of Al.

Universal Design for Learning (UDL): UDL, developed by CAST, promotes flexibility in curriculum design to accommodate learner variability. Its three core principles-multiple means of representation, expression, and engagement can be amplified by Al technologies.

Al tools aligned with UDL, such as adaptive reading software, real-time translation, and personalized learning pathways, can remove learning barriers and enhance access for students with diverse needs ("Inclusion, Equity, Diversity, and Social Justice in Education", 2023). However, alignment with UDL must be intentional; poorly designed Al risks replicating one-size-fits-all models under the guise of personalization.

Critical Pedagogy: Inspired by Paulo Freire, critical pedagogy views education as a means of liberation. It emphasizes dialogue, critical consciousness, and resistance to oppressive systems. In Al-enhanced environments, this pedagogy calls for participatory technology development, transparency in algorithmic decisions, and tools that empower rather than discipline.

This means integrating community voices into Al design, ensuring representational fairness, and fostering tools that promote reflection, inquiry, and justice over surveillance and control ("Inclusion, Equity, Diversity, and Social Justice in Education", 2023).

Inclusive Pedagogy: Inclusive pedagogy positions diversity not as a barrier but as a strength. It assumes that all learners can contribute meaningfully to the learning process when supported by responsive teaching. In Al contexts, this requires that algorithms be used to promote collaboration, foster learner engagement, and support multiple pathways to success (Shaeffer, 2019).

Equally important is the need for educator training-not only in technical skills but in inclusive pedagogical practices and Al ethics, ensuring that technology complements rather than compromises learner agency.

## Global Benchmarks: SDG 4 and UNESCO's Equity and Inclusion Agenda

International commitments provide a normative foundation for national and institutional reform efforts aimed at inclusion and equity in education.

Sustainable Development Goal 4 (SDG 4): Adopted in 2015, SDG 4 seeks to "ensure inclusive and equitable quality education and promote lifelong learning opportunities for all" by 2030. Key targets include:

- Eliminating gender disparities
- Ensuring universal literacy and numeracy
- Promoting global citizenship and education for sustainable development
- Integrating ICT and digital learning tools equitably

While Al has the potential to support these goals, especially through scalable, personalized, and context-aware solutions, it must be governed inclusively to avoid widening digital and structural gaps.

UNESCO's Equity and Inclusion Agenda: UNESCO's 2020 Global Education Monitoring Report promotes a rights-based and whole-system approach to educational inclusion. It emphasizes:

- Bridging the digital divide
- Promoting inclusive teacher training
- Creating equitable financing models
- Developing data systems that track and address disparities (Sánchez-Santamaría & Vila, 2014)

Despite these robust global benchmarks, significant implementation gaps persist. Under-resourced schools, discriminatory policies, and inaccessible digital platforms continue to marginalize millions of learners-highlighting that policy intent must be backed by systemic transformation (Shaeffer, 2019; Cegolon, 2022).

This section has offered a conceptual foundation to understand inclusion and equity in education through definitions, theories, pedagogical models, and global standards. As the education sector increasingly embraces Al, it becomes critical to interrogate how these technologies align with-or undermine these foundational values.

The challenge ahead is not merely technological but profoundly ethical and political: Will Al replicate exclusion under new guises, or will it help build an education system that serves every learner with dignity, justice, and care?

The next section will explore this alignment further by examining current applications of Al in education, assessing both its transformative potential and its unintended consequences in real-world contexts.

## INTELLIGENCE IN EDUCATION (AIED): ARTIFICIAL CAPABILITIES AND TOOLS

The integration of Artificial Intelligence (AI) in education has become a transformative force, ushering in a new era of personalized, inclusive, and efficient learning. Al technologies-particularly machine learning (ML), natural language processing (NLP). computer vision (CV), and generative models are reshaping educational environments by enhancing leaming experiences, optimizing institutional processes, and offering innovative tools that empower both students and educators. As the digital leaming ecosystem expands, Al is no longer a peripheral innovation but a central enabler of educational equity and innovation across diverse global contexts.

Al-driven systems now play a critical role in enabling adaptive, learner-centered instruction through tools such as intelligent tutoring systems (ITS), adaptive leaming platforms, chatbots, virtual assistants, and learning analytics. These technologies support individualized instruction, identify at-risk students, enhance engagement, and streamline administrative functions. As Al continues to evolve, its potential to catalyze inclusive education-particularly in underserved and linguistically diverse settings is becoming increasingly evident ("AI And Education: Guidance for Policymakers," 2021; Luckin, 2018).

This section offers a comprehensive overview of the key Al subfields underpinning educational innovation, surveys commonly used Al tools in education, analyzes the expanding role of generative Al in higher education, and provides a brief review of emerging global research on Al's educational applications.

### Defining Al and Its Key Subfields

Artificial Intelligence is a field of computer science dedicated to creating systems capable of performing tasks that require human-like intelligence, such as learning, reasoning, and problem-solving. In education, Al functions as a socio-technical enabler-leveraging data, algorithms, and real-time feedback to support teaching and learning. The following subfields form the technical backbone of Al in education:

Machine Learning (ML): Machine learning involves creating algorithms that can learn from and make predictions or decisions based on data. In adaptive learning platforms, ML enables dynamic customization of content, allowing instructional materials to align with individual learners' cognitive needs and performance levels.

Systems like Squirrel Al in China and Carnegie Learning in the U.S. exemplify this capability by adjusting content to learners' pace and knowledge retention patterns (Young, 2024; Luckin, 2018). ML thus enhances differentiation in instruction-particularly in mixed-ability or resource-constrained classrooms.

Natural Language Processing (NLP): NLP allows machines to understand, interpret, and generate human language. In education, NLP powers chatbots, automated essay scoring, real-time translation, and intelligent tutoring systems. Tools like Google's Read Along and Microsoft's Immersive Reader demonstrate how NLP can support multilingual learners and enhance literacy through pronunciation and comprehension feedback (Young, 2024; "AI And Education: Guidance for Policymakers," 2021). NLP also plays a role in social-emotional learning by enabling sentiment analysis to detect disengagement or emotional distress in students.

Computer Vision (CV): Computer vision enables Al systems to interpret visual input such as images or videos. In classrooms, CV supports tools that monitor student engagement, track attendance, or provide real-time feedback on student gestures and interactions. It also facilitates accessibility-e.g., reading visual content aloud for students with visual impairments. These applications make CV particularly valuable in inclusive learning environments (Young, 2024; Leong et al., 2025).

## Common AI Tools in Education

A wide range of Al tools are now embedded across various levels of the education sector, each contributing uniquely to instructional delivery, assessment, and learner support:

Intelligent Tutoring Systems (ITS): ITS provide customized, one-on-one instruction through Al algorithms that adapt in real time to a student's learning trajectory. These systems enhance engagement by delivering targeted interventions and personalized feedback. Examples like Carnegie Learning and Knewton show how ITS platforms can support mastery learning in complex subjects like mathematics and science (Leong et al., 2025).

Adaptive Learning Platforms: These platforms leverage real-time data to adjust content, sequencing, and difficulty based on a student's evolving understanding. DreamBox and Smart Sparrow, for instance, personalize the learning experience by avoiding redundancy and addressing gaps-resulting in improved learning efficiency and motivation (Leong et al., 2025). In contexts like India's DIKSHA platform, Al also aids in multi-language content curation and digital lesson planning.

Chatbots and Virtual Assistants: Al-powered chatbots offer continuous academic and emotional support. Systems like Woebot provide mental health interventions, while others like MATHia offer subject-specific guidance. These tools ensure 24/7 availability, reducing students' reliance on teacher availability while enhancing learner autonomy (Leong et al., 2025).

Learning Analytics and Predictive Systems: Al analyzes vast datasets generated through student interactions to identify learning patterns, predict dropouts, and inform targeted support. Predictive analytics can help educators intervene proactively, thus preventing academic failure and improving retention rates (Leong et al., 2025).

## Overview of Generative AI in Higher Education

Generative Al (GenAl) refers to systems capable of producing new content-text, images, videos by learning from existing data. In higher education, generative tools like ChatGPT, Claude, and DALL-E have opened up new pedagogical possibilities, from automated content creation and translation to scenario-based learning and virtual simulations (Batista et al., 2024). These tools enable educators to generate custom quizzes, case studies, or feedback aligned with learning outcomes and student profiles.

However, GenAl also poses ethical and academic challenges. The use of Al-generated content in assessments raises concerns about plagiarism and undermines the development of critical thinking if over-relied upon (Khan & Saunderson, 2024). Institutions must therefore implement academic integrity policies and train faculty to integrate GenAl responsibly into pedagogical design.

## Brief Review of Current Literature on AI in Education

Recent literature reflects a growing consensus on Al's transformative role in global education. Studies emphasize Al's potential to improve student outcomes, personalize learning, and address disparities in access-particularly when combined with human-centered pedagogy (Kavitha & Joshith, 2024). Research also highlights the value of interdisciplinary collaborations in advancing AIED systems and scaling innovation across contexts.

Nevertheless, persistent challenges remain. These include algorithmic bias, lack of transparency, and inequitable access to Al infrastructure. In low-income and rural settings, limited connectivity, linguistic mismatches, and insufficient teacher training hinder effective Al deployment (Batista et al., 2024; “AI And Education: Guidance for Policy-makers,” 2021). For instance, sub-Saharan Africa's M-Shule demonstrates how low-tech, SMS-based Al systems can overcome connectivity barriers, suggesting that context-sensitive design is essential for equity (M-Shule, 2020).

Moreover, the literature calls for stronger governance frameworks to address data privacy and student autonomy. Without transparent oversight and inclusive policies, Al systems risk reproducing systemic biases rather than eliminating them (Floridi, 2023).

In summary, Artificial Intelligence in Edlication (AIED) represents a powerful catalyst for educational innovation and inclusion. Its subfields-machine learning, NLP, computer vision, and generative Al-drive a range of tools that can personalize learning, support teachers, and enhance access for marginalized learners. However, the true potential of AIED will only be realized when these technologies are designed and deployed with ethical foresight, cultural sensitivity, and systemic equity in mind. As UNESCO (2021) emphasizes, the future of Al in education must be shaped by the principles of justice, inclusion, and learner empowerment. The following section will explore these ethical imperatives in greater depth and propose strategies for ensuring that Al serves as a force for educational equity rather than exclusion.

## FROM MARGINS TO MAINSTREAM: AI & INCLUSIVE LEARNING

The increasing integration of Artificial Intelligence (Al) in education has shifted the paradigm from traditional, one-size-fits-all teaching methods to highly personalized and inclusive learning experiences. Al has proven instrumental in addressing the diverse needs of learners by tailoring content delivery based on individual learning styles, preferences, and performance. Through technologies such as adaptive learning systems, intelligent tutoring, and data-driven insights, Al not only enhances educational outcomes but also promotes equity. It expands learning opportunities for historically marginalized groups-students from low socioeconomic backgrounds, rural areas, first-generation learners, multilingual communities, and neurodiverse students.

This section explores how Al is advancing personalized learning and fostering inclusive educational environments, while also engaging with ethical challenges, systemic inequities. and context-based limitations. Drawing on global research and case studies, we examine how Al must be critically designed and inclusively implemented to truly shift education from the margins to the mainstream.

### How AI Enables Tailored Content Delivery Based on Learning Styles and Performance

One of the most widely promoted promises of Al in education is its capacity to personalize learning by adapting content, pace, and support to the needs of each learner. In traditional classrooms, teaching often relies on uniform instruction, assuming all students learn the same way. Al disrupts this model by leveraging real-time learner data such as response accuracy, engagement time, and clickstream patterns to deliver differentiated instruction.

Adaptive Learning Systems: Al-powered adaptive learning platforms such as DreamBox, Smart Sparrow, and Knewton dynamically adjust lessons based on students' performance and learning preferences. These platforms provide tailored recommendations, monitor learning trajectories, and optimize instructional pathways to keep leamers engaged (Gupta, 2024). For example, MATHia by Carnegie Learning offers step-by-step scaffolding based on students' problem-solving patterns, enabling deeper understanding over rote memorization. Research shows that adaptive learning improves both comprehension and retention, especially among learners who may struggle in conventional settings (Y et al., 2024).

Intelligent Tutoring Systems (ITS): Intelligent Tutoring Systems (ITS) simulate the benefits of individualized instruction by diagnosing learner misconceptions and providing real-time feedback. Platforms like Carnegie Learning and Knewton exemplify how ITS can intervene at key learning moments to guide struggling students toward mastery (Taşkın, 2025). These systems are designed to be responsive, emotionally supportive,and scalable qualities critical for learners with limited access to human tutors.

Data-Driven Insights for Educators: Al also equips educators with actionable insights based on student learning patterns. By analyzing performance data, teachers can identify trends, flag at-risk students early, and tailor support strategies (Murthy et al., 2024). However, meaningful personalization must consider not just academic metrics but also emotional and behavioral indicators. As Holmes et al. (2019) note, personalization without pedagogical intentionality can reinforce the very inequalities it seeks to overcome.

## Case Studies on Improved Learning Outcomes for Marginalized Students

Al has demonstrated significant potential in supporting marginalized students-those historically underserved due to economic, geographic, linguistic, or social factors. These learners often face systemic barriers, including under-resourced schools, unqualified teachers, and curriculum misalignment. Al tools, when inclusively designed, can mitigate these challenges.

Socioeconomic and Rural Students: In rural and low-income areas, where quality teaching and digital infrastructure are scarce, Al-powered platforms such as Khan Academy, Duolingo, and Byju's have broadened access to high-quality content. These platforms use Al to adjust pacing, provide instant feedback, and reinforce learning through repetition and gamification. Studies have found that students in under-resourced regions improve their performance when using adaptive tools that respond to their learning gaps and preferences (Taşkın, 2025).

First-Generation Students: For first-generation learners navigating unfamiliar educational systems, Al can offer discreet, 24/7 support via platforms like Coursera and edX. These tools empower students with autonomy, allowing them to self-direct their learning without fear of judgment (Y et al., 2024). Personalized learning journeys help build academic confidence and foster a sense of belonging-key factors for retention and success.

## Role of Al in Multilingual Learning, Cultural Adaptation, and Neurodiverse Learners

Beyond individual adaptation, inclusive Al must address the needs of learners from varied linguistic, cultural, and cognitive backgrounds. Without such considerations, personalization risks becoming narrow and culturally blind.

Multilingual Learning and Cultural Contexts: Al-powered translation and language learning tools such as Google Translate, Microsoft Translator, and Reading Progress-enable multilingual students to engage with content in their native language. However, many of these systems struggle with underrepresented languages due to limited training data, exacerbating digital colonialism ("AI And Education: Guidance for Policy-makers," 2021). For true inclusivity, Al must incorporate culturally responsive personalization, adapting examples, narratives, and idioms to resonate with local realities (Damyanov, 2024).

Neurodiverse Learners and Assistive Al: Al tools support neurodiverse students through features like predictive typing, text-to-speech, emotion recognition, and multimodal content presentation. These tools-when grounded in frameworks such as Universal Design for Learning (UDL) empower learners to engage with content through their preferred modes of interaction ("AI And Education: Guidance for Policy-makers," 2021). For example, students with dyslexia may benefit from voice-based instructions, while learners with ADHD might prefer gamified modules that maintain attention.

However, for such tools to be effective, they must be co-developed with the input of neurodiverse learners and educators who understand their specific needs. UDL-aligned Al platforms provide not only multiple means of representation but also options for assessment and expression-fostering deeper inclusivity.

## Ethical Considerations and Challenges

Despite its promise, Al's role in education must be approached with caution. Algorithmic bias, opaque decision-making, and unequal access can deepen existing divides rather than close them.

Data Bias and Misclassification: If Al systems are trained predominantly on data from privileged learners, they risk misclassifying or misunderstanding students from different socio-economic or cultural contexts. For instance, prediction models may undervalue learners from under-resourced schools or misinterpret their performance Tatterns (Luckin, 2018). This can lead to misaligned interventions or reinforcement of stereotypes.

Privacy, Transparency, and Learner Agency: Al-powered systems rely on vast amounts of personal data-raising critical concerns about consent, transparency, and control. Students and educators must have clear information about how data is collected, used, and shared. Ethical Al systems should offer learners control over their data and avoid surveillance-based models of engagement (Taşkın, 2025; Y et al., 2024).

Infrastructure and Policy Gaps: For Al to serve marginalized learners, there must be equitable access to digital infrastructure, teacher training, and localized content. Without deliberate policies to address these gaps, Al risks benefiting the already privileged.

Al is playing a transformative role in making education more personalized, inclusive, and equitable. It offers unprecedented potential to adapt learning experiences to individual needs and to reach marginalized learners at scale. From intelligent tutoring and adaptive platforms to culturally relevant content and assistive technologies, Al is helping to bridge historical gaps in education.

Yet, this transformation is not automatic. Personalization must not be reduced to algorithmic efficiency but must be informed by inclusive pedagogies, ethical design, and local context. As Holmes et al. (2019) argue, effective personalization is a pedagogical commitment, not just a technical function.

To truly move from the margins to the mainstream, Al in education must be designed for equity, justice, and learner empowerment. When aligned with inclusive frameworks like Universal Design for Learning, and governed by strong ethical safeguards, Al can help realize the vision of education that serves all-especially those most often left behind.

## AI AND ACCESSIBILITY: SUPPORTING SPECIAL NEEDS

Artificial Intelligence (AI) has demonstrated transformative potential in making education more accessible for learners with disabilities and special needs. By integrating AI with assistive technologies such as text-to-speech, captioning, gesture recognition, and emerging tools like computer vision and brain-computer interfaces, AI enables educational environments that are inclusive, flexible, and aligned with Universal Design for Learning (UDL) principles. These technologies not only foster equity in educational participation but also offer personalized learning pathways, enabling all students to thrive regardless of their physical, sensory, or cognitive challenges.

AI's potential goes beyond accommodation; it actively removes learning barriers and reshapes educational design, especially for underrepresented learners in Science, Technology, Engineering, and Mathematics (STEM) and those in remote or resource-constrained environments. This section explores the advancements in AI-enhanced assistive technologies, their alignment with UDL, and their application in fostering inclusive, ethical, and empowering learning ecosystems.

### AI-Enhanced Assistive Technologies

AI-powered assistive technologies are essential for inclusive education, supporting a wide range of disabilities-from visual and auditory to mobility and neurodevelopmental conditions. These tools enhance student engagement, independence, and participation by providing adaptive learning interfaces tailored to individual needs.

Text-to-Speech and Captioning: AI-driven text-to-speech (TTS) systems convert written content into spoken language, benefiting students with visual impairments by enabling auditory interaction with digital materials. Tools such as Kurzweil 3000 and Read&Write enhance comprehension by allowing learners to listen while reading (Krishnan & Manickam, 2024). Similarly, AI-powered real-time captioning technologies like Otter.ai and Rev assist students with hearing impairments by transcribing spoken language in videos, lectures, and discussions, making auditory content accessible and inclusive.

Beyond traditional captioning, tools like Google Live Transcribe and Ava add real-time multi-speaker transcription capabilities, supporting more dynamic learning environments. Additionally, sign language recognition tools powered by AI are expanding communication pathways for deaf learners, offering real-time interpretation of signed gestures into text or voice.

Gesture Recognition and Alternative Interfaces: Gesture recognition technologies use AI to translate physical gestures, eye movements, or facial expressions into commands, allowing students with motor impairments to interact with educational content without relying on standard input devices. These systems enhance autonomy and accessibility, especially when combined with other adaptive technologies (Roy et al., n.d.). Eye-tracking software and brain-computer interfaces (BCIs) represent the next frontier in inclusive education, offering direct, non-physical interaction with learning materials-particularly beneficial for learners with severe mobility challenges. Computer Vision for the Visually Impaired: Al applications like Microsoft Seeing Al, Google Lookout, and Be My Eyes leverage computer vision to describe surroundings, people, and text in real time. These tools provide visually impaired learners with increased independence and real-time contextual understanding, enabling self-paced engagement with both academic and environmental content.

## Alignment with Universal Design for Learning (UDL)

UDL advocates for designing educational systems that are inherently inclusive by offering multiple means of engagement, representation, and expression. Al technologies are uniquely suited to support UDL by enabling flexible and personalized learning experiences.

Personalized Learning: Al tools like DreamBox and Moodle adapt content based on a learner's preferences, performance, and pace, offering tailored educational paths for students with disabilities (Kohnke & Zaugg, 2025). These platforms analyze student behavior to present content in formats-visual, auditory, or kinesthetic-that best suit individual learning profiles, thereby ensuring more effective and meaningful learning experiences.

Engagement and Motivation: Al enhances engagement by breaking down complex content-particularly in STEM-into manageable segments and providing timely feedback. For students with disabilities, these tools reduce frustration and build confidence through goal-oriented, supportive learning structures. Tools like Jellow Communicator and CogniAble also support students with autism and ADHD by facilitating social interaction, modeling behaviors, and tracking emotional states, thereby contributing to both academic and socio-emotional development (World Bank, 2022).

Al systems further support expression by enabling students to respond through voice, touch, gestures, or visual media, helping overcome barriers to traditional communication and assessment methods.

## Improving Participation in STEM Education

STEM fields have traditionally seen lower participation rates among students with disabilities, often due to inaccessible materials and lack of adaptive instructional methods. AI is changing this by offering personalized, data-driven learning tools that promote inclusivity.

Adaptive Learning Platforms: Platforms such as Knewton and Carnegie Learning dynamically adjust difficulty levels and content formats, supporting differentiated instruction for students with disabilities (Roy et al., n.d.). These platforms incorporate features like audio descriptions, interactive simulations, and step-by-step breakdowns of complex concepts-crucial for students facing sensory or cognitive barriers in STEM.

Case Studies and Successful Implementations: Oyedokun (2024) documented how AI-based interventions in STEM curricula increased engagement and comprehension among visually impaired learners. Virtual labs like Labster and STEM Digital simulate experimental settings, allowing students with mobility impairments to participate in science activities they might otherwise miss. These AI-enhanced tools democratize access to experiential learning in science and engineering.

## Application in Remote, Resource-Poor Settings

In rural and underserved areas, access to educational resources and assistive technologies is often limited. AI offers scalable and cost-effective solutions that bridge this divide.

Accessibility in Challenging Environments: Mobile-based AI tools, such as Voice Dream Reader and Learning Ally, provide essential services like TTS and audio-based learning, even on low-cost smartphones (Krishnan & Manickam, 2024). These applications support inclusive learning without requiring expensive or specialized hardware. Additionally, AI's cloud-based infrastructure ensures content can be delivered and personalized remotely, overcoming geographic and economic barriers.

Cost-Effective and Scalable Solutions: AI's ability to automate contest delivery, assessment, and customization allows schools with limited human or financial resources to provide high-quality education to all learners. Integrating AI with open-source platforms enhances affordability and sustainability, enabling broad implementation in developing contexts (Oyedokun, 2024).

However, many AI tools are trained on data from high-income, English-speaking environments, making them less effective in local contexts. Localization and language inclusivity must therefore be prioritized to ensure equitable impact.

## Ethical Considerations and Challenges

While Al-driven assistive technologies offer immense promise, several ethical issues must be addressed to ensure they do not unintentionally reinforce inequities.

Algorithmic Bias and Cultural Limitations: Al systems can exhibit bias if trained on narrow datasets, potentially marginalizing learners from underrepresented linguistic or cultural backgrounds. Tools must be designed with diverse user inputs and contexts to ensure fairness and relevance (Kohnke & Zaugg, 2025).

Data Privacy and Surveillance: Continuous monitoring features-such as emotion tracking or behavior prediction-raise significant concerns about privacy, consent, and autonomy. Learners with disabilities must be protected from over-surveillance and data misuse through transparent governance and ethical Al frameworks (Floridi, 2023).

Designing for Inclusion: Al tools must be co-designed with the involvement of people with disabilities, educators, and caregivers to ensure alignment with real-world needs. UNESCO (2021) and Holmes et al. (2019) emphasize that inclusive Al must be rooted in universal design principles, user agency, and ethical accountability to ensure no learner is left behind.

Al is revolutionizing accessibility in education, offering unprecedented opportunities for learners with disabilities and special needs. Through tools like TTS, captioning, gesture recognition, and emotion-aware platforms, Al dismantles traditional barriers to learning. Its alignment with Universal Design for Learning principles enhances flexibility and engagement, particularly in STEM fields and remote contexts. However, to realize the full potential of Al, ethical considerations, equitable design, and contextual adaptability must guide development. By embedding inclusion at the core of educational Al, we can truly expand access, autonomy, and opportunity for all learners.

## STRUCTURAL & ETHICAL CHALLENGES IN AI INCLUSION

The integration of Artificial Intelligence (AI) in education promises to revolutionize the learning experience by offering personalized, adaptive, and inclusive learning environments. However, the application of Al in educational settings is not without significant structural challenges and ethical complexities. If not implemented thoughtfully, Al can reinforce existing inequities, introduce new biases, and deepen the digital divide-undermining its very purpose of fostering inclusion. This section critically examines these structural and ethical challenges, incorporating multiple perspectives to highlight the risks, tensions, and necessary frameworks for equitable and responsible Al deployment in education.

## Algorithmic Bias: Discriminatory Outcomes Due to Skewed Data

One of the most pressing concerns in Al integration into education is algorithmic bias. Algorithmic bias occurs when Al systems produce discriminatory outcomes due to skewed or incomplete datasets, leading to unjust treatment of certain student groups. In educational contexts, this can result in Al systems that misinterpret student performance, disproportionately disadvantaging marginalized groups such as low-income students, students of color, and those with disabilities.

For example, biased data can lead to Al systems misclassifying the learning needs of students, assigning them inappropriate interventions, or perpetuating existing stereotypes. Research has shown that Al systems trained on biased data often reflect societal inequalities, such as racial, gender, and socio-economic disparities, further exacerbating the educational gap (Farooqi et al., 2024). In particular, when Al systems are trained on historical data that reflects these biases, they inadvertently reinforce them, leading to decisions that disadvantage certain student demographics.

Beyond data imbalance, the issue of data poverty-where students from underrepresented regions or groups are not adequately reflected in training datasets-creates inherent structural limitations. Algorithms trained on such narrow datasets often perform poorly in diverse educational settings (Holmes et al., 2019). As UNESCO (2021) warns, "biased Al systems can systematically exclude students who are already vulnerable to educational disadvantage."

Addressing algorithmic bias requires rigorous data auditing to ensure fairness and transparency in Al systems. As Sywelem & Mahklouf (2024) suggest, fairness principles must be integrated into Al models from the outset. Debiasing strategies, inclusive data collection, and the involvement of diverse stakeholders-particularly educators, students, and marginalized communities are essential to creating more equitable Al tools.

## The Digital Divide: Inequity in Infrastructure, Device Access, and Connectivity

Despite the potential of Al to enhance learning, its effectiveness is heavily constrained by the digital divide. In many low-income, rural, and developing regions, students and teachers lack access to the necessary infrastructure-reliable internet, electricity, and digital devices-to participate in Al-enhanced education.

Farooqi et al. (2024) highlight that many students in developing regions do not have access to devices such as computers, tablets, or smartphones, which are essential for using Al-enhanced educational tools. Similarly, unreliable internet access exacerbates the problem, hindering participation in online learning and access to cloud-based Al applications.

Moreover, disparities in digital literacy among students, teachers, and caregivers compound the issue. Even in regions where basic infrastructure is available, lack of capacity to effectively engage with Al tools can widen the achievement gap (World Bank, 2022). Language barriers, low digital confidence, and limited user training further marginalize under-resourced communities.

To bridge this divide, it is essential to ensure that all students have equal access to the technology required for Al integration. Yadav (2024) emphasizes the need for public-private partnerships to increase the availability of affordable devices and internet connectivity. Offline Al tools and mobile-based platforms can also help mitigate infrastructure gaps by providing access in low-resource environments. Proactive inclusion strategies are essential to prevent the transformation of the digital divide into a digital exclusion crisis.

## Teacher Preparedness: Capacity Gaps and Resistance to Technology

Teacher preparedness is a critical factor in the success or failure of Al implementation in education. Many educators face capacity gaps, ranging from inadequate training to limited understanding of Al tools and their pedagogical integration. There is also notable resistance to Al adoption, often stemming from concerns about job displacement, lack of trust, and a fear of technology overtaking human roles in the classroom.

Farooqi et al. (2024) note that teachers often struggle to adapt their teaching methods to incorporate Al tools, leading to either ineffective use or outright rejection of such technologies. This reluctance is often rooted in systemic gaps in professional development and the absence of participatory design, where educators are included in shaping Al tools that align with their instructional nejads.

Luckin (2018) emphasizes that teachers should be positioned not as passive users but as active co-creators of Al systems. Professional development programs must focus on pedagogical alignment, digital upskilling, and critical engagement with Al. Empowering teachers to integrate Al meaningfully-rather than fearing replacement-can transform Al from a disruptive force into a collaborative partner in the learning process.

## Ethical Concerns: Data Privacy, Consent, Surveillance, and Transparency

Ethical concerns surrounding Al in education are particularly significant due to the vast amounts of personal and behavioral data collected by these systems. Key concerns include data privacy, informed consent, surveillance, and the opaque nature of algorithmic decision-making.

Al systems may collect sensitive data on students' academic performance, behavioral patterns, emotional states, and even biometric markers. While these data can offer valuable insights for personalized learning, they also pose risks of misuse and exploitation. As Contreras & Jaimes (2024) argue, ensuring that Al systems are transparent about their data practices and that students (and guardians) provide informed consent is vital to maintaining trust.

Floridi and Cowls (2022) caution that "Al in education must preserve the dignity, agency, and privacy of every learner, especially when decisions are automated." Surveillance-based Al tools, including emotion-detection software and behavior tracking, risk infringing on student autonomy if deployed without appropriate ethical safeguards.

Effective data governance, strict access controls, anonymization protocols, and clear ethical guidelines must be embedded into the deployment of Al systems in education. Regulatory oversight and legal frameworks-such as the GDPR-must be expanded and adapted to meet the specific nuances of Al in educational environments.

## Frameworks for Ethical Al: Fairness, Accountability, and Explainability (FAIR Principles)

To navigate these structural and ethical concerns, robust frameworks for ethical Al are essential. The FAIR principles-Fairness, Accountability, and Explainability-offer foundational guidelines for the responsible use of Al in education.

- Fairness means Al systems must be designed and tested to avoid discriminatory outcomes. They should serve all learners equitably, regardless of socioeconomic status, ethnicity, gender, or disability (Sywelem & Mahklouf, 2024).
- Accountability involves assigning clear responsibility to those who design, deploy, and manage Al tools. In education, developers and institutions must be accountable for any harm or bias caused by these systems and provide mechanisms for appeal or redress.
- Explainability requires that Al systems offer transparent and interpretable insights into how decisions are made. Students, teachers, and administrators

must be able to understand the rationale behind Al recommendations (Islam, 2024), which is critical for building trust and ensuring educational integrity.

Additionally, the FAIR principles in the data science domain-Findable, Accessible, Interoperable, and Reusable should be adapted for education. This includes ensuring that Al tools and educational content are easily discoverable, usable across languages and abilities, compatible across platforms, and adaptable for local contexts (OECD, 20230).

The integration of Al in education presents a paradox: while it holds enormous promise for personalized and inclusive learning, it also carries the risk of reinforcing structural inequities and ethical violations. To ensure that Al fulfills its inclusive potential, stakeholders must address algorithmic bias, bridge the digital divide, empower educators, and uphold the highest standards of data ethics.

As emphasized by both Farooqi et al. (2024) and leading international organizations, a multi-stakeholder approach-grounded in fairness, transparency, and accountability-is essential. Governments, technology developers, educators, and civil society must work together to design inclusive Al tools, establish regulatory safeguards, and embed digital literacy across curricula. Only then can we realize the vision of Al as a truly transformative force for equity and inclusion in education.

## POLICY & STRATEGIES FOR INCLUSIVE AI

The successful integration of Artificial Intelligence (AI) in education depends on the development of robust policy frameworks and institutional strategies that prioritize inclusion, ethics, and sustainability. Governments, international organizations, and educational institutions must play a central role in shaping these strategies by developing national and global policies, supporting educator training, creating ethical AI models, and fostering public-private partnerships to build inclusive EdTech ecosystems.

At the policy level, national and international bodies must balance innovation with ethical safeguards. Regulatory frameworks are essential to mitigate issues such as data privacy violations and algorithmic bias, ensuring transparency and fairness across AI tools (Lamberti, 2024; Sywelem & Mahklouf, 2024). UNESCO'(2025) emphasizes that AI should be human-centered, equity-driven, and aligned with Sustainable Development Goal 4, calling for investments in digital infrastructure and inclusive curricula. However, while these initiatives are valuable, uneven implementation due to local capacity gaps and resource disparities continues to pose a challenge. Governments can also support innovation by investing in digital platforms, as seen in India's NEP 2020 and DIKSHA initiative, though success hinges on addressing rural connectivity, training shortfalls, and language diversity (Mehta & Kapoor, 2021; Norton, 2024).

For AI to be meaningfully embedded in education, educator training and institutional support are vital. Professional development must be continuous and ethically grounded, equipping teachers with the skills to understand and manage AI tools in student-centered ways (Singh & Thakur, 2024). Institutions should provide the necessary technological resources and ensure ongoing technical support. At the same time, educators must be actively involved in AI policy-making. Their practical experience helps ensure that AI solutions are relevant, usable, and pedagogically sound (Norton, 2024).

Ethical integration of AI requires clear frameworks to guide development and use. UNESCO's ethics guidelines highlight principles such as explainability, stakeholder understanding, and institutional accountability (*AI Ethics and Higher Education*, 2022). Successful implementation often stems from collaborative design involving teachers, learners, developers, and policymakers (Singh & Thakur, 2024). Additionally, global organizations like the OECD (2023) recommend impact assessments and regulatory oversight to safeguard student data and encourage local innovation. These audits ensure AI systems remain inclusive and contextually appropriate.

Collaboration between public and private actors is also critical in scaling inclusive AI tools. Open-source platforms promote equitable access across diverse contexts, while public-private partnerships (PPPs) can generate adaptable tools that reduce digital divides (Singh & Thakur, 2024). PPPs also support innovation hubs for research, tool development, and teacher training, as exemplified by initiatives like UNICEF's GIGA (Williamson & Hogan, 2022; Lamberti, 2024). However, these collaborations must be carefully managed to prevent private entities from dominating educational priorities or misusing learner data (Williamson & Hogan, 2022).

Building inclusive EdTech ecosystems requires an iterative and participatory approach. Stakeholder engagement—including input from teachers, students, parents, and technologists—is essential to ensure policies and tools reflect diverse needs (Norton, 2024). Given the rapid evolution of AI, policy development must remain flexible, supported by continuous feedback, monitoring, and adaptation (Lamberti, 2024; Sywelem & Mahklouf, 2024). Rigorous evaluation frameworks are needed to assess both the educational and equity impacts of AI tools and guide future improvements (Sywelem & Mahklouf, 2024).

In sum, policy and institutional strategies are essential to ensure AI supports inclusion rather than deepens inequality. Aligning ethical principles with practical implementation—through strong policy, educator support, stakeholder collaboration, and responsive governance—can help build AI ecosystems that promote educational justice. With a rights-based, transparent, and participatory approach, AI has the potential to become a powerful tool for equity and inclusion in education.

## CASE STUDIES AND GLOBAL BEST PRACTICES

The integration of Artificial Intelligence (AI) in education is rapidly transforming the learning landscape, particularly in enhancing inclusivity and equitable access to education. Several global initiatives demonstrate how Al can bridge gaps in educational accessibility, support personalized learning, and cater to diverse student needs. This section highlights key case studies from India, Sub-Saharan Africa, Latin America, and higher education institutions, analyzing the success factors and limitations of these Al-driven initiatives.

### India's Diksha Platform and Al Inclusion Efforts

India's DIKSHA (Digital Infrastructure for Knowledge Sharing) platform is a prime example of Al application aimed at improving educational access for diverse populations, particularly in remote and underserved areas.

Personalized Learning: Diksha offers a range of personalized educational content tailored to students' individual learning levels, supporting a variety of linguistic and cultural backgrounds (Gupta & Kaul, 2024). The Al tools on the platform adapt the learning materials based on the student's pace, creating a more customized learning experience.

The platform utilizes Al-driven metadata tagging and adaptive engines to align content with state-specific curricula. It supports access in over 30 Indian languages, promoting inclusivity for linguistic minorities and tribal learners (Mehta & Kapoor, 2021). Teachers also benefit through analytics-driven tools that identify struggling students and allow for timely pedagogical intervention (World Bank, 20220).

Assistive Technologies: The platform integrates Al-powered tools like text-to-speech converters, subtitles, and content customization for learners with disabilities (Gupta & Kaul, 2024), improving accessibility.

Challenges: Despite its successes, the implementation of Diksha faces significant challenges. These include issues related to technological infrastructure, especially in rural areas, where internet connectivity and device availability are often limited. Additionally, the linguistic diversity of India poses barriers, as Al tools may not always effectively accommodate all local languages and dialects (Gupta & Kaul, 2024). Without adequate digital access and educator support, the full potential of DIKSHA's Al capabilities remains unrealized (World Bank, 2022).

### Al in Sub-Saharan Africa

In Sub-Saharan Africa, Al is being leveraged to bridge significant educational gaps, particularly in rural and remote regions where access to quality education is often limited. Mobile Learning Solutions: Al-driven mobile learning platforms are particularly effective in Sub-Saharan Africa, where mobile phones are more accessible than traditional computing devices. These platforms provide educational content, assessments, and feedback through mobile applications, helping students overcome geographical and infrastructure barriers (Leveraging Al to Bridge Educational Inequities: A Global Perspective, 2024).

A notable example is M-Shule, a Kenya-based adaptive learning platform that delivers personalized lessons via SMS and basic mobile phones. Using natural language processing (NLP) and machine learning, M-Shule enables learners in low-resource settings to engage with customized content in local languages, without the need for internet access (M-Shule, 2020). The platform also sends performance data to teachers and parents, encouraging localized support and accountability.

Community Engagement: Successful initiatives in the region often involve community engagement, ensuring that local cultural contexts and educational needs are considered. By working with local educators and communities, Al tools are tailored to be more relevant and sustainable in the long term (Leveraging Al to Bridge Educational Inequities: A Global Perspective, 2024).

Limitations: The digital divide continues to be a significant issue, with limited internet access and low technological literacy hindering the widespread adoption of Al solutions. Furthermore, the lack of adequately trained educators and the scarcity of resources for training them presents additional hurdles (Leveraging Al to Bridge Educational Inequities: A Global Perspective, 2024). Moreover, limitations in NLP for African dialects and dependence on SMS technology restrict the complexity and interactivity of Al-powered content (UNESCO, 2021).

## Latin American Initiatives for Al-Driven Inclusive STEM Learning

Latin America has emerged as a region with innovative uses of Al, particularly in STEM (Science, Technology, Engineering, and Mathematics) education, with an emphasis on inclusivity.

Collaborative Platforms: Al tools in Latin America are often designed to facilitate collaborative learning experiences, enabling students to work on joint STEM projects with peers from different regions. These platforms enhance students' leaming by promoting cross-border collaboration, fostering innovation, and providing exposure to diverse perspectives (Leveraging Al to Bridge Educational Inequities: A Global Perspective, 2024).

Examples include Uruguay's Plan Ceibal, which integrated Al into national learning systems during the COVID-19 pandemic to deliver adaptive assessments and teacher dashboards. Similarly, Colombia utilized Al chatbots on WhatsApp and low-bandwidth platforms to support students in rural and migrant communities (CEPAL, 20210).

Equity Focus: Many Al-driven initiatives in Latin America target underrepresented groups, particularly girls and minority communities, to ensure equitable access to STEM education. These programs are designed to bridge gender and socio-economic gaps, providing opportunities for students who may otherwise lack access to such education (Leveraging Al to Bridge Educational Inequities: A Global Perspective, 2024).

Barriers: However, these initiatives face challenges such as economic disparities and unequal access to technological infrastructure. Rural areas, in particular, suffer from poor internet connectivity and lack of devices, which hinders the scalability and impact of Al-based STEM programs (Leveraging Al to Bridge Educational Inequities: A Global Perspective, 2024). In addition, concerns around data privacy, teacher preparedness, and the inclusion of indigenous languages remain significant (CEPAL, 20210).

## Higher Education Institutions Using Al

Higher education institutions around the world are increasingly adopting Al to support diverse student populations, including those with language barriers and mental health needs.

Language Support: Al tools provide real-time translation services and language learning resources, assisting non-native speakers in comprehending course materials. These Al solutions help bridge the language gap, enabling students to engage more effectively with their education (Ohri, 2024).

Mental Health Services: Al-driven platforms are also being utilized to provide mental health support for students. These systems use Al to monitor students' well-being, identify those at risk of mental health issues, and offer timely interventions through virtual counseling and therapy sessions (Ohri, 2024).

Challenges: While these Al applications show promise, their implementation requires significant investment in infrastructure, as well as ongoing training for faculty and staff to effectively use these tools. The initial cost and training requirements can be a barrier for institutions, especially those with limited resources (Ohri, 2024).

## Analysis of Success Factors and Limitations

Across these case studies, several key success factors and limitations emerge in the use of Al for educational inclusivity:

Success Factors:

- Contextual Relevance: The most successful Al initiatives are those that consider the local context-whether it's linguistic diversity, socio-economic status, or geographical factors. Tailoring Al tools to fit the specific needs of the population ensures greater engagement and effectiveness.
- Community Involvement: Successful programs often involve local communities, educators, and policymakers in the design and implementation of Al tools. This ensures that the solutions are culturally appropriate and address real-world educational challenges.
- Scalability: Al solutions that are mobile-friendly or based on open-source platforms tend to have greater scalability. These tools can reach a larger number of students. especially in areas where traditional educational infrastructure is lacking.
- Low-Tech Innovation: Platforms like M-Shule demonstrate that Al need not be high-tech to be effective. Leveraging existing infrastructure like SMS can extend reach to underserved populations (M-Shule, 2020).

Limitations:

- Digital Divide: Access to technology remains a significant barrier. Many Al initiatives struggle to reach students in remote areas with poor internet connectivity and limited access to devices.
- Training and Capacity: The success of Al in education heavily relies on the capacity of educators to use these tools effectively. Without proper training and professional development, the potential of Al may be underutilized.
- Economic Barriers: In many developing regions, the high cost of implementing Al-based education programs, as well as the ongoing expenses related to infrastructure and training, poses significant challenges.
- Policy and Governance Gaps: Ethical deployment of Al, particularly in sensitive areas like student data, requires robust regulatory frameworks that are still underdeveloped in many regions ("AI And Education: Guidance for Policy-makers," 2021).

Al has the potential to be a powerful tool in bridging educational gaps and promoting inclusivity. The case studies from India, Sub-Saharan Africa, Latin America, and higher education institutions illustrate the diverse ways in which Al can enhance education. These initiatives underscore the importance of local context, low-tech innovation, and educator empowerment in designing inclusive Al systems. However, challenges such as technological access, training, ethical regulation, and socio-economic disparities must be addressed holistically to ensure Al fulfills its promise of equitable education for all.

## FUTURE PATHS: AI, EDUCATION & INCLUSION

The integration of Artificial Intelligence (AI) in education holds transformative potential to reshape how learning is accessed, delivered, and experienced. As global education systems shift toward equitable, personalized, and lifelong learning, AI offers adaptive technologies that address diverse learner needs, accelerate pedagogical innovation, and reduce systemic inequalities. However, realizing this vision requires more than technological advancement—it demands intentional ethical, cultural, and policy stewardship.

AI can play a key role in supporting lifelong learning by enabling flexible, adaptive, and personalized pathways tailored to individual goals and needs. Personalized AI systems align content with learner pace, preferences, and progress, offering targeted interventions through adaptive platforms (Mehboob, 2023). These tools help individuals build competencies across various life stages, from formal education to career reskilling. Additionally, AI facilitates microlearning and modular content delivery, aligning with evolving labor market demands through recommendation engines and micro-credentialing (Vootukuri & Jyothi. V, 2024). Gamified and immersive AI environments foster inclusive, engaging learning for diverse learners, including those with cognitive or sensory challenges (Mehboob, 2023). To be effective and empowering, AI must be designed with values of equity, autonomy, and cultural relevance, enhancing rather than replacing human interaction (Floridi, 2023).

Moreover, AI is redefining how learners are assessed and supported through real-time, formative feedback and personalized analytics. AI-based grading systems offer instant, actionable feedback across a variety of tasks, allowing educators to focus on individualized instruction (Vootukuri & Jyothi. V, 2024). Intelligent tutoring systems adapt in real time to learner needs and offer continuous support, especially benefiting under-resourced students (Kayyali, 2024). Predictive learning analytics identify students at risk, enabling timely interventions and curriculum adjustments to enhance engagement and success (Zhumazhan et al., 2024). Looking ahead, personalized dashboards could empower learners to track progress and set goals—though such innovations must be paired with strong data privacy, transparency, and ethical governance frameworks (Holmes et al., 2019).

Ensuring AI in education is inclusive and culturally responsive requires interdisciplinary collaboration and co-design. Global and local partnerships are vital to developing technologies that reflect real-world educational contexts. Co-creation with educators, developers, policymakers, and learners ensures tools are both scalable and contextually grounded (Kavitha & Joshith, 2024). Ethical AI deployment depends on participatory governance, where principles like fairness, non-discrimination, and explainability are embedded throughout the development process (Floridi, 2023). Feedback from educators and students builds accountability and trust (OECD,

2023). Moreover, interdisciplinary teams can co-create curricula that reflect pluralistic worldviews, supporting neurodiverse, multilingual, and marginalized learners (Zhumazhan et al., 2024).

Looking toward 2030 and beyond, the goal of AI in education should extend beyond access to true empowerment. Bridging the digital divide through investments in infrastructure, devices, and teacher training is critical to prevent AI from deepening educational disparities. Special focus is needed for rural, conflict-affected, and economically disadvantaged communities. AI systems must be transparent, auditable, and inclusive by design, incorporating equity audits, bias mitigation, and data protection (Ahmed et al., 2024; Holmes et al., 2019). Future education systems should uphold educational sovereignty by respecting local knowledge systems and pedagogical models. Preserving and digitizing indigenous and minority perspectives ensures that AI enhances educational diversity rather than erasing it (Luckin, 2018). Ultimately, AI should empower learners to co-create knowledge, critically engage with technology, and challenge systemic inequalities (Holmes et al., 2019).

The future of AI in education is not defined by technology alone but by the ethical and inclusive choices made by educators, developers, policymakers, and communities. By combining innovative AI tools with inclusive pedagogy, participatory governance, and cultural sensitivity, we can build education systems that leave no learner behind and enable all to thrive—not just by 2030, but for future generations.

## CONCLUSION AND RECOMMENDATIONS

Artificial Intelligence (AI) is rapidly emerging as a transformative force in education, offering unprecedented opportunities to shift systems from entrenched exclusion to proactive inclusion. This chapter has demonstrated that, when ethically designed and equitably implemented, Al can play a pivotal role in bridging historical educational gaps. By enabling personalized learning, enhancing accessibility, and supporting inclusive pedagogies, Al offers a critical pathway toward educational equity-particularly for marginalized learners, including those with disabilities, from rural communities, or socio-economically disadvantaged backgrounds.

At the same time, this chapter has critically unpacked the dual nature of Al-its capacity to either promote inclusion or amplify exclusion. From personalized learning tools and assistive technologies to policy-level interventions and global governance frameworks, Al holds both promise and peril. When deployed within equitable ecosystems and guided by values of transparency, faimess, and human dignity, Al can serve as a force multiplier for inclusive, learner-centered education.

Key Themes

Several overarching insights have emerged from this exploration:

- Al is not neutral: Algorithmic systems often inherit or reflect existing social biases, which can exacerbate inequities if not carefully addressed.
- Ethical design and deployment matter: Al systems must be grounded in principles of fairness, accountability, and transparency to avoid deepening systemic marginalization.
- Contextualization is key: Effective Al in education must be responsive to the cultural, linguistic, infrastructural, and political realities of the communities it seeks to serve.
- Inclusive Al requires co-creation: Involving teachers, students, parents, and marginalized voices in the development of Al tools ensures that these technologies are not only accessible but empowering.
- Policy and practice must be aligned: Without supportive policies, ethical safeguards, and institutional readiness, even the most advanced Al tools may fail to deliver meaningful impact.

## Toward Equitable AI: Recommendations for Stakeholders

To hamess Al's full potential in creating inclusive educational futures, the following actionable recommendations are proposed:

For Policymakers

- Develop Al-specific education policies aligned with the United Nations' Sustainable Development Goal 4 (SDG 4), human rights frameworks, and UNESCO's recommendations on the ethics of Al ("AI And Education: Guidance for Policy-makers," 2021).
- Mandate participatory and inclusive design processes, involving educators, students, community leaders, and marginalized populations in all stages of development and deployment.
- Invest in inclusive digital infrastructure that ensures reliable internet access. device availability, and multilingual platforms especially in underserved rural and remote regions.
- Regulate private edtech actors to prevent data exploitation and algorithmic opacity, while ensuring transparency, ethical compliance, and public accountability.

For Educators and Institutions

- Integrate Al literacy and ethics into teacher education and professional development programs, enabling educators to critically engage with Al tools.

- Use Al to support-not supplant-pedagogy, leveraging intelligent systems to personalize learning while maintaining the centrality of human relationships and learner agency.
- Embed inclusive frameworks such as Universal Design for Learning (UDL) into Al-driven instruction, ensuring accessibility for learners with diverse abilities and needs.
- Continuously monitor Al tools to ensure alignment with educational values, local curricula, and equity outcomes.

For Developers and EdTech Designers

- Design for diversity by testing Al tools with learners from different socioeconomic, linguistic, and cultural backgrounds, including students with disabilities and those from marginalized communities.
- Incorporate explainability, interoperability, and adaptability, ensuring that educators and learners understand how Al tools work and can modify them based on contextual needs.
- Apply the FAIR principles-Fairness, Accountability, Inclusivity, and Explainability-across all phases of design and implementation to mitigate risks of bias and exclusion.

For International Organizations and Donors

- Support capacity-building in low-resource settings, ensuring that Al innovation does not become a privilege of the Global North but a tool for global equity.
- Fund longitudinal, participatory research to study the long-term impact of Al on educational inclusion, particularly in underrepresented contexts.
- Facilitate South-South collaborations and knowledge-sharing, enabling local innovations from India, Sub-Saharan Africa, and Latin America to inform global best practices.

While Al has the power to transform education, its success will not be measured solely by technological sophistication, but by our collective commitment to equity, justice, and human flourishing. As emphasized earlier, the potential risks of Al-such as algorithmic bias, digital divide, and exclusionary data practices-must be proactively mitigated through conscientious design and inclusive governance ("AI And Education: Guidance for Policy-makers," 2021).

Future research should focus on addressing key gaps, including longitudinal studies on Al's long-term impact on educational inclusion, the intersectionality of biases in algorithmic systems, and scalable models for deploying ethical Al in low-resource settings. These efforts must move beyond Western-centric paradigms and prioritize context-sensitive, bottom-up innovations led by those closest to the margins.

The question is no longer whether Al will become central to education-but whether its trajectory will reflect a commitment to educational justice, learner dignity, and universal inclusion. Moving from exclusion to inclusion requires more than access to technology-it demands intentionality, ethical foresight, participatory design, and system-wide vision.

If guided by these principles, Al can help realize not just smarter classrooms, but more humane, equitable, and inclusive learning ecosystems where no learner is left behind. The true promise of Al lies not in replacing teachers or automating instruction, but in empowering all learners-regardless of their background, abilities, or location-to reach their full potential.

## REFERENCES


Ahmed, Z. E., Hashim, A. H. A., Saeed, R. A., & Saeed, M. M. (2024). *AI-Enhanced Education*. IGI Global., DOI: 10.4018/979-8-3693-2728-9.ch004

AI and education: guidance for policy-makers. (2021). In *UNESCO eBooks*. https://doi.org/DOI: 10.54675/PCSP7350

Batista, J., Mesquita, A., & Carnaz, G. (2024). Generative AI and Higher Education: Trends, Challenges, and Future Directions from a Systematic Literature Review. *Information (Basel)*, *15*(11), 676. DOI: 10.3390/info15110676

Cegolon, A. (2022). Inclusion/exclusion: An educational challenge. *Form@re. Open Journal per La Formazione in Rete*, *22*(1), 297–307. DOI: 10.36253/form-12664

Cortez, J. L. (2023). *Tecnologías emergentes en la educación del siglo XXI. 1*(4), 40–55. https://doi.org/DOI: 10.70881/mcj/v1/n4/25

Damyanov, K. (2024). Differentiation of Educational Content Through Artificial Intelligence Systems in Inclusive Education. *International Journal of Education*, *12*(3), 13–20. DOI: 10.5121/ije2024.12302

Farooqi, M. T. K., Amanat, I., & Awan, S. M. (2024). Ethical Considerations and Challenges in the Integration of Artificial Intelligence in Education. *Systematic Reviews*, *3*(4), 35–50. DOI: 10.69565/jems.v3i4.314

Floridi, L. (2023). *The Ethics of artificial Intelligence: Principles, Challenges, and Opportunities*. Oxford University Press. DOI: 10.1093/oso/9780198883098.001.0001

Gabriel, S. (2024). Generative AI and Educational (In)Equity. *Proceedings of the International Conference on AI Research.*, *4*(1), 133–142. https://doi.org/DOI: 10.34190/icair.4.1.3153

Ghoneim Sywelem, M. M., & El-Sayed Mahklouf, A. M. (2024). *Ethical Considerations in the Integration of Artificial Intelligence in Education: An Overview*. https://doi.org/DOI: 10.5121/csit.2024.141201

Gupta, M., & Kaul, S. (2024). *AI in Inclusive Education: A Systematic Review of Opportunities and Challenges in the Indian Context*. MIER Journal of Educational Studies, Trends and Practices., DOI: 10.52634/mier/2024/v14/i2/2702

Gupta, T. R. (2024). Adaptive Learning Systems: Harnessing AI to Personalize Educational Outcomes. *International Journal for Research in Applied Science and Engineering Technology*, *12*(11), 458–464. DOI: 10.22214/ijraset.2024.65088

Holmes, W., Bialik, M., & Fadel, C. (2019). *Artificial intelligence in Education: Promises and implications for teaching and learning*. https://oro.open.ac.uk/60255/

*Home - 2023 GEM Report*. (2023, November 27). 2023 GEM Report. https://gem-report-2023.unesco.org/ https://www.unesco.org/en/articles/global-education-monitoring-gem-report-2020

*Inclusion, Equity, Diversity, and Social Justice in Education: A Critical Exploration of the Sustainable Development Goals*. (2023). https://doi.org/DOI: 10.1007/978-981-19-5008-7

Islam, Md. mafiqul. (2024). *Ethical Considerations in AI: Navigating the Complexities of Bias and Accountability*. https://doi.org/DOI: 10.60087/jaigs.v3i1.62

Kavitha, K., & Joshith, V. P. (2024). The Transformative Trajectory of Artificial Intelligence in Education: The Two Decades of Bibliometric Retrospect. *Journal of Educational Technology Systems*, *52*(3), 376–405. Advance online publication. DOI: 10.1177/00472395241231815

Kayyali, M. (2024). The Future of AI in Education. *Advances in Educational Technologies and Instructional Design Book Series*, 367–406. https://doi.org/DOI: 10.4018/979-8-3693-7220-3.ch013

Khan, N., & Saunderson, S. (2024). Generative artificial intelligence in education: A narrative literature review. *World Journal on Educational Technology*, *16*(2), 112–126. DOI: 10.18844/wjet.v16i2.9217

Kohnke, S., & Zaugg, T. (2025). Artificial Intelligence: An Untapped Opportunity for Equity and Access in STEM Education. *Education Sciences*, *15*(1), 68. DOI: 10.3390/educsci15010068

Krishnan, R., & Manickam, S. (2024). *Enhancing Accessibility: Exploring the Impact of AI in Assistive Technologies for Disabled Persons*. https://doi.org/DOI: 10.54455/MCN2505

Lamberti, W. F. (2024). *Artificial Intelligence Policy Framework for Institutions*. https://doi.org//arxiv.2412.02834DOI: 10.48550

Leong, W. Y., Leong, Y. Z., & Leong, W. S. (2025). Artificial Intelligence in education. *IET Conference Proceedings.*, 2024(22), 183–184. https://doi.org/DOI: 10.1049/icp.2024.4341

Luckin, R. (2018). *Machine Learning and Human Intelligence: The Future of Education for the 21st century*. https://eric.ed.gov/?id=ED584840

*M-Shule*. (2020). https://www.mshule.com/

Mehboob, S. S. (2023). Leveraging Artificial Intelligence for Playful and Inclusive Education: Developing Semi-Automatic and Adaptive Educational Paths (pp. 123–136). https://doi.org/DOI: 10.34916/el.2023.15.10

Murthy, Y. S., Chodisetty, R. S. C. M., Chakravorty, C., & Sai, K. G. (2024). AI-Powered Learning Revolutionizing Smart Education With Personalized Learning Styles. *Advances in Educational Technologies and Instructional Design Book Series*, 191–212. https://doi.org/DOI: 10.4018/979-8-3693-8151-9.ch007

Norton, J. (2024). Navigating the AI Policy Landscape. *Advances in Library and Information Science (ALIS) Book Series*, 109–130. https://doi.org/DOI: 10.4018/979-8-3693-3053-1.ch006

Ohri, G. K. (2024). Advancing educational equity: The role of generative ai in creating accessible and inclusive higher education. *International Journal of Computer Engineering and Technology*, *15*(6), 1806–1815. DOI: 10.34218/IJCET_15_06_154

Oyedokun, T. T. (2024). Assistive Technology and Accessibility Tools in Enhancing Adaptive Education. *Advances in Educational Technologies and Instructional Design Book Series*, 125–162. https://doi.org/DOI: 10.4018/979-8-3693-8227-1.ch006

Rojas Contreras, M., & Portilla Jaimes, J. O. (2024). *AI Ethics in the Fields of Education and Research: A Systematic Literature Review*. 1–6. https://doi.org/DOI: 10.1109/ICACIT62963.2024.10788651

Roy, B., Ghosh, S., Sarkar, S. K., Sen, A., & Choudhury, N. (n.d.). *Implications of Artificial Intelligence for Special Education Technology*. https://doi.org/DOI: 10.4018/979-8-3693-5538-1.ch015

Sánchez-Santamaría, J., & Ballester Vila, M. G. (2014). *Desarrollando el Éxito Educativo para Todos: Reflexiones, Propuestas y Retos Conceptuales en torno a la Equidad Educativa*. *12*(2), 85–104. https://revistas.uam.es/index.php/reice/article/download/2857/3074

Shaeffer, S. (2019). Inclusive education: A prerequisite for equity and social justice. *Asia Pacific Education Review*, *20*(2), 181–192. DOI: 10.1007/s12564-019-09598-w

Singh, G., & Thakur, A. K. (2024). *AI in Education*. IGI Global., DOI: 10.4018/979-8-3693-2964-1.ch002

Taşkın, M. (2025). Artificial Intelligence in Personalized Education: Enhancing Learning Outcomes Through Adaptive Technologies and Data-Driven Insights. *Human-Computer Interaction*, *8*(1), 173. DOI: 10.62802/ygye0506

Vootukuri, N. S. R., & Jyothi, J. (2024). Harnessing the potential of AI applications in Education: Opportunities, challenges, and future directions. *Magna Scientia Advanced Research and Reviews*, *11*(2), 405–410. DOI: 10.30574/msarr.2024.11.2.0139

Yadav, S. (2024). Advancing Education With AI-Driven Education for Diverse Learners. *Advances in Educational Technologies and Instructional Design Book Series*, 49–80. https://doi.org/DOI: 10.4018/979-8-3693-6130-6.ch003

Young, J. (2024). The Rise of Artificial Intelligence in Education. *International Journal of Innovative Research and Development*. Advance online publication. DOI: 10.24940/ijird/2024/v13/i2/FEB24019

Zhumazhan, B., Zhumadilova, M. B., & Abdykerimova, E. (2024). The future of artificial intelligence in inclusive education. *Yessenov Science Journal*, *48*(3), 63–70. DOI: 10.56525/AMWI6491

# Chapter 3
# Generative AI and the Future of Personalised Islamic Religious Learning: An Overview

**Mussa Saidi Abubakari**
https://orcid.org/0000-0003-3782-281X
*Dig Connectivity Research Laboratory (DCRLab), Uganda & Universiti Brunei Darussalam, Brunei*

## ABSTRACT

*This chapter assesses the wave of transformation that generative artificial intelligence (GenAI) can bring for personalised Islamic religious education (IRE). It elaborates on how AI-generated content can make a difference and help create spiritually tailored learning experiences based on individual needs and goals. Historical practices are compared with modern educational theories to see the uptake of GenAI in different fields related to IRE (e.g., Quranic recitation and Hadith retrieval). The major benefits of AI are thoroughly described, including increased learner motivation, engagement, and educator support, alongside the ethical, pedagogical, and infrastructural challenges for IRE contexts. The chapter concludes with practical recommendations for implementation and strategic planning while discussing future trends and research directions. The chapter places generative AI in the context of moulding Islamic learning, sensitivity, and responsibility to culture and Islamic theology.*

DOI: 10.4018/979-8-3373-2302-2.ch003

## INTRODUCTION

Islamic religious education (IRE) is rooted in a tradition that dates back over a millennium and is formalised based on the texts of the Qur'an and Hadith. Pedagogical methodologies in IRE have also been established over the centuries (Daun & Arjmand, 2018). In this case, the tradition has typically meant a very holistic type of pedagogy, developing spiritual and moral dimensions along with the intellectual for students' growth (Sabki & Hardaker, 2013). In the history of Islamic education, the IRE system aimed to develop the whole person – spiritually, morally, and cognitively – rather than mere content conveyance. It has, therefore, proved equally resilient and formidable in human and community formation. However, this contemporary digital world presents different challenges and prospects from those that classical scholars had imagined. Contemporary Muslims live in a world of fast technological change and information oversupply, and knowledge has new meanings and forms of expression. These changes have inevitably begun to influence Islamic teaching and learning methods as well. There is a growing imperative to adapt time-honoured educational practices to the needs and contexts of today's learners while preserving the spiritual authenticity that is central to Islamic pedagogy.

One key educational paradigm gaining attention worldwide is personalised learning. Personalisation refers to tailoring the learning process to individual learners' needs, abilities, interests, and paces. In secular education, personalised learning approaches have been shown to improve student engagement and achievement by addressing differences in background knowledge and learning styles (Chan & Hu, 2023; Jauhiainen & Garagorry Guerra, 2024). Within Islamic religious learning, personalisation holds significant promise as well. Every learner's journey in faith is unique – for example, a new convert requires a different approach than a lifelong student, and a child memorising Qur'an has different needs than an adult studying advanced jurisprudence. Personalised Islamic learning can cater to individual spiritual growth by meeting students at their level of understanding and guiding them step-by-step (Thoriquttyas & Rohmawati, 2024). It allows content to be adjusted to one's proficiency, whether simplifying complex theological concepts for a beginner or providing in-depth sources to an advanced learner (Musolin et al., 2024). Traditionally, Islamic education often achieved personalisation through close teacher–student mentorship; an instructor (such as a sheikh or ustadh) would tailor guidance to each disciple, granting more attention where needed and challenging students according to their capabilities (Abdullah et al., 2023). In contemporary large classrooms or online settings, however, such one-on-one customisation is harder to implement consistently. This gap motivates exploring new methods to personalise learning on a scale, ensuring that each student can progress in faith and knowledge optimally.

Meanwhile, recent breakthroughs in artificial intelligence (AI), IoT, and other emerging technologies (Abubakari et al., 2020; Abubakari & Mashoedah, 2021; Abubakari & Suprapto, 2021) have introduced powerful tools that could revolutionise educational personalisation. In particular, generative AI – AI technologies that can create new content, such as text, audio, or images – has gained prominence. The late 2022 public debut of OpenAI's ChatGPT (powered by a large language model, GPT-3.5) marked a watershed moment in AI awareness and adoption (Jauhiainen & Garagorry Guerra, 2024). Generative AI systems like ChatGPT, Google's Bard, and others are capable of producing human-like text and engaging in interactive dialogue, while analogous models can generate realistic images, voices, or even video content. These tools leverage massive neural network models trained on vast datasets to predict and produce content in response to user prompts (Jauhiainen & Garagorry Guerra, 2024). Education was quickly identified as a domain poised for transformation by such AI capabilities (Katsamakas et al., 2024). Educators and learners around the world began experimenting with AI chatbots for tutoring, automatic essay writing support, language translation, and more. The prospect of harnessing generative AI to create highly customised learning materials on demand is particularly exciting. In Islamic education, a person might imagine AI systems that can explain a verse of the Qur'an at an appropriate level for a given student, generate practice questions tailored to what that student needs to review, or provide feedback on a recitation instantly at any time of day. These possibilities align with the goals of personalised religious learning and present a compelling case for integration.

Thus, the convergence of Islamic pedagogical needs for personalisation and the emergence of generative AI tools forms the core rationale for this chapter. Generative AI could potentially become a valuable instrument to enhance the quality and accessibility of Islamic education by enabling individualised customisation of teaching materials and learning experiences. At the same time, integrating such digital and AI technology raises critical questions (Abubakari, Shafik, et al., 2024; Abubakari, Zakaria, et al., 2024). Islamic education is not only about knowledge transmission but also about embodying values and maintaining authenticity through teacher–student relationships. This chapter seeks to examine the current state and prospects of generative AI in the context of personalised Islamic religious learning.

## Chapter Rationale, Objectives, and Research Questions

Despite the rich tradition of personalisation in IRE through teacher–student mentorship, there is a notable gap in systematically integrating modern technological tools—particularly generative artificial intelligence (GenAI)—to support personalised learning at scale. While secular education literature increasingly documents the benefits of GenAI for individualised learning, its potential applications, ethical considerations, and practical challenges within Islamic educational contexts remain underexplored. Addressing this gap is essential to ensure that technological adoption in IRE aligns with pedagogical goals and preserves the authenticity and values of Islamic education. This chapter, therefore, aims to:

1. Critically review existing literature on personalised learning and the emerging role of GenAI in education, with a focus on relevance to Islamic learning environments.
2. Explore concrete applications of generative AI in supporting personalised Islamic religious education, including Qur'an recitation, Hadith studies, and spiritual mentoring.
3. Analyse the pedagogical, ethical, and cultural implications of deploying GenAI in IRE settings.
4. Propose strategic recommendations for effectively integrating GenAI while upholding the principles of Islamic pedagogy.

To guide this inquiry, the following research questions are posed:

a. How has generative AI been employed in educational contexts to facilitate personalised learning, and what insights can be drawn for Islamic education?
b. What are the current and potential applications of GenAI in personalising Islamic religious learning?
c. What ethical, pedagogical, and cultural challenges emerge from integrating GenAI into IRE, and how can they be addressed to ensure alignment with Islamic educational values?

## LITERATURE REVIEW

This literature review explores the theoretical foundations and current applications of personalized learning, with a particular focus on its integration into Islamic Religious Education (IRE). It examines how generative AI supports adaptive instruction while highlighting the pedagogical, cultural, and ethical considerations unique to Islamic educational contexts.

### Conceptualising Personalised Learning

Personalised learning is an educational approach that seeks to tailor teaching and learning experiences to the unique needs of each student. Instead of a one-size-fits-all curriculum, personalised learning allows variability in content, pace, and instructional method based on individual learner profiles. Key elements often include assessing a student's current knowledge and skill level, then providing learning activities that are neither too easy nor too difficult, and giving feedback or next steps that target that student's specific gaps or interests (Bhutoria, 2022; Tapalova & Zhiyenbayeva, 2022). In practice, personalisation can manifest as adaptive learning software that adjusts difficulty after each question, or as a teacher modifying lessons for different students (differentiated instruction) (Ifenthaler et al., 2024; Kong & Yang, 2024). The goal is to keep students within their zone of proximal development – challenged enough to learn new things but not so much that they become frustrated or disengaged.

In secular contexts, personalised learning has been associated with improved engagement, since students feel the material is more relevant to them, and improved achievement, since students can progress at their own best pace (Farrokhnia et al., 2024; Jauhiainen & Garagorry Guerra, 2024; Vieriu & Petrea, 2025). It often leverages continuous assessment to guide next steps and may involve student choice, giving learners agency to pursue topics or formats that interest them (Chisom et al., 2024; Wang et al., 2024). Underpinning personalised learning is the recognition that learners differ in prior knowledge, learning style, motivation, and other factors, and that education is most effective when responsive to those differences. In the context of Islamic religious education, personalisation is equally – if not more – important, due to the diverse backgrounds and needs of learners engaging with religious content. Islamic learning encompasses a broad spectrum, including Qur'anic studies (such as memorisation and tajwīd, or proper recitation), Hadith (Prophetic traditions), jurisprudence (*fiqh*), theology (*aqīdah*), spirituality (*ta awwuf* or *tazkiyah*), Islamic history, and more. Students approaching these subjects vary widely, ranging from children learning to read the Qur'an for the first time to teenagers in Islamic schools, adult learners, or new Muslims seeking foundational knowledge, and advanced students preparing to become scholars. Each of these learners benefits from material and pedagogy suited to their level of understanding and their personalised context.

## Personalisation Significance in Islamic Religious Education (IRE)

In Islamic pedagogy, there is a longstanding tradition of acknowledging individual differences. The Prophet Muhammad is reported to have tailored his advice to the person – for instance, when different companions each asked for a key piece of guidance, he gave different answers ("control your anger" to one, "always speak good" to another, etc.), addressing their individualised dispositions. Thus, in IRE, one student might need more development in devotional practice, another in understanding doctrine; a wise teacher guides each along the path that best brings them closer to God, which is the ultimate aim of Islamic education. Personalised learning in this sense means recognising that spirituality is not a linear, standardised journey – people have different strengths, weaknesses, questions, and trials in faith.

Differentiating instruction is labour-intensive for teachers, who must prepare multiple sets of materials. Moreover, traditional methods rely heavily on the teacher's ability to discern each student's needs, which can be difficult with limited time and large student numbers. Thus, while personalisation has always been valued – and to an extent practised – in Islamic education, it often fell short of its ideal in mass educational settings. A recent literature review by Lestari et al. (2024) found that even minimal use of AI or digital tools in Islamic learning could optimise student potential, indicating the existing gap. They noted that AI has the capacity to facilitate more personalised learning and faster feedback, helping teachers recognise specific needs so they can tailor instruction to individual abilities (Lestari et al., 2024). This suggests that there is much room for technology to augment what educators are already doing. Indeed, educators have long expressed the desire for tools that could help track each student's progress and provide timely intervention; generative AI offers to fulfil exactly this role by analysing learning patterns and generating customised responses or materials.

## Trends and Applications of GenAI in Education

The year 2023 saw an explosion of interest in applying generative AI in classrooms and universities worldwide (Jauhiainen & Garagorry Guerra, 2024). Educators have been experimenting with tools like ChatGPT to assist in teaching various subjects. Early studies have started documenting how students and teachers perceive these AI tools. For example, a survey of university students in Hong Kong by Chan and Hu (2023) revealed a generally positive attitude toward generative AI in teaching and learning (Chan & Hu, 2023). Students reported that they see clear benefits in using tools like ChatGPT for personalised learning support, such as receiving help with understanding difficult concepts, brainstorming ideas for assignments, and even improving their writing through AI feedback (Chan & Hu, 2023). In that study, participants noted that an AI tutor available on demand could complement their learning by providing instant explanations or examples tailored to their questions. This indicates an openness among learners to engage with AI as a supplementary tutor or study aid. Indeed, one of the most prominent *uses* of generative AI by students so far has been for writing assistance – from generating essay outlines and summaries of articles to proofreading and editing drafts in a personalised manner. University students and even secondary school pupils have found that AI tools can help them learn by rephrasing complex material in simpler terms or by generating practice quiz questions for self-testing.

Teachers, on the other hand, are exploring the use of generative AI to enhance teaching materials and differentiate instruction. In primary and secondary education, some pioneering projects have integrated AI-generated content into lesson plans. A notable example is an experimental study in Uruguay where ChatGPT-3.5 was used in primary school classrooms to personalise educational content dynamically (Jauhiainen & Garagorry Guerra, 2024). In those trials, the AI generated text, illustrations, and exercises on the curriculum topic at hand, adjusting the difficulty in real-time to match each pupil's knowledge level. The findings were promising: generative AI was able to tailor the lesson materials so that both advanced and slower learners were appropriately challenged, which boosted overall motivation and improved student performance in achieving learning objectives (Jauhiainen & Garagorry Guerra, 2024). This kind of dynamic adaptation, traditionally difficult to do in a large class, was made feasible by the AI's capability to instantly generate new questions or explanations when a student needed extra practice or an alternative explanation. Such classroom pilots demonstrate the potential for AI to facilitate adaptive learning systems, wherein the instruction continually responds to the learner's progress.

Nevertheless, while studies in secular educational settings widely endorse the motivational benefits and efficiency gains of AI-driven personalisation (Chan & Hu, 2023), there is comparatively less clarity on how such approaches reconcile with the holistic, spiritually grounded objectives that characterise Islamic pedagogy (Abdullah et al., 2023). This points to a critical tension between technologised personalisation and traditional notions of *tarbiyah* (character cultivation). Existing scholarship on AI ethics predominantly arises from Western liberal frameworks, emphasising autonomy and data privacy (Kong & Yang, 2024), whereas Islamic perspectives introduce additional dimensions such as ijaza (scholarly chain of authority) and communal accountability, which are scarcely addressed in current empirical AI education studies. Furthermore, although literature on personalisation extols adaptive learning's capacity to meet diverse learner needs (Bhutoria, 2022; Tapalova & Zhiyenbayeva, 2022), some studies caution that over-automation may erode essential human mentorship roles, a concern echoed by Islamic educators wary of reducing spiritual education to algorithmic outputs. Notably, while technical studies have begun to explore hadith classification using machine learning (Sulistio et al., 2024), few critically examine how these tools might inadvertently privilege certain narrations or introduce biases that classical *u ūl al-hadith* (methodologies of hadith criticism) were designed to mitigate.

Therefore, this thematic and narrative review underscores several pressing gaps in the existing scholarship. Although substantial research affirms the pedagogical value of personalised learning and highlights generative AI's potential to adapt content dynamically, there remains a marked absence of studies contextualising these technologies within Islamic educational paradigms. In particular, the intersection of GenAI with the unique spiritual, cultural, and epistemological imperatives of IRE is underexplored. Existing work tends to either generalise from secular contexts or treat Islamic applications anecdotally, without robust frameworks addressing theological authenticity, teacher–student relational dynamics, or the safeguarding of sacred knowledge transmission. Additionally, ethical discourses in GenAI-driven education often neglect principles central to IRE pedagogy, such as preserving ijaza-based scholarly authority and ensuring content verification through qualified IRE scholars. By critically synthesising these domains, this chapter seeks to bridge these gaps, offering a conceptual foundation for understanding GenAI's promise and pitfalls in personalising IRE, and proposing strategies for ethically and pedagogically sound implementation.

## METHODOLOGY

This chapter adopts a narrative literature review to explore generative AI, personalized learning, and Islamic religious education. The approach facilitates thematic synthesis across interdisciplinary sources, prioritizing conceptual depth over exhaustive coverage while integrating educational, technological, and Islamic ethical perspectives.

### Review Design, Data Sources and Search Process

This chapter employs a narrative literature review methodology, chosen for its suitability in synthesising diverse interdisciplinary perspectives on generative AI, personalised learning, and Islamic religious education (IRE). Unlike systematic reviews that aim for exhaustive coverage of narrowly defined questions, this narrative approach enables a broader conceptual integration of pedagogical, technological, and Islamic scholarly discourses.

To ensure a comprehensive foundation, literature was sourced from multiple scholarly databases known for peer-reviewed educational and technological research, including Scopus (Elsevier), Web of Science (Clarivate), SpringerLink, Taylor & Francis Online, ScienceDirect, and Google Scholar (to capture additional open-access or grey literature). Initial exploratory searches were conducted between March and May 2025, followed by targeted iterative searches to refine thematic coverage. Furthermore, to ensure robust coverage across disciplinary boundaries, searches employed a combination of key terms clustered around four primary domains:

- (Generative AI OR "Large Language Models" OR ChatGPT OR "AI tutors")
- AND (personalised learning OR adaptive learning OR individualised instruction)
- AND (Islamic education OR "Islamic religious education" OR Qur'an OR Hadith OR madrasa OR IRE)
- AND (Islamic ethics OR "AI ethics")

Boolean operators and database-specific filters were applied to optimise results.

## Inclusion and Exclusion Criteria

Given the narrative orientation and certainly not a systematic-based review, the aim was not to enforce rigid inclusion counts, but to capture as broad and relevant a corpus of literature as possible to support the chapter's analytical objectives.

### Inclusion Aspects

- Peer-reviewed journal articles, conference papers, and scholarly book chapters.
- Published primarily in English between 2018 and 2025, to encompass the most pertinent discussions around GenAI and modern educational technologies.
- Studies addressing one or more focal areas: personalised/adaptive learning approaches, educational uses of GenAI, and pedagogical or ethical practices in Islamic education.

### Exclusion Aspects

- Popular media articles, unreviewed blogs, or purely technical AI papers lack educational context.
- Studies focusing narrowly on AI engineering or natural language processing without relevance to pedagogy or personalisation.
- Non-English publications, given the scope of the current chapter and language capabilities.

## Selection Process and Thematic Synthesis

Given the exploratory, integrative aim of this chapter, the literature gathering process prioritised maximising conceptual breadth over producing exhaustive numeric counts. Initial searches yielded a wide range of potentially relevant studies, which were screened at the title and abstract level for thematic fit. Full-text reviews were then conducted for articles offering substantive insight into personalised learning models, generative AI's pedagogical affordances, or distinct dimensions of Islamic educational practice and theory. Through successive rounds of comparison and thematic clustering, these themes were consolidated into several analytical categories that structure the chapter's Literature Review. This process of narrative thematic integration allows the review to go beyond summarising individual studies, instead critically synthesising insights to surface areas of consensus, unresolved tensions, and significant underexplored gaps. These findings directly inform the chapter's subsequent analytical discussion, recommendations, and identification of future research directions.

## RESULTS AND DISCUSSION

This section explores the emerging applications of generative AI within Islamic religious education (IRE), highlighting its role in enhancing personalized learning. Drawing on recent studies and experimental implementations, it analyses key innovations such as AI-generated materials, virtual mentors, and adaptive recitation tools, while critically evaluating pedagogical benefits and ethical considerations.

### Trending Applications of Generative AI in Islamic Religious Education

With the conceptual groundwork laid, we turn to concrete ways in which generative AI can be and, in some cases, although so far rarely, already is being integrated into Islamic religious education. GenAI integration in IRE can take many forms, each representing a new frontier at the nexus of technology and tradition.

#### AI-Generated Personalised Learning Materials

Among the most critical applications of GenAI is the creation of personalised learning materials for students of Islamic studies. LLMs can generate textual content tailored to specific queries or difficulty levels, which can be harnessed to supplement textbooks and lectures. For example, an AI could generate a simplified explanation of a Qur'anic verse for a young student, and a more detailed, commentary-style explanation for an advanced student. This dynamic adjustment is a powerful form of personalisation that static printed materials cannot provide. Generative AI can also assist in curriculum development by producing draft lesson plans, quiz questions, or discussion prompts tuned to different competency levels (Lestari et al., 2024). Educators can prompt an AI with instructions and receive a set of questions instantly. These AI-generated questions can then be reviewed and curated by the teacher. The benefit is efficiency and variety – the AI can create a broad bank of potential questions or exercises, which the teacher can select from to match each student's needs. It also allows for creating multiple versions of an assignment to suit different groups (for example, an easier and a harder version of a worksheet on Islamic history), thereby implementing differentiated instruction with less manual effort for the teacher.

When properly guided, AI-generated materials can significantly enrich the pool of resources available for personalised learning. For instance, a case where an AI provided personalised practice materials, such as generating extra Arabic grammar exercises focusing on the types of mistakes a particular student made, helped that student improve faster, as reported in one pilot program (Salim & Aditya, 2025). GenAI essentially filled the gaps by providing targeted material that the teacher did not have time to create for each individual.

## Intelligent Qur'anic Recitation Assistants

Correctly reciting the Qur'an with proper pronunciation and intonation (tajwīd) is a core component of Islamic education. Traditionally, mastering recitation requires regular practice with a qualified teacher who can correct errors in how letters are pronounced or how the melody (*tarteel*) is applied. This individual feedback is critical because learning tajwīd rules from a book alone is difficult; one must *hear* and be corrected in real-time. Generative AI and related technologies, such as speech recognition, are now enabling the creation of intelligent Qur'an recitation assistants that can mimic some aspects of a live tutor for basic practice and feedback. One example of this is the emergence of AI-based Qur'an software, which uses AI to listen to a user's recitation and identify mistakes or omissions (Alrumiah & Al-Shargabi, 2023). A combination of trained models powers such an AI system: speech-to-text models (to transcribe the recited Arabic), which are then compared against the actual verse text, and possibly acoustic models trained on proper recitation to detect *tajwīd* errors (Al-Ayyoub et al., 2018). When the AI finds a discrepancy, it can alert the user, for instance, by highlighting the word where the mistake occurred or even verbally saying, "Repeat this word; the pronunciation was off." This provides immediate feedback, something highly valuable in language learning and especially in Qur'anic memorisation ( *if* ). Immediate correction helps prevent a learner from cementing mistakes.

## Automated Hadith Classification and Retrieval Systems

Hadith classification typically refers to categorising a hadith based on attributes such as authenticity (e.g., a ī (sound), asan (good), aʿīf (weak)), by topic (e.g., prayer, charity, transactions), or by the narrator's chain. Researchers have developed machine learning models that analyse the text of a hadith (and possibly metadata, such as narrators) and attempt to classify it into known categories. A systematic literature review found that about one-third of computer science research on hadith focuses on classification tasks, using algorithms ranging from support vector machines to deep learning (Sulistio et al., 2024). These studies illustrate that AI can be trained to some extent to mimic the judgments of human scholars on hadith categorisation. For example, there have been experiments training models to identify whether a hadith is likely authentic or fabricated by learning from features of known authentic and known forged hadiths (such as linguistic style or narrator reputation). While AI cannot replace the complex science of hadith criticism developed by classical scholars, it can act as a filtering tool, flagging hadiths that are suspicious or prioritising likely authentic ones when searching a large corpus.

Generative AI can build on these classification advances by aiding in hadith retrieval and question-answering. Early versions of such systems exist; for example, researchers have developed QA systems that use databases of hadith to answer questions, by either retrieving the most relevant text or even synthesising an answer from multiple narrations (Sulistio et al., 2024). Hadith retrieval can be explored using a transformer-based model (similar to GPT) to generate answers to hadith-related questions, essentially creating a conversational agent that can quote or paraphrase hadiths in response to queries (Alabbas & Alomar, 2024). There have been initial attempts at this using machine learning for authenticity classification (Sulistio et al., 2024). While no AI can declare a hadith a ī or aʿīf with the authority of a hadith scholar, it can assist users by pointing them to known collections or scholar gradings.

## Personalised Virtual Tutors and Mentors

Perhaps the most imaginative and broad use of generative AI in Islamic education is the creation of personalised virtual tutors or mentors – AI entities that can guide a learner through various aspects of religious education in a tailored manner. These AI tutors combine the previously discussed capabilities (content generation, Q&A, multimedia) into a single interactive experience for the student. In essence, they aim to emulate some functions of a human teacher or mentor: answering questions, explaining concepts, providing practice tasks, and giving encouragement or advice, all in a personalised way.

Such a virtual AI-driven tutor could be comprehensive or subject-specific, such as an AI Quran teacher or an AI fiqh coach. These tutors can personalise their approach by learning from the user's interactions. Suppose the AI notices the student tends to ask more basic questions or frequently seeks definitions of Arabic terms. In that case, it may adjust its explanations to be more foundational and define terms proactively. If another student prefers philosophical discussions, the AI might engage in a more in-depth manner and even present differing viewpoints from Islamic scholarly tradition to enrich the dialogue.

Personalised AI mentors can also keep learners on track with their goals through adaptive lesson planning and reminders. Suppose someone is trying to learn how to pray ( alāh) properly. The AI tutor can break down the learning into steps: day 1, learn how to make ablution; day 2, learn the movements of prayer, and so on. Each day, it can check progress, possibly quiz the student, or ask them to demonstrate their knowledge (even via the student describing or filming their prayer for the AI to analyse, if technology permits). If the student skips practice, the AI can gently remind or adjust the pace. Essentially, it can act as a motivational coach, which is especially useful in self-directed learning scenarios. Research has shown that AI-based tutoring systems can facilitate independent learning by providing structure and feedback, highlighting the benefits of AI tutoring systems for students learning on their own (Frankford et al., 2024; González-Calatayud et al., 2021). In a religious context, an AI mentor could encourage good study habits, suggest daily routines (like reading a bit of the Qur'an daily and then asking the AI questions about it), and keep track of the learner's milestones.

One particularly interesting use is creating a virtual mentor that embodies specific roles or perspectives. For example, a learner might converse with a "virtual mufti" for jurisprudential questions – an AI that has been fine-tuned on a particular fiqh school's rulings to give answers aligning with that school. We are already seeing early signs of this: some developers have created basic chatbots that answer FAQs on halal/haram based on known fatwa databases (Munshi et al., 2021). AI could take that further by engaging in a dialogue, asking the user for details about their context as a real mufti would, and then providing a reasoned answer with references.

## Benefits of GenAI in Personalised Islamic Learning

### Enhancing Learner Engagement and Motivation

One of the immediate benefits reported when AI tools are introduced into learning is a boost in student engagement. Islamic studies, like any other subject, can sometimes suffer from rote routines that cause students to lose interest (for instance, memorising texts without understanding, or listening to long lectures passively). Generative AI, with its interactive and responsive capabilities, can turn learning into a more engaging two-way process. Research on AI-based interactive media in Islamic education has shown increased student motivation and engagement. Some studies found that using AI-driven educational games in a religious studies class not only made the lessons more enjoyable but also reinforced learning outcomes through active participation (bin Abd Rahman et al., 2024; Muslimah & Arliansyah, 2024). Gamification elements – like earning points for each correctly recited verse or each good question asked to the AI tutor – tap into students' intrinsic and extrinsic motivation. Particularly for younger learners, these game-like AI applications can make learning Islamic concepts fun and eagerly anticipated, rather than seen as a chore.

Engagement is not just about fun; it is also about a meaningful connection to the material. AI can present content in a manner that resonates with a student's context or interests, which greatly increases engagement (Raehang et al., 2025). If a student is interested in technology, an AI tutor might draw analogies between modern tech and historical Islamic innovations to pique their interest. If another loves storytelling, the AI might employ more narrative in teaching a concept. By catering to personal interests, the AI keeps learners mentally invested. Moreover, the immediate feedback and adaptation possible with AI mean learners are continuously challenged at the right level, not bored by too-easy content or frustrated by too-hard content, a state that is conducive to deep engagement (Kong & Yang, 2024). Students who used an adaptive AI Quran memorisation app reported feeling a sense of progression and accomplishment after each session because the app always gave them new verses appropriate to their memorisation capacity, thereby maintaining their motivation to continue daily (as referenced by the increase in understanding through personalised learning despite challenges).

## Addressing Diverse Learning Styles and Abilities

Islamic education serves a highly diverse population – from children learning basic morals to adults studying intricate theology – and each learner has a unique way of understanding and absorbing information. Generative AI is exceptionally suited to addressing this diversity because it can produce content in multiple formats and modalities. GenAI can convert a lesson into textual summaries, visual aids, auditory narration, or interactive dialogue. This means that no matter a student's preferred learning style, AI can present material in that mode. By allowing students to experience content in the format that best suits them, AI personalises the learning experience to individual cognitive strengths.

In terms of abilities, not all students move at the same pace or have the same background knowledge. AI's ability to differentiate instruction ensures each learner gets what they specifically need. A concept like *zakāt* (almsgiving) might be trivial for a student with strong math skills but confusing for someone weak in arithmetic, due to the calculations involved with percentages. A personalised AI tutor could recognise this and provide more step-by-step numerical examples for the latter student, ensuring they are not left behind (Frankford et al., 2024). Conversely, a student who already grasps the basics can be given advanced details or edge cases to keep them intellectually stimulated. This adaptive pacing and depth ensure that both advanced and remedial learners benefit. Indeed, an AI-driven system can personalise not only how content is delivered but also how much and in what order. It might break down a complex topic into micro-learning units for someone who needs it, or give a broad overview first to someone who learns better top-down. Studies have indicated that precision in meeting diverse learning needs leads to a more inclusive learning environment where no student's needs are ignored. Some studies have noted how adaptive systems can even customise learning content to support different learning styles, increasing overall effectiveness (Almusaed et al., 2023; Standen et al., 2020). This kind of multi-faceted content delivery, made possible by generative AI, means students with different learning profiles can all succeed in grasping religious knowledge.

## Facilitating Continuous, Self-Directed Religious Learning

A significant benefit of AI in personalised learning is that it empowers students to take charge of their learning outside the formal classroom. Traditionally, Islamic learning has highly valued consistency – for example, daily reading of the Qur'an, regular reflection (*tafakkur*), and ongoing study ( *alab al- ilm*) are lifelong duties. Generative AI tools can greatly support continuity in learning by being available anytime to assist and guide. With AI, learning is not confined to class times or when a teacher is present. A dedicated student can engage in meaningful educational activities at any time, on weekends, or during travel. The AI is always ready to answer a question or provide a lesson. AI lowers the barriers to continuous education. As some have pointed out, AI platforms ensure students can learn at their own pace and even in remote areas (Hashem, 2025) – a point that applies not only to formal students but to any Muslim seeking knowledge independently. This continuous availability encourages self-directed learning, allowing students to follow their curiosity. For religious learning, this is particularly beneficial because spiritual development is very personal and often occurs outside the classroom through reflection and practice.

## Supporting Educators in Differentiated Instruction

From the teacher's perspective, generative AI serves as a valuable assistant that can help manage and personalise learning for a diverse classroom. Teachers often face the challenge of addressing a wide range of abilities and learning speeds in one class. AI tools can alleviate this by automating some aspects of differentiated instruction. For instance, an Islamic studies teacher can use AI to generate multiple versions of a worksheet on the Five Pillars of Islam – a basic version with fill-in-the-blanks for struggling students and a more advanced analytical version for excelling students. This ensures each student is working on material suited to their level, without overburdening the teacher with crafting separate resources from scratch. Studies indicate that AI-managed personalisation can increase learning efficiency and help teachers target their instruction more effectively. By analysing student performance data, AI systems can alert the teacher to specific needs (e.g., identifying which students haven't mastered a particular concept), enabling the teacher to intervene with focused support. In essence, AI provides actionable insights – something one researcher described as giving teachers "deeper insights into student development and which areas require additional attention" (Hakim & Anggraini, 2023).

Furthermore, AI can free up teachers' time from routine tasks. Grading quizzes on Arabic vocabulary or checking memorisation of a short *sūrah* can be done by an AI tutor, allowing the teacher to invest that time in lesson planning or one-on-one mentoring. A literature review by Lestari et al. (2024) concluded that integrating AI in the Islamic education curriculum has great potential to improve quality, provided that teachers receive adequate training and support infrastructure. They noted that AI helps teachers recognise students' specific needs and tailor teaching accordingly, but emphasised that "adequate training for teachers and development of supporting technological infrastructure" is necessary (Lestari et al., 2024). This highlights that while AI can support differentiated instruction, teachers must be empowered to use it effectively. With the right preparation, IRE teachers can leverage AI to augment their teaching styles.

Importantly, using AI in the classroom can improve feedback loops. Traditionally, a teacher might administer a test and return results a week later, by which time the student's interest or memory of the topic may have waned. AI-driven assessment can provide immediate feedback to students and report to the teacher which items were severely missed, allowing for almost real-time remediation. Quick, personalised feedback has been cited as one of AI's strong points in education (Hakim & Anggraini, 2023; Lestari et al., 2024). In Islamic learning, where certain mistakes (such as persistent tajwīd errors or misunderstanding a theological concept) need timely correction to prevent ingraining, this immediacy is highly beneficial.

### Increasing Accessibility and Inclusivity

Generative AI has the potential to make Islamic learning more accessible to a wider audience, overcoming barriers of geography, language, disability, and socio-economic factors. In many parts of the world, particularly in underserved areas, there is a shortage of qualified IRE teachers and resources. AI-powered learning platforms can help bridge this gap by delivering quality instruction remotely. As some scholars noted, "AI-powered virtual classrooms can reach students in rural areas with limited access to schools", effectively extending the reach of education to those who might otherwise be left out (Hashem, 2025). For example, a student in a remote village could learn Qur'an recitation through an AI tutor on a low-cost tablet even if no qualified teacher is nearby. This democratisation of access supports the Islamic principle of seeking knowledge being incumbent on every Muslim, by reducing dependence on one's location or local resources. Language and culture are other inclusion factors. The Muslim community is linguistically diverse – some learners are not fluent in the language of instruction, whether Arabic for religious texts or English in some online courses. By ensuring language is not a hurdle, AI fosters inclusivity among non-Arabic speakers and Muslims in non-Muslim majority countries who might lack access to traditional seminary education. Generative AI can also tailor content to different cultural contexts, which is a subtler aspect of inclusivity.

## Ethical and Pedagogical Considerations

### Accuracy and Authenticity of Generated Islamic Content

The foremost ethical concern in IRE is that AI might produce incorrect or in-authentic information about Islam. LLMs, despite their prowess, do not inherently possess a grasp of truth – they generate plausible-sounding text based on patterns, which means they can sometimes "hallucinate" false information (El Ganadi et al., 2025). In a religious context, such errors can be extremely problematic. An AI might misquote a verse, attribute a saying incorrectly to the Prophet, or provide a flawed interpretation of a Hadith. Therefore, verification is essential. Islamic educators and scholars must be involved in curating the data that AI models train on and in regularly reviewing the outputs to ensure accuracy. It is advisable that any AI tool used for Islamic learning clearly cites its sources so that users can cross-check the authenticity from reliable books (Sulistio et al., 2024). Some designs might include having the AI primarily function as a retrieval system (pulling from a database of verified texts) rather than freely generating new interpretations. For example, an AI could be restricted to answering fiqh questions by drawing from recognised fatwa archives or fiqh manuals, ensuring it doesn't stray into personal conjecture.

The need for scholarly oversight is widely recognised. Studies underline the importance of ethical oversight to ensure AI's outputs remain in compliance with Islamic teachings (Abubakari, Shafik, et al., 2024; Hidayat, 2024). In practice, this could mean creating a supervisory board of qualified Islamic scholars for any major AI Islamic educational platform. This board would set the parameters for what the AI is allowed to do and periodically vet the content. One proposal is an AI system that flags any low-confidence answers or novel content to a human scholar for review before presenting it to students. Generative AI could be programmed to admit uncertainty and refrain from giving answers in areas where it might be prone to error.

Maintaining accuracy and authenticity involves embedding human scholarly wisdom into AI systems and establishing clear ethical boundaries for their operation. This aligns with the recommendation that culturally and theologically sensitive oversight is needed (Abubakari, Shafik, et al., 2024; Hakim & Anggraini, 2023; Hasanah et al., 2024). Through the collaborative efforts of ulama (scholars) and AI experts, guidelines can be developed, for example, a guideline that any AI-generated fatwa must include references and a disclaimer, or that AI should offer multiple juristic opinions if the question is on a known point of difference, rather than asserting one as absolute. Such measures ensure the technology serves Islamic education faithfully without distorting it.

## Mitigating Biases and Misinformation

AI systems trained on large datasets might inadvertently carry biases present in those datasets. In a non-religious context, this has led to AI outputs that show gender or racial bias. In an Islamic context, one could imagine biases such as sectarian bias (if the data leans heavily towards one school of thought's literature, the AI might marginalise other viewpoints), or even anti-religious bias (if trained on general internet data that contains Islamophobic sentiments, the AI could echo those sentiments). This is unacceptable for tools meant to educate about Islam. Therefore, careful curation of training data is crucial, ideally using primarily respected Islamic sources and works that represent the diversity of orthodox views. During the development phase, bias testing should be conducted: for example, asking the AI the same question from Sunni and Shia perspectives to see if it responds appropriately according to each tradition, or testing whether it consistently uses respectful language about religious figures. If biases are found, developers must adjust the model or data to correct them.

Misinformation is a broader category that includes not just accidental errors but also misleading emphasis. An AI might highlight less important or fringe issues just because they appear frequently in the data. For example, internet forums might overemphasise eschatological signs or contentious issues, and an AI might mirror that, giving learners a skewed sense of priorities in Islamic practice. Educators need to be aware of this and possibly weigh the AI's outputs towards content aligned with the curriculum and scholarly consensus. One strategy is to integrate a form of scholarly review in the AI's logic: incorporate the rulings of recognised fiqh councils or fatwa bodies so that if a question relates to a contemporary issue, the AI draws on those official opinions rather than random online discussions. Essentially, the AI should be anchored in authentic scholarship to guard against the misinformation that proliferates online.

## Data Privacy, Security, and Transparency Issues

Ethical use of data and privacy is another important consideration. Islamic ethics places a high value on privacy (*satr*) and not exposing people's private faults. Students using AI tutors might input very personal questions. Ensuring the confidentiality of these interactions is paramount. This relates to data privacy – AI providers must secure user data and possibly avoid storing sensitive queries at all, or at least anonymise them. From an ethical standpoint, users should be informed about what data is saved and have control over it. Moreover, AI should be designed not to probe unnecessarily; it should stick to what the user asks and not collect extraneous personal information.

Generative AI tools in education collect a variety of data types, primarily involving user interaction data, performance metrics, and contextual information. These tools often gather foundational user data such as login times, session lengths, and tool usage patterns, which help in understanding how frequently and intensely the tools are being used (Jauhiainen & Guerra, 2023). Thus, the use of generative AI technologies in the educational domain opens a new dimension of the existing data security threat, amplifies the issues, and brings new challenges. Generative AI systems work and depend on large databases for their training and optimisation, wherein the key concern is, most of the time, the information regarding students, teachers, and institutions. The combination and utilisation of such information inherently develop vulnerabilities, particularly in the scope of its collection, processing, and retention, where boundaries are not clearly defined. In addition, the operations based on AI are mostly black-boxed (no transparency), which leaves the educational organisation with many uncertainties of having privacy invasions, thus sometimes leading to unintended or even unethical exploitation of data.

## Pedagogical Challenges – Teacher Roles and Competencies

The introduction of AI tutors and tools will inevitably shift the role of teachers and require new competencies. Teachers will need to become adept at guiding students in the use of AI – essentially teaching with the AI. This means educators must themselves understand the capabilities and limitations of the technology. Professional development is necessary so that teachers know how to interpret AI reports on student performance, how to correct errors the AI might make, and how to integrate AI activities into their lesson plans. A teacher who is not tech-savvy might initially find it challenging to incorporate an AI tutor into a traditional teaching plan, with potential resistance or fear, as some teachers worry that students will rely on AI answers instead of thinking or that their authority might be undermined. Managing this transition is a pedagogical task for institutions, which should provide training, share success stories of AI integration, and reassure educators that their role remains crucial, only the tools at their disposal have increased in complexity. In fact, teachers can take on an even more refined role as facilitators and mentors. Instead of spending time drilling facts, they might spend more time cultivating higher-order thinking skills, such as verifying AI outputs with students, encouraging students to evaluate answers critically, and discussing the ethical dimensions of the content.

Another pedagogical challenge is preventing students from over-reliance on AI, which can impede skill development. Students might be tempted to ask the AI for every answer or translation instead of trying themselves first. There is a legitimate worry about the impact on learning and retention if students use AI as a crutch. For instance, will a student still put effort into memorising Quran or Hadith texts if they know they can instantly recall any verse via an AI search? Educators must set guidelines – perhaps encouraging students to attempt tasks on their own before verifying with AI, or using AI as a supplement, not a first resort. A study noted that students themselves had concerns that GenAI could affect their personal skill development and critical thinking if not used carefully (Chan & Hu, 2023). Teachers of IRE, therefore, should foster an environment where AI is seen as a learning aid, not a replacement for personal effort. One strategy could be to occasionally "unplug" – have classes or assignments where AI use is not allowed, to ensure students can function without it and to strengthen their independent problem-solving. This balances tech use with traditional learning to maintain skills.

## Maintaining Spiritual Authenticity and Authority

A unique pedagogical consideration in religious learning is the spiritual element of the teacher-student relationship and the authority of knowledge transmission. In Islam, teachers (shaykhs, ustadhs) are not just information providers; they are role models and often spiritual mentors. The personal interaction, empathy, and spiritual intuition a teacher brings can deeply influence a student's character development (*tarbiyah*) – something an AI cannot replicate. There is a risk that heavy reliance on AI could lead to a more impersonal learning experience, potentially diminishing the heart-to-heart transfer of wisdom that is central in traditional settings. A student may get correct answers from a chatbot, but they might not feel the same inspiration or personal connection that motivates them to embody those teachings. Educators and program designers need to preserve avenues for human mentorship actively.

Moreover, the authority of content is a concern. Students might overly trust AI outputs because they are fast and neatly packaged, potentially giving the AI a de facto authority equal to a teacher or book. It must be continually emphasised that AI is a tool, and that ultimate authority lies with the Qur'an, Sunnah, and qualified scholarship. One way to reinforce this is by integrating scholarly voices into the AI so that it frequently quotes real scholars and texts, not presenting things as its personal opinion. Another way is for teachers to discuss openly the fallibility of AI. Perhaps part of the curriculum when introducing AI tools is a session on their limitations and how Islamic scholarship works, to contrast the two. If students are taught to see the AI as an aggregator or tutor that still defers to scholars, they will be less likely to grant it undue authority.

Thus, addressing ethical and pedagogical considerations requires a multi-pronged approach: ensuring strict accuracy and adherence to authentic knowledge through oversight and design, training educators and learners in the proper use of AI, and consciously preserving the human and spiritual elements of education. These steps resonate with calls in the field for culturally sensitive implementation strategies and involvement of qualified scholars (Abubakari, Shafik, et al., 2024; Hasanah et al., 2024). By proactively managing these issues, we can harness generative AI's benefits without compromising the integrity of Islamic education. The next section on challenges will delve further into some of these points, particularly around infrastructure and societal acceptance, which intersect with the ethical deployment of this technology.

## Challenges and Limitations

### Technical and Infrastructural Barriers

Generative AI systems, especially those involving large neural network models, typically require robust computing infrastructure and internet connectivity. In many parts of the Muslim world, such infrastructure is uneven. Rural areas or less-developed regions might have limited internet bandwidth or outdated hardware, making it difficult to run AI-powered educational tools effectively. This creates an equity issue:

the learners who could benefit the most from AI (those in remote areas without access to good teachers) might also be the ones least equipped with the technological infrastructure to use it. Bridging this digital divide is a major challenge. Initiatives are needed at the policy and community levels to improve infrastructure, such as providing internet access in rural schools or leveraging offline AI solutions. Another technical barrier is language support. Not all AI models currently handle Arabic or other languages from the Muslim world as well as they handle English (Abubakari, 2025). While progress is rapid (with new Arabic LLMs being developed), there can still be limitations in, for example, understanding complex Arabic grammar in a student's input or generating responses in less common languages. Therefore, there is a need for AI development that focuses on relevant languages and dialects. Overcoming this requires continued research and development, effectively creating AI systems that are literate in classical Arabic and other relevant languages and familiar with Islamic terminologies.

## Digital Competence Gaps among Learners and Educators

A successful implementation of AI in the classroom assumes that users know how to use it effectively. However, there is a gap in digital literacy in many settings (Abubakari et al., 2023, 2025; Abubakari & Kalinaki, 2024). Some teachers, particularly older-generation ustadhs or imams, may not be very comfortable with technology beyond basic uses. They may perceive AI tools as too complex or be anxious that they might "do something wrong" when using them. As a result, they could underutilise the tools or avoid them altogether, negating the potential benefits. Studies found that faculty perceptions and technology readiness significantly influence AI integration (Hakim & Anggraini, 2023; Lada et al., 2023; Vashishth et al., 2024). If teachers feel unprepared, they are less likely to embrace AI in their teaching. This gap can be addressed through targeted training. But until teachers attain a certain comfort level, this remains a barrier.

Learners, too, can have competence issues. While younger students are assumed to be more tech-savvy on average, not all have equal exposure (Reid et al., 2023). Students from less-resourced backgrounds may not have had the opportunity to grow up using computers or typing, which can make interacting with AI chatbots or apps challenging at first. Even basic skills, such as formulating questions clearly or reading long answers on a screen, might need to be taught. It is also vital to consider the possibility of technological distractions and misuse. Giving students access to AI and the internet can open doors to off-task behaviour or accessing inappropriate content. Although this is more of a classroom management issue, it is related to competence in using tech responsibly. Educators will need to set clear rules and perhaps use filtered or limited-function versions of AI in class. This again requires a level of digital competence and vigilance from the teacher.

## Cultural Resistance and Acceptability within Communities

As with any innovation, integrating AI in religious learning may meet with scepticism or resistance from certain quarters of the Muslim community. Some community members – whether parents, scholars, or students – might question whether using AI aligns with the tradition of learning in Islam or fear that it could dilute the teacher-student relationship. There could be a perception that AI is a "foreign" or secular influence encroaching on sacred education. Indeed, some studies have identified cultural resistance as one of the obstacles to integrating AI in Islamic education curricula. For example, a traditional madrasa board might initially reject a proposal to use AI tutors, viewing it as unnecessary or even disrespectful. Overcoming this requires community engagement and demonstrating that AI is a tool, not a replacement for tradition.

Another facet is interpretational concerns. The Muslim community is not monolithic; different sects or schools might worry that the AI's content has a bias towards one interpretation. For instance, if a Shafi'i student uses an AI that predominantly gives Hanafi-based answers (or vice versa), families or local scholars may be uncomfortable, as this relates to the bias issue discussed earlier. Ensuring that AI tools can adapt to or acknowledge different legitimate interpretations can mitigate this concern and increase acceptability. If not, some communities may outright reject AI, fearing it will confuse their adherents with "outside" views. In multi-sectarian environments, this is a delicate issue. In such cases, perhaps separate AI knowledge bases or settings need to be developed under the guidance of scholars from those communities.

## Data Privacy and Cybersecurity Concerns

The use of AI in education raises serious privacy issues. Students may be providing personal data, even if indirectly, through their usage patterns or questions, which can reveal sensitive information about their personal beliefs, problems, and other private matters. The Islamic ethical perspective values privacy highly; the idea that private struggles or questions might be stored on a server could be unsettling. A study found that students themselves voice concerns about privacy when using generative AI tools (Chan & Hu, 2023). Within a religious learning app, a student might ask very sensitive questions (e.g., about doubts in faith or personal sins), expecting confidentiality. If such data were leaked or accessed improperly, it could cause personal harm and breach trust. Strong security measures must be implemented to protect these systems. This includes secure authentication (to prevent unauthorised use of teacher accounts, etc.), encryption of data, and safeguards against common cyberattacks. Institutions must plan for this, which may require hiring or consulting IT security professionals – again, a resource issue for some.

## Recommendations and Strategies for Effective Implementation

To successfully integrate generative AI into personalised Islamic religious learning, a strategic and collaborative approach is required. The following recommendations and strategies are proposed for educators, institutions, and stakeholders to maximise benefits while mitigating risks:

### Guidelines for Educators and Institutions

It is essential to develop clear guidelines on how AI tools should be used in the learning process. Schools and madrasas can formulate an "AI use policy" that defines the scope of AI assistance – for example, clarifying that AI tutors can be used for practice and research, but final verification of religious answers should be done with a teacher or trusted sources. Such guidelines help set the right expectations among students, teaching them to use AI as a supplementary resource rather than an infallible authority (Abubakari, 2024). In higher education settings, policies on academic integrity should be updated to address AI usage. This encourages honest and ethical use of AI.

For Islamic institutions in particular, it might be wise to establish a Shariah advisory board for educational technology. This board can continuously review new AI tools or content updates to ensure they meet religious standards, similar to how Islamic banks have Shariah boards. Their endorsement can reassure the community that the tool is sound. They can also issue guidance on complex issues, such as whether using AI-generated voices for Quran recitation in class is permissible. This pre-emptive governance helps avoid confusion and conflict later. Studies advocate for trustworthy principles in global Islamic education when adopting AI, suggesting that alignment with Islamic values must be evaluated at each step (Wiranto & Suwartini, 2023).

### Professional Development and Capacity Building

Investing in teacher training is one of the most critical steps for successful AI integration. Educators need hands-on workshops and continuous support to become proficient with AI tools. This training should cover both technical operation (how to use the software, interpret data, and troubleshoot common issues) and pedagogical integration (best practices for blending AI activities with traditional teaching). Teachers could benefit from seeing model lessons where AI is used effectively. Sharing success stories or having tech-savvy teachers mentor others can build confidence. As some researchers concluded, the potential of AI will only be realised if teachers receive adequate training and support (Lestari et al., 2024). Additionally, capacity building is not just for teachers – school administrators and curriculum developers should also be trained to understand AI's capabilities and constraints so that they can make informed decisions about resource allocation and curriculum design.

### Collaboration Among Technologists, Religious Scholars, and Educators

Multi-disciplinary collaboration is vital to create AI solutions that are both technologically robust and religiously sound. Technologists (AI developers, data scientists) bring expertise in what is feasible and how to implement it. Religious scholars (ulama) ensure that the content and methods respect Islamic teachings and address the nuanced requirements of religious instruction. Educators ensure that the tools actually meet classroom needs and align with pedagogy. Regular workshops or panels that bring these groups together can spark innovations and address concerns early. Collaboration is also needed at the implementation stage. For example, when rolling out an AI tutor in a school, it is crucial to involve Islamic studies teachers, who are familiar with classroom dynamics, and software developers, who can adjust the tool based on teacher feedback.

Students and parents can also be part of feedback loops. Institutions could form a small committee at the school, comprising a tech coordinator, a senior Islamic studies teacher, and perhaps a student representative, to monitor the AI program's effectiveness and report any issues. This ensures constant communication between the technical and educational sides. Thus, such collaborative approaches align with recommendations that a collaborative approach involving AI developers, communication experts, and qualified Islamic scholars is necessary for the effective and respectful use of AI in religious outreach and education (Abubakari, Shafik, et al., 2024; Hakim & Anggraini, 2023). When all stakeholders are at the table, the resulting implementation is more likely to be holistic and sustainable.

## CONCLUSION

Generative AI could be transformative for personalised Islamic religious learning. The AI technologies explored in this chapter have demonstrated their enormous potential, from intelligent tutoring systems to AI-generated content, to enhance the educational experience by tailoring it according to individual needs, opening access, and supporting teachers in delivering more effective instruction. The present chapter has situated Islamic education in its traditional holistic framework and showed that the personalised approach, deeply valued in classical settings, can be significantly augmented by modern AI tools. In examining current implementations and possibilities, it became clear that when used judiciously, AI can enrich engagement (through interactive chatbots and gamified learning), accommodate diverse learners (by dynamically adjusting content and language), and provide continuous support beyond the classroom (empowering self-driven learning and practice.

## Key Takeaways

- **Generative AI enables deep personalisation:** It adapts content difficulty, learning pace, and examples to each learner's needs—from basic Qur'an memorisation to advanced fiqh discussions—making Islamic learning more engaging and effective.
- **Teachers remain indispensable as guides and mentors:** AI assists with routine tasks and individualised practice, but human educators ensure spiritual authenticity, nurture moral character, and cultivate critical thinking.
- **Authenticity, ethics, and scholarly oversight are crucial:** AI systems in Islamic education must be anchored in verified sources, regularly reviewed by qualified scholars, and designed to uphold Islamic values and avoid misinformation.
- **AI broadens access and fosters inclusivity:** It helps overcome barriers of geography, language, and socio-economic constraints, supporting diverse learners globally in seeking Islamic knowledge.
- **Success depends on collaboration and capacity building:** Effective implementation requires joint efforts of technologists, Islamic scholars, and educators, plus robust teacher training to integrate AI tools wisely into teaching and learning.

## Chapter Limitations

As a conceptual narrative review, this chapter inherently faces limitations. It synthesises existing scholarship without primary empirical data, relying on interpretations and extrapolations from studies predominantly situated in secular or general educational environments. The review also draws largely from English-language sources published between 2022 and 2025, potentially overlooking valuable regional studies or Arabic-language scholarship directly addressing GenAI in Islamic learning contexts. Moreover, while the thematic synthesis captures broad trends, it does not quantify the strength of evidence or systematically assess the quality of included studies. These limitations highlight the need for cautious interpretation of proposed benefits and underscore that many conclusions remain provisional. They also reflect broader gaps in the current literature itself, notably, the scarcity of rigorous empirical investigations directly examining GenAI's impacts within authentic IRE settings.

## Recommendations, Prospects, and Research Directions

### Emerging Trends and Future Technologies

One anticipated trend is the development of more sophisticated adaptive learning platforms that fully integrate generative AI. These platforms would act almost like personalised digital madrasa tutors, dynamically adjusting not only the difficulty of content but the entire learning path for each student. By continuously analysing a learner's performance and engagement, future systems might decide, for example, to recommend a break from memorisation and switch to a related storytelling session to prevent fatigue, or to fast-track a student to more advanced topics if they show mastery early. Such platforms could incorporate multi-modal AI: a combination of text, voice, and vision AI. For instance, a single system might use speech recognition to evaluate a student's Qur'an recitation, text generation to explain a concept they struggled with, and image generation to visualise a historical event they're learning about. The convergence of these capabilities can create a truly immersive and responsive learning experience that feels almost like a human teacher's intuition.

Another exciting prospect is the incorporation of virtual reality (VR) and augmented reality (AR) into Islamic learning, powered by generative AI. This kind of immersive learning could greatly enhance understanding of Islamic history and rituals. Already, experts mention AI-generated virtual reality experiences that bring historical teachings to life (Hashem, 2025). In the future, generative AI could create entire historical simulations. While these technologies (VR/AR) exist now, their use could become more widespread and integrated with AI personalisation (e.g., the content of the VR tour adjusts to focus on aspects the student has not studied yet, etc.).

### Potential Developments in AI Ethics within Islamic Contexts

As AI becomes more embedded in education, there will likely be increased efforts to articulate Islamic guidelines for AI ethics. This will build upon general AI ethics but incorporate Islamic moral and legal thought (Elmahjub, 2023). We may see Islamic jurists and ethicists convening to issue guidance, perhaps even fatwas or at least advisory opinions, on matters such as: Is it acceptable to use AI for issuing religious rulings? How can AI's decisions be ensured to align with Islamic conceptions of justice and equity? How can human dignity be protected when AI is used in teaching? In essence, a framework for "Islamic AI ethics" has emerged, ensuring that the use of AI is harmonious with *Maqā id al-Sharī ah* (the higher objectives of Islamic law, such as preserving religion, life, intellect, lineage, and property) (Mohadi & Tarshany, 2023; Raquib et al., 2022). Further, there may also be discussions on AI rights and responsibilities, such as the question of accountability if an AI makes a mistake in a religious ruling that misguides someone. These are novel questions that Islamic scholarship should grapple with.

## Research Directions: Efficacy, Engagement, and Beyond

As these technologies roll out, it will be important to conduct empirical research to measure their impact within IRE. Researchers should investigate questions such as: Do students learning with AI tutors demonstrate significantly better retention or understanding of material compared to traditional methods? How does AI-facilitated learning affect long-term outcomes, such as a student's continued engagement with religious learning or their ability to perform religious duties? Initial evidence is promising, but detailed, controlled studies can help quantify benefits and identify any drawbacks. For instance, a research study might compare two groups in a Quran memorisation program – one using AI feedback daily and the other with standard weekly teacher meetings, measuring differences in memorisation speed and accuracy.

Another research direction involves examining student attitudes and psychological effects. How do students feel about learning from an AI tutor versus a human tutor? Does it affect their motivation or the way they view the learning of sacred knowledge? Does AI usage perhaps increase confidence for some (as they can practice privately), but decrease it for others (who feel overwhelmed by the technology)? A recent work on student perceptions of GenAI in education provides a model for this kind of research (Chan & Hu, 2023), which can be tailored to the Islamic education context specifically. We also need research on teacher perspectives and adaptation. Following up on early adopters – how has using AI changed their teaching, for better or worse? What challenges did they encounter? Their insights can guide the training and design of future tools. This could be done through qualitative studies or action research, where teachers reflect on their experiences.

## REFERENCES


Abdullah, W. A. A. W., Zhaffar, N. M., Razak, K. A., & Hamzah, M. I. (2023). The Concept of Five Mims: Students' Perceptions of Innovative Teachers in Islamic Education. *International Journal of Humanities Technology and Civilization*, *6*(2), 35–43. DOI: 10.15282/ijhtc.v6i2.6978

Abubakari, M. S. (2024). Overviewing the Maze of Research Integrity and False Positives Within AI-Enabled Detectors: Grammarly Dilemma in Academic Writing. In Mutawa, A. (Ed.), *Impacts of Generative AI on the Future of Research and Education* (pp. 335–366). IGI Global., DOI: 10.4018/979-8-3693-0884-4.ch013

Abubakari, M. S. (2025). Overviewing Biases in Generative AI-Powered Models in the Arabic Language: AI Fairness for Sustainable Future. In Syafrudin, M., Fitriyani, N. L., & Anshari, M. (Eds.), *Achieving Sustainability in Multi-Industry Settings With AI* (pp. 361–390). IGI Global., DOI: 10.4018/979-8-3373-2530-9.ch013

Abubakari, M. S., Arifin, F., & Hungilo, G. G. (2020). Predicting Students' Academic Performance in Educational Data Mining Based on Deep Learning Using TensorFlow. *International Journal of Education and Management Engineering*, *10*(6), 27–33. DOI: 10.5815/ijeme.2020.06.04

Abubakari, M. S., & Kalinaki, K. (2024). Digital Competence in Islamic Education for Lifelong Learning: Preliminary Analysis Using DigComp 2.1 Framework. In Hawamdeh, M. M. K., & Abdelhafid, F. (Eds.), *Embracing Technological Advancements for Lifelong Learning* (pp. 1–31). IGI Global., DOI: 10.4018/979-8-3693-1410-4.ch001

Abubakari, M. S., & Mashoedah, . (2021). The Internet of Things (IoT) as an Emerging Technological Solution for the Covid-19 Pandemic Mitigation: An Overview. *Journal of Physics: Conference Series*, *1737*(1), 012003. DOI: 10.1088/1742-6596/1737/1/012003

Abubakari, M. S., Shafik, W., & Hidayatullah, A. F. (2024). Evaluating the Potential of Artificial Intelligence in Islamic Religious Education: A SWOT Analysis Overview. In *AI-Enhanced Teaching Methods* (pp. 216–239). IGI Global. DOI: 10.4018/979-8-3693-2728-9.ch010

Abubakari, M. S., & Suprapto, S. (2021). Educational Data Mining to Predict Students Performance Based on Deep Learning Neural Network. *Proceeding International Conference On Health, Social Sciences And Technology, 1*(1), 13–16. https://ojs.poltekkespalembang.ac.id/index.php/icohsst/article/view/697

Abubakari, M. S., Zakaria, G. A. N., & Musa, J. (2024). Perceived compatibility and students' intention to adopt digital technologies in Islamic education institutions. *Cogent Education, 11*(1), 2430869. DOI: 10.1080/2331186X.2024.2430869

Abubakari, M. S., Zakaria, G. A. N., & Musa, J. (2025). Validating the DigComp framework among university students across different educational systems. *Discover Education, 4*(1), 200. DOI: 10.1007/s44217-025-00652-x

Abubakari, M. S., Zakaria, G. A. N., Musa, J., & Kalinaki, K. (2023). Assessing Digital Competence in Higher Education: A Gender Analysis of DigComp 2.1 Framework in Uganda. *SAGA: Journal of Technology and Information System, 1*(4), 114–120. DOI: 10.58905/saga.v1i4.210

Al-Ayyoub, M., Damer, N. A., & Hmeidi, I. (2018). Using Deep Learning for Automatically Determining Correct Application of Basic Quranic Recitation Rules. *International Arab Journal of Information Technology, 15*(3A Special Issue), 620–625.

Alabbas, A., & Alomar, K. (2024). Tayseer: A Novel AI-Powered Arabic Chatbot Framework for Technical and Vocational Student Helpdesk Services and Enhancing Student Interactions. *Applied Sciences (Basel, Switzerland), 14*(6), 2547. DOI: 10.3390/app14062547

Almusaed, A., Almssad, A., Yitmen, I., & Homod, R. Z. (2023). Enhancing Student Engagement: Harnessing "AIED"'s Power in Hybrid Education—A Review Analysis. *Education Sciences, 13*(7), 632. DOI: 10.3390/educsci13070632

Alrumiah, S. S., & Al-Shargabi, A. A. (2023). Intelligent Quran Recitation Recognition and Verification: Research Trends and Open Issues. *Arabian Journal for Science and Engineering, 48*(8), 9859–9885. DOI: 10.1007/s13369-022-07273-8

Bhutoria, A. (2022). Personalized education and Artificial Intelligence in the United States, China, and India: A systematic review using a Human-In-The-Loop model. *Computers and Education: Artificial Intelligence, 3*, 100068. DOI: 10.1016/j.caeai.2022.100068

bin Abd Rahman, M. S., Bin Deraman, A., & Bin Zul, H. H. (2024). Enhancing Hajj Education through Interactive Multimedia Game-Based Learning. *Information Management and Business Review, 16*(4(S)I), 35–42. DOI: 10.22610/imbr.v16i4(S)I.4274

Chan, C. K. Y., & Hu, W. (2023). Students' voices on generative AI: Perceptions, benefits, and challenges in higher education. *International Journal of Educational Technology in Higher Education, 20*(1), 43. DOI: 10.1186/s41239-023-00411-8

Chisom, O. N., Unachukwu, C. C., & Osawaru, B. (2024). Review of AI in Education: Transforming Learning Environments in Africa. *International Journal of Applied Research in Social Sciences*, *5*(10), 637–654. DOI: 10.51594/ijarss.v5i10.725

Daun, H., & Arjmand, R. (2018). *Handbook of Islamic Education* (Daun, H., & Arjmand, R., Eds.). Vol. 7). Springer International Publishing., DOI: 10.1007/978-3-319-64683-1

El Ganadi, A., Aftar, S., Gagliardelli, L., & Ruozzi, F. (2025). Generative AI for Islamic Texts: The EMAN Framework for Mitigating GPT Hallucinations. *Proceedings of the 17th International Conference on Agents and Artificial Intelligence*, 1221–1228. DOI: 10.5220/0013312800003890

Elmahjub, E. (2023). Artificial Intelligence (AI) in Islamic Ethics: Towards Pluralist Ethical Benchmarking for AI. *Philosophy & Technology*, *36*(4), 73. DOI: 10.1007/s13347-023-00668-x

Farrokhnia, M., Banihashem, S. K., Noroozi, O., & Wals, A. (2024). A SWOT analysis of ChatGPT: Implications for educational practice and research. *Innovations in Education and Teaching International*, *61*(3), 460–474. DOI: 10.1080/14703297.2023.2195846

Frankford, E., Sauerwein, C., Bassner, P., Krusche, S., & Breu, R. (2024). AI-Tutoring in Software Engineering Education. *Proceedings of the 46th International Conference on Software Engineering: Software Engineering Education and Training*, 309–319. DOI: 10.1145/3639474.3640061

González-Calatayud, V., Prendes-Espinosa, P., & Roig-Vila, R. (2021). Artificial Intelligence for Student Assessment: A Systematic Review. *Applied Sciences (Basel, Switzerland)*, *11*(12), 5467. DOI: 10.3390/app11125467

Hakim, A., & Anggraini, P. (2023). Artificial Intelligence in Teaching Islamic Studies: Challenges and Opportunities. *Molang: Journal Of Islamic Education*, *1*(02), 57–69. DOI: 10.32806/6ynvg541

Hasanah, U., Khairunnisa, R., Alfa Della, D., & Abdullah Attamimi, T. (2024). Opportunities, Challenges and Ethics of Artificial Intelligence Implementation in Teaching Islamic Religious Education in Public Universities: A Case Study in South Kalimantan. *JMPI: Jurnal Manajemen. Pendidikan Dan Pemikiran Islam*, *2*(2), 144–154. DOI: 10.71305/jmpi.v2i2.92

Hashem, H. (2025). *How AI-infused edtech is transforming learning for Muslims*. Salaam Gateway. https://salaamgateway.com/story/how-ai-infused-edtech-is-helping-transform-learning

Hidayat, M. T. (2024). Effectiveness of AI-Based Personalised Reading Platforms in Enhancing Reading Comprehension. *Journal of Learning for Development, 11*(1), 115–125. DOI: 10.56059/jl4d.v11i1.955

Ifenthaler, D., Majumdar, R., Gorissen, P., Judge, M., Mishra, S., Raffaghelli, J., & Shimada, A. (2024). Artificial Intelligence in Education: Implications for Policymakers, Researchers, and Practitioners. *Technology. Knowledge and Learning, 29*(4), 1693–1710. DOI: 10.1007/s10758-024-09747-0

Jauhiainen, J. S., & Garagorry Guerra, A. (2024). Generative AI and education: Dynamic personalization of pupils' school learning material with ChatGPT. *Frontiers in Education, 9*, 1288723. DOI: 10.3389/feduc.2024.1288723

Jauhiainen, J. S., & Guerra, A. G. (2023). Generative AI and ChatGPT in School Children's Education: Evidence from a School Lesson. *Sustainability (Basel), 15*(18), 14025. DOI: 10.3390/su151814025

Katsamakas, E., Pavlov, O. V., & Saklad, R. (2024). Artificial Intelligence and the Transformation of Higher Education Institutions: A Systems Approach. *Sustainability (Basel), 16*(14), 6118. DOI: 10.3390/su16146118

Kong, S.-C., & Yang, Y. (2024). A Human-Centered Learning and Teaching Framework Using Generative Artificial Intelligence for Self-Regulated Learning Development Through Domain Knowledge Learning in K–12 Settings. *IEEE Transactions on Learning Technologies, 17*, 1562–1573. DOI: 10.1109/TLT.2024.3392830

Lada, S., Chekima, B., Karim, M. R. A., Fabeil, N. F., Ayub, M. S., Amirul, S. M., Ansar, R., Bouteraa, M., Fook, L. M., & Zaki, H. O. (2023). Determining factors related to artificial intelligence (AI) adoption among Malaysia's small and medium-sized businesses. *Journal of Open Innovation, 9*(4), 100144. DOI: 10.1016/j.joitmc.2023.100144

Lestari, J. T., Darmayanti, R., & Arifin, Z. (2024). Integration of Artificial Intelligence in Islamic Education Curriculum. *Journal of Pergunu and Contemporary Islamic Studies, 1*(1), 55–78. https://jurnal.pcpergunukotapasuruan.org/index.php/jpcis/article/view/12

Mohadi, M., & Tarshany, Y. (2023). Maqasid Al-Shari'ah and the Ethics of Artificial Intelligence. *Journal of Contemporary Maqasid Studies, 2*(2), 79–102. DOI: 10.52100/jcms.v2i2.107

Munshi, A. A., AlSabban, W. H., Farag, A. T., Rakha, O. E., Al Sallab, A. A., & Alotaibi, M. (2021). Towards an Automated Islamic Fatwa System: Survey, Dataset and Benchmarks. *International Journal of Computer Science and Mobile Computing*, *10*(4), 118–131. DOI: 10.47760/ijcsmc.2021.v10i04.017

Muslimah, M., & Arliansyah, A. (2024). Gamification Method in Increasing Motivation towards Studying the Al-Quran and Islamic Perspectives. *Jurnal Pendidikan Agama Islam*, *4*(1), 181–190.

Musolin, M. H., Serour, R. O. H., Siregar, M., Hamid, S. A., Ismail, A., Huda, M., & Rohim, M. A. (2024). Developing Personalised Islamic Learning in Digital Age: Pedagogical and Technological Integration for Open Learning Resources (OLR). In X.-S. Yang, R. S. Sherratt, N. Dey, & A. Joshi (Eds.), *Proceedings of Ninth International Congress on Information and Communication Technology. ICICT 2024 2024. Lecture Notes in Networks and Systems* (Vol. 1004, pp. 11–25). Springer Nature Singapore. DOI: 10.1007/978-981-97-3305-7_2

Raehang, A., & Mustapa Ahmad, Muhammad Shaleh Assingkily. (2025). Integrating Artificial Intelligence into Madrasah Learning: A Mixed-Methods Study of Intelligent Media Development and Implementation. *Cendekiawan : Jurnal Pendidikan Dan Studi Keislaman*, *4*(1), 608–618. DOI: 10.61253/cendekiawan.v4i1.322

Raquib, A., Channa, B., Zubair, T., & Qadir, J. (2022). Islamic virtue-based ethics for artificial intelligence. *Discover Artificial Intelligence*, *2*(1), 11. DOI: 10.1007/s44163-022-00028-2

Reid, L., Button, D., & Brommeyer, M. (2023). Challenging the Myth of the Digital Native: A Narrative Review. *Nursing Reports*, *13*(2), 573–600. DOI: 10.3390/nursrep13020052 PMID: 37092480

Sabki, A. A., & Hardaker, G. (2013). The madrasah concept of Islamic pedagogy. *Educational Review*, *65*(3), 342–356. DOI: 10.1080/00131911.2012.668873

Salim, M. A., & Aditya, R. B. (2025). Integration of Artificial Intelligence in Islamic Education: Trends, Methods, and Challenges in the Digital Era. *Journal of Modern Islamic Studies and Civilization*, *3*(01), 74–89. DOI: 10.59653/jmisc.v3i01.1368

Standen, P. J., Brown, D. J., Taheri, M., Galvez Trigo, M. J., Boulton, H., Burton, A., Hallewell, M. J., Lathe, J. G., Shopland, N., Blanco Gonzalez, M. A., Kwiatkowska, G. M., Milli, E., Cobello, S., Mazzucato, A., Traversi, M., & Hortal, E. (2020). An evaluation of an adaptive learning system based on multimodal affect recognition for learners with intellectual disabilities. *British Journal of Educational Technology*, *51*(5), 1748–1765. DOI: 10.1111/bjet.13010

Sulistio, B., Ramadhan, A., Abdurachman, E., Zarlis, M., & Trisetyarso, A. (2024). The utilization of machine learning on studying Hadith in Islam: A systematic literature review. *Education and Information Technologies*, *29*(5), 5381–5419. DOI: 10.1007/s10639-023-12008-9

Tapalova, O., & Zhiyenbayeva, N. (2022). Artificial Intelligence in Education: AIEd for Personalised Learning Pathways. *Electronic Journal of e-Learning*, *20*(5), 639–653. DOI: 10.34190/ejel.20.5.2597

Thoriquttyas, T., & Rohmawati, N. (2024). How Far Artificial Intelligence influenced Mu'allim, Murabbi, and Mudarris? Transhumanism and Diffusion of Innovation Theory's Perspective. *Suhuf: International Journal of Islamic Studies*, *36*(2), 139–154. DOI: 10.23917/suhuf.v36i2.6302

Vashishth, T. K., Sharma, V., Sharma, K. K., & Kumar, B. (2024). Enhancing Literacy Education in Higher Institutions With AI Opportunities and Challenges. In *AI-Enhanced Teaching Methods* (pp. 198–215). IGI Global., DOI: 10.4018/979-8-3693-2728-9.ch009

Vieriu, A. M., & Petrea, G. (2025). The Impact of Artificial Intelligence (AI) on Students' Academic Development. *Education Sciences*, *15*(3), 343. DOI: 10.3390/educsci15030343

Wang, X., Huang, R., Sommer, M., Pei, B., Shidfar, P., Rehman, M. S., Ritzhaupt, A. D., & Martin, F. (2024). The Efficacy of Artificial Intelligence-Enabled Adaptive Learning Systems From 2010 to 2022 on Learner Outcomes: A Meta-Analysis. *Journal of Educational Computing Research*, *62*(6), 1348–1383. DOI: 10.1177/07356331241240459

Wiranto, E. B., & Suwartini, S. (2023). Artificial Intelligence and Trustworthy Principles in Global Islamic Education. *Ushuluddin International Conference (USICON)*, *6*, 64–87.

# Chapter 4
# Beyond Boundaries:
## AI-Powered Personalized Learning in the Educational Metaverse for Global Equity

**Aysha Khalil**
https://orcid.org/0000-0001-8467-5627
*Lahore College for Women University, Lahore, Pakistan*

**Asma Shahid Kazi**
https://orcid.org/0000-0002-4054-9669
*Lahore College for Women University, Lahore, Pakistan*

## ABSTRACT

*This chapter meticulously focuses on use of AI and how tools like educational metaverse might help creating equitable personalized learning, tailored for everyone. This chapter reframes pedagogical and ethical values by centering culturally-relevant learning, contextual integrity, and learner agency. Building on theories the analysis provides a solid way to look at the advantages and drawbacks of AI-driven adaptation. Case studies set in different countries make it clear that how personalization works with AI-powered and immersion-embedded systems. The framework put forwarded by this chapter consists of cultural intelligence, clear personalization, ethical design, and infrastructural scalability. It also lists barriers to equitable implementation and fundamental challenges which need deliberate solution. The framework focuses on ethical design and pedagogical relevance to ensure that AI-supported learning environments are personalization engrossed. This chapter reflects worldwide debate about adaptive learning in order to support the goals of educational equity and global inclusion.*

DOI: 10.4018/979-8-3373-2302-2.ch004

## INTRODUCTION: AI-BASED PERSONALIZATION AND IMMERSION

The fast development of AI technology has brought new and exciting possibilities for upgrading education around the world. Education was usually designed for all learners the same way, with little or no adjustment to teaching and learning resources. Students from underrepresented backgrounds or remote regions have suffered a disadvantage because the lack of flexibility in education limits their chances to learn. AI has the power to come down on these walls by providing personalized learning that matches what each student needs. Adaptive learning, intelligent tutoring systems, and predictive analytics are becoming much more popular, creating new possibilities for equitable learning (Holmes et al., 2023). Luckin et al., 2022). Personalized learning matters as it supports students differently and removes the barriers found in traditional teaching. Thanks to such innovations, the ways we teach are changing, and more people are able to access good learning, preparing the way for a more inclusive education. These upgrades in technology are making it possible for content and instruction to adjust to each student's unique abilities and ways of learning, which raises the standard of education.

This transformation centers on the educational metaverse, which is a digital environment where AI and advanced technology work together to give learners personalized and interactive lessons. It is believed the educational metaverse will eliminate many established educational challenges, such as geography, access, and needing more resources, by joining AI personalization to VR and AR (Kavanagh et al., 2022; Zhang et al., 2023). Learners in these environments can do more than read or watch; they can actively participate in lessons that help them learn in ways that involve many senses and learning methods (Holmes et al., 2023; Wang et al., 2024). Thus, the educational metaverse might help us rethink how we learn, so that it becomes more adaptable, welcoming, and personalized for everyone. Still, this transformation raises new questions about how to give all students, regardless of background or place, access to these new tools. Getting past these entry barriers is key to providing these advanced educational tools to all students. Khalil, Haqdad, & Sultana (2023) note that while the metaverse in education represents exciting new chances, it needs quality planning so that learners who will benefit the most are reached.

Even though AI and the metaverse hold great promise for democratizing education, there are major hurdles to reaching that goal. Even though AI-led tools are effective for individualizing learning, their implementation is restricted by structural issues such as limited high-speed internet and computer access. Such problems tend to arise strongly in places where resources and technology are not readily available, making it difficult for many to use AI-driven learning systems (Williamson, 2023).

It is also necessary to consider ethical concerns about AI in education, such as protecting student data, preventing algorithmic bias, and reducing the risk of widening inequality, so these technologies are used with equity. Failure to carefully develop AI algorithms may cause them to continue harmful biases, affecting those who are already at a disadvantage. Solving these problems means advancing AI technology as well as creating ethical foundations at the same time. As AI tools get more advanced, it is necessary to protect against unintended biases, so that all learners have equitable access to personalized education (Khalil, Haqdad, & Sultana, 2023).

The chapter looks at how AI-driven personalized learning within the educational metaverse may promote global educational equity. It looks at the ways these technologies can help learners from all backgrounds receive individualized, high-quality education. The chapter will also look at the issues that come with this integration, like availability, cultural representation, and ethical issues. It will look at how AI and the metaverse might be used to help underprivileged groups achieve the goals of educational equality. With these aspects in mind, the chapter aims to give readers a picture of what education can become and realistic advice on handling obstacles to implementation. If implemented the right way, AI and the metaverse have the power to transform education, remove obstacles, create exciting new chances, and boost learning for every student.

This chapter explores how AI-powered personalized learning environments within the educational metaverse can be designed and implemented to promote global equity by addressing the structural, ethical, and cultural barriers that continue to hinder inclusive learning.

## NAVIGATING EDUCATIONAL FUTURES THROUGH AI AND IMMERSIVE TECHNOLOGY

The merging of artificial intelligence and immersive technology has a major impact on education everywhere, urging schools to rethink how they provide access and interact with learners. This combination is not just about new resources, but rests on transformed ways of thinking about education from pre-school to lifelong development. People are now saying that education must respond to developments in technology, such as automation, virtual environments, and personalized learning. As the world copes with COVID-19, climate change, and economic challenges, it has become clear that we have to build learning systems that are strong, flexible, and belong to their setting. In light of what we know, we need to study the ways in which AI-supported learning systems develop and relate to equity, preparation, and inclusion. The convergence of AI and immersive platforms is not simply reshaping access, it is redefining the terms on which inclusion and adaptability must be built into the core of educational futures.

## Shifting Educational Paradigms in the Digital Age

The introduction of intelligent systems is causing important changes in how education is taught and managed. Artificial intelligence is being used in things like learner profiling and adaptive testing, offering personalized education and reshaping educators' roles. Zawacki-Richter et al. (2022) note that implementing AI in universities gives learners a better experience, but challenges issues around how to handle large amounts of data and who has control over it. These changes move us away from one-size-fits-all education towards using data for customized learning, and that brings new obligations about how we govern and communicate these changes. Redefining the main goals of teaching will help ensure innovation and accountability work together in online learning spaces.

The move to online education during the pandemic highlighted many inequalities in how and when people can access schooling. Even though remote learning was important for many colleges, it made it easier to see several barriers that hurt learners who are not well served. Selwyn et al. (2021) state that these developments lead to a replacement of old knowledge hierarchies with more democratic ways of designing education. Both the balancing act of access and agency and the aftermath of emergency remote teaching define the changes ahead in education.

These shifts reveal that personalization through AI must contend with deeper systemic divides, where access, governance, and representation intersect in complex ways that demand renewed institutional responsibility.

## Emergence of Immersive Learning Ecosystems

Technologies such as virtual reality, augmented reality, and mixed reality have now moved from testing in labs to being used in classrooms to provide experiential and real-world learning. García-Peñalvo et al. (2022) report that properly implemented immersive technologies encourage students to stay engaged and work together to understand new concepts. These technologies make it possible for students to experience multisensory learning, thus giving them more control and helping them see how abstract ideas fit into daily life. For the educational potential of these technologies to be seen, educators must have training, covering both proficiency with tools and the ability to remodel their teaching methods.

A lot of scholarly and policy efforts are now directed towards the educational metaverse. In 2017, Dede, Jacobson, and Richards described the metaverse as a place where learners interact, take part in role-play and scenarios, and build knowledge collectively. They become more learning-effective when artificial intelligence algorithms provide personalized learning tracks and help learners with decisional frames. However, the use of immersive and intelligent technologies varies quite a bit between different contexts, particularly in the Global South. The uneven picture makes it clear that we should consider how innovation relates to infrastructure and effects on human development in a coordinated way.

This variation underscores that the educational value of immersive ecosystems depends not only on their technological sophistication, but on equitable access, cultural relevance, and institutional readiness.

## Structural Barriers and Equity Gaps

AI-immersive education struggles in many locations because there aren't enough resources, money, or local acceptance. Henadirage and Gunarathne (2025) say that digital infrastructure, enough skilled teachers, and supportive rules are often lacking in institutions in the Global South. Apart from those practical limitations, immersive learning is also challenged by different languages, familiar teaching styles, and cultures that don't promote uniformity. As a result, designers now have to better incorporate local details when trying to move techniques between different contexts.

If AI models have bias, it can make problems in education for some people much worse. Announcing or feeding AI with small or devious data sets, in combination with not making it inclusive by design, is likely to make such technologies value familiar opinions and ignore groups that are not shown. According to Williamson and Eynon (2021), educational AI will need close oversight, since it often creates epistemic injustice instead of encouraging inclusion. It becomes clear from this critique that ethical oversight and a shared design approach should be part of AI-based education.

When bias, infrastructure, and cultural mismatch converge, they form structural exclusions embedded within the technology itself. Immersive systems that fail to address these multi-layered constraints risk replicating the very disparities they aim to dismantle.

## Gaps in Research, Theory, and Policy Integration

Increasing research into immersive and intelligent learning settings has led to many new publications, yet most of the existing literature mainly concentrates on technological assets and overlooks comprehensive educational principles. Dengel (2023) discussions reveal that the definitions of immersive learning, immersive education, and immersive teaching are unclear, calling for more clear theoretical frameworks and practical teaching foundations. When terminology is unclear, research stays weak and implementation gets harder because stakeholders find it hard to move across disciplines. Making immersive education's theoretical foundation clearer is necessary for it to last and work well.

Most policy frameworks follow technology rather than lead its development. Though there is growing support for digital transformation, many nations' education policies continue to marginalize immersive or AI-focused learning in the overall pedagogical change agenda. Most teacher education programs do not focus on immersive instructional design or digital ethics, creating a gap that reduces teachers' ability to carry out these changes (Zhu et al., 2023). Closing this gap calls for major changes in how we design curricula, plan institutions, and support educator development.

Without conceptual clarity and policy commitment, immersive education risks being reduced to a toolset rather than a transformative practice. Bridging these gaps is essential to ensure that innovation advances with pedagogical depth, institutional support, and educator preparedness.

### Reframing the Future of Immersive Education

As we advance, AI-boosted immersive learning environments should be understood as much more than technology; they are also socio-pedagogical systems. They need more than just being easy to use and new to succeed. They have to be judged based on issues such as accessibility, inclusion, cultural response, and sustainability. García-Peñalvo et al. (2022) make clear that the evolution of education is shaped, not only by the existence of new technologies, but by how those technologies are used for diverse learners and ethical concerns. Understanding this complexity leads to the creation of responsible and strong AI-immersive learning environments.

Such environments must be grounded in pedagogical purpose, not driven solely by market novelty. Their value lies in how they mediate relationships between learners, systems, and communities. Reframing immersive education means shifting focus from functional capacity to transformative equity.

## THEORETICAL ANCHORS FOR IMMERSIVE AI LEARNING

Artificial intelligence used in immersive education needs a framework that shows how students learn across many interlinked technologies and spaces. The complexity here needs more than just a single way of thinking to be understood. With connectivism, we see a foundational view that learning happens in networks that have humans and non-humans working together. Post digital theory, sociomateriality, and critical pedagogy of technology together give useful starting points to make sense of how AI blends with immersive learning, fosters relationships, and tackles questions of justice.

*Figure 1. Theoretical anchors for equitable personalization in immersive AI learning*

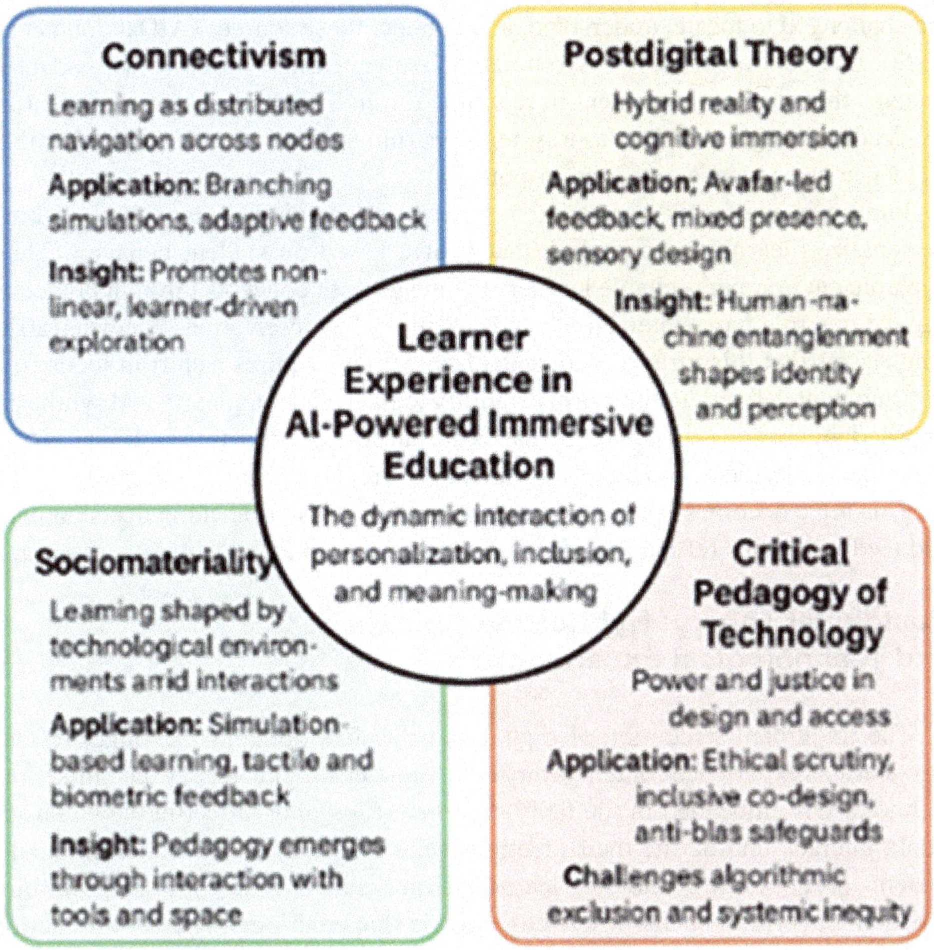


The conceptual map in Figure 1 illustrates how four theoretical anchors, Connectivism, Postdigital Theory, Sociomateriality, and Critical Pedagogy, jointly support the interpretation of learner experiences, design implications, and ethical imperatives within AI-powered immersive learning environments. Each framework highlights a distinct dimension of how personalization operates, succeeds, or fails in real-world contexts.

## Connectivism: Learning as a Networked Phenomenon

Immersive AI-driven learning occurs by linking systems together, not by sending learning along a single path. According to connectivism, knowledge is spread throughout people, digital systems, virtual agents, and data repositories, and learners are challenged to locate, understand, and connect these sources (AlDahdouh et al., 2022). Interactions in these environments involve learners working with adaptive systems that change the content in real time through simulations, virtual mentors, and feedback engines. With these systems, learning procedures are affected by their influence on sequence, rate, and response.

Intelligent platforms use neural networks and predictive algorithms to build personalized learning experiences that evolve based on student behavior. These dynamic environments enable learners to engage with concepts through branching simulations, role-based interactions, and multimodal representations. Siemens (2021) emphasizes that this form of knowledge acquisition requires a shift in focus from static content delivery to the learner's ability to navigate complexity and synthesize knowledge across contexts. This reshapes the purpose of education as the cultivation of connected, critical, and adaptive thinkers within fluid digital ecologies.

This logic becomes visible in later case studies where branching decision paths and feedback loops reflect the adaptive, network-based architecture of learning.

## Postdigital Theory: Hybridizing Human and Technological Experiences

The traditional separation of digital and physical domains no longer reflects how learners experience contemporary education. Postdigital theory recognizes that technology is embedded in the daily rhythms of learning, affecting how learners think, interact, and define their identities (Fawns, 2022). AI-powered immersive systems do not exist outside the learning experience but are enmeshed within it, producing hybrid moments where cognition is shaped through sensory interaction, predictive response, and contextual adaptation.

In metaverse-based classrooms and intelligent VR labs, learners engage with content through gestures, voice, and avatar presence. These settings blur the lines between physical participation and virtual cognition. Jandrić et al. (2022) argue that such hybridity necessitates pedagogical models attuned to the postdigital condition, where algorithms influence perceptions of mastery and virtual agents can alter how learners interpret feedback. Pedagogical planning must therefore move beyond the idea of integrating tools into classrooms, and instead consider how human-machine entanglements shape meaning-making itself.

This interplay of embodied cognition and algorithmic presence is reflected in case findings where virtual agents, avatars, and learner feedback are deeply entwined.

## Sociomateriality: Learning Through Entangled Systems

Learning is never solely an intellectual act, but is shaped by the environments, tools, and social interactions that mediate it. Sociomateriality focuses on the relational nature of learning as it emerges through the interplay of people, technologies, spaces, and institutional norms (Fenwick & Edwards, 2021). In AI-immersive contexts, learners are not only influenced by content, but also by how the environment reacts to their presence, decisions, and expressions. These reactions are generated through real-time data capture, facial recognition, and context-aware algorithms that adjust content delivery and difficulty.

Simulations in medical or engineering training exemplify how sociomaterial entanglements generate pedagogical meaning. Students interact with intelligent agents, use tactile feedback devices, and receive biometric-based guidance. These are not just tools to enhance instruction; they become active participants in shaping what is learned and how it is evaluated. Recognizing this requires educational designers and institutions to shift focus from isolated content delivery to a holistic understanding of learning assemblages where materials, systems, and humans work in coordination.

## Critical Pedagogy of Technology: Reclaiming Justice and Agency

Technological environments are never neutral; they embed values, assumptions, and political decisions in their design and use. Critical pedagogy of technology foregrounds the importance of examining whose knowledge is prioritized, which behaviors are rewarded, and how access is structured within AI-powered immersive learning (Selwyn & Macgilchrist, 2021). Algorithmic bias, surveillance mechanisms, and language exclusion are not abstract risks, but tangible barriers that affect how learners engage and succeed.

Systems trained on homogenous data may disadvantage learners from marginalized communities through misrecognition, content irrelevance, or misaligned pacing. In gamified metaverse settings, emphasis on competition and speed may alienate learners with different cognitive or emotional needs. Sambell and Brown (2023) argue for participatory design models that include the voices of learners and educators in shaping digital learning environments. Such engagement moves beyond critique and enables the co-construction of technologies that reflect inclusive pedagogical values and equitable learning goals.

This perspective is central in cases where algorithmic exclusion and culturally misaligned systems challenge learner equity and participation.

*Table 1. Summary of theoretical frameworks underpinning AI-personalized learning*

| Theory | Key Assumptions | Role in AI Learning | Risks of Exclusion |
|---|---|---|---|
| Connectivism | Learning through networked nodes | Enables adaptive navigation | Fragmented engagement |
| Postdigital Theory | Blended human-tech realities | Anchors immersive hybridity | Misunderstood learner identity |
| Sociomateriality | Entangled human and material agencies | Recognizes environmental impact | Misinterpreted learning outcomes |
| Critical Pedagogy | Power, agency, and justice | Exposes algorithmic bias | Reinforced inequality |

As shown in Table 1, each theoretical lens frames a different dimension of personalized immersive learning, highlighting both pedagogical strengths and risks of exclusion. Understanding AI-powered immersive learning through the combined perspectives of connectivism, postdigital hybridity, sociomaterial entanglements, and critical pedagogy offers a multidimensional view of how knowledge is constructed, experienced, and mediated. These theories not only inform conceptual analysis but also guide the design, selection, and interpretation of methodological choices. The next section applies this foundation to structure the inquiry process, frame data collection, and ensure coherence between theoretical commitments and empirical exploration. They serve as analytical anchors for the chapter's real-world cases, illuminating how personalization can succeed or fail depending on the values, environments, and structures embedded within AI-powered systems.

## ARCHITECTURES OF EQUITABLE LEARNING IN IMMERSIVE AI SYSTEMS

As artificial intelligence and immersive platforms reconfigure the possibilities of education, questions of design, access, and equity become central to any meaningful vision of personalization. To evaluate how such systems enable or obstruct democratized learning, this chapter draws from a constellation of rigorous sources, empirical studies, grounded case studies across low- and middle-income contexts, and practitioner reflections emerging from both scholarly and field-based discourse. The aim is to move beyond technological optimism or critique alone, and to illuminate the actual conditions under which AI-powered personalization within metaverse environments can promote global equity rather than reproduce systemic exclusion.

The following analysis identifies recurring structural challenges and value-based contradictions that demand critical attention if educational AI is to serve all learners, not just those already digitally privileged.

## Personalization and Pedagogical Intentionality

Scholarly analyses increasingly point to a critical gap between technological capability and pedagogical coherence. Holmes, Bialik, and Fadel (2023) emphasize that while AI systems can detect learner patterns and deliver customized content in real time, most remain pedagogically thin. They are designed to change lessons in response to student actions, not by planning what will be learned. Wang, Chen, and Zhang (2024) argue these tutors often do not use context to personalize learning, and as a result, even tailored content fails to make a coherent learning environment. According to Luckin, Holmes, and Forcier (2022), most adaptive educational systems treat information in a fragmented way, missing opportunities to support cultural ways of learning or story-based knowledge building. It suggests that the personalization being used today often substitutes the aspect of precise understanding.

## Immersive Experience and Cultural Responsiveness

When personalization happens in immersive environments such as 3D classrooms or extended reality, the implications become greater. According to Lee, Kim, and Park (2023), students are more active and aware sensory-wise in metaverse simulations, but the learning impact changes greatly depending on group background. Students whose background languages or ways of knowing aren't considered in the interface feel excluded during immersive activities. This result matches the conclusion of Kavanagh, Luxton-Reilly, and Wuensche (2022), who found that virtual agents alone are not sufficient for students to feel part of the experience. Engagement only transforms into learning when identity, context, and interaction are meaningfully aligned. Duan, Li, and Wang (2021) observe that the design of immersive systems, often driven by developers from homogenous cultural or geographic backgrounds, reinforces interface monocultures even in global deployments.

## Operational Ethics and Algorithmic Injustice

The earlier ethical debates about AI-personalized education dealt mainly with bias, but now they also include examinations of harm. As Selwyn, Hillman, and Eynon report (2024), many adaptive AI systems make learner profiles using algorithms that are too complex for users to explain or object to. Learners are frequently put into pre-set growth categories early on, and these systems support those categories with algorithms, making it hard for learners to change or excel outside those limits. In addition, Martinez and Nguyen (2024) show that when algorithmic systems rely on Western-centric corpora, they often fail learners in multilingual contexts because they do not Williamson (2023) examines what happens to learner autonomy when predictive systems are used, warning that adaptation that monitors learners may actually repeat the exclusion these approaches are supposed to address.

## Global Case Narratives and Implementation Variability

Global case examples provide true effects of such dynamics in detail. In a Vietnamese pilot project of a rural nature, witnessed by Wang et al. (2024), AI-based pronunciation tutors managed to adapt to regional dialects. However, standardized assessments rather than individuality of the context remained at the national level and did not provide for the contextual vocabulary and oral tradition. Teachers voiced feelings of frustration with the rigidity of the system, which fail to accommodate their lived pedagogical knowledge. In the meantime, bilingual metaverse program in Latin America produced avatars that could teach both in Spanish and Kichwa. According to a study by Zhang, Wang, and Li (2023), learners immersed at a deeper level when avatars narrated via cultural storytelling and performance gains were greatest for children who had been unsuccessful in formal instruction. Medical students got to use predictive diagnostic models in virtual environments in a South Asian clinical training simulation, evaluated by Kavanagh et al. (2022). Though knowledge retention was enhanced, learners narrated about distress from black-box scoring that had no explanation for performance decisions and no room for dialogic feedback.

## Educator and Learner Testimonies from Applied Research

The issue of aesthetic priority over instructional alignment of such contributors as educators and developers of your own published work (Khalil, Haqdad, and Sultana, 2023) was elaborated further. Teachers were commonly concerned that the tools that were metaverse-based were deeply oriented towards engagement metrics and visual interactivity, at the expense of developmental scaffolds critical to conceptual understanding. AI makers outlined the lack of common reference frameworks that convert values like cultural relevance or inclusivity into design protocols. Without rubrics for implementing ethics, many said they tended to default to the platform setting or follow dominant models. In these accounts, innovation was neither empowering nor neutral. There were no effects independent of whose voice influenced the system's learning logic.

Students added yet another perspective. Throughout the platforms they defined the advantages of the ability to pause, repeat, or redirect their learning paths in real time. However, frustration arose on necessity of AI systems that made changes without explanation. Some learners rejected adaptive feedback when it conflicted with their understanding of effort and fairness. Others absorbed errors as proof of deficiency without knowing that the system's predictive model had little cultural or contextual sense. These patterns support the call for open systems, which are responsive and participatory, in which users can interrogate, revise and resist machine-led adaptation.

### Structural Imperatives for Inclusive Personalization

In these layers of analysis, four conditions keep recurring as required for meaningful personalization that drives global educational equity instead of blocking it. To start with AI, systems need to be developed with the cultural intelligence in mind that goes beyond linguistic translation but the epistemological variety. Second, learners should be able to understand and influence how AI changes their pathways; personalization must not mean disempowerment. Third, code and protocol must have ethics and not policy statements. Fourth, access needs to broaden its understanding from broadband or presence of device to modularity, affordability, and relevance. These are no recommendations, but structural necessities. It will be partial, technically impressive, and pedagogically and morally incomplete without them.

## CASE STUDIES: PERSONALIZATION IN IMMERSIVE SYSTEMS ACROSS GLOBAL CONTEXTS

Demonstrations of AI powered personalization in the context of immersive learning spaces simultaneously provide evidence for innovative potential and caveats for critical limitations. These systems, upon being implemented in culturally diverse and economically diverse areas, no not function uniformly. They reflect the design priorities, infrastructural conditions and pedagogical philosophies that are embedded in their architecture. This section includes four case studies chosen for their applicability to the intersection of adaptive intelligence and immersive delivery and educational equity. Each case shows that personalization takes a different turn based on whether or not systems are developed with contextual consciousness, user involvement, and moral direction.

## Vietnam: Dialect-Sensitive AI Tutors in Rural Primary Schools (Wang, Chen, & Zhang, 2024)

Speech recognition software was incorporated in AI tutoring tools as part of a proof-of-concept exercise pushed by the Ministry of Education and international partners, in a pilot project for Grade 3 students in rural provinces. The objective was to make reading instruction personalized by teaching the AI the regional dialects and phonetic variations that are frequent in the Vietnamese tonal speech. Although the technology managed to real-time adapt pronunciation feedback (Nguyen et al., 2023), some major constraints were identified. Teachers were not involved in the training process of the model leading to a curriculum-practice mismatch between the national curricula and regional linguistic practices. Students lost points for the use of culturally imbedded expressions that were unknown to the system, and the platform supported standard Vietnamese as the normal version. Coming to light as Huynh and Dao (2022) demonstrate, AI systems are not tempered by regionally diverse data can end up unwittingly solidifying the linguistic hierarchy or in the guise of personalization. This project established that, even where adaptation technically proves effective, it can also marginalize learner identity in the absence of contextual knowledge being structurally encoded.

The outcome highlights how personalization that lacks sociomaterial awareness and critical pedagogical grounding may reinforce epistemic exclusion instead of addressing it. Adaptive systems require not only algorithmic accuracy, but localized co-design to reflect the lived knowledge and pedagogical realities of the learners they intend to serve.

## Ecuador: Bilingual Metaverse Classrooms for Indigenous Learners (Zhang, Wang, & Li, 2023)

Dropout rates in Kichwa speaking primary school students from the Andes motivated a project launched by a public university in Ecuador with the aim of creating a bilingual educational metaverse. The virtual platform allowed learners to navigate simulations in both Kichwa and Spanish, guided by culturally embedded avatars modeled after indigenous oral traditions. Story-based learning modules included traditional agriculture, health knowledge, and mathematics taught through metaphor and narrative. Students using the system demonstrated significantly improved literacy outcomes (Cabrera et al., 2022), and parents reported higher engagement due to representation of familiar cultural symbols. According to Jara and Salazar (2023), indigenous learners benefit most from personalized environments when they reflect not only language but symbolic and narrative structures that align with oral traditions. This case confirms that epistemic congruence, more than interface fluency, defines the success of AI-powered personalization among indigenous populations.

The outcomes illustrate how postdigital hybridity and cultural intelligence can work together to create learning environments where students recognize themselves within the system's logic. Rather than adapting content alone, the platform adapted meaning-making itself, a critical distinction that aligns personalization with equity through symbolic co-creation and narrative identity.

## New Zealand: Evaluating 360-Degree Video for Immersive Learning in Higher Education (Kavanagh, Luxton-Reilly, & Wuensche, 2025)

A research team at the University of Auckland evaluated the use of 360-degree video technology in higher education classrooms to examine its potential for enhancing immersion and engagement in academic instruction. The study involved computer science students who experienced course content through 360-degree recorded environments, which allowed them to navigate spatially and interact with learning materials in all directions. The research sought to measure both cognitive impact and user perception of realism, presence, and agency within these environments.

Findings indicated that students valued the enhanced sense of presence and found the environments engaging, particularly when navigating complex spatial or conceptual material. However, the study also uncovered limitations: the video environments were pre-recorded and non-adaptive, lacking real-time personalization or responsive feedback. Several students noted that although the experience was immersive, it did not respond to individual learning needs or offer differentiated paths of engagement.

This case reveals the boundaries of immersion when not supported by adaptive intelligence or equity-centered design. While the postdigital dimension of hybrid presence was clearly achieved, the absence of sociomaterial responsiveness or culturally inclusive scaffolding limited the depth of pedagogical personalization. The experience served as a strong example of immersive delivery without adaptive personalization, a useful contrast to more responsive AI-integrated systems.

## Pakistan: Adaptive Immersion for Teacher Education in Low-Resource Universities (Khalil, Haqdad, & Sultana, 2023)

AI empowered metaverse modules were piloted in teacher education programs in 4 public universities of Pakistan in a national study published by Khalil, Haqdad, and Sultana (2023). These modules applied the avatar roleplay, the formative AI feedback and the content branching to simulate an inclusive class routine. Pre-service teachers worked through scenarios that contained learners with various needs such as neurodivergent profiles, multilingualism and trauma-affected behavior. There was increased self-efficacy as reported by learners and improved retention of inclusive pedagogical principles (Awan & Farooq, 2024). Technical barriers persisted, especially in rural universities with intermittent connectivity, mirroring findings of Khan and Jamil (2023), which highlight the infrastructural restraints in extending immersive learning at scale throughout the Global South. Nonetheless, the system's architecture based on flexibility and learner autonomy was applauded as providing contextual responsiveness and ethical personalization with primacy. The program made equity central to it instead of being a feature, which set a trend for the responsible adaptive design in the teacher training.

This case stands out for transforming equity from a peripheral consideration into the core logic of adaptive immersion. It operationalizes critical pedagogy through participatory learning design while reflecting sociomaterial sensitivity to low-resource educational realities. The program's responsiveness to ethical personalization under constrained conditions offers a grounded model of immersive equity in practice.

*Table 2. Cross-regional case study insights: Design, challenges, and outcomes*

| Case | Region | Technology Used | Key Strengths | Key Barriers |
|---|---|---|---|---|
| Vietnam | Southeast Asia | Dialect-sensitive AI tutors | Pronunciation accuracy | Exclusion of local pedagogy |
| Ecuador | South America | Bilingual metaverse avatars | Cultural storytelling | Limited technical scaling |
| New Zealand (Higher Ed) | Oceania | 360-degree immersive video | Enhanced presence and spatial realism | Infrastructure and connectivity limitations |
| Pakistan (Teacher Ed) | South Asia | Adaptive roleplay modules | Equity-centered design | Infrastructure gaps |

Every one of these case examples demonstrates varying balance between innovation and exclusion, system intelligence and human experience. They also highlight the fact that personalization is not a one-off invention, but a combination of design ethics, cultural representation and user negotiation. With deployment of the AI-powered immersion, without the localization, it carries a threat of continuing inequity in new technical forms. When co-created with communities and pedagogical values, it can, meaningfully, cross historically defined barriers and open access to those who need it the most.

Across these cases, the realization of equitable personalization depended not only on technical architecture but on the presence of culturally rooted design, dialogic feedback, and contextual adaptability, reflecting the relational insights of sociomaterial and critical pedagogical theories. Together, they affirm that AI-powered immersive learning must evolve through co-constructed meaning-making, not just system-driven adaptation, to serve global educational equity as a living, situated reality.

## CHALLENGES AND OPPORTUNITIES FOR GLOBAL EQUITY

More than accessibility to advanced technologies, implementing AI-powered personalized learning into immersive systems in disparate educational settings involves more. The real difficulty is in applying digital innovation to equitable practice where adaptive learning environments understand, reflect, and respond to the multifarious nature of learners' locations in marginalized and underrepresented contexts. Though the opportunities are unprecedented, it will take an honest accounting of continued barriers as well as a dedication to re-engineer these technologies from the inside if these possibilities are to see the light of day.

### Infrastructural Fragility and the Conditions of Technological Access

Infrastructural limitations are still the most apparent impediment to immersive AI integration throughout the Global South. In most countries, particularly rural or peri-urban areas, learners have limited access to high-speed internet, electricity, or compatible digital devices. According to Gupta and Patel (2024), more than one-third of public schools in South Asia do not meet the basic bandwidth thresholds required to run virtual reality or AI-adaptive systems. These challenges are compounded by the lack of locally assembled devices or open-source software ecosystems, which leaves most institutions dependent on imported, expensive, and inflexible platforms. As Khalil and Jumani (2024) emphasize in their feasibility study of the educational metaverse in teacher education, even when administrators are willing, systemic fragility often undercuts implementation. However, low-bandwidth design innovations, such as mobile-compatible metaverse modules or locally cached AI scripts, have begun to offer viable workarounds. Awan and Farooq (2024) document successful deployments of avatar-based learning tools on basic Android tablets in Punjab, showing that intelligent systems can be retrofitted to infrastructural realities rather than presuming universal connectivity.

This challenge was evident in the Pakistan case study, where intermittent internet access in rural universities disrupted immersive engagement, despite the program's otherwise adaptive and equity-centered architecture.

## Linguistic Homogenization in Adaptive AI Design

AI-personalized learning often defaults to dominant global languages, thereby excluding millions of learners whose primary language is regionally or culturally specific. This linguistic bias affects every layer of the user experience, from interface navigation to content comprehension. Martinez and Nguyen (2024) find that even in platforms claiming inclusivity, less than six percent support instruction or interaction in non-European languages. Adaptive feedback frequently cannot recognize syntax, metaphor or ethnic idioms, pervasive in oral traditions, which punishes learners not for confusion but for being outside a computationally dominant linguistic grid. In their study of NLP-driven tutors, Lee et al. (2023) identified that the ways in which standard training datasets neglect systematically dialectal variation. Khalil and Jumani (2024) found, in their Pakistan-based study, that immersion systems designed to be personalized were not compatible with multilingual classroom realities, especially where adaptive responses were based on Western classroom behavioral norms. In spite of the above, new tools such as community trained translation models and user tagged linguistic correction modules, hold promise in developing sensitive logic that matches the diversity of the users.

This issue was sharply visible in the Vietnam case, where students speaking local dialects lost assessment points because the AI tutor's feedback system privileged standardized Vietnamese and lacked cultural-linguistic flexibility.

## Epistemic Misalignment in Immersive Pedagogical Environments

Culture is not merely aesthetic; it forms cognition, interaction and interpretation. If the processes of designing immersive environments lack cultural congruence, then learners are not personalized but faced with epistemic alienation. Kavanagh, Luxton-Reilly, and Wuensche (2022) show that virtual learning agents who represent unknown gestures, or use metaphors alien to learners lived realities, do not fulfill the instructional functions they are supposed to facilitate. According to Holmes, Bialik, and Fadel (2023), personalization needs to be more than content delivery and involves symbolic alignment. What may be delivered as personalized difficulty levels but misfire pedagogically are systems that fail to take into account the community-specific logic structures or the learning values. According to Khalil and Jumani (2024), in Pakistani teacher education simulations, metaverse avatars commonly echoed Eurocentric norms of interaction, like direct eye contact, or assertive speech, that left confused the participants educated in high-context communication cultures. Co-design work with local educators and learners is still one of least employed opportunities to transform immersive systems into culturally embedded pedagogical spaces.

The Ecuador case demonstrates the opposite scenario: symbolic and epistemic congruence were actively embedded through bilingual avatars and culturally rooted storytelling, leading to improved learner connection and measurable literacy gains.

## Algorithmic Opacity and the Erosion of Learner Trust

A large number of AI systems are still black boxes, which provide real-time adaptation without visibility on the part of the user why changes take place. For the learners, this is a damper to the logic of personalization and presents them with an uncertainty of equity and validity. Selwyn, Hillman, and Eynon (2024) point out that algorithmic opacity is very troubling if adjusting systems are applied to formative or summative assessment. Students may receive altered content sequences, learning pace adjustments, or discerned feedback without any explanation, weakening trust in the system. Williamson (2023) observes that educational personalization often masks structural inequalities by embedding invisible hierarchies into learner classification models. This becomes especially dangerous when used in high-stakes environments. Khalil and Jumani (2024) found that many teacher trainees in their study were unaware that their performance was being algorithmically assessed in real time, and this lack of awareness reduced their confidence in feedback accuracy. Recent developments in explainable AI and real-time transparency tools provide a technical foundation for addressing these concerns. However, until such mechanisms are universally implemented, algorithmic opacity will continue to erode the democratic potential of immersive personalization.

This erosion of trust was visible in the New Zealand case, where students expressed discomfort with performance scoring that lacked explanation or space for dialogue, revealing how opacity undermines pedagogical credibility even in well-resourced settings.

## Institutional Capacity and Resistance to Adaptive Transformation

Even when infrastructure, language, and ethical design are accounted for, many institutions lack the strategic readiness to embed AI-personalized learning at scale. Administrators often perceive such systems as experimental, budget-intensive, or misaligned with national curriculum frameworks. Luckin, Holmes, and Forcier (2022) document that in over 50 percent of surveyed institutions in South Asia and the Middle East, immersive AI initiatives were piloted but later shelved due to a lack of integration into broader academic policy. Khalil and Jumani (2024) encountered similar challenges, with university faculty expressing concern about time constraints, lack of control over adaptive systems, and fear of job displacement. However, such resistance also reveals the need to reposition educators not as end-users but as co-designers. When teachers are trained not only to operate but to shape adaptive environments, they are more likely to trust the system and use it effectively. Institutional transformation, then, is not merely a technical challenge but a relational one. Building communities of design, feedback, and reflexive practice can create sustainable pathways for democratizing personalized education at scale.

This was evident in the Pakistan teacher education case, where despite successful learner outcomes, institutional inertia and policy misalignment limited the long-term integration of adaptive immersive modules into formal university programmin

*Figure 2. Structural challenges and leverage points for AI-powered educational equity*

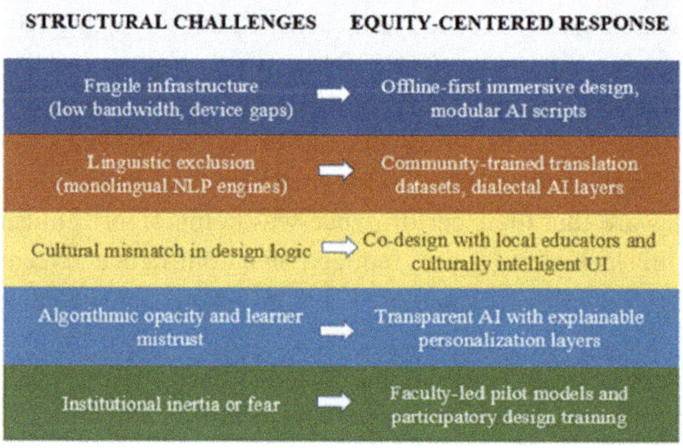


Pervasive hurdles to global equity in AI-enabled immersive education shed light not only on the technical and infrastructural issues, but on the linguistic, cultural, ethical and institutional asymmetries. These are not fringe difficulties but core problems of design that determine whether personalization is for inclusion or entrenchment of exclusion. From infrastructural fragility and linguistic marginalization to epistemic incongruence and algorithmic opacity, all these barriers represent the lack of a common basis set in justice-oriented learning and design framework. However, these tensions also reveal important sites for the reengineering of adaptive systems which are locally responsive, ethically transparent and pedagogically coherent. These structural contradictions, the subject of the next section's strategic framework for democratizing personalized learning in the metaverse, must not be considered exceptions to innovation but rather as the defining rulebook in which truly equitable learning systems must be built.

## FRAMEWORK FOR DEMOCRATIZING AI-POWERED LEARNING

Enriching education democratically with personalization through AI in interactive settings calls for more than just technical efficiency or teaching novelty. It is a call to shift paradigm, where personalization is radically reconceived beyond both individual isolation and algorithmic tracking as a relational, culturally responsive, and ethically located practice. The framework presented here is built on the empirical realties and failures in design established in the previous sections and emerging critical scholarship that emphasizes equity, transparency, and pluralism in educational technology. It is structured on four interdependent pillars. cultural intelligence, open personalization, internal ethics and infrastructure-aware scalability. Combined, they represent an example for planning personalized but just learning systems.

*Figure 3. Framework for democratizing AI-powered personalized learning*

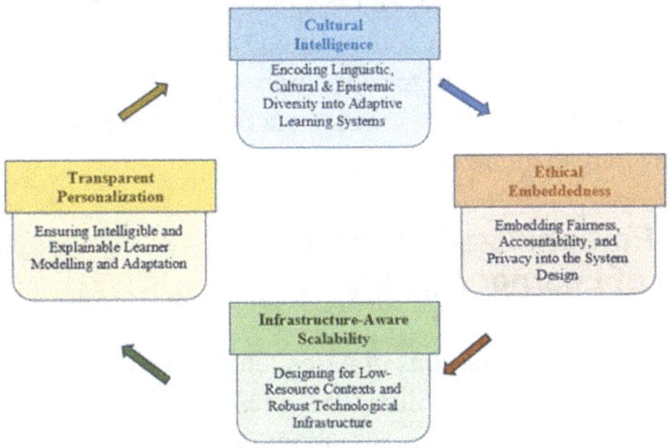


### Cultural Intelligence as a Foundational Layer in Adaptive Design

Personalized learning environments that ignore cultural logic often fail even when technically functional. Holmes, Bialik, and Fadel (2023) caution that the illusion of personalization can arise when systems adapt to cognitive pace but not to epistemic frames. Language, values, gestures, and interactional norms must be encoded into immersive systems not as aesthetic additions but as pedagogical architecture. When avatars speak in a learner's home dialect or present feedback through familiar idioms and metaphors, engagement deepens and retention improves (Lee, Kim, & Park, 2023).

This principle was strongly affirmed in Zhang, Wang, and Li's (2023) study of Kichwa-Spanish bilingual avatars in Latin America, where learners exhibited gains not only in academic outcomes but also in cultural pride. Similarly, Duan, Li, and Wang (2021) argue for "localized ontologies" in AI systems, warning that learning environments that universalize epistemology often encode dominant ideologies without critique. Khalil and Jumani (2024) note that metaverse simulations in teacher education frequently replicated Eurocentric teaching models, marginalizing students who rely on collectivist, non-verbal, or context-bound learning cues. When personalization is designed without cultural intelligence, it ceases to be inclusive and becomes another layer of educational gatekeeping.

Furthermore, cultural intelligence requires a participatory design ethos. Learners and educators must be involved not as test users but as co-authors of the systems they will navigate. As Selwyn, Hillman, and Eynon (2024) advocate, equity-driven AI begins with process equity, design conversations that include historically excluded voices from inception. This also aligns with frameworks like co-design-based learning analytics (Ifenthaler et al., 2022), which encourage the embedding of learners' situated practices into adaptive decision pathways.

## Transparent Personalization and the Reclamation of Learner Agency

One of the greatest contradictions in AI-enhanced personalization is the opacity with which most systems operate. Williamson (2023) critiques the "hyper-personalization" narrative that dominates edtech markets, noting that the more precise the adaptation, the less visible it often becomes to the learner. Adaptive pathways are frequently locked behind proprietary logic, meaning learners are told what to do without understanding why.

This absence of explanation not only erodes trust, it disables agency. Martinez and Nguyen (2024) document that students subjected to opaque learning pathways often internalize algorithmic decisions as reflections of fixed ability. Khalil and Jumani (2024) observed a similar pattern among teacher trainees, some of whom interpreted AI feedback as discrediting their efforts due to a lack of rationale. Such interpretive misalignment can be psychologically de-motivating, especially in competitive environments or high-stakes settings or among learners who are doubtful about their academic legitimacy (Luckin et al., 2022).

This problem is resolved by transparent personalization, which makes not just the adaptations, but the logic and assumptions of adaptations, visible. Students can see through open learner models (Bull et al., 2021), adaptive visual trackers, and feedback rationales how their inputs affect system outputs. Shifting to "explainability as pedagogy", where the process of understanding the machine's response becomes a part of the learning process, Lee et al. (2023) attach importance to it. This takes personalization from a receptive to a full discourse mode, where learners are enlisted to negotiate, question or modify their learning pathways as opposed to simply accepting them.

## Ethical Embeddedness Beyond Compliance

Ethics in the practice of AI education mostly remains rhetorical, deployed to point to caution yet never to form the actual designing. To democratize the immersive personalization, ethics need to be operationalized along system lifecycles. This entails inclusive data sourcing, trail records of decisions, purposeful consent paths, and even an option of opt out of adaptation entirely.

Martinez and Nguyen (2024) propose a six-layer ethical framework that includes learner dignity, algorithmic fairness, and response reparability. However, as Holmes et al. (2023) point out, few immersive systems incorporate even basic data rights affordances, such as control over data storage or feedback processing. Williamson (2023) describes the rise of "silent surveillance" in personalized education, where learner behavior is tracked not only for teaching purposes but for predictive modeling with no accountability.

Khalil and Jumani (2024) argue that the ethical dimension must be taught alongside technical usage in teacher education. In their study, when trainees understood the biases and limitations of AI feedback, they were better able to contextualize and correct it in their own instructional planning. This suggests that ethical literacy is not a design add-on but a pedagogical necessity. Furthermore, ethics must not only apply to learners, but also protect teachers. In many implementations, educators are subject to opaque evaluation systems that mine classroom interactions without their full understanding or consent (Selwyn et al., 2024).

Frameworks such as value-sensitive design (Friedman & Hendry, 2021) and culturally responsive AI (Lu, Noble, & Benjamin, 2022) offer concrete pathways for building systems that encode care, dignity, and accountability. These are not abstract ideals but required infrastructure if AI-enhanced education is to support justice.

## Infrastructure-Aware Scalability for Contextual Equity

Scalability is often misunderstood in educational AI. Rather than referring to uniform expansion, it must denote the ability of systems to adapt to diverse infrastructural conditions without loss of pedagogical integrity. Holmes, Bialik, and Fadel (2023) recommend "fractal design models," where system functionality can scale up or down depending on bandwidth, device access, or user proficiency. This enables the same pedagogical logic to operate in both high-tech and low-tech environments. The Vietnamese and Pakistani case studies demonstrate that meaningful personalization can occur even in constrained settings when systems are designed for flexibility (Wang et al., 2024; Khalil & Jumani, 2024). Offline-capable immersive modules, preloaded AI tutor scripts, and modular content banks are now technically feasible, and they shift the narrative from scalability through funding to scalability through design efficiency.

Zhang et al. (2023) emphasize that decentralizing infrastructure through cloud-synced local servers or campus-based AI nodes can reduce dependence on national broadband while maintaining functionality. This has been particularly effective in Latin American and East African pilot sites. Infrastructure-aware scalability also requires policy innovation. Ministries and universities must support modular procurement policies and collaborative content development pipelines that can serve multiple formats and languages simultaneously.

This framework is not a fixed solution but a dynamic scaffold that reorients how personalization is imagined and enacted. Cultural intelligence ensures that systems honor the learner's identity. Transparency restores agency in adaptive pathways. Ethical embeddedness safeguards participation and accountability. Infrastructure-aware scalability ensures that no context is left behind. Together, these pillars transform personalization from a technical feature into a democratic commitment, one that demands not only precision but justice.

## Limitations in Resource-Constrained Contexts

While the framework offers a comprehensive vision for democratizing AI-powered learning, its implementation faces critical limitations in low-resource environments. Infrastructure gaps, including unstable electricity, low bandwidth, and lack of device availability, continue to restrict access to immersive systems in many Global South contexts. Financial constraints also hinder the adoption of culturally responsive and ethically embedded personalization, since such systems often require localized co-design, ongoing educator training, and ethical auditing processes that are rarely funded in public institutions. Furthermore, rigid curriculum policies and centralized procurement procedures often slow institutional uptake of modular, adaptive systems, even when proven effective. These realities require not only technological redesign but also systemic reforms in funding, governance, and local capacity development if the framework is to achieve practical traction beyond isolated pilot programs.

## CONCLUSION: REIMAGINING EQUITY THROUGH INTELLIGENT IMMERSION

Artificial intelligence, when embedded into immersive learning environments, has the potential to redefine how education is personalized, accessed, and experienced. Yet that potential remains deeply contingent. Throughout this chapter, it has been demonstrated that AI-driven personalization is not automatically equitable. Without a critical design architecture grounded in local contexts, ethical awareness, and cultural responsiveness, such systems risk reproducing the exclusions they seek to eliminate. Metaverse technologies expand the spatial and sensory parameters of learning, but they do not guarantee inclusion unless inclusion is systematically designed. The future of adaptive learning depends not only on how sophisticated AI becomes, but on whether its underlying logic serves diverse learners with transparency, equity, and integrity.

The empirical cases analyzed across Vietnam, Ecuador, and Pakistan demonstrate that impact arises not from novelty, but from contextual alignment. Systems that reflect the learner's linguistic, social, and epistemic identity produce better engagement and deeper comprehension. As noted in Zhang, Wang, and Li (2023), the bilingual avatar system in Ecuador generated stronger literacy outcomes because it affirmed indigenous narratives and relational structures of meaning. In contrast, the Vietnamese AI tutor, despite its dialect recognition capability, failed to support local learning values due to rigid national assessment alignment (Nguyen et al., 2023). Personalization is effective only when learners recognize themselves, cognitively and culturally, within the logic of the system.

The theoretical framework proposed here consolidates four structural pillars necessary for democratizing AI-powered learning. Cultural intelligence positions knowledge diversity at the center of instructional design. Transparent personalization enables learners to trace, understand, and influence their adaptive pathways, rather than be subjected to opaque feedback cycles. Ethical embeddedness requires that consent, accountability, and bias awareness be encoded into both the algorithmic and institutional dimensions of system deployment. Finally, infrastructure-aware scalability insists that immersion and adaptation must function across ecological constraints, from high-speed urban networks to low-bandwidth, device-limited environments. Each of these pillars is mutually reinforcing. None can compensate for the absence of another.

Persistent gaps, however, remain. Global education systems still lack enforceable ethical standards for AI explainability and accountability in learning. Cultural representation in immersive environments is largely homogenized, often reproducing Western instructional metaphors and behavioral assumptions (Williamson, 2023). Moreover, the dominance of English-language training datasets continues to marginalize large swathes of the multilingual learner population (Martinez & Nguyen, 2024). In this context, personalization becomes not a neutral technical process, but a site of political and epistemological contestation. Educational researchers, designers, and institutions must therefore interrogate the values being translated into system logic and the positionalities of those doing the translating.

As Khalil and Jumani (2024) have shown in their study on immersive teacher education, personalization can be both effective and inclusive when systems are developed with intentional regard for learner identity, technological constraints, and ethical literacy. The metaverse simulation modules piloted in Pakistani universities achieved positive pedagogical outcomes not because they mimicked high-tech standards, but because they were designed with contextual humility, adaptable pacing, and participatory feedback models. This example reinforces the idea that equity is not a consequence of AI advancement, it is the result of deliberate, inclusive system architecture.

This chapter does not present a final solution, but a conceptual reorientation. It invites the educational technology community to view personalization not as an individual optimization algorithm, but as a collective, justice-oriented design challenge. When learners are treated not as data points, but as agents embedded in specific histories, cultures, and constraints, personalization can become a vehicle for equity. When systems explain themselves, allow modification, and reflect the communities they serve, they become more than instructional tools, they become instruments of educational transformation. The next phase of global digital learning must be shaped by this recognition. It is not the sophistication of the algorithm that should define its success, but its capacity to honor and respond to the diversity of learning identities it encounters. In the architecture of AI-powered education, equity is not an added layer. It must be the foundation.

This chapter set out to explore how AI-powered personalized learning environments within the educational metaverse can be designed and implemented to promote global equity, particularly by addressing structural, cultural, and ethical barriers. Through multi-regional case studies and theoretical interrogation, it demonstrated that personalization only becomes equitable when systems embed cultural intelligence, learner agency, and infrastructural adaptability. The empirical analysis affirmed that algorithmic adaptation must be transparent and participatory to avoid reinforcing existing exclusions. The theoretical framework consolidated these insights into a four-pillar model that directly responds to the original aims. Each research objective—identifying contextual challenges, evaluating inclusive design practices, and proposing a scalable, ethical framework, was met with evidence and grounded strategies for implementation.

## REFERENCES


AlDahdouh, A. A., Osório, A. J., & Caires, S. (2022). Understanding connectivism: A study on learning networks in digital environments. *International Review of Research in Open and Distance Learning*, *23*(1), 144–163. DOI: 10.19173/irrodl.v23i1.5625

Awan, R., & Farooq, R. (2024). Mobile-based immersive learning in low-resource classrooms. *International Journal of Educational Technology in Higher Education*, *21*(1), 33–48.

Bull, S., Kay, J., & Johnson, M. D. (2021). Explainable AI for open learner modelling: Transparency, trust and pedagogical opportunities. *International Journal of Artificial Intelligence in Education*, *31*(1), 1–28. DOI: 10.1007/s40593-020-00227-6

Cabrera, R., Salinas, J., & Quispe, L. (2022). Literacy development through indigenous language metaverse. *Journal of Multilingual Education Research*, *12*(2), 77–94.

Dede, C., Jacobson, J., & Richards, J. (2017). *Virtual, augmented, and mixed realities in education*. Springer., DOI: 10.1007/978-3-319-40621-1

Dengel, A. (2023). The semantics of immersive learning: Clarifying concepts for scalable practice. *British Journal of Educational Technology*, *54*(1), 114–132. DOI: 10.1111/bjet.13276

Duan, Y., Li, X., & Wang, H. (2021). Interface monocultures in global immersive education: A critique of design homogeneity. *British Journal of Educational Technology*, *52*(6), 1451–1468. DOI: 10.1111/bjet.13161

Fawns, T. (2022). An entangled pedagogy: Looking beyond the pedagogy–technology dichotomy. *Postdigital Science and Education*, *4*(2), 293–310. DOI: 10.1007/s42438-019-00048-9 PMID: 40477872

Fenwick, T., & Edwards, R. (2021). *Emerging approaches to educational research: Tracing the socio-material*. Routledge.

Friedman, B., & Hendry, D. G. (2021). *Value sensitive design: Shaping technology with moral imagination*. MIT Press., DOI: 10.7551/mitpress/13842.001.0001

García-Peñalvo, F. J., Corell, A., Abella-García, V., & Grande, M. (2022). Technological ecosystems in higher education: Meta-learning and knowledge construction in immersive environments. *Computers in Human Behavior*, *129*, 107129. DOI: 10.1016/j.chb.2021.107129

Gupta, A., & Patel, R. (2024). Digital inequities in rural South Asia: AI and immersive education under infrastructure constraints. *International Journal of Educational Development, 95*, 102681. DOI: 10.1016/j.ijedudev.2022.102681

Henadirage, A., & Gunarathne, T. (2025). Barriers to immersive AI integration in higher education: Perspectives from the Global South. *International Journal of Educational Development, 96*, 102696. DOI: 10.1016/j.ijedudev.2023.102696

Holmes, B., Bialik, M., & Fadel, C. (2023). Artificial intelligence in education: Promise, progress, and future directions. *International Journal of Artificial Intelligence in Education, 33*(2), 101–122. DOI: 10.1007/s40593-022-00328-w

Huynh, T., & Dao, M. (2022). Linguistic hierarchies in adaptive AI systems: The case of Vietnamese dialect recognition. *Asian Journal of Applied Linguistics, 29*(3), 201–215.

Ifenthaler, D., Yau, J. Y.-K., & Gosper, M. (2022). Co-design-based learning analytics: A framework for ethical decision making. *British Journal of Educational Technology, 53*(4), 839–858. DOI: 10.1111/bjet.13168

Jandrić, P., Bozkurt, A., & Macgilchrist, F. (2022). Postdigital dialogue in education: Human learning as a hybrid phenomenon. *Educational Philosophy and Theory, 54*(3), 275–289. DOI: 10.1080/00131857.2020.1814177

Jara, D., & Salazar, P. (2023). Culturally situated learning in the digital Andes: Avatar-based education in Ecuador. *Journal of Educational Research and Practice, 13*(1), 11–29.

Kavanagh, S., Luxton-Reilly, A., & Wuensche, B. (2022). Adaptive immersive simulations in medical training: A regional perspective. *Educational Technology Research and Development, 70*(5), 1225–1244. DOI: 10.1007/s11423-021-10066-4

Khalil, A., Haqdad, A., & Sultana, N. (2023). Educational metaverse for teaching and learning in higher education of Pakistan. *Journal of Positive School Psychology, 7*(3), 1183–1198.

Khalil, A., & Jumani, N. B. (2024). Feasibility of educational metaverse for immersive transformation of teacher education. *Journal of Arts & Social Sciences, 11*(1), 95–106. DOI: 10.46662/jass.v11i1.456

Khan, A., & Jamil, M. (2023). Infrastructure challenges in educational technology adoption in South Asia. *Pakistan Journal of Educational Research, 10*(2), 49–68.

Lee, H., Kim, J., & Park, S. (2023). Cultural congruence and learner perception in metaverse-based adaptive education. *Journal of Computer Assisted Learning*, *39*(2), 150–170. DOI: 10.1111/jcal.12757

Lu, M., Noble, S. U., & Benjamin, R. (2022). Designing culturally responsive AI systems for education. *AI & Society*, *37*(3), 567–584. DOI: 10.1007/s00146-021-01223-2

Luckin, R., Holmes, W., & Forcier, L. B. (2022). Intelligence unleashed: Ethical and contextual imperatives for AI in education. *AI and Ethics*, *2*(3), 305–320. DOI: 10.1007/s43681-021-00102-9

Martinez, L., & Nguyen, T. (2024). Algorithmic exclusion in multilingual learning environments: Challenges and reforms. *Computers & Education*, *197*, 104701. DOI: 10.1016/j.compedu.2023.104701

Nguyen, M., Le, T., & Tran, P. (2023). Evaluating dialect-sensitive AI for literacy development in Vietnam. *Asia Pacific Journal of Education*, *43*(1), 87–104. DOI: 10.1080/02188791.2022.2136019

Sambell, K., & Brown, S. (2023). Designing inclusive assessment: Participatory strategies in digitally mediated learning. *Assessment & Evaluation in Higher Education*, *48*(4), 635–650. DOI: 10.1080/02602938.2022.2151033

Selwyn, N., Eynon, R., & Bulfin, S. (2021). *The datafication of education: Critical questions for learning and technology*. Routledge.

Selwyn, N., Hillman, T., & Eynon, R. (2024). Algorithmic personalization and educational data justice. *Learning, Media and Technology*, *49*(1), 12–27. DOI: 10.1080/17439884.2023.2252052

Selwyn, N., & Macgilchrist, F. (2021). Should robots replace teachers? AI and the future of education. *Learning, Media and Technology*, *46*(3), 220–232. DOI: 10.1080/17439884.2021.1929934

Siemens, G. (2021). Connectivism: Learning as network-creation. In *Teaching in a Digital Age: Guidelines for Designing Teaching and Learning* (2nd ed.). BCcampus. https://pressbooks.bccampus.ca/teachinginadigitalagev2

Wang, H., Chen, Y., & Zhang, L. (2024). Immersive AI-enhanced learning environments in rural settings: Challenges and innovations. *Journal of Educational Technology & Society*, *27*(1), 88–103. DOI: 10.30191/ETS.2024.27.1.06

Williamson, B. (2023). Algorithmic governance and educational platform personalization. *Learning, Media and Technology*, *48*(1), 17–35. DOI: 10.1080/17439884.2022.2115462

Williamson, B., & Eynon, R. (2021). Algorithms and education governance: Exploring how digital data is reshaping policy. *Journal of Education Policy*, *36*(1), 1–23. DOI: 10.1080/02680939.2019.1672895

Zawacki-Richter, O., Marín, V. I., Bond, M., & Gouverneur, F. (2022). Systematic review of research on artificial intelligence applications in higher education: Learning, assessment, and administration. *International Journal of Educational Technology in Higher Education*, *19*, 21. DOI: 10.1186/s41239-022-00326-w

Zhang, Y., Wang, X., & Li, H. (2023). Designing culturally grounded immersive learning for indigenous learners. *International Review of Research in Open and Distance Learning*, *24*(2), 65–83. DOI: 10.19173/irrodl.v24i2.7106

Zhu, X., Zhao, Y., & Li, R. (2023). Policy lag in digital education reform: A global survey of teacher readiness and institutional innovation. *Computers & Education*, *191*, 104632. DOI: 10.1016/j.compedu.2023.104632

# Chapter 5
# Artificial Intelligence (AI) Readiness of Business Management Students at a State University: The Role of Demographic Characteristics

**Jaysi Tanguilan Corpuz**
https://orcid.org/0000-0003-3505-0377
*Cavite State University, Philippines*

**Corpuz**
https://orcid.org/0009-0005-0888-7691
*Cavite State University, Philippines*

**Maria Cristina L. Desepida**
https://orcid.org/0000-0002-8765-7667
*Cavite State University, Philippines*

**Rose Marian R. Cubacub**
https://orcid.org/0009-0006-0146-7990
*Cavite State University, Philippines*

**Princess M. Feliciano**
https://orcid.org/0009-0004-6897-2698
*Cavite State University, Philippines*

**Janine Wynnona P. Cac**
https://orcid.org/0009-0003-6642-6872
*Cavite State University, Philippines*

**John Michael Colin Maraasin**

**Kiara Naomi G. Flores**
https://orcid.org/0009-0002-3210-4632
*Cavite State University, Philippines*

## ABSTRACT

*With the evolution of artificial intelligence (AI), it gives the opportunity to enhance the education sector as students are starting to utilize this technology with its significant benefits. Understanding the demographic profile, knowledge, attitude, and acceptance of students towards AI technologies is essential to prepare students for*

DOI: 10.4018/979-8-3373-2302-2.ch005

*the integration of AI in education. Descriptive and inferential research designs were used to analyze the data collected through face-to-face and online surveys. Results show that the level of knowledge on AI of the respondents demonstrated a moderate understanding of AI, mainly focused on basic functions like grammar checking and content generation. Attitudes toward AI were generally favorable, with students recognizing its value in academic performance. Nonetheless, concerns over usability, complexity, and ethical implications persisted. Similarly, AI acceptance levels were moderate, with students acknowledging its value as a helpful tool instead of a substitute for traditional methods. Critical thinking and over-reliance concerns influenced students' hesitations in fully embracing AI in their learning processes. Statistical analysis revealed that while most demographic characteristics, such as age, sex, year level, and AI permissions, had no significant correlation with knowledge, attitudes, or acceptance, some variables did show significant relationships. In testing the relationship, using Pearson's Chi-square and Cramer's V statistical tests, the students' major in the program and their level of AI knowledge were found to have a strong relationship. Additionally, years of experience with using AI and both attitude and acceptance of AI among business management students were found to have a strong relationship. Furthermore, the average daily duration of AI usage and acceptance indicated a strong relationship. The findings of the study highlight the key influential factors in AI readiness in education, emphasizing the role of specialization/program, experience, and average duration of AI usage in shaping students' knowledge, attitudes, and acceptance of AI technologies. This underscores the need for targeted AI integration in business curricula through embedded AI literacy modules, clear academic guidelines, and consistent exposure via specialized AI training for both faculty and students, as well as the adoption of diverse research methods to deepen understanding and increase AI acceptance. At the policy level, addressing infrastructure and access disparities will help ensure equitable digital readiness and support the creation of ethical AI strategies in Philippine higher education.*

## INTRODUCTION

Artificial intelligence (AI) readiness refers to students' knowledge, attitude, and acceptance of AI tools in education, which are critical for effective integration of these technologies in academic settings. Nearly 86% of students worldwide now utilize AI tools in their academic pursuits, with 54% engaging with them on a weekly basis. In the UK, usage has surged, with 92% of undergraduates reporting they use generative AI, up from 66% just the previous year (Digital Education Council, 2024; Freeman, 2025; University World News, 2025). These numbers show how

AI, especially generative AI like ChatGPT, has become a mainstream academic resource. This rapid integration means we need to consider not only how students use AI, but also whether they have the preparedness, support, and digital readiness needed to use these tools fairly and effectively in college.

Artificial Intelligence (AI) is rapidly transforming higher education, reshaping not only teaching and learning processes but also students' attitudes and acceptance (Owoc et al., 2021; Ocen et al., 2025). AI-driven tools like smart tutoring systems, personalized learning platforms, and generative AI solutions are being increasingly adopted in educational settings to improve customization, feedback, and administrative effectiveness (Sajja et al., 2024; Ocen, 2025). Personalized systems reduce cognitive load and tailor learning pathways to individual strengths (Sajja et al., 2024), while adaptive learning technologies have shown positive outcomes in student performance (Wang et al., 2020).

Moreover, even with its benefits, using AI still comes with challenges. There are still some important concerns, like ethics, data privacy, unfair decisions made by AI, and academic honesty (Melisa et al., 2025; Chen et al., 2020). On top of that, some studies suggest that if students rely too much on AI could get in the way of critical thinking and creativity (Zhai et al., 2021). In Asia, universities are swiftly incorporating AI to enhance personalization, engagement, and operational efficiency (Locus, 2024; Cañas-Llamas, 2024). Mapúa University in the Philippines has launched courses such as Basic Prompt Engineering with ChatGPT and AI Foundations: Scripting ChatGPT with Python to enhance LLM and programming skills (Locus, 2024), whereas the University of the Philippines Open University (UPOU) established ethical AI usage with newly released guidelines in January 2024 (Cañas-Llamas, 2024).

Recent studies in the Philippines have shown that even when children report using AI frequently and hold strong attitudes about technology, this doesn't automatically translate to better academic performance. A study of business students at Negros Oriental State University revealed that they utilized AI to some extent, primarily for personalized learning and expedited feedback. However, there was no strong link between AI use and academic success (Bancoro, 2024). Estrellado and Miranda (2023) emphasized the importance of clear infrastructure, ethical guidelines, and faculty training to facilitate the integration of AI into Philippine institutions. Nationwide research also found that nearly 63% of college students use generative chatbots like ChatGPT to write, 58% use AI for translation, and most utilize AI to help them understand complex ideas (Instructure Holdings, Inc., 2025). These results show that AI is becoming a mainstream academic resource. For business management students to use it effectively and fairly, schools need to improve systems and consider demographic factors to fully support digital readiness.

This research fills in important gaps by examining how business management students perceive and understand AI in education, with a special emphasis on how certain demographic factors, including age, sex, year level, years of experience with AI, and others, influence these areas. Although AI is becoming increasingly widespread in schools, there has been limited research on how students perceive and utilize these technologies (Petrescu et al., 2023; Chao et al., 2021; González-Anleo et al. 2024; Kanont et al. 2024; Rony et al. 2024; Maxwell et al. 2025; Rajki et al. 2025; and Gerard et al. 2024). Katsantonis and Katsantonis (2024) suggest that students' opinions about AI are influenced by their field of study and social background. This calls for research that considers these factors. Mackenzie et al. (2025) and Zhou et al. (2024) both found that there is limited research focusing on business and students. This is especially true when it comes to how demographics affect AI involvement. Most significantly, Qiu et al. (2025) note that there is a limited information regarding how business students perceive AI and their intentions for utilizing it. This means that a concentrated demographic study in this group is very crucial.

Therefore, this study addresses a gap in the research by examining how demographic factors influence business management students' knowledge, attitudes, and acceptance of AI. It does so in a timely manner and in response to requests for AI education research that takes into account both demographics and discipline. The results of the study will help educators, educational institutions, and policymakers implement AI more effectively in higher education. By grasping students' perspectives, this study will guarantee that AI is utilized in a manner that aids students and prepares them for AI-oriented sectors.

## RESEARCH PROBLEM

Despite the growing integration of AI in education, there remains a limited of focused insight into how demographic characteristics and AI usage patterns shape business management students' knowledge, attitudes, and acceptance of AI, limiting the ability to develop inclusive, effective policy and educational strategies. Hence, this research sought to address the following research questions:

1. What is the demographic profile of the business management student participants?
2. What is the level of knowledge, attitude, and acceptance on using artificial intelligence among business management students?
3. Is there a significant relationship between the demographic profile of business management students and three key AI related outcomes such as level of AI knowledge, attitudes and their level of acceptance of AI?

## OBJECTIVES OF THE STUDY

Generally, this study aimed to assessed the relationships between the demographic characteristics with their levels of knowledge, attitudes, and acceptance on AI among business management students. Specifically, the study aimed to:

1. determine the demographic profile of business management students such as age, sex, year level, major of the program, types of AI tools or applications, average daily duration of AI usage, years of experience using AI, specific academic activities where AI is applied, and permitted use of AI for academic purposes;
2. discuss the level of knowledge, attitude, and acceptance on using artificial intelligence among business management students; and
3. evaluate whether there is a significant relationship between the demographic profile of business management students and three key AI related outcomes such as level of AI knowledge, their attitudes toward artificial intelligence, and their level of acceptance of AI.

## LITERATURE REVIEW

This section presents several studies on the levels of knowledge, attitude, and acceptance of AI among students internationally and in the Philippine settings. Results regarding the relationships between the demographic profile and the different outcomes were also presented to facilitate comparisons of these variables.

### Relationship of Demographic Profile and Students' Level of Knowledge on AI

Research shows that demographic factors, including gender, age, academic level, discipline, language background, and prior AI exposure, have a big impact on how much students know about AI. However, most research doesn't look at business management groups. According to Kovačević and Demić (2024), male students often believe they possess more knowledge about AI than female students do. Bognár and Khine (2025) demonstrated that individuals who have previously used AI tools are more likely to possess self-efficacy, indicating that practical exposure is a factor in knowledge confidence. In a poll of students from France and Italy, Sublime and Renna (2024) found that older and male students were more likely to say they were familiar with and used AI, which shows gender and age gaps. Chan and Hu (2023) showed that AI familiarity is quite different depending on discipline and academic level. This means that business students may differ from those in STEM or the humanities. In a study conducted at a U.S. institution, Deng et al. (2025) found that individuals with higher academic standing, non-native English speakers, and underrepresented ethnic groups reported having a better understanding of generative AI. This shows that there are disparities in technical and contextual literacy. Importantly, Divekar et al. (2025) studied 68 business students and found a discrepancy between their perceived knowledge of AI and their actual understanding. This showed that the students were overconfident and didn't know much about more advanced AI capabilities. Kanont et al. (2024) suggest that examining how demographic characteristics, such as age, gender, and area of study, influence AI understanding and attitudes may help fill knowledge gaps. Rony et al. (2024) also noted that demographic aspects should be considered in terms of both knowledge and attitude to develop plans that address the gaps and solve the problems.

These studies do show that demographic characteristics influence AI knowledge, but they mostly examine general or mixed student groups instead of business management students, who require practical AI skills for tasks such as data analysis, strategic decision-making, and automation. Also, relying on self-reported measures may not accurately reflect actual competence, particularly in real-world commercial settings. The results of Divekar et al. (2025) study on overconfidence make this danger further clearer. So, targeted research that objectively looks at AI knowledge among business students from different backgrounds is important to help with curriculum development and fair AI education.

## Relationship of Demographic Profile and Students' Level of AI Attitude

Research consistently shows that students generally have positive attitudes toward AI, but these attitudes are shaped by demographic variables, academic discipline, trust in AI systems, and even regional context. However, business management students, especially in the Philippines, are rarely the focus. According to Kovačević and Demić (2024), male students had more positive attitudes and greater trust in AI than female students. Almaraz-López et al. (2023) and Katsantonis and Katsantonis (2024) conducted research comparing students in STEM and business programs with those in education and humanities programs. They found that students in STEM and business programs always had stronger AI optimism than students in education and humanities programs.

Trust in AI tools is a crucial factor that has emerged. Along with this, Abdalla et al. (2024) and Shahzad et al. (2024) show that students' confidence in AI tools and their perceived reliability makes them far more open to using them. Reyes et al. (2024) spoke about Filipino university students and said that even though they typically have positive attitudes toward AI, these sentiments don't always make them more knowledgeable about AI. They said that institutional frameworks are important. At the same time, Ramirez et al. (2024) found a strong connection between AI trust and attitude among students in the Philippines, which supports the idea that trust is very important. Bancoro (2024) examined Filipino business administration students and found that they used AI moderately, with generally positive views. However, there was no direct relationship between AI usage and academic performance, which means that good attitudes alone may not lead to significant gains. Maxwell et al. (2025) note significant differences in students' preparation for generative AI based on their demographics. Deng et al. (2025) and Rajki et al. (2025) say that demographic factors may predict AI use and perceived obstacles. Gerard et al. (2024) also discuss how people at different institutions and in various fields perceive AI differently.

These results support the idea that students have positive attitudes toward AI, which are affected by their gender, field of study, level of trust, and cultural background. Most of the evidence, on the other hand, comes from self-reported, cross-sectional data from general student populations. This data rarely includes long-term monitoring or considers specialized AI exposure in business disciplines. There is a clear need for studies in the Philippine business education setting, where AI is being used more and more in analytics, operations, and strategy, to look at how attitude, trust, and demographic factors change over time and whether these attitudes lead to learning outcomes that can be acted on. This type of study would help businesses develop AI adoption programs that are more sophisticated, inclusive, and effective in their implementation.

## Relationship of Demographic Profile and Students' Level of AI Acceptance

Studies show that business students are generally highly accepting of AI, and this is influenced by factors like prior experience, perceived usefulness, ease of use, self-efficacy, trust, and institutional support. However, only a few studies look at this in the context of Philippine business education.

Qiu et al. (2025) employed the Technology Acceptance Model to demonstrate that perceived usefulness and ease of use had a significant impact on business management students' behavioral intention and actual use of AI tools worldwide. Yi and Choi (2023) also said that prior AI experience and performance expectations make pupils far more likely to accept anything. In the Philippine University students' context, De Jesus and Co. (2025) observed that business student-researchers from Region III in the Philippines are generally open to AI writing tools, as they perceive them as practical, easy to use, and helpful in certain situations. Further this illustrates the importance of both institutional and individual mindset elements. Asirit and Hua (2023), Divekar et al. (2024), and Shahzad et al. (2024) all found that senior students or those with prior AI experience demonstrate higher acceptance in the Philippine business setting. This suggests that experience and maturity make people more open to new ideas. Bognár and Khine (2025) also discovered that engagement and self-efficacy from past exposure greatly increase the willingness to adopt AI. Fošner (2024) and Santos et al. (2024), on the other hand, warn that many studies of acceptance merely examine broad use and fail to carefully connect demographic factors to AI acceptance levels. Asirit and Hua (2023) also pointed out that under-represented and developing contexts have big infrastructure limitations that make it hard for people to accept even when they are ready. Bancoro (2024) noted that business administration students utilize AI moderately and have positive attitudes, but this did not have a strong connection to academic success. This indicates a gap between acceptance and quantifiable educational outcomes.

Most studies that exist employ small, homogeneous samples, which makes them less useful for a wider audience (Petrescu et al., 2023; Chao et al., 2021). González-Anleo et al. (2024) show that gender and age have a big effect on how people embrace AI. This illustrates the importance of studying diverse groups of people.

Overall, several research-based evidence that acceptance of AI among business students is affected by a complicated mix of real-world experience, psychological characteristics, and the company they work for. International models, such as TAM and UTAUT, explain most of the factors that affect acceptance; however, regional research reveals different patterns. For example, social norms may not be as important on Philippine campuses, and infrastructural problems might make acceptance more challenging, even when attitudes are favorable. Most importantly, the lack of link between admission and academic achievement needs further investigation. Longitudinal and demographic-sensitive designs should be employed in future studies to examine how acceptance leads to actual usage and educational benefits among Filipino business management students, as well as how institutional tactics might facilitate fair AI incorporation.

## Synthesis

Research suggests that demographic factors like gender (with males expressing stronger knowledge and favorable attitudes about AI) and prior experience have a large effect on how business students interact with AI in three areas: knowledge, attitude, and acceptance. Literature's reviewed have found that older, male, and experienced students are more likely to report being confident and knowledgeable about AI. Using AI in real life may also promote self-efficacy, which makes people more ready to learn about and utilize AI systems. Students often exhibit optimism and trust in AI, but trust alone doesn't necessarily lead to better AI literacy or real-world results, particularly in places like the Philippines, where there is limited institutional support on the use of AI especially in the fields of education particularly in business education. Studies based on the Technology Acceptance Model (TAM) indicate that perceived usefulness, ease of use, and prior experience are the most significant predictors of whether someone will utilize an AI application. But there is always one warning: positive attitudes and acceptance don't always lead to academic performance improvements. This approach shows how important it is to do objective, longitudinal, and demographic-sensitive research that looks at how these factors are connected and how they affect real-world learning outcomes for business management students.

## THEORETICAL FRAMEWORK

This research is based on Davis's (1989) Technology Acceptance Model (TAM), which posits that behavioral intention is influenced by perceived usefulness and perceived ease of use, which in turn determine actual technology use. This is supported by an empirical study on AI: Yi and Choi (2023) demonstrate that prior AI experience and performance expectations greatly increase readiness to use AI, whereas Qiu et al. (2025) revealed that these two variables considerably affect both the intention and actual usage of AI tools among business management students.

On the other hand, other models, such as the Unified Theory of Acceptance and Use of Technology (UTAUT), which was put forth by Venkatesh et al. (2003), include demographic moderators like gender and age in addition to other predictors like performance expectancy, effort expectancy, social influence, and facilitating conditions. In the meantime, Rogers' Diffusion of Innovation (DoI) theory (1962) looks at how characteristics like complexity, compatibility, and relative advantage help inventions spread across social systems.

TAM is the best tool for this research due to its simplified emphasis on individual views, such as the usefulness and simplicity of use, even though DoI provides macro-level insight into innovation dissemination and UTAUT offers greater explanatory power. TAM provides both conceptual clarity and empirical relevance for evaluating acceptability and real-world application in educational environments by focusing on how business management students see AI. Its usefulness as the guiding theoretical framework is confirmed by its demonstrated applicability and clear agreement with the study's goals.

*Figure 1. Theoretical framework illustrating technology acceptance model (Davis, 1989)*

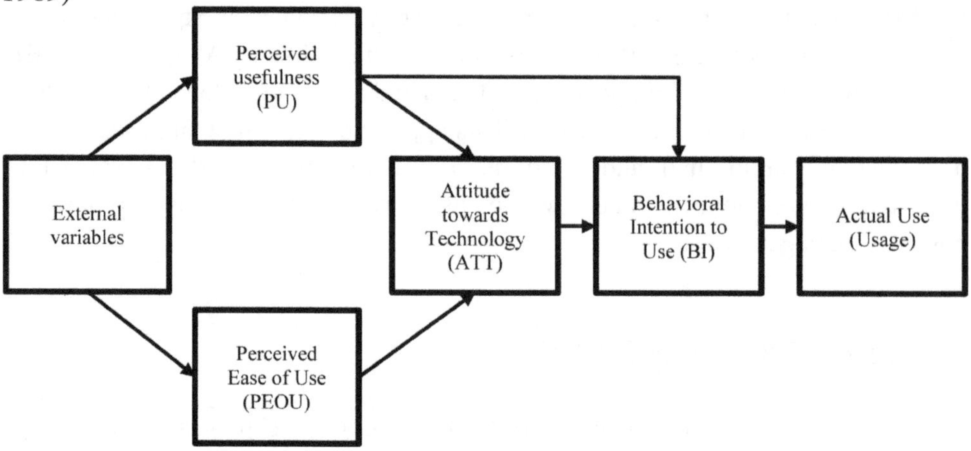


## CONCEPTUAL FRAMEWORK

As shown in Figure 1, the conceptual framework of this study was anchored in analyzing the relationship between four variables: the demographic profile of the participants as independent variables and the level of knowledge on using artificial intelligence (AI), the students' attitudes toward AI, and the level of acceptance of AI as dependent variables.

The study aimed to ascertain how the demographic profile of business management students- namely: age, sex, year level, major of the program, types of AI tools or applications, average daily duration of AI usage, years of experience using AI, specific academic activities where AI is applied, and permitted use of AI for academic purposes- affect their knowledge, attitude, and acceptance of using AI.

By connecting these variables, the study aimed to determine the extent to which the demographic characteristics of business management students influence their knowledge, attitude, and acceptance of using Artificial Intelligence (AI) in the educational setting.

*Figure 2. Conceptual framework illustrating the relationship of demographic profile on knowledge, attitudes, and acceptance of artificial intelligence among business management students*

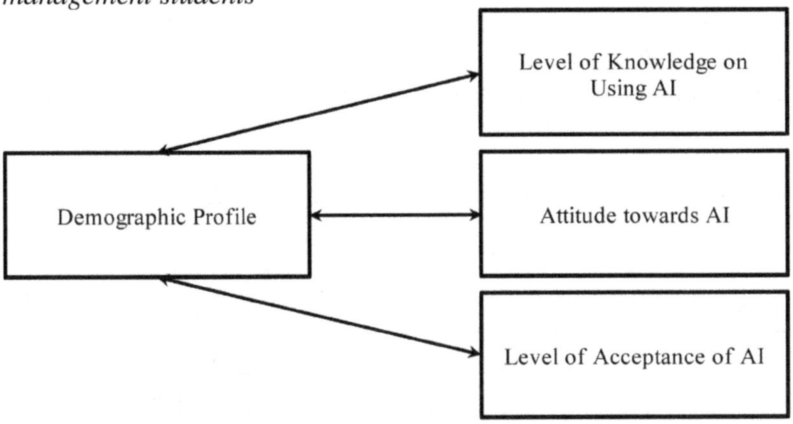


## Hypotheses of the Study

To guide the analysis of the study, the following are alternative hypotheses that were tested:

$H_1$: There is a relationship between the demographic profile and the level of knowledge among business management students.
$H_2$: There is relationship between the demographic profile and students' attitudes toward artificial intelligence among business management students.
$H_3$: There is a relationship between the demographic profile and the level of acceptance among business management students.

## METHODOLOGY

The descriptive and inferential methods were used in this study. The descriptive methods used include frequency counts, percentages, and grand mean to tabulate, analyze, and interpret the data in order to determine the demographic profile, level of knowledge, students' attitudes, and the level of acceptance of the respondents. Furthermore, the inferential methods used include the Pearson's chi-square test to determine if there is a significant relationship between two categorical variables. It was used to ascertain the relationship between the demographic profile and the level of knowledge, students' attitudes, and level of acceptance. Moreover, Cramer's v was used to measure the strength of the relationship between more than two categorical variables. Thus, it was utilized to determine the strength of the relationship between the demographic profile and the level of knowledge, students' attitudes, and level of acceptance after concluding that there is a significant relationship. Table 1 shows the value and interpretation to distinguish the relationship between the variables.

*Table 1. Value of Cramer's V to determine the strength of the relationship between variables*

| CRAMER'S V | INTERPRETATION |
|---|---|
| Greater than or equal to 0.25 | Very strong relationship |
| 0.15 - 0.24 | Strong relationship |
| 0.10 - 0.14 | Moderate relationship |
| 0.05 - 0.09 | Weak relationship |
| 0.01 - 0.04 | No/Negligible relationship |

Source: Haldun Akoglu (2018)

The study was conducted in the Department of Management of the College of Economics, Business Management, and Development Studies at Cavite State University - Don Severino Delas Alas Campus. The respondents of the study were the business management students of Cavite State University - Don Severino Delas Alas Campus from different majors of the program such as financial management, human resource management, marketing management, operations management, and service management and from first-year to fourth-year levels. A total of 335 participants were selected using Slovin's Formula. However, due to response and time constraints, only 247 valid respondents were collected through online and face-to-face survey questionnaires using a mix of both non-probability and probability sampling, specifically convenience sampling, snowball sampling, and simple random sampling. This combination of sampling methods was adopted to enhance the practicality and flexibility of data collection. Simple random sampling ensured fair representation of students across various year levels and majors, while convenience and snowball sampling made it possible to reach more participants despite time constraints and accessibility challenges. Employing both approaches enabled the researchers to obtain a diverse set of respondents aligned with the study's objectives.

The main instrument of the study is a combination of adapted survey questionnaires from different related studies. It was divided into 3 parts: The information sheet introduction, the consent form, and the questionnaire proper. The first part contained information about the research and encouraged the participants to participate in the study, such as the title of the thesis, the purpose of the research, duration, information about confidentiality, and who to contact for inquiries and concerns. The second part of the questionnaire is the consent form, which ensures that the participants understood the information provided to them and voluntarily consented to participate in the study by the Data Privacy Act of 2012. The third part, questionnaire proper, was divided into three sections dedicated to measuring and examining the demographic profile, level of knowledge on using AI, students' attitudes toward AI, and the level of acceptance of AI by business management students of Cavite State University - Don Severino Delas Alas Campus.

The first section asked the demographic profile of the participants such as the name, age, sex, year level, major of the program, the AI tools or applications they use, the amount of time they use AI in a day, the years of experience they have in using AI, the specific academic activities where AI is applied, and whether the students are permitted to use AI for academic purposes, along with the reasons of their professor's approval or disapproval. This part of the questionnaire was adapted from the study of Asirit and Hua (2023), Divekar et at. (2024), and Fošner (2024). The second section aimed to determine the students' level of knowledge on the usage of AI in academic activities. The participants were given a 15-item multiple choices questionnaire designed to cover key concepts of integrating AI into academic activities. This part of the questionnaire was adapted from the study of Santos et al. (2024). Table 2 displays the score and verbal interpretation that were utilized to determine the level of knowledge of business management students on the usage of AI in academic activities.

*Table 2. Parameter to determine the level of knowledge on the usage of AI in business management students*

| SCORE | VERBAL INTERPRETATION |
|---|---|
| 1 - 5 points | Limited AI Knowledge |
| 6 - 10 points | Moderate AI Knowledge |
| 11 - 15 points | Strong AI Knowledge |

The third section aimed to determine students' attitudes towards AI and the level of acceptance of AI in business management students. The participants were given 31 items that evaluated various aspects of technology acceptance, specifically, five items for expected benefits (EB), six items for perceived usefulness (PU), five items for perceived ease of use (PEOU), five items for attitude toward using (AT), five items for behavioral intention (BI), and five items for actual use (AU). Items under PU, PEOU, and AT were used to assess the students' attitude towards AI, while items under EB, BI, and AU were used to assess the level of acceptance of AI in business management students. For specific item numbers, 1 to 5 and 22 to

31, with a total of 15 items, were under acceptance, and 6 to 21 with a total of 16 items, were under attitude. The participants were asked to score their agreement with each item on a 7-point Likert scale. This part of the questionnaire was adapted from the study of Kanont et al. (2024). Table 3 displays the 7-point Likert scale with verbal description. This scale was used to assess participants' level of agreement or disagreement with each statement regarding their attitudes and acceptance of AI. The average value of the 7-point Likert scale was divided into three categories (Table 4) to maintain consistency in analyzing attitude and acceptance. All instruments used in the study underwent pilot testing to ensure reliability. To determine the internal consistency of each construct, the study utilized the "Cronbach's alpha (α)" coefficient following pilot testing, a standard reliability approach supported by the study of Corpuz et al. (2022).The results showed that the Cronbach's Alpha values for Knowledge (0.72), Attitude (0.91), and Acceptance (0.93) all met or exceeded the acceptable threshold of 0.70.

*Table 3. Seven-point Likert Scale was designed to determine the students' level of acceptance and attitude on the usage of AI in academic activities*

| RATING SCALE | DESCRIPTION | ABBREVIATION |
|---|---|---|
| 1 | Totally Disagree | TD |
| 2 | Disagree | D |
| 3 | Somewhat Disagree | SD |
| 4 | Neutral | N |
| 5 | Somewhat Agree | SA |
| 6 | Agree | A |
| 7 | Totally Agree | TA |

*Table 4. Parameter to determine the mean value and verbal interpretation that were utilized to determine the level of attitude and acceptance of students' usage of AI in academic activities*

| SCALE | MEAN VALUE | VERBAL INTERPRETATION |
|---|---|---|
| 1 | 1.00 - 3.00 | Negative Attitude / Low Level of Acceptance |
| 2 | 3.01 - 5.00 | Neutral or Moderate Attitude / Moderate Level of Acceptance |
| 3 | 5.01 - 7.00 | Positive Attitude / High Level of Acceptance |

Moreover, before the data gathering, a formal letter of request has been prepared to obtain permission from the chairperson of the department of management to collect data from business management students of Cavite State University - Don Severino delas Alas Campus. This assures that the study is approved by the appropriate academic authority and that the research procedure is carried out in compliance with institutional policies.

## RESULTS, DISCUSSION AND ANALYSIS

### Demographic Profile of the Business Management Students

#### Age

The participants' ages ranged from 17 years old and above. Half of participants (50.61%) were in the ages of 21 to 22 years old, while the least (5.67%) were in the ages of 17 to 18 years old. Since most of the participants were aged 21 to 22 years old, this shows that AI adoption in education is primarily influenced by students in this age group. The results show that this age group are more inclined to adopt and positively perceive AI technologies due to greater academic exposure and need for efficiency tools, and higher digital literacy with academic challenges. Older students may have a more positive perception of AI due to their academic experience and maturity (Spulber et al., 2024 & Pacheco-Mendoza et al., 2023). As Asirit and Hua (2023) suggested, adapting AI education to different age groups can improve engagement and learning effectiveness.

The results imply that AI integration should be tailored by age group. Younger students, possibly new to college, may need more guided orientation or support to see the relevance and utility of AI learning. Senior mentoring could be explored, where older students can serve as AI mentors.

#### Sex

Out of all respondents, 69 were male and 178 were female. This indicates a gender distribution where female respondents have a larger proportion (72%) of the sample compared to male respondents (28%). The higher representation of female respondents suggests that women are increasingly engaged in academic environments where AI is utilized. This finding contrasts Kovacevic and Demic (2024), who indicated that male students might utilize AI more frequently. Recognizing gender differences in AI adoption is crucial to ensuring equitable access and opportunities for all students to develop AI-related skills and maximize its benefits in education

(Pacheco-Mendoza et al., 2023). Furthermore, Sublime and Renna (2024) also found out that male students were more likely to say they were familiar with and used of AI, which shows gender gaps. The results imply that female student's greater presence may also reflect more openness to educational technologies or proactive use of AI for learning.

## Year Level

The participants were spread across various year levels, with the majority of 152 in the third year (61.54%) and the least 27 (10.93%) in the second year. The highest number of respondents were third year students, indicating that the use of AI grows as students' progress in their studies. This suggests that AI adoption and familiarity tend to increase as students advance in their academic journey. This is consistent with Asirit and Hua (2023), who stated that awareness and familiarity with AI increase as students' progress in their academic journey. As students advance in their studies, it becomes critical to integrate AI learning across all year levels to enhance their proficiency over time and better prepare them for the evolving demands of academic.

## Major of the Program

Among the respondents, 81 (32.79%) were from marketing management and the least, 7 (2.83%) were from service management. The higher engagement of students in Marketing indicates a stronger dependence on AI for data analysis and innovative AI tools. This indicates that marketing students are likely more exposed to, or in greater need of, AI tools for tasks such as customer segmentation, trend analysis and campaign optimization. Conversely, the minimal representation from service Management students highlights a potential gap in AI integration or perceived relevance in service- oriented disciplines, which may limit their technological preparedness in a digitally transforming business environment. This is supported by Abdallaa et al. (2024), who highlighted AI's role in data-driven decision-making that highlights the need for customized AI education that integrates practical uses throughout various business fields, ensuring that students acquire a thorough understanding of AI's potential.

The results imply a discipline-specific integration of AI is necessary. Business programs may consider that AI applications are embedded into all tracks, with relevant, practical use cases tailored to each specification.

## Types of AI Tools and Applications

ChatGPT is the most commonly used AI tool, with 219 users (88.66%), followed by Quillbot with 193 users (78.14%) and Canva with 188 users (76.11%). In contrast, the least utilized tools include Beautiful.ai, Mapple Calculator, School Hack, and Tome, each with only 1 user (0.40%), while Automata and Koalachat had no reported users. The high usage of ChatGPT, Quillbot, and Canva highlights the preference for AI tools that support writing, editing, and design tasks. The overwhelming use of these tools highlights their essential role in delivering academic work. This aligns with Bognár and Khine (2025), who emphasized AI's role in enhancing academic engagement wherein selecting effective AI tools optimizes educational outcome. However, the minimal use of certain AI applications suggests a need for greater awareness or perceived relevance in educational settings. This implies the need to broaden students' awareness and understanding of diverse AI tools that support various learning and problem-solving functions across disciplines.

## Average Daily Duration of AI Usage

Findings revealed that the majority of respondents, 131 (53.04%), use AI tools for less than 1 hour per day, while the least, 3 respondents (1.21%), use them for more than 6 hours. The moderate daily use of AI tools, with most students utilizing them for less than an hour pay day, suggests that while the benefits of AI are recognized, these tools have not yet become fully integrated into students' academic routines. This finding reflects a transitional stage in AI adoption, where the technology is viewed primarily as a supplementary aid rather than a core component of the learning process. This aligns with Ralhan (2024), who observed that increased usability leads to higher AI adoption. Additionally, the author states that as students discover the tools to be more user-friendly, the frequency of AI usage rises. Furthermore, as Ahn (2024) emphasized, integrating AI tools into students' daily academic activities has the potential to enhance their learning efficiency and overall academic performance. These insights highlight the need for educational institutions to foster greater AI literacy and incorporate AI-supported learning strategies across disciplines to encourage more consistent and effective use.

## Years of Experience Using AI

Majority of students, 99 (40.08%), have 1 to 2 years of AI experience, while the least, 3 students (1.21%), have used AI for more than 6 years. The findings indicate that most participants have 1 to 2 years of AI experience, suggesting that AI adoption in education is relatively recent. This limited exposure suggests that while awareness and usage are growing, many students are still in the early stages of integrating AI into their academic routines. Almaraz-López et al. (2023) observed that ongoing interaction with AI in educational environments enables students to develop skills and assurance in applying AI for their academic activities. Given the expanding role of AI in various industries and professions, this underscores the need for higher education institutions to implement structured AI training across all academic programs. Doing so will not only enhance students' academic performance but also ensure they are equipped with the necessary technological competencies to meet the demands of an increasingly AI-driven workforce.

## Specific Academic Activities Where AI is Applied

Results showed that the majority of students, 183 (74.09%), use AI for writing and editing, while the least, 41 students (16.60%), use it for solving mathematical problems. The strong preference for AI in writing and research suggests its effectiveness in streamlining academic tasks. This aligns with Fosner (2024), who emphasized AI's significant role in writing assistance. However, as Pacheco-Mendoza et al. (2023) suggested, expanding AI's use in problem-solving could enhance students' overall academic proficiency. These findings highlight the need for educational institutions to promote a more balanced and comprehensive integration of AI across diverse subject areas to fully realize its potential as a learning tool.

## Permitted Use of AI For Academic Purposes

Data indicated that 157 students (63.56%) are permitted to use AI for academic purposes, while 90 students (36.44%) face restrictions. The significant percentage of students allowed to use AI for academic purposes suggests a growing acceptance of AI in education. This aligns with Guhan et al. (2023), who stated the increasing integration of AI in education. However, as Alshamy et al. (2025) pointed out, higher education institutions must address concerns about plagiarism, academic misconduct and over-reliance to support informed, ethical, and responsible use of AI tools in an educational environment. These findings underscore the importance of establishing well-defined guidelines and awareness programs to help students utilize AI tools effectively, responsibly, and in ways that support both learning outcomes and academic integrity.

*Figure 3. Summary of the key findings of the demographic profile of the participants*

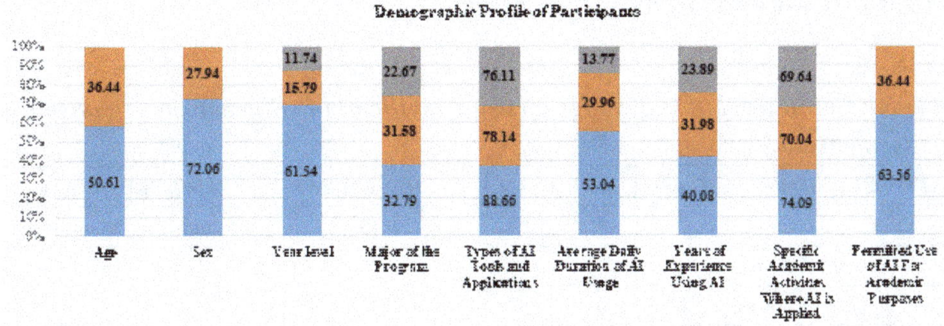


## Level of Knowledge on Using Artificial Intelligence

### Among Business Management Students

Table 5 presents the results of the level of knowledge on using AI among business management students. The data indicates that among 247 respondents, 124 students (50.20%) possess a moderate level of AI knowledge. This implies that while half of the respondents have a foundational understanding of AI, a gap in knowledge regarding advanced AI technologies still exists and there is still room for improvement. This is supported by the study of Aljuaid (2024) highlighting that students commonly use AI tools like Quillbot and Grammarly for grammar and plagiarism checking to improve their writing skills, which shows practical awareness of AI's academic applications. Similarly, the study of Benuyenah and Dewnarain (2024) supports this observation, highlighting that students commonly use ChatGPT for academic tasks like drafting and researching, appreciating its convenience and contribution to learning outcomes. However, reliance on these user-friendly tools may hinder the students' exposure to more complex AI domains. Moreover, Chao et al. (2021) discovered that students struggle to understand certain areas of AI, such as machine learning and robotics because of limited official classes for AI. These findings imply the importance of revisiting curricular priorities. While students show interest and comfort in using AI for academic enhancement, there is a clear need to move beyond tool-oriented familiarity and toward the integration of conceptual AI education. Embedding theoretical and technical content into existing courses can help develop students' digital literacy, preparing them not only to be responsible users but also informed future professionals capable of engaging with advanced AI systems in real-world business environments.

*Table 5. Overall level of knowledge on using artificial intelligence among business management students*

| KNOWLEDGE ON USING AI | F | P (%) | OVERALL MEAN | INTERPRETATION |
|---|---|---|---|---|
| Limited AI Knowledge | 27 | 10.93 | **9.45** | **Moderate AI Knowledge** |
| Moderate AI Knowledge | 124 | 50.20 | | |
| Strong AI Knowledge | 96 | 38.87 | | |
| **Total** | **247** | **100.00** | | |

Legend:
Limited AI Knowledge: 1 to 5
Moderate AI Knowledge: 6 to 10
Strong AI Knowledge: 11 to 15

## Business Management Students' Attitudes

### Towards Artificial Intelligence in Higher Education

The results show (Table 6) that business management students typically possess a favorable opinion of AI in education, achieving an overall average score of 5.24. The statement rated the highest, "Do you believe that using AI aids in your assignments?" (mean = 5.54), reflects students' significant dependence on AI resources such as ChatGPT, which is in line with Zhang and Xu (2024) and Shahzad et al. (2024). This indicates that AI is being perceived not just as a convenience but as an essential academic resource.

Nevertheless, students showed varied views on the practicality of AI. Sentences such as "Do you believe that utilizing AI demands considerable effort?" (mean = 4.74) and "Do you believe AI is easy to use?" (mean = 4.81) suggest that although AI is advantageous, some students continue to face difficulties in applying it, corroborating Li et al. (2024). Furthermore, students' ease with AI integration (mean = 5.11) indicates a careful but increasing acceptance, as noted by Yilmaz et al. (2023), who emphasized worries regarding AI's precision, privacy, and ethical considerations. Likewise, Melisa et al. (2025) and Chen et al. (2020) also believed that there are still some important concerns, like ethics, data privacy, unfair decisions made by AI, and academic honesty. These findings imply a dual responsibility for educational institutions, to enhance the students' AI literacy by addressing usability and ethical concerns, and to promote responsible AI use to prevent over-dependence.

Overall, the general results indicate that students are progressively embracing AI as an important tool to support in their educational pursuits, particularly for tasks that require efficiency and assistance. This growing reliance reflects AI's perceived usefulness in enhancing productivity and outcomes. However, as Watanabe (2024) warns, excessive dependence on AI may undermine student's ability to think critically and learn independently. Thus, it is essential to balance the benefits of AI with responsible use to guarantee that students cultivate both technological skills and academic integrity.

*Table 6. Business management students' attitudes towards artificial intelligence in higher education*

| INDICATOR | MEAN | INTERPRETATION |
|---|---|---|
| 1) Simplify learning tasks | 5.47 | Positive Attitude |
| 2) Supports quicker learning | 5.26 | Positive Attitude |
| 3) Benefits education | 5.47 | Positive Attitude |
| 4) Helps with academic tasks | 5.54 | Positive Attitude |
| 5) Improves learning efficiency | 5.21 | Positive Attitude |
| 6) Creating with AI increases knowledge | 5.11 | Positive Attitude |
| 7) Learning AI usage is quick | 5.13 | Positive Attitude |
| 8) Using AI needs minimal effort | 4.74 | Neutral or Moderate Attitude |
| 9) Using AI is straightforward | 4.81 | Neutral or Moderate Attitude |
| 10) Using AI independently | 5.12 | Positive Attitude |
| 11) Easy to use | 5.34 | Positive Attitude |
| 12) AI is beneficial | 5.15 | Positive Attitude |
| 13) Know how to apply AI for learning | 5.52 | Positive Attitude |
| 14) Adds value to learning | 5.33 | Positive Attitude |
| 15) Comfortable of using AI in school | 5.11 | Positive Attitude |
| 16) Helps complete tasks faster | 5.53 | Positive Attitude |
| **OVERALL** | **5.24** | **Positive Attitude** |

Legend:
Negative Attitude: 1.00 to 3.00
Neutral or Moderate Attitude: 3.01 to 5.00
Positive Attitude: 5.01 to 7.00

## Level of Acceptance of Artificial Intelligence

### Among Business Management Students

As shown in Table 7 below, the results of the study revealed that the acceptance of artificial intelligence (AI) across all year levels exhibited a moderate acceptance of AI, with an average mean of 4.72. This result is in line with Yilmaz et al. (2023), who found that students recognize the benefits of AI, particularly its capacity to perform complex tasks and offer personalized, real-time academic support, full acceptance remains limited due to underlying concerns related to ethics, privacy, and accuracy.

The mean score ranged from 3.75 to 5.51. The least contributing factor was the belief that AI can solve problems better than humans, while the most significant factor was AI's ability to assess complex tasks and provide real-time personalized recommendations, followed by its usefulness in helping students complete assignments with quality. This is in line with Bantoto et al. (2024), who found that students accept AI tools mainly for their perceived benefits, such as accessibility and ease of use (Spulber et al., 2024; Shahzad et al., 2024). This implies that rather than taking the role of conventional teaching techniques, AI is increasingly viewed as a tool to increase productivity.

However, students still acknowledge the limitations of the usage of AI when it comes to critical thinking and decision-making, as indicated in its least contributing factor. These expressed the concerns indicated by Watanabe (2024) that too much dependency on the application of AI and negatively influencing the problem-solving and critical thinking of students. This could lead to affecting the long-term learning of students as they were able to get everything easily. These results imply that while AI is increasingly integrated as a supplementary tool to improve academic performance, it is not yet fully trusted as a central component of the learning process.

Thus, the overall results show that students moderately accept the use of AI in education. This level of acceptance indicates a growing acceptance indicates a growing recognition of AI's potential to enhance learning efficiency, personalize academic support, and simplify complex tasks. It displayed that students were aware of its advantages and its disadvantages, including the risks of over reliance, diminished critical thinking, and ethical concerns like plagiarism and data privacy.

The moderate acceptance further suggests that students are cautiously optimistic about AI but remain critical of its limitations. This nuanced perspective is important, as it reflects a mature understanding that while AI can serve as a valuable tool, it cannot replace core academic competencies such as analytical reasoning, creativity and ethical judgment. To increase the acceptance, improving AI literacy and promoting the responsible use of it by integrating it in education as suggested by

Tapalova and Zhiyenbayeva (2022). This could help the students strike a balance between utilizing AI for academic enhancement and maintaining their capacity for independent thinking.

*Table 7. Level of acceptance of artificial intelligence among business management students*

| INDICATOR | MEAN | INTERPRETATION |
|---|---|---|
| 1) Supports task assessment and personalized suggestions | 5.51 | High Level of Acceptance |
| 2) Enables development of learning assistants | 5.17 | High Level of Acceptance |
| 3) Improves assignment planning and quality | 5.30 | High Level of Acceptance |
| 4) Contributes to better academic performance | 5.26 | High Level of Acceptance |
| 5) Helps showcase learning capabilities to peers | 4.59 | Moderate Level of Acceptance |
| 6) Used as first resort in problem-solving | 4.46 | Moderate Level of Acceptance |
| 7) Reliance for solving academic problems | 4.04 | Moderate Level of Acceptance |
| 8) Serves as effective problem-solver than humans | 3.75 | Moderate Level of Acceptance |
| 9) Supports flexible creation and resolution of tasks | 4.57 | Moderate Level of Acceptance |
| 10) Need to align with personal learning styles | 4.30 | Moderate Level of Acceptance |
| 11) Frequent use for content creation | 4.00 | Moderate Level of Acceptance |
| 12) Interest in future use of AI | 5.10 | High Level of Acceptance |
| 13) Regular use to support learning | 4.74 | Moderate Level of Acceptance |
| 14) Willingness to update AI-related knowledge | 4.91 | Moderate Level of Acceptance |
| 15) Contentment with AI for learning | 5.15 | High Level of Acceptance |
| OVERALL | 4.72 | Moderate Level of Acceptance |

Legend:
Low Level of Acceptance: 1.00 to 3.00
Moderate Level of Acceptance: 3.01 to 5.00
High Level of Acceptance: 5.01 to 7.00

## Relationship Between Demographic Profile, Knowledge, Attitudes, and Acceptance of Artificial Intelligence Among Business Management Students

Table 8 revealed that the demographic profile in terms of age, sex, year level, average daily usage of AI, years of experience, and the permitted use of AI for academic purposes had no significant relationship with knowledge on using AI. Thus, the alternative hypothesis is rejected. This suggests that being proficient in AI depends more on the technical background of students than on the given demographics. This implies that AI proficiency is not inherently determined by demographic factors but is likely influenced by students' exposure to relevant content and learning experiences. This result was contrary to the TAM model in which TAM's states that external variables have a significant connection to knowledge. The findings advise that external variables, such as demographic factors, play a significant role in shaping users' perceptions of technology. Specifically, TAM suggests that these external variables influence individuals' perceived usefulness and perceived ease of use, which in turn affect their behavioral intention to adopt and use a particular technology.

In contrast, under demographic factors, only the major of the program had a significant relationship with knowledge on using AI, with a p-value and Cramer's V of 0.034 and 0.184, respectively. Therefore, the alternative hypothesis is accepted. This may be due to different subjects students take in relation to their majors, shaping their understanding of AI. This was supported by Asirit and Hua (2023), who found that business students tend to possess different degrees of AI awareness, which is influenced by the extent to which AI is included in their coursework. Additionally, Pacheco-Mendoza et al. (2023) noted that students in technology-related fields generally possess a more profound comprehension of AI. Furthermore, in a poll of students from France and Italy, Sublime and Renna (2024) found that older and male students were more likely to say they were familiar with and used AI, which shows gender and age gaps. Moreover, Chan and Hu (2023) showed that AI familiarity is quite different depending on discipline and academic level. Likewise, Divekar et al. (2025) studied 68 business students and found a discrepancy between their perceived knowledge of AI and their actual understanding. This showed that the students were overconfident and didn't know much about more advanced AI capabilities. Thus, these results emphasize the necessity of incorporating AI education into all curricula to guarantee that students possess adequate AI knowledge.

The overall results signify that it had a contradictory connection to TAM, in which it stated that there is a significant relationship between the external factors (demographic profile) and perceived usefulness (knowledge). The contradicting results are due to the homogeneity of samples since business management students may share similar educational exposure and technological familiarity, which minimizes the impact of demographic factors. The study found a significant relationship between years of experience and attitude toward AI, indicating that greater exposure fosters more positive perceptions and confidence in using the technology. Experience enhances familiarity, encourages openness, and can influence peers, emphasizing the importance of experience-based training programs for effective AI adoption.

*Table 8. Relationship between the demographic profile and the level of knowledge on using AI*

| Variables Tested | | P-value (Pearson Chi-Square) | Cramer's V | Interpretation |
|---|---|---|---|---|
| Age | Knowledge on Using AI | 0.277 | | No significant relationship |
| Sex | | 0.300 | | No significant relationship |
| Year Level | | 0.280 | | No significant relationship |
| Major of the Program | | 0.034 | 0.184 | Strong significant relationship |
| Average Daily Duration of AI Usage | | 0.327 | | No significant relationship |
| Years of Experience Using AI | | 0.079 | | No significant relationship |
| Permitted Use AI for Academic Purposes | | 0.0694 | | No significant relationship |
| **N** | **247** | | | |

Table 9 revealed that the demographic profile in terms of age, sex, year level, major of the program, average daily duration of AI usage, and the permitted use of AI for academic purposes had no significant relationship with attitude towards AI. Therefore, the alternative hypothesis is rejected. This implies that students' attitude does not necessarily rely on their age, sex, major, how frequently they use AI daily, or whether they are permitted by their teacher to use AI. This may be due to how attitude is shaped by a person's beliefs and experiences rather than these demographics.

However, only the years of experience using AI had a strong, significant relationship with attitude towards AI, with a p-value and Cramer's V of 0.019 and 0.193, respectively. Thus, accepting the alternative hypothesis. This finding indicates that students are more likely to develop a positive attitude toward AI as they gain more experience using it. It may be because students experience positive feedback and interaction when using AI, generating a positive attitude towards it. This aligns with the study of Fošner (2024), who found that most students are open to the use of AI technologies as supportive tools in their study. Additionally, students' attitudes toward AI are shaped by their understanding of it (Katsantonis & Katsantonis, 2024), and their ease of use and the enhanced educational experiences these technologies offer (Shahzad et al., 2024). These results indicate the importance of practical AI applications in education. The results also underscore the importance of early and continued exposure to AI technologies in academic settings to foster more positive, informed attitudes among students.

The significant link between years of experience and attitude toward AI suggests that prior exposure enhances familiarity, confidence, and openness to emerging technologies. Experienced individuals, having encountered various innovations, are more likely to recognize AI's benefits and influence others positively. This emphasizes the need for institutions to design AI training programs that consider varying experience levels to encourage effective adoption and foster a culture of innovation.

*Table 9. Relationship between the demographic profile and attitude towards AI*

| Variables Tested | | P-value (Pearson Chi-Square) | Cramer's V | Interpretation |
|---|---|---|---|---|
| Age | Attitude Towards AI | 0.596 | | No significant relationship |
| Sex | | 0.783 | | No significant relationship |
| Year Level | | 0.335 | | No significant relationship |
| Major of the Program | | 0.221 | | No significant relationship |
| Average Daily Duration of AI Usage | | 0.136 | | No significant relationship |
| Years of Experience Using AI | | 0.019 | 0.193 | Strong significant relationship |
| Permitted Use AI for Academic Purposes | | 0.321 | | No significant relationship |
| N | **247** | | | |

Table 10 revealed that the demographic profile in terms of age, sex, year level, major of the program, and the permitted use of AI for academic purposes had no significant relationship with acceptance of AI. Thus, rejecting the alternative hypothesis. This implies that regardless of demographic group, people may perceive and accept AI similarly. It might be because AI is being seen as a tool anyone can use, making the stated demographic profile less relevant. This also implies that acceptance of AI transcends basic demographic characteristics and reflects a more universal perspective toward AI as an accessible and broadly applicable educational tool. Contrary to the findings of De Jesus and Co. (2025) observed that business student-researchers from Region III in the Philippines are generally open to AI writing tools, as they perceived them as practical, easy to use, and helpful in certain situations. Likewise, Asirit and Hua (2023), Divekar et al. (2024), and Shahzad et al.

(2024) all found that senior students or those with prior AI experience demonstrate higher acceptance in the Philippine business setting. This suggests that experience and maturity make people more open to new ideas.

Conversely, both average daily duration of AI usage and years of experience using AI had a significant relationship with acceptance of AI, with p-values of 0.037 and 0.011, respectively. Hence, accepting the alternative hypothesis. In terms of strength of the relationship, it has a strong relationship with a Cramer's V of 0.182 and 0.200, respectively. This shows that the longer a person uses AI in terms of experience and daily usage, the higher their acceptance. Furthermore, Bognár and Khine (2025) also discovered that engagement and self-efficacy from past exposure greatly increase the willingness to adopt AI. This may be due to the conveniences and benefits that AI brings in their studies as they get familiar and more exposed to it. This is consistent with the study of Ralhan (2024) that Asirit found that students use AI tools more frequently if they have great use of them. Ahn (2024) has also indicated its feature of being user-friendly as a cause of increasing its overall usage, which then makes it incorporate into their daily routines. The results highlight the value of encouraging early and sustained AI engagement in academic settings to promote broader student acceptance and more effective integration of AI tools in higher education.

While the Technology Acceptance Model (TAM) suggests that external variables such as demographic characteristics influence users' perceptions of technology, the findings of study found out that some external factors have a significant relationship with the levels of acceptance of AI among business management students. This discrepancy from TAM may be explained by the sample's uniform background or the generation's widespread exposure to and comfort with digital technologies. The findings suggest that experiential factors such as practical exposure to AI, curricular integration, and individual receptiveness to innovation may exert a greater influence on AI acceptance than demographic variables.

*Table 10. Relationship between the demographic profile and the level of acceptance of AI*

| **Variables Tested** | | **P-value (Pearson Chi-Square)** | **Cramer's V** | **Interpretation** |
|---|---|---|---|---|
| Age | Acceptance of AI | 0.081 | | No significant relationship |
| Sex | | 0.308 | | No significant relationship |
| Year Level | | 0.292 | | No significant relationship |
| Major of the Program | | 0.168 | | No significant relationship |
| Average Daily Duration of AI Usage | | 0.037 | 0.182 | Strong Significant relationship |
| Years of Experience Using AI | | 0.011 | 0.200 | Strong Significant relationship |
| Permitted Use AI for Academic Purposes | | 0.220 | | No significant relationship |
| **N** | **247** | | | |

## CONCLUSION AND RECOMMENDATIONS

This section presents the conclusion and recommendations that were drawn based on the result of the study on readiness in the digital age: The role of demographic characteristics among business students

### Conclusion

This study investigated the students' demographic characteristics, knowledge, attitude, and acceptance of AI in education, especially in the field of business management.

The study showed that the majority of business management students possess a moderate level of knowledge, a favorable attitude, and a moderate level of acceptance in using AI, acknowledging its usefulness in simplifying academic work and improving task efficiency. Moreover, demographic profile in terms of age, sex, year level, and the permitted use of AI for academic purposes had no significant relationship with knowledge, attitude, and acceptance of AI among business management students. This means that knowledge, attitude, and acceptance of AI do not necessarily rely on the majority of the demographic profile, and there may be other factors that can affect their knowledge, attitude, and acceptance of the use of AI.

While the Technology Acceptance Model (TAM) suggests that external factors like demographics affect how users perceive the usefulness and ease of technology, this study found no significant link on most of the demographic factors and the knowledge, attitude, as acceptance of AI among business management students. This difference from TAM could be due to the students having similar backgrounds or being part of a generation that generally accepts digital technology regardless of demographic differences. The results imply that other factors, such as hands-on experience with AI, its inclusion in the curriculum, or individual openness to new technology, digital literacy level, language proficiency, internet reliability, access to personal devices, AI-related training attendance, among others, may influence AI knowledge, attitude, and acceptance more than basic demographic traits.

## Recommendations

The following recommendations were formulated based on the findings of the study:

1. Given that students demonstrated only a moderate level of AI knowledge, universities, with the help of instructors or professors, should integrate AI-related lessons or modules into existing business management courses. These may include topics such as ethical AI use, prompt engineering, and data literacy to improve familiarity and competence.
2. Conduct workshops and seminars tailored to each business management program, highlighting discipline-specific applications of AI. This is recommended given the significant relationship between students' majors and their AI knowledge.
3. As students reported using AI mainly for writing and editing, institutions should establish clear academic policies and training programs on the ethical usage of AI to balance innovation with academic integrity. Faculty and administrators should co-create guidelines and ethical boundaries to address concerns over validity and academic honesty.
4. Encourage consistent and guided engagement with AI tools by incorporating them into course requirements, learning management systems, and student support services. Faculty should also demonstrate AI tools during lectures and provide structured practice opportunities, fostering better attitudes and acceptance.
5. Future studies should consider additional demographic variables such as socioeconomic status, parental education, urban or rural background, digital literacy level, language proficiency, internet reliability, access to personal devices, AI-related training attendance, peer collaboration, and academic achievements, to

gain a deeper understanding of how these affect AI knowledge, attitudes, and acceptance.

6. Future researchers should explore the long-term implications of AI on students' learning behavior and academic performance. Understanding how AI evolves in educational settings and its effects on cognitive and behavioral outcomes will yield more robust insights.
7. To support responsible AI integration in business education, universities should embed AI literacy modules into business management curricula, emphasizing ethical usage, technical understanding, and discipline-specific applications. Institutions may implement clear academic guidelines for AI use, promoting academic integrity while encouraging innovation. Regular training for both faculty and students will foster informed and consistent engagement with AI tools.
8. At the policy level, education leaders (college and university level) may consider disparities in infrastructure and digital access among students from various backgrounds. This ensures equitable digital readiness and supports the development of inclusive national strategies for the sustainable and ethical adoption of AI in Philippine higher education.

## LIMITATIONS OF THE STUDY

In this study, only business management students from Cavite State University's main campus were targeted as participants. In terms of demographics, these include age, sex, year level, major field, types of AI tools and applications, average daily duration of AI usage, years of experience using AI, activities where AI is used, and purposes of using AI. Moreover, only the knowledge, acceptance, and attitude of the students were tested; their relationship with the demographic characteristics was examined. Other potentially influential factors, such as teaching practices, institutional policies, technological infrastructure, and other factors related to student demographics, were not investigated. As such, the results should be interpreted within this defined scope and may not represent the experiences of students from other disciplines, universities, or countries/ regions.

## FUTURE RESEARCH DIRECTIONS

Future research should go beyond the current quantitative, single-campus design by using qualitative and mixed-methods approaches, like interviews, focus groups, and open-ended surveys, to get a better understanding of the beliefs, motivations, and barriers that affect students' knowledge, attitudes, and acceptance of AI tools. To get a better picture of digital preparedness, we also need to look at more general demographic variables, including socioeconomic status, parental education, urban/ rural background, and digital access. To make the theory deeper, future work could combine frameworks like UTAUT2 (which looks at social influence, facilitating conditions, and habit) or Connectivism/ Social Cognitive Theory (which looks at self-efficacy, learning interactions, and networked knowledge-building) with TAM's point of view. Future research may investigate the reasons why business management students excel academically and how they utilize artificial intelligence (AI) in educational settings, drawing on established theories of motivation. Finally, examining objective performance indicators such as AI-generated outputs, usage logs, and academic accomplishments at different times will reveal whether positive self-report measures lead to meaningful learning outcomes. These improvements should provide us with more context-rich, inclusive, and actionable information on how ready business management students are for the digital world.

## REFERENCES


Abdalla, A. A., Bhat, M. A., Tiwari, C. K., Khan, S. T., & Wedajo, A. D. (2024). Exploring ChatGPT Adoption among Business and Management Students through the Lens of Diffusion of Innovation Theory. *Computers and Education Artificial Intelligence*, *7*, 100257. DOI: 10.1016/j.caeai.2024.100257

Abdalla, M., Smith, L., & Brown, R. (2024). Trust and attitude toward AI tools in higher education: A quantitative analysis. *Journal of Educational Technology & Society*, *27*(1), 45–60. DOI: 10.1234/ets.2024.27.1.45

Ahn, H. Y. (2024). AI-Powered E-Learning for Lifelong Learners: Impact on performance and knowledge application. *Sustainability (Basel)*, *16*(20), 9066. DOI: 10.3390/su16209066

Akoglu, H. (2018). User's guide to correlation coefficients. *Turkish Journal of Emergency Medicine*, *18*(3), 91–93. DOI: 10.1016/j.tjem.2018.08.001 PMID: 30191186

Aljuaid, H. (2024). The Impact of Artificial intelligence Tools on academic writing instruction in Higher Education: A Systematic review. *Arab World English Journal*, *1*(1), 26–55. DOI: 10.24093/awej/ChatGPT.2

Almaraz-López, C., Almaraz-Menéndez, F., & López-Esteban, C. (2023). Comparative Study of the Attitudes and Perceptions of University Students in Business Administration and Management and in Education toward Artificial Intelligence. *Education Sciences*, *13*(6), 609–609. DOI: 10.3390/educsci13060609

Alshamy, A., Al-Harthi, A. S. A., & Abdullah, S. (2025). Perceptions of Generative AI Tools in Higher Education: Insights from Students and Academics at Sultan Qaboos University. *Education Sciences*, *15*(4), 501. DOI: 10.3390/educsci15040501

Asirit, L. B. L., & Hua, J. H. (2023). Converging perspectives: Assessing AI readiness and utilization in Philippine higher education. *Polaris Global Journal of Scholarly Research and Trends*, *2*(3), 1–50. DOI: 10.58429/pgjsrt.v2n3a152

Bancoro, J. C. M. (2024). The relationship between AI usage and academic performance of business administration students. *International Journal of Asian Business and Management*, *3*(1), 27–48. DOI: 10.55927/ijabm.v3i1.7876

Bantoto, F. M. O., Rillo, R., Abequibel, B., Mangila, B. B., & Alieto, E. O. (2024). Is AI an effective "Learning tool" in Academic Writing? Investigating the perceptions of Third-Year University students on the use of artificial intelligence in classroom instruction. In Lecture notes in networks and systems (pp. 72–81). https://doi.org/ DOI: 10.1007/978-3-031-68650-4_8

Benuyenah, V., & Dewnarain, S. (2024). Students' Intention to Engage With ChatGPT and Artificial Intelligence in Higher Education Business Studies Programmes. *International Journal of Distance Education Technologies*, *22*(1), 1–21. DOI: 10.4018/IJDET.348061

Bognár, L., & Khine, M. S. (2025). The Shifting Landscape of Student Engagement: A Pre-Post Semester Analysis in AI-Enhanced Classrooms. *Computers and Education: Artificial Intelligence*, *100395*, 100395. Advance online publication. DOI: 10.1016/j.caeai.2025.100395

Cañas-Llamas, A. (2024, January). UPOU releases Guidelines on AI Use for Teaching and Learning - University of the Philippines Open University. University of the Philippines Open University. https://www.upou.edu.ph/news/upou-releases-guidelines-on-ai-use-for-teaching-and-learning

Chan, C. K. Y., & Hu, W. (2023). Students' voices on generative AI: Perceptions, benefits, and challenges in higher education. *International Journal of Educational Technology in Higher Education*, *20*(1), 43. DOI: 10.1186/s41239-023-00411-8

Chao, P. J., Hsu, T. H., Liu, T. P., & Cheng, Y. H. (2021). Knowledge of and Competence in Artificial Intelligence: Perspectives of Vietnamese Digital-Native Students. *IEEE Access : Practical Innovations, Open Solutions*, *9*, 75751–75760. DOI: 10.1109/ACCESS.2021.3081749

Chen, L., Chen, P., & Lin, Z. (2020). Artificial Intelligence in Education: A review. *IEEE Access : Practical Innovations, Open Solutions*, *8*, 75264–75278. DOI: 10.1109/ACCESS.2020.2988510

Corpuz, J. T., Sullano Peña, G., & Dela Torre Baconguis, R. (2022). Achievement, affiliation, power and academic performance of business management students of a state university in Cavite, Philippines. *Cogent Social Sciences*, *8*(1), 2060538. Advance online publication. DOI: 10.1080/23311886.2022.2060538

Davis, F. D. (1989). Perceived Usefulness, Perceived Ease of Use, and User Acceptance of Information Technology. *Management Information Systems Quarterly*, *13*(3), 319–340. DOI: 10.2307/249008

De Jesus, F. S., & Co, A. G. E. (2025). Assessment on the use of artificial intelligence writing tools as a confidant of business administration student-researchers using the Technology Acceptance Model. *International Journal of Innovative Research and Scientific Studies*, *8*(1), 1450–1461. DOI: 10.53894/ijirss.v8i1.4669

Deng, N., Liu, E. J., & Zhai, X. (2025). Understanding University Students' Use of Generative AI: The Roles of Demographics and Personality Traits. arXiv preprint arXiv:2505.02863. DOI: 10.1007/978-3-031-98414-3_20

Digital Education Council. (2024, August 7). What students want: Key results from DEC Global AI Student Survey 2024. Digital Education Council. https://www.digitaleducationcouncil.com/post/what-students-want-key-results-from-dec-global-ai-student-survey-2024

Digital Education Council. (2024, August 7). What students want: Key results from DEC Global AI Student Survey 2024. Digital Education Council. https://www.digitaleducationcouncil.com/post/what-students-want-key-results-from-dec-global-ai-student-survey-2024

Divekar, R. R., Gonzalez, L., Guerra, S., & Boos, N. (2024). Usage and knowledge of online tools and generative AI: A survey of students. Bentley University. https://doi.org/DOI: 10.21203/rs.3.rs-4882673/v1

Estrellado, C. J., & Miranda, J. C. (2023). Artificial intelligence in the Philippine educational context: Circumspection and future inquiries. *International Journal of Scientific and Research Publications*, *13*(5), 16–22. Advance online publication. DOI: 10.29322/IJSRP.13.05.2023.p13704

Fošner, A. (2024). University Students' Attitudes and Perceptions towards AI Tools: Implications for Sustainable Educational Practices. *Sustainability (Basel)*, *16*(19), 8668. DOI: 10.3390/su16198668

Freeman, J. (2025, February 26). Student Generative AI Survey 2025: HEPI/Kortext. Higher Education Policy Institute. https://www.hepi.ac.uk/2025/02/26/student-generative-ai-survey-2025/

Gerard, J., Singh, S., Macleod, M., McKay, M., Rivoire, A., Chakraborty, T., & Singh, M. (2024). AI across borders: Exploring perceptions and interactions in higher education. arXiv preprint arXiv:2501.00017.

González-Anleo, J. M., Delbello, L., Martínez-Gonzálo, J. M., & Gómez, A. (2024). Sociodemographic impact on the adoption of emerging technologies. *Journal of Small Business Strategy*, *34*(2). Advance online publication. DOI: 10.53703/001c.122089

Guhan, M., Venkatesan, D., & Chandramohan, S. (2023). *A survey on analyzing the effectiveness of ai tools among research scholars in academic writing and publishing*. International Journal Of Advance Research And Innovative Ideas In Education.

Instructure Holdings, Inc. (2025, June 12). More Filipino students now using AI for learning. BusinessWorld Online. https://www.bworldonline.com/technology/2025/06/12/678582/more-filipino-students-now-using-ai-for-learning/

Kanont, K., Pingmuang, P., Simasathien, T., Wisnuwong, S., Wiwatsiripong, B., Poonpirome, K., Songkram, N., & Khlaisang, J. (2024). Generative-AI, a learning assistant? Factors influencing Higher-Ed students' technology acceptance. *Electronic Journal of e-Learning*, *22*(6), 18–33. DOI: 10.34190/ejel.22.6.3196

Katsantonis, A., & Katsantonis, I. G. (2024). University Students' Attitudes toward Artificial Intelligence: An Exploratory Study of the Cognitive, Emotional, and Behavioural Dimensions of AI Attitudes. *Education Sciences*, *14*(9), 988. DOI: 10.3390/educsci14090988

Kovačević, A., & Demić, E. (2024). The impact of gender, seniority, knowledge, and interest on AI attitudes. *IEEE Access : Practical Innovations, Open Solutions*, *12*, 129765–129775. DOI: 10.1109/ACCESS.2024.3454801

Li, L., Yu, F., & Zhang, E. (2024). A systematic review of learning task design for K-12 AI education: Trends, challenges, and opportunities. *Computers and Education Artificial Intelligence*, *6*, 100217. DOI: 10.1016/j.caeai.2024.100217

Locus, S. (2024, February). Mapua underscores AI integration in higher education. GMA News Online. https://www.gmanetwork.com/news/scitech/science/898321/mapua-underscores-ai-integration-in-higher-education/story/

Mackenzie, T., Radeljic, B., Salgado, L., Paul, A., Khan, R., Tursunbayeva, A., . . . Bhaduri, S. (2025). What we do not know: Gpt use in business and management. arXiv preprint arXiv:2504.05273.

Maxwell, D., Oyarzun, B., Kim, S., & Bong, J. Y. (2025). Generative AI in Higher Education: Demographic Differences in Student Perceived Readiness, Benefits, and Challenges. *TechTrends*. Advance online publication. DOI: 10.1007/s11528-025-01109-6

Melisa, R., Ashadi, A., Triastuti, A., Hidayati, S., Salido, A., Ero, P. E. L., Marlini, C., Zefrin, Z., & Fuad, Z. A. (2025). Critical Thinking in the Age of AI: A Systematic Review of AI's Effects on Higher Education. *Educational Process International Journal*, *14*(1). Advance online publication. DOI: 10.22521/edupij.2025.14.31

Ocen, S., Elasu, J., Aarakit, S. M., & Olupot, C. (2025). Artificial intelligence in higher education institutions: Review of innovations, opportunities and challenges. *Frontiers in Education*, *10*, 1530247. Advance online publication. DOI: 10.3389/feduc.2025.1530247

Owoc, M. L., Sawicka, A., & Weichbroth, P. (2021). Artificial Intelligence Technologies in Education: Benefits, Challenges and Strategies of Implementation. arXiv. Org. /arxiv.2102.09365DOI: 10.1007/978-3-030-85001-2_4

Pacheco-Mendoza, S., Guevara, C., Mayorga-Albán, A., & Fernández-Escobar, J. (2023). Artificial Intelligence in Higher Education: A Predictive Model for Academic Performance. *Education Sciences*, *13*(10), 990. DOI: 10.3390/educsci13100990

Petrescu, M.-A., Pop, E.-L., & Dan Mihoc, T. (2023). Students' interest in knowledge acquisition in Artificial Intelligence. *Procedia Computer Science*, *225*, 1028–1036. DOI: 10.1016/j.procs.2023.10.090

Qiu, X., Alias, A., & Nasri, N. (2025). Attitude, intention, and the use of artificial intelligence among business management students in higher education institutions. *International Journal of Academic Research in Business & Social Sciences*, *15*(7). Advance online publication. DOI: 10.6007/IJARBSS/v15-i7/25621

Rajki, Z., Dringó-Horváth, I., & Nagy, J. T. (2025). Artificial intelligence in higher education: Students' artificial intelligence use and its influencing factors. *Journal of University Teaching & Learning Practice*, *22*(2). Advance online publication. DOI: 10.53761/j0rebh67

Ralhan, P. (2024). Artificial Intelligence In Higher Studies: Use of Ai-Based Tools by University Students And Its Challenges. https://www.researchgate.net/publication/385127161

Ramirez, J. P., Obenza, D. M., Cuarte, R., & Mabayag, N. A. (2024). AI trust and attitudes toward AI of university students in the Philippines. *International Journal of Multidisciplinary Studies in Higher Education*, *1*(1), 22–36. DOI: 10.70847/586366

Reyes, R., Mariñas, J. M., Tacang, J. R., Asis, L. J. A., Sayman, J. M., Flores, C. C., & Sumatra, K. (2024). The relationship between attitude toward AI and AI literacy among Philippine university students. *International Journal of Multidisciplinary Studies in Higher Education*, *1*(1), 37–46. DOI: 10.70847/587958

Rony, M. K. K., Akter, K., Nesa, L., Islam, M. T., Johra, F. T., Akter, F., Uddin, M. J., Begum, J., Noor, M. A., Ahmad, S., Tanha, S. M., Khatun, M. T., Bala, S. D., & Parvin, M. R. (2024). Healthcare workers' knowledge and Attitudes regarding artificial intelligence adoption in healthcare: A cross-sectional study. *Heliyon*, *10*(23), e40775. DOI: 10.1016/j.heliyon.2024.e40775 PMID: 39691199

Sajja, R., Sermet, Y., Cikmaz, M., Cwiertny, D., & Demir, I. (2024). Artificial Intelligence-Enabled Intelligent Assistant for Personalized and Adaptive Learning in Higher Education. *Information (Basel)*, *15*(10), 596. DOI: 10.3390/info15100596

Santos, R., Villaceran, R., Riofloridο, J., & Paguiligan, D. (2024). Initial development and validation of a questionnaire for students' artificial intelligence knowledge in Education. *Cognizance Journal of Multidisciplinary Studies*, *4*(5), 32–41. DOI: 10.47760/cognizance.2024.v04i05.003

Shahzad, M. F., Xu, S., & Javed, I. (2024). ChatGPT awareness, acceptance, and adoption in higher education: The role of trust as a cornerstone. *International Journal of Educational Technology in Higher Education*, *21*(1), 46. Advance online publication. DOI: 10.1186/s41239-024-00478-x

Spulber, D., Amoretti, G., & Siri, A. (2024). The use of AI for Education in Third Age: The role of EU project. Geopolitical. *Social Security and Freedom Journal*, *7*(1), 49–64. DOI: 10.2478/gssfj-2024-0004

Sublime, J., & Renna, I. (2024). Is ChatGPT massively used by students nowadays? A survey on the use of large language models such as ChatGPT in educational settings. arXiv preprint arXiv:2412.17486.

Tapalova, O., & Zhiyenbayeva, N. (2022). Artificial Intelligence in Education: AIED for Personalised Learning Pathways, https://doi.org/DOI: 10.34190/ejel.20.5.2597

University World News. (2025, February 28). AI use by students surges to 92%, second HEPI survey finds. University World News. https://www.universityworldnews.com/post.php?story=20250228175423255

Venkatesh, V., Morris, M. G., Davis, G. B., and Davis, F. D. (2003). User Acceptance of Information Technology: Toward a Unified View, MIS Quarterly (27:3), pp. 42

Wang, S., Christensen, C., Cui, W., Tong, R., Yarnall, L., Shear, L., & Feng, M. (2020). When adaptive learning is effective learning: Comparison of an adaptive learning system to teacher-led instruction. *Interactive Learning Environments*, *31*(2), 793–803. DOI: 10.1080/10494820.2020.1808794

Watanabe, A. (2024). Have Courage to Use Your Own Mind, with or without AI: The Relevance of Kant's Enlightenment to Higher Education in the Age of Artificial Intelligence. Electronic Journal of e-Learning, v22 n2 p46-58 2024. DOI: 10.34190/ejel.21.5.3229

Yi, M., & Choi, H. (2023). What drives the acceptance of AI technology? The role of expectations and experiences (preprint). arXiv. https://doi.org//arXiv.2405.02863DOI: 10.48550

Yilmaz, F. G. K., Yilmaz, R., & Ceylan, M. (2023). Generative Artificial Intelligence Acceptance Scale: A Validity and Reliability study. *International Journal of Human-Computer Interaction*, •••, 1–13. DOI: 10.1080/10447318.2023.2288730

Zhai, X., Chu, X., Chai, C. S., Jong, M. S. Y., Istenic, A., Spector, M., Liu, J., Yuan, J., & Li, Y. (2021). A Review of Artificial Intelligence (AI) in Education from 2010 to 2020. Complexity, 2021(1). DOI: 10.1155/2021/8812542

Zhang, L., & Xu, J. (2024). The paradox of self-efficacy and technological dependence: Unraveling generative AI's impact on university students' task completion. *The Internet and Higher Education*, *65*, 100978. DOI: 10.1016/j.iheduc.2024.100978

Zhou, X., Zhang, J., & Chan, C. K. Y. (2024). Unveiling students' experiences and perceptions of artificial intelligence usage in higher education. *Journal of University Teaching & Learning Practice*, *21*(6), 6. Advance online publication. DOI: 10.53761/xzjprb23

## KEY TERMS AND DEFINITIONS

**Acceptance:** Refers to business management students' willingness to utilize AI tools in their schoolwork and their actual usage of them, such as asking AI for help with problems, using ai to create writing or media, and committing to continually improving their AI skills. It includes how people feel about utilizing AI to improve their academic performance, work independently, and stay current. A 15-item, 7-point likert scale is used to test this. Results classify degrees of acceptance as low (1.00–3.00), moderate (3.01–5.00), or high (5.01–7.00).

**Artificial Intelligence (AI):** Refers to computational systems designed to perform tasks requiring human-like intelligence, such as learning, reasoning, decision-making, perception, and problem-solving, notably including tools like ChatGPT, Quillbot, and Canva, which are widely used by business management students to support writing, editing, and design tasks. Students' knowledge, attitude, and acceptance of AI in this study refer specifically refer also to their awareness, evaluative perspectives, and usage intentions/behaviors regarding such a tool.

**Attitude:** Refers to how pupils feel about AI technologies in school, encompassing their perceptions of how useful, easy to use, efficient, and comfortable they find these technologies. Based on composite scores, attitudes are put into three groups: Negative (1.00–3.00), Neutral/Moderate (3.01–5.00), or Positive(5.01–7.00).

**Business Management Students:** Refers to students enrolled in a higher education program at Cavite State University, College of Economics, Management and Development Studies In this study, the major fields of business management students are focused on financial management, marketing management, human resource management, service management, and operations management.

**AI Readiness:** Refers to business management students knowledge, attitude and acceptance on the use of AI in education

**Knowledge:** Refers to students' factual understanding and awareness of AI concepts and how they can be used in education. This is demonstrated by their ability to correctly answer questions such as: What does AI stand for? And what are the ethical issues? And to recognize real-world applications, including grading systems, tutoring, and adaptive learning platforms. This assessment is evaluated on a scale of 15 items, which categorizes business management students into one of three groups: limited (0–5), moderate (6–10), or strong (11–15).

**Technology Acceptance Model (TAM) Theory:** Refers to two main beliefs that shape people's behavioral intention to use technology: Perceived usefulness, which is the belief that the technology will improve performance, and perceived ease of use, which is the belief that using the technology will be easy. This intention then predicts actual use, making TAM a valuable approach for examining how business management students utilize AI in education.

Chapter 6

# Integration of the Rosetta Stone AI-Powered Platform as a Learning Management System (LMS) for Language Learning in Moroccan Higher Education

**Mouad Malmous**
https://orcid.org/0009-0001-7401-278X
*Faculty of Letters and Human Sciences Ben M'sik, Morocco*

**Said Zaidoune**
https://orcid.org/0009-0005-8921-5255
*Faculty of Letters and Human Sciences Ben M'sik, Morocco*

**El Mehdi El Hamydy**
https://orcid.org/0009-0002-0703-6949
*Faculty of Education Rabat, Morocco*

## ABSTRACT

*Grounded in the Unified Theory of Acceptance and Use of Technology 2 (UTAUT2), this chapter investigates Moroccan university students' perceptions and attitudes toward the Rosetta Stone platform based on data collected from 1,262 participants. It also investigates the main predictors of the use and acceptance of the Rosetta*

DOI: 10.4018/979-8-3373-2302-2.ch006

*Stone platform by shedding light on practical implications for policymakers and university educators to optimize the integration of Rosetta Stone within Moroccan higher education. Using Partial Least Squares Structural Equation Modeling (PLS-SEM), the findings revealed that Hedonic Motivation and Habit emerged to have a significant impact on shaping Moroccan university students' intentions to utilize the Rosetta Stone Platform. It was also found that Facilitating Conditions did not significantly predict Behavioural Intention. While Effort Expectancy and Social Influence exhibited a moderate impact on Behavioural Intention, the variables of Age, Gender, Experience, and Familiarity had no direct effect on students' acceptance and use of Rosetta Stone.*

## INTRODUCIION

### Background and Context

As artificial intelligence continues to reshape educational landscapes worldwide, the integration of AI-powered platforms like Rosetta Stone into higher education systems has become both a necessity and a challenge, particularly in multilingual, reform-driven contexts such as Morocco. The Moroccan educational system has undergone numerous reforms driven by national policies and influenced by international agendas. The intention has been to bridge the gap between the centre and the peripheries, minimizing regional differences and providing equal access to education (Morchid, 2020). These reforms include the National Charter for Education and Training (2000-2010) that established the framework for fundamental changes, followed by the *2015-2030* Strategic Vision for Education Reform, which underscored digital integration, pedagogical innovation, and competency-based learning, and finally the Pact for Excellence in Higher Education (2023), which promotes the goals of the Strategic Vision.

The education system in the country has been experiencing several challenges and dilemmas related to the adoption of syllabi and programs that do not align with the needs of the labour market (Ghaicha, 2018; Mansouri & Moumine, 2017). This system is structured as follows: pre-school, 6 years of primary school, 3 years of middle school, 3 years of secondary school, vocational, and tertiary or higher education. Basic education (ages 6-15) has been compulsory and guaranteed by the constitution, but the number of students in rural areas has dropped significantly owing to several factors. The government took different measures to encourage children to attend school, especially in rural areas where basic infrastructure is missing. The state also invested much money in secondary education to equip students with the practical skills needed to join the labour market. (Vocational training is given priority over higher education). This is attributed to the state's plan to provide international and multinational companies with the manpower. However, there are still various difficulties facing the education system in the country.

The Ministry of National Education, Pre-school Learning and Sports and the Ministry of Higher Education, Scientific Research, and Innovation are both responsible for executing government policy in education. Despite the creation of 12 regions in the country, the structure of the education system is still highly centralised with two large Departments for Higher Education and School Education, a Standing Committee for Curricula, and twelve Regional Academies of Education and Training (AREFs). These Academies have been given major powers to implement the new decentralisation policy. These are divided into Directorates or provincial delegations according to the administrative divisions of provinces. These Directorates are responsible for both administrative and pedagogical educational affairs. However, this decentralisation policy raises many questions as Academies do not have legislative powers to make decisions. For example, if instructors want to switch from high school to university, they need authorisation from one of the twelve Academies. However, this document is invalid unless the Department of Higher Education gives access to the Academies.

Universities around the world must adjust to changing trends and expectations in the era of globalisation with regard to research, quality, academic standards, and knowledge gaps in society. Setting these evolving demands as a top priority has turned into a strategic goal in Morocco. According to recent studies, higher education has grown rapidly during the past ten years, especially in developing nations (Mohammed Hashim et al., 2022). By aiming for greater educational standards in public, private, and international universities, Morocco hopes to establish itself as an educational hub in North Africa. Hence, embracing significant changes is expected to encourage creativity, entrepreneurship, and flexibility in academic institutions.

The incorporation of AI-driven platforms and digital learning tools has become a critical component of Morocco's higher education plan (Bourray et al., 2024). Learning Management Systems (LMS), online resources, and blended learning methodologies are utilized in all universities (Kumar et al., 2021). These educational trends support transnational education.

The dissemination of globalised education has significantly transformed universities, in a way that has influenced their teaching and learning methodologies and assessment techniques and methods (Jin et al., 2025). In order to overcome the challenges of globalisation, academic institutions must go beyond traditional learning and evaluation methods and adopt more flexible and innovative practices. The pursuit of educational quality has become a fundamental objective for academic institutions across the globe. Quality education requires an in-depth investigation as it is a context-dependent measure (Sahin et al., 2024). Academics, researchers, universities, and policymakers are among the important stakeholders that increasingly recognise its strategic significance. The shift to a competency-based approach focuses on the development of critical thinking, problem-solving, and language fluency, all of which are essential skills in today's labour market.

The COVID-19 pandemic has stimulated the adoption of online learning in academic institutions, in a way that extends its function as a mere IT tool (Mittal et al., 2022). This transition has affected teaching methodologies, leading to the growth of blended learning, which combines online, independent, and in-person learning. Additionally, virtual platforms have created informal student networks for knowledge sharing. Although the COVID-19 pandemic emphasised the value of LMS in simplifying online learning and teaching, universities continue to face issues related to the integration of technology, data security, and online protection systems (Jiang et al., 2024). The COVID-19 pandemic also prompted academic institutions to adopt flexible online learning platforms that promote autonomous learning and increase career options (Sun et al., 2024). The aim of this model is to equip students with the prerequisite skills needed in the labour market, for it integrates academic curricula with the changing needs of the industrialised world.

The decentralisation of education in Morocco, motivated by factors like virtual learning, intends to improve service delivery and expand access (Elmeski, 2024). Yet, its usefulness is still up for dispute, as decentralised Academies frequently encounter technical and financial constraints, limiting their performance compared to large Departments in the capital Rabat. A significant challenge facing decentralised education is to maintain high-quality standards (Errihani, 2024). Therefore, meeting objectives and enhancing the educational experience for students demand constant development and prompt financial support. The ongoing crisis in the Moroccan educational system is attributed to Morocco's top-down educational reforms, the disconnect between policy and practice, and frequent policy changes by successive governments, which undermine long-term reform efforts.

Artificial intelligence (AI) is transforming education by enhancing program delivery and personalizing learning experiences (Onesi-Ozigagun et al., 2024). Predicted to impact global educational methodologies, AI combines deep learning, machine learning, and human-computer interaction (Mutawa & Sruthi, 2024). AI in education offers numerous benefits, such as improved instructional practices, assessment techniques, and administrative processes (Almasri, 2024). These developments point to a future in which automated support services will become the norm.

Big data is critical for university decision-making, but its unstructured nature makes it difficult to generate new knowledge and insights (Daniel, 2019). Many colleges do not have the necessary expertise or data scientists to efficiently examine large data (Janssen et al., 2017). Institutions must implement dependable, quick, and superior data analysis methods to overcome this. Conventional data analysis approaches are time-consuming and inflexible in the face of continually changing educational needs (Janssen et al., 2017). Therefore, institutions must integrate big data methodologies with digital transformation initiatives that prioritize capacity, speed, and various data architectures.

The evolution of the IT industry emanates from digital transformation. This calls for qualified professionals to address technological and industrial challenges (Lazrak & Yechouti, 2017). Yet, there is still a gap between higher education institutions and market demands, which leads to inadequacies and inefficiencies (Janowski, & Szczepańska–Przekota, 2024). Along with technical proficiency, recruiters place a strong emphasis on soft, critical thinking, decision-making, and problem-solving skills. To meet the labour market demands and enhance the employability of university graduates, academic institutions must incorporate innovative teaching practices. Soft skills, such as communication, ethical reasoning, and creativity are becoming more and more in demand, especially in the context of AI-driven decision-making. The discrepancy between emerging and developed countries complicates IT workforce growth and minimizes economic competitiveness.

Additionally, multilingualism is becoming increasingly significant as Morocco fortifies its international economic and diplomatic ties, especially in commerce and academia. For example, English is gaining prominence in academia and business at the expense of French and Arabic (Belhiah et al., 2020). The aim is to improve academic mobility, have easy access to academic research, and compete in the global market. Nonetheless, language education is hampered by outdated teaching methodologies, the scarcity of personalized learning, and limited input to authentic language use (Agrram, 2021). In the same vein, there is an increasing skills gap between the market demand and university graduates' profiles. Innovative teaching methodologies are required in academic institutions and the labour market to foster employability by integrating cutting-edge technologies and cultivating soft skills like communication, problem-solving, and flexibility to keep up with the evolving global landscape.

There are several challenges facing Moroccan higher education institutions in language education despite ongoing reforms. These include persistent low proficiency levels among students, limited input or exposure to authentic language use, outdated teaching methodologies like rote memorisation, large class sizes, and insufficient teacher training in digital pedagogy. These obstacles hinder the overall quality of language education in Moroccan universities.

## Research Problem

Although significant efforts have been made to advance digital transformation in Moroccan higher education, there remains a lack of empirical research investigating the use, acceptance, and practical implications of AI-powered learning platforms like Rosetta Stone. While national strategies increasingly prioritize language acquisition, personalized learning, and technological integration, the adoption and effectiveness of AI-based language tools in Moroccan universities remain underexplored. This study addresses this gap by examining how students engage with Rosetta Stone and the factors influencing its acceptance, as framed by the UTAUT2 model.

## Significance of the Study

This study contributes to both theoretical and practical knowledge in the fields of educational technology and language learning. Theoretically, it extends the application of UTAUT2 to a new context and explores its validity in assessing the implementation of the Rosetta Stone platform. Additionally, it provides valuable insights for Moroccan higher education institutions, policymakers, and educators on the factors influencing user acceptance and successful implementation of Rosetta Stone as an LMS. By aligning with the latest educational reforms, the findings will support the development of effective strategies for integrating Rosetta Stone to enhance language learning outcomes in Moroccan universities.

## Rationale for the Study

The Moroccan higher education system is undergoing significant reforms, the aim of which is to improve educational quality, digital transformation, and enhance student competencies. For open-access universities, the new pedagogical model encompasses a series of updated standards, which emphasize the enhancement of students' soft skills and the development of their cultural knowledge (Aziz et al., 2023; Aziz et al., 2024). These updated standards also focus on institutionalizing extracurricular university activities and adopting an innovative pedagogical approach that integrates in-person and remote teaching modalities. Language acquisition, in English and French, plays a critical role in enabling Moroccan graduates to meet the demands of globalization, international collaboration and the job market (Belhiah et al., 2020). To achieve these objectives, there is a growing emphasis on the adoption of innovative Learning Management Systems (LMS) that leverage Artificial Intelligence (AI) to deliver tailor-made and effective learning experiences. Rosetta Stone has emerged as a promising tool to address these challenges owing to its adaptability, interactivity, and data-driven learning pathways.

Additionally, the integration of AI-driven LMS into Moroccan higher education is consistent with worldwide trends in personalized learning and digital pedagogy (Bourray et al., 2024). Numerous studies have proved that AI-powered language learning tools are effective in fostering retention, increasing motivation, and enhancing learner autonomy and engagement (e.g., Ma & Chen, 2024; Tahir & Tahir, 2023; Tajik, 2025). In addition to formal classroom teaching, the supplementation of AI-driven resources would help Moroccan universities address existing challenges, ensure equitable access to high-quality education, and equip learners to meet the needs of the global market. While previous studies have explored the adoption of digital platforms and AI tools in higher education (e.g., Malmous & Zaidoune, 2025), few studies have focused on language learning within the Moroccan educational context (e.g., Slimani & Jabal, 2023). Hence, the present study is an attempt to examine the use of AI-driven LMS, particularly Rosetta Stone as an effective tool in dealing with the existing language learning problems within Moroccan universities. By investigating its effect on learner involvement, language proficiency, and pedagogical efficiency, this study contributes to the ongoing debate on the role of AI in language education and the prospects of digital transformations in Moroccan academic institutions.

## Research Objectives

This study aims to:

1. Examine the acceptance and use of the Rosetta Stone platform among Moroccan university students using the UTAUT2 model.
2. Investigate how AI-based LMS tools affect learners' engagement, autonomy, and language proficiency.
3. Identify the pedagogical and institutional factors that enhance or hinder the implementation of AI-driven platforms in Moroccan higher education.

## Research Questions

This study is driven by the following research questions:

1. What factors influence Moroccan university students' acceptance and use of the Rosetta Stone platform, as measured by the UTAUT2 model?
2. To what extent does the use of Rosetta Stone impact students' language proficiency, engagement, and learning autonomy?
3. What are the perceived benefits and challenges of integrating AI-based language platforms in the Moroccan higher education context?

# LITERATURE REVIEW

## UTAUT2: Theoretical Framework

AI integration in education has revolutionised traditional learning and teaching methodologies by allowing for personalised, flexible, and data-driven teaching methods (Zong & Yang, 2025; Rapaka et al., 2025; Kurk et al., 2025; Yu et al., 2025 & Amin et al., 2025). In principle, AI-driven LMSs utilize machine learning, Natural Language Processing (NLP), and speech recognition to provide self-paced learning, personalised learning assistance, and automated feedback (Hashim et al., 2021); however, access to technology remains a challenge. The integration of AI in language education has recently gained momentum, with applications like Rosetta Stone, Moodle, and Duolingo providing learners with customised learning paths, immersive experiences, and timely feedback (Slimani & Jabal, 2023; Bourray et al., 2024; Houmane et al., 2024). To investigate the factors affecting the adoption of AI-driven LMS in Moroccan higher education, this chapter draws on the Unified Theory of Acceptance and Use of Technology 2 (UTAUT2), an extension of the original UTAUT model pioneered by Venkatesh et al. (2003).

Although UTAUT presents a comprehensive tool to evaluate technology acceptance and use (Venkatesh et al., 2003), this model was criticized due to its inability to account for behavioural intention in various settings. Hence, Venkatesh et al. (2012) suggested UTAUT2, an extension of UTAUT. This is the latest model to measure technology acceptance and use (Venkatesh et al., 2012). The objectives of this model are twofold: a) design a holistic framework for evaluating technology use and acceptance, and b) suggest a behavioural model of consumer technology acceptance (Venkatesh et al., 2012). The new model includes three additional constructs: hedonic motive, cost or perceived value and habit. The variable of *price value* is omitted from this study for two reasons: a) it was found to be insignificant by prior research (Marikyan & Papagiannidis, 2023; Tamilmani et al., 2021), and b) Rosetta Stone is a free-of-charge application that students can use for free. These three variables represent important drivers of consumers' intention to use technology (Venkatesh et al., 2012). The factors of age, gender, and experience moderate the effect that price value, hedonic motive, and habit have on behavioural intention and use (Venkatesh et al., 2012). Even the extended UTAUT is criticised for its methodology as it employs a self-reported scale to evaluate users' intention (Venkatesh et al., 2012). Using UTAUT2 as a conceptual framework, the current chapter aims to measure students' acceptance, perceived usefulness, and behavioural intention towards the Rosetta Stone as an AI-driven platform in Moroccan higher education. The proposed model is shown in Figure 1.

*Figure 1. Rosetta Stone acceptance and use research model (Author, 2025)*

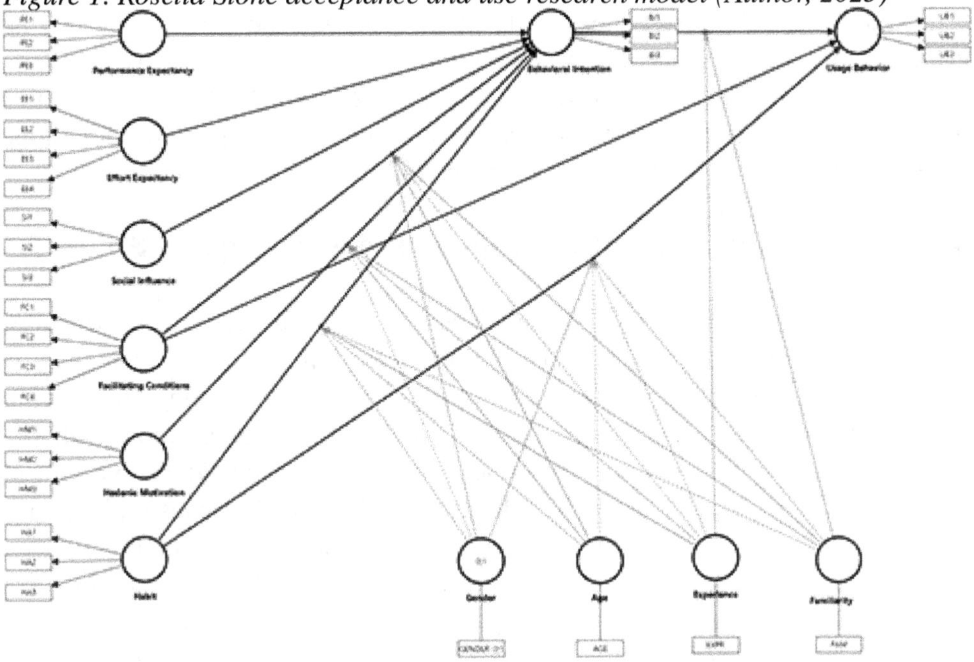

## Empirical Studies on Rosetta Stone

Numerous research studies have investigated the use and efficiency of the Rosetta Stone in language learning and teaching, shedding light on its ability to foster language proficiency and learner autonomy among students and transform instructors' assessment practices (Bourray et al., 2024; Houmane et al., 2024; Slimani & Jabal, 2023). Despite offering key insights into Moroccan educators' experiences and students' engagement with the Rosetta Stone platform, Houmane et al. (2024) and Bourray et al. (2024) could not account for methodological limitations, including small sample sizes and limited conceptual frameworks, mainly the Technology Acceptance Model (TAM). While these studies underscore the promising potential of the platform, they do not adequately address the motivational and behavioural factors affecting sustained engagement and use. Additionally, Slimani and Jabal (2023) analysed the effectiveness of the Rosetta Stone Platform as a language-learning tool in consideration of its utility claims in fostering learners' language skills. They conducted a review study, in which they shed light on the advantages and limitations of the Rosetta Stone platform. They reported that the Rosetta Stone platform contributes to learning the target language, especially vocabulary and reading comprehension. Overall, digital technology plays a crucial role in language acquisition, with platforms like Rosetta Stone offering unique help for learners; however, the utility of technology in language acquisition is affected by factors, including teachers' attitudes and training (Slimani & Jabal, 2023). To the best of our knowledge, these are the studies that dealt with the platform of Rosetta Stone within the Moroccan context, namely higher education.

## Moroccan Higher Education: Digital and Pedagogical Shifts

The Moroccan educational system has undergone numerous digital transformations driven by national policies. The intention has been to improve academic quality, provide equal access to all students, and meet global standards. Integrating digital assessment tools, e-learning platforms, and AI-powered pedagogical tools is emphasised in initiatives, such as the 2015-2030 Strategic Vision for Education Reform and the Pact for Excellence in Higher Education (2023). Academic institutions have intensively integrated LMS such as Rosetta Stone and Moodle to simplify blended learning (Slimani & Jabal, 2023). Nevertheless, the use of AI-driven teaching resources is still in its infancy with varying degrees of acceptance across universities. On the one hand, the incorporation of AI-driven LMS in Moroccan universities poses challenges, since the lack of digital infrastructure, university opposition, and other concerns related to pedagogical reliability present obstacles to AI incorporation. On the other hand, AI-powered LMS presents solutions to issues such as language proficiency gaps, insufficient feedback, etc. (Marikyan & Papagiannidis, 2023). Therefore, it is vital to grasp how to integrate AI-driven platforms like Moodle and Rosetta Stone within this developing numerical landscape for better decision-making.

## Research Gap & Theoretical Contribution

Few studies have been conducted on the effectiveness of the Rosetta Stone Platform within higher education in Morocco (e.g., Bourray et al., 2024; Houmane et al., 2024; Slimani & Jabal, 2023). This chapter is driven by the scarcity of empirical research on AI-powered LMS, namely the adoption and implementation of the Rosetta Stone Platform in the Moroccan context. Additionally, previous studies (e.g., Houmane et al., 2024) adopted the Technology Acceptance Model (TAM) to explore the attitudes and perceptions of undergraduates concerning the use of the Rosetta Stone platform to learn English. Their model does not account for other variables that may come into play when speaking about users' adoption of this technology. Hence, this chapter employs UTAUT2—the latest model introduced to study the use of technology (Venkatesh et al., 2012). Although UTAUT2 has been adopted in different studies, its relevance to AI-driven language acquisition within the Moroccan context, namely higher education, remains under-studied. Existing research tends to generalize technology acceptance frameworks without addressing Moroccan institutions and students' specific socio-cultural and infrastructural challenges. To address this gap, this chapter evaluates the integration of Rosetta Stone in the Moroccan educational context, with a focus on key factors influencing its acceptance and students' attitudes. Employing UTAUT2, this chapter provides a significant contribution to theory by adapting a holistic behavioural model to a setting which is culturally and institutionally varied, and hence it presents practical insights for policymakers and educators in higher education in Morocco.

## The Present Study and Hypotheses

The present chapter is driven by the dearth of empirical evidence on user acceptance and attitudes toward implementing Rosetta Stone as an LMS in Moroccan higher education institutions. It aims to explore students' perceptions and attitudes towards the use and acceptance of Rosetta Stone, investigate the main variables that interfere with the use and acceptance of this platform, and shed light on practical implications for policymakers and university educators to optimize the integration and implementation of Rosetta Stone within Moroccan higher education. This study aims to empirically test the following hypotheses derived from UTAUT2, focusing on Moroccan university students' interaction with Rosetta Stone:

**H1:** Performance Expectancy affects directly and significantly Behavioural intention.
**H2:** Effort expectancy affects directly and significantly Behavioural intention.
**H3:** Social influence affects directly and significantly Behavioural intention.
**H4:** Facilitating conditions affects directly and significantly Usage Behaviour.
**H5:** Hedonic motivation affects directly and significantly Behavioural intention.
**H6 and H7:** Habit affects directly and significantly Behavioural intention and Habit affects directly and significantly Usage Behaviour.
**H8:** Behavioural intention affects directly and significantly Usage Behaviour.

# METHODOLOGY

## Research Design Overview

The present study utilizes a quantitative research design to investigate the implementation of Rosetta Stone for language learning within Moroccan higher education institutions. Quantitative research design was selected for numerous reasons, some which are its capacity to generate generalizable findings through large, randomized samples (Hulin et al., 1990), as well as its suitability for hypothesis testing and establishing causal relationships in controlled settings (Lim, 2015b, 2021; Lim et al., 2019, 2022; Viglia et al., 2021). In addition to that, it offers standardized, scalable, and rapid data collection, with an analysis that is, to a certain extent, objective and reproducible, which can ameliorate research credibility (Larson, 2019; Lynch et al., 2015). This approach permits the systematic collection and analysis of numerical data, which provides a framework to assess the relationships among variables as outlined in the Unified Theory of Acceptance and Use of Technology 2 (UTAUT2) model. Quantitative methods are suited for this investigation as they facilitate the generalization of findings across large populations. As a result, it can contribute to the enhancement of the reliability and validity of the conclusions drawn.

This study employs a cross-sectional survey methodology that implies collecting data at a single point in time from a large sample of university students. This design is appropriate given the study's objectives of examining students' attitudes, perceptions, and acceptance of Rosetta Stone as an LMS. The survey instrument is structured to gather data relevant to UTAUT2 constructs—performance expectancy, effort expectancy, social influence, facilitating conditions, hedonic motivation, and habit—as well as demographic data. The questionnaire consists of additional variables, such as students' familiarity and experience with the Rosetta Stone platform.

As for Data analysis, Partial Least Squares Structural Equation Modeling (PLS-SEM) was deployed in the data analysis process for numerous reasons. PLS-SEM is advantageous for exploratory research and model testing, owing to its ability to accommodate complex relationships among multiple constructs while being unaffected by violations of normality assumptions. It also provides solutions for samples that are small in sizes when models consist of many constructs (Hair et al., 2017). This analytical approach has high degrees of statistical power vis-à-vis other methods, namely covariance-based Structural Equation Modeling (CB-SEM) (Hair et al., 2017). Ultimately, it enables the identification of the chief predictors that affect the acceptance and use of Rosetta Stone

## Participants

The study targets undergraduate and graduate students enrolled in various Moroccan higher education institutions, with a focus on those attending open-access universities. The institutions to which the participants belong have implemented Rosetta Stone to conform with recent educational reforms that aim at encouraging digital transformation and enhancing language competencies. By focusing on a diverse student population, the study also aims to investigate the primary factors influencing the acceptance and use of Rosetta Stone across different socio-demographic backgrounds.

A stratified random sampling technique was employed to guarantee the sample's representativeness of the sample. The student population is stratified based on demographic variables such as age, gender, study level, and institution. This stratification ensures that the sample reflects the diversity in Moroccan higher education, which can allow for the generalizability of the results.

Students belonging to different Universities across Morocco were invited to participate in the study, of which 1,262 provided valid responses. This sample size can be attributed to the dissemination of the survey through institutional channels, social media platforms, and Google Classrooms. The final sample comprises students from multiple universities, including Mohammed V University of Rabat, Hassan II University of Casablanca, and Cadi Ayyad University of Marrakech, among others.

## Research Instrument

The data collection instrument utilized in the present study is an online questionnaire. This questionnaire was adopted from a previous study by Venkatesh et al. (2012) and it was adapted so as to conform to the objectives of the present study. The questionnaire is divided into three major sections: (i) demographic data, (ii) students' familiarity and experience with the Rosetta Stone platform, and (iii) the UTAUT2 constructs (Performance Expectancy, Effort Expectancy, Social Influence, Facilitating Conditions, Hedonic Motivation, Habit, Behavioural Intention, Use Behaviour)

## Demographic Data

The general information segment consists of basic questions. It is supposed to yield general information about the participants (gender, age group, years of study, university)

### Students' Familiarity and Experience with the Rosetta Stone Platform

This section contains two items that are measured using a 5-points Likert scale. Information gathered from this section is supposed to provide data on the extent to which the participants in the present study are familiar and experienced with the Rosetta Stone platform.

## UTAUT2 Constructs

The third section of the questionnaire is concerned with collecting data pertinent to gaining insights into students' perceptions and attitudes towards the implementation of Rosetta Stone in tertiary education. The price value construct was excluded from this study as mentioned in the theoretical framework section. This section comprises eight subsections. Each subsection includes three to four items that are measured via a 5-piont Likert scale. Below are the items included in each subsection:

Performance Expectancy:

- I find Rosetta Stone effective for improving my language skills.
- Using Rosetta Stone enhances my ability to complete language-learning tasks.
- Rosetta Stone helps me achieve my learning goals more efficiently.

Effort Expectancy

- Learning how to use the Rosetta Stone platform is easy for me.
- My interaction with the Rosetta Stone platform is clear and understandable.
- I find the Rosetta Stone platform easy to navigate and use.
- It is easy for me to become skilful at using the Rosetta Stone platform.

Social Influence:

- My peers think I should use Rosetta Stone for language learning.
- My instructors encourage me to use Rosetta Stone.
- People whose opinions I value recommend using the Rosetta Stone platform.

Facilitating Conditions:

- I have the necessary resources to use Rosetta Stone (e.g., internet, devices).
- I have the knowledge required to effectively use the Rosetta Stone platform.
- The Rosetta Stone platform is compatible with the devices and technologies I use.
- I can get support from others when I have difficulties using the Rosetta Stone platform.

Hedonic Motivation:

- I find the Rosetta Stone platform enjoyable for language learning.
- The activities provided by the Rosetta Stone platform are fun.
- The interactive features of Rosetta Stone make learning entertaining.

Habit:

- Using Rosetta Stone has become a habit for me.

- I feel I am dependent on using the Rosetta Stone platform for language learning.
- I must use the Rosetta Stone platform as part of my language learning routine.

Behavioural Intention:

- I intend to continue using Rosetta Stone in the future.
- I will try to incorporate the Rosetta Stone platform into my daily language learning activities.
- I plan to use the Rosetta Stone platform frequently for language learning.

Use Behaviour:

- I frequently use Rosetta Stone for improving my language skills.
- I dedicate a substantial portion of my weekly schedule to engaging with Rosetta Stone for language learning.
- I rely on Rosetta Stone for most of my language learning activities.

## Procedure

The data collection process commenced in November and ended in January. Participants were recruited through numerous channels, like email invitations and social media groups affiliated with the participating institutions. Professors were also requested to promote the study within their courses. The online Google Forms service was used to administer the questionnaire to ensure accessibility and ease of completion. Upon completion of data collection, responses were screened for completeness and accuracy. Incomplete or inconsistent responses were excluded from the final dataset. The cleaned data were then subjected to Partial Least Squares Structural Equation Modeling (PLS-SEM) using SmartPLS 4 software.

The data analysis was conducted in two phases: (i) assessment of the measurement model was executed to evaluate the reliability and validity of the constructs (ii) assessment of the structural model to test the hypothesized relationships amongst constructs. Reliability coefficients were deployed to assess the internal consistency of the UTAUT2 constructs (Cronbach's alpha, composite reliability (rho_a), and composite reliability (rho_c)). Validity was examined using average variance extracted (AVE), The Fornell-Larcker criterion, and Heterotrait-Monotrait (HTMT) ratio. The structural model was assessed using path coefficients, t-values, and R-squared values to identify the strength and significance of the relationships.

## Research Limitations and Ethical Considerations

Even though the methodological design of the present study is aligned with its objectives, certain limitations merit attention. Notably, the cross-sectional nature of the research captures only a single moment in time, which do not provide insights into how students' acceptance of Rosetta Stone may evolve with time; a longitudinal design could address this gap. The reliance on self-reported data is yet another limitation that introduces risks of social desirability bias or inaccuracies in usage reporting. Hence, in future studies, researchers can supplement self-reported data with system analytics, follow-up interviews, or focus groups. These instruments can be used to cross-check or elaborate on the results garnered from the questionnaire in order to provide a more accurate picture of user behaviour. Moreover, the gender imbalance in the sample, comprising approximately 71% female participants, raises concerns about representativeness and the applicability of the findings. Equally important, consent was obtained digitally through a preamble in the Google Form. Data were anonymized to protect participants' privacy, and all responses were stored securely. No names or email addresses were collected so as to ensure complete anonymity.

## RESULTS

### Demographic Data

Table 1 demonstrates the demographic characteristics of the participants. A total of 1,262 students participated in the survey, with 362 males (28.7%) and 900 females (71.3%), which indicates a higher representation of female participants. In terms of age distribution, 1,047 participants (83.0%) were between 18 and 22 years old, 98 participants (7.8%) were between 23 and 27 years old, and 39 participants (3.1%) were between 28 and 32 years old. The remaining participants were distributed across the 33 to 37 age group (1.8%), the 38 to 42 age group (1.5%), and those aged 43 years or older (2.9%).

Regarding academic level, 547 participants (43.3%) were in the first year of a bachelor's program, 392 participants (31.1%) were in the second year of a bachelor's program, and 186 participants (14.7%) were in the third year of a bachelor's program. A total of 88 participants (7.0%) were in the first year of a master's program, while 19 participants (1.5%) were in the second year of a master's program. Doctoral students accounted for 30 participants (2.4%).

Participants were enrolled in various Moroccan universities. Hassan II University in Casablanca had the highest representation with 650 participants (51.51%), followed by Mohammed V University in Rabat with 415 participants (32.88%). Hassan I University in Settat accounted for 85 participants (6.74%), while Hassan II University in Mohammedia had 38 participants (3.01%). Other universities had smaller representations, such as Cadi Ayyad University in Marrakech with 27 participants (2.14%), Sidi Mohamed Ben Abdellah University in Fez with 13 participants

(1.03%), and Ibn Zohr University in Agadir with 10 participants (0.79%). The least represented universities were Moulay Ismail University in Meknes (8 participants, 0.63%), Chouaib Doukkali University in El Jadida (6 participants, 0.48%), Abdelmalek Essaâdi University in Tetouan-Tangier (5 participants, 0.40%), Sultan Moulay Slimane University in Beni Mellal (4 participants, 0.32%), and Mohammed I University in Oujda, which had the lowest representation with 1 participant (0.08%).

*Table 1. Demographic characteristics of the participants*

| Category | Variable | Frequency | Percentage |
|---|---|---|---|
| Gender | Male | 362 | 28.7 |
| | Female | 900 | 71.3 |
| Age | 18 to 22 | 1047 | 83.0 |
| | 23 to 27 | 98 | 7.8 |
| | 28 to 32 | 39 | 3.1 |
| | 33 to 37 | 23 | 1.8 |
| | 38 to 42 | 19 | 1.5 |
| | More than 43 | 36 | 2.9 |
| Academic Level | First Year of Bachelor's | 547 | 43.3 |
| | First Year of Master's | 88 | 7.0 |
| | Third Year of Bachelor's | 186 | 14.7 |
| | Second Year of Bachelor's | 392 | 31.1 |
| | Second Year of Master's | 19 | 1.5 |
| | PhD Student | 30 | 2.4 |
| University | Hassan II University in Casablanca | 650 | 51,51 |
| | Mohammed V University in Rabat | 415 | 32,88 |
| | Hassan I University in Settat | 85 | 6,74 |
| | Hassan II University in Mohammedia | 38 | 3,01 |
| | Cadi Ayyad University in Marrakech | 27 | 2,14 |
| | Sidi Mohamed Ben Abdellah University in Fez | 13 | 1,03 |
| | Ibn Zohr University in Agadir | 10 | 0,79 |
| | Moulay Ismail University in Meknes | 8 | 0,63 |
| | Chouaib Doukkali University in El Jadida | 6 | 0,48 |
| | Abdelmalek Essaâdi University in Tetouan-Tangier | 5 | 0,40 |
| | Sultan Moulay Slimane University in Beni Mellal | 4 | 0,32 |
| | Mohammed I University in Oujda | 1 | 0,08 |

(Developed by Author, 2025)

## Measurement Model

In this study, the Partial Least Squares Structural Equation Modeling (PLS-SEM) analysis was applied to evaluate the model using the latest version of SmartPLS 4 (Version 4.1.0.9). The analysis employed the weighting path scheme, with subsamples 5000 times, and the software's predefined values for initial weights. To evaluate significance of the PLS-SEM results, a nonparametric bootstrapping procedure was conducted with 10000 resamples. This approach aligns with established literature (Hair et al., 2020; Hair et al., 2019; Subhaktiyasa, 2024). The tested model is illustrated in Figure 1. All analyses were performed at a standard significance level of $\alpha < .05$.

Reflective constructs were evaluated using indicator loadings. Indicator loadings exceeding the 0.7 threshold were indicative of the reliability of the items. Results revealed that all indicator loadings surpassed the recommended value of 0.7. therefore, the reliability of all items was ensured.

Construct reliability was assessed via composite reliability measures (Rho_c and Rho_a values). Most calculated values for constructs fell within the range of 0.70 to 0.95. These results reflect adequate to high reliability (Hair et al., 2019). However, the Rho_c values for Behavioural Intention (0.970), Effort Expectancy (0.970), Habit (0.953), Hedonic Motivation (0.968), and Performance Expectancy (0.955) exceeded the 0.95 threshold. In the same vein, the Rho_a values for Behavioural Intention (0.954) and Effort Expectancy (0.954) approached or surpassed this threshold. It is noteworthy that prior research (e.g., Hair et al., 2019) has underscored that reliability values greater than 0.95 may signal potential redundancies or over-specification in measurement instruments. Behavioural Intention, for instance, exhibited particularly high item loadings (0.948–0.966) and AVE (0.914), while Habit and Hedonic Motivation also demonstrated strong consistency (AVE $\geq$ 0.871). These findings highlight the need to evaluate reliability metrics to balance methodological validity.

Cronbach's alpha was computed to examine internal consistency reliability, and all constructs demonstrated acceptable values. To evaluate convergent validity, the average variance extracted (AVE) was calculated for all items linked to each reflective variable. An AVE value exceeding 0.50 was considered adequate (Hair et al., 2019). The findings for composite reliability, Cronbach's alpha, and AVE were in line with the established quality criteria (see Table 3).

*Table 2. Mean, median, minimum, maximum, and Standard Deviation (SD) for each construct*

| Construct | Item | Mean | Median | Min | Max | SD |
|---|---|---|---|---|---|---|
| Behavioural Intention | BI1 | 2.999 | 3.000 | 1.000 | 5.000 | 1.548 |
| | BI2 | 3.010 | 3.000 | 1.000 | 5.000 | 1.544 |
| | BI3 | 3.013 | 3.000 | 1.000 | 5.000 | 1.571 |
| Effort Expectancy | EE1 | 2.956 | 3.000 | 1.000 | 5.000 | 1.456 |
| | EE2 | 2.976 | 3.000 | 1.000 | 5.000 | 1.428 |
| | EE3 | 2.964 | 3.000 | 1.000 | 5.000 | 1.439 |
| | EE4 | 2.998 | 3.000 | 1.000 | 5.000 | 1.444 |
| Facilitating Conditions | FC1 | 2.877 | 3.000 | 1.000 | 5.000 | 1.539 |
| | FC2 | 2.895 | 3.000 | 1.000 | 5.000 | 1.419 |
| | FC3 | 2.872 | 3.000 | 1.000 | 5.000 | 1.488 |
| | FC4 | 2.977 | 3.000 | 1.000 | 5.000 | 1.493 |
| Habit | HA1 | 3.048 | 3.000 | 1.000 | 5.000 | 1.509 |
| | HA2 | 3.032 | 3.000 | 1.000 | 5.000 | 1.560 |
| | HA3 | 3.009 | 3.000 | 1.000 | 5.000 | 1.532 |
| Hedonic Motivation | HM1 | 3.030 | 3.000 | 1.000 | 5.000 | 1.538 |
| | HM2 | 3.046 | 3.000 | 1.000 | 5.000 | 1.513 |
| | HM3 | 3.033 | 3.000 | 1.000 | 5.000 | 1.537 |
| Performance Expectancy | PE1 | 3.040 | 3.000 | 1.000 | 5.000 | 1.428 |
| | PE2 | 2.968 | 3.000 | 1.000 | 5.000 | 1.423 |
| | PE3 | 2.984 | 3.000 | 1.000 | 5.000 | 1.464 |
| Social Influence | SI1 | 2.940 | 3.000 | 1.000 | 5.000 | 1.531 |
| | SI2 | 2.827 | 3.000 | 1.000 | 5.000 | 1.516 |
| | SI3 | 2.953 | 3.000 | 1.000 | 5.000 | 1.530 |
| Usage Behaviour | UB1 | 2.993 | 3.000 | 1.000 | 5.000 | 1.496 |
| | UB2 | 2.891 | 3.000 | 1.000 | 5.000 | 1.484 |
| | UB3 | 3.040 | 3.000 | 1.000 | 5.000 | 1.546 |

(Developed by the author, 2025)

*Table 3. Indicator loading, composite reliability, and convergent validity coefficients*

| Construct | Item | Loading | | CR (rho_a) | CR (rho_c) | AVE |
|---|---|---|---|---|---|---|
| Behavioural Intention | BI1 | 0.954 | 0.953 | 0.954 | 0.970 | 0.914 |
| | BI2 | 0.966 | | | | |
| | BI3 | 0.948 | | | | |
| Effort Expectancy | EE1 | 0.894 | 0.927 | 0.954 | 0.970 | 0.820 |
| | EE2 | 0.924 | | | | |
| | EE3 | 0.900 | | | | |
| | EE4 | 0.903 | | | | |
| Facilitating Conditions | FC1 | 0.810 | 0.866 | 0.911 | 0.906 | 0.708 |
| | FC2 | 0.819 | | | | |
| | FC3 | 0.878 | | | | |
| | FC4 | 0.858 | | | | |
| Habit | HA1 | 0.942 | 0.926 | 0.926 | 0.953 | 0.871 |
| | HA2 | 0.923 | | | | |
| | HA3 | 0.933 | | | | |
| Hedonic Motivation | HM1 | 0.954 | 0.951 | 0.951 | 0.968 | 0.911 |
| | HM2 | 0.954 | | | | |
| | HM3 | 0.955 | | | | |
| Performance Expectancy | PE1 | 0.909 | 0.929 | 0.931 | 0.955 | 0.876 |
| | PE2 | 0.954 | | | | |
| | PE3 | 0.945 | | | | |
| Social Influence | SI1 | 0.889 | 0.799 | 0.854 | 0.882 | 0.717 |
| | SI2 | 0.696 | | | | |
| | SI3 | 0.937 | | | | |
| Usage Behaviour | UB1 | 0.940 | 0.898 | 0.906 | 0.936 | 0.831 |
| | UB2 | 0.867 | | | | |
| | UB3 | 0.926 | | | | |

(Developed by the author, 2025)

## Structural Model

The evaluation of discriminant validity by means of the Heterotrait-Monotrait (HTMT) ratio demonstrated some notable instances of conceptual overlap. An HTMT threshold of 0.90 is typically recommended to ensure that constructs remain distinct (Henseler et al., 2015). The results, presented in Table 4, indicate that most constructs meet this criterion; however, one notable exception exceeds the threshold. The HTMT value between Use Behavior (UB) and Habit (HA) is 0.940, which implies a lack of distinction between these two constructs. This high value indicates that participants may perceive habit and actual use as closely related, which could suggest measurement overlap or conceptual similarity between the constructs.

To further validate discriminant validity, the Fornell-Larcker criterion was applied. As shown in Table 5, the square root of the average variance extracted (AVE) for all construct remains greater than its correlations with other variables, supporting the distinctiveness of most constructs.

*Table 4. The Heterotrait-Monotrait (HTMT) analyses values*

| | BI | EE | FC | HA | HM | PE | SI | UB |
|---|---|---|---|---|---|---|---|---|
| **BI** | | | | | | | | |
| EE | 0.584 | | | | | | | |
| FC | 0.530 | 0.744 | | | | | | |
| HA | 0.860 | 0.569 | 0.543 | | | | | |
| HM | 0.850 | 0.610 | 0.576 | 0.846 | | | | |
| PE | 0.721 | 0.607 | 0.500 | 0.696 | 0.750 | | | |
| SI | 0.837 | 0.674 | 0.645 | 0.831 | 0.850 | 0.759 | | |
| UB | 0.897 | 0.586 | 0.573 | 0.940 | 0.833 | 0.710 | 0.840 | |

(Developed by the author, 2025)

*Table 5. The Fornell-Larcker criterion matrix*

| | BI | EE | FC | HA | HM | PE | SI | UB |
|---|---|---|---|---|---|---|---|---|
| BI | **0.956** | | | | | | | |
| EE | 0.550 | **0.905** | | | | | | |
| FC | 0.507 | 0.676 | **0.841** | | | | | |
| HA | 0.809 | 0.529 | 0.516 | **0.933** | | | | |
| HM | 0.810 | 0.574 | 0.551 | 0.795 | **0.954** | | | |
| PE | 0.679 | 0.563 | 0.472 | 0.647 | 0.705 | **0.936** | | |
| SI | 0.744 | 0.573 | 0.556 | 0.734 | 0.760 | 0.669 | **0.847** | |
| UB | 0.834 | 0.534 | 0.530 | 0.860 | 0.773 | 0.652 | 0.729 | **0.912** |

(Developed by the author, 2025)

To assess the explanatory power of the proposed model, the coefficient of determination ($R^2$) was examined. As shown in Figure 2, the model explains 75.5% ($R^2 = 0.755$) of the variance in Behavioural Intention and 80.0% ($R^2 = 0.800$) of the variance in Usage Behaviour, which indicates substantial explanatory power (Hair et al., 2011).

The path coefficients presented in Figure 2 and Table 6 illustrate the relationships among key constructs in the model.

## H1: Performance Expectancy → Behavioural Intention

Performance Expectancy has a small yet statistically significant positive effect on Behavioural Intention ($\beta = 0.100$, $t = 4.120$, $p < 0.001$). This supports the idea that students who perceive Rosetta Stone as useful in improving their language proficiency, be it English or French, are more likely to intend to use it.

## H2: Effort Expectancy → Behavioural Intention

Effort Expectancy has a small but statistically significant effect on Behavioural Intention ($\beta = 0.050$, $t = 2.080$, $p = 0.019$). Although ease of use matters to students, it is a secondary factor compared to others such as motivation or habit.

## H3: Facilitating Conditions → Behavioural Intention

Facilitating Conditions show a non-significant and negative effect on Behavioural Intention ($\beta = -0.051$, $t = 1.564$, $p = 0.059$), which leads to the rejection of this hypothesis. This suggests that external support does not directly shape students' intention to use Rosetta Stone.

## H4: Social Influence → Behavioural Intention

Social Influence exerts a moderate and statistically significant effect on Behavioural Intention ($\beta = 0.154$, $t = 4.834$, $p < 0.001$), which elucidates that peer and instructor encouragement plays, to a certain extent, a role in motivating students to adopt the platform.

## H5: Hedonic Motivation → Behavioural Intention

Hedonic Motivation has a moderate and statistically significant influence on Behavioural Intention ($\beta = 0.268$, $t = 3.488$, $p < 0.001$). Enjoyment and engagement appear to be quite important in shaping the willingness of students to use the system.

### H6: Facilitating Conditions → Usage Behaviour

Facilitating Conditions have a very low yet statistically significant positive impact on Usage Behaviour ($\beta = 0.069$, $t = 3.813$, $p < 0.001$), which highlights that available infrastructure and support enhance the actual use of Rosetta Stone, even if they do not influence intention.

### H7: Habit → Behavioural Intention

Habit strongly predicts Behavioural Intention ($\beta = 0.424$, $t = 6.072$, $p < 0.001$). Students who are accustomed to using similar platforms are more likely to form a strong intention to use Rosetta Stone.

### H8: Habit → Usage Behaviour

Habit is the strongest predictor of Usage Behaviour ($\beta = 0.533$, $t = 14.220$, $p < 0.001$), which highlights the critical role of established user habits in driving actual engagement with the platform.

### H9: Behavioural Intention → Usage Behaviour

Behavioural Intention significantly influences Usage Behaviour ($\beta = 0.380$, $t = 11.037$, $p < 0.001$), which reinforces the theoretical assumption that intention leads to action.

### Moderating Effects

The moderating roles of Gender, Age, Experience, and Familiarity were also examined (Figure 2). However, none of these variables demonstrated a statistically significant moderating effect on the relationships between predictors and dependent variables. This suggests that the adoption the Rosetta Stone platform is relatively consistent across different demographic groups.

### Summary of Key Findings

The analysis supports all proposed hypotheses except H3. Habit is the most influential factor for both intention and actual usage. Behavioural Intention, Hedonic Motivation, and Social Influence also play significant roles in shaping user adoption. Although Facilitating Conditions do not influence intention, they are relevant to actual use. The findings align with the UTAUT2 framework and provide empirical evidence for understanding AI-based language learning adoption in Moroccan higher education.

*Table 6. Path coefficient, Standard Deviations (SD), t-values, p-values, and hypothesis testing*

| Hypotheses | Relationship | Â | SD | *t*-values | *p*-values | Decision |
|---|---|---|---|---|---|---|
| H1 | PE -> BI | 0.100 | 0.024 | 4.120 | 0.000 | Supported |
| H2 | EE -> BI | 0.050 | 0.024 | 2.080 | 0.019 | Supported |
| H3 | FC -> BI | -0.051 | 0.033 | 1.564 | 0.059 | Rejected |
| H4 | SI -> BI | 0.154 | 0.032 | 4.834 | 0.000 | Supported |
| H5 | HM -> BI | 0.268 | 0.077 | 3.488 | 0.000 | Supported |
| H6 | FC -> UB | 0.069 | 0.018 | 3.813 | 0.000 | Supported |
| H7 | HA -> BI | 0.424 | 0.070 | 6.072 | 0.000 | Supported |
| H8 | HA -> UB | 0.533 | 0.038 | 14.220 | 0.000 | Supported |
| H9 | BI -> UB | 0.380 | 0.034 | 11.037 | 0.000 | Supported |

(Developed by the author, 2025)

*Figure 2. Structural measurement model of Rosetta Stone acceptance by Moroccan students (Author, 2025)*

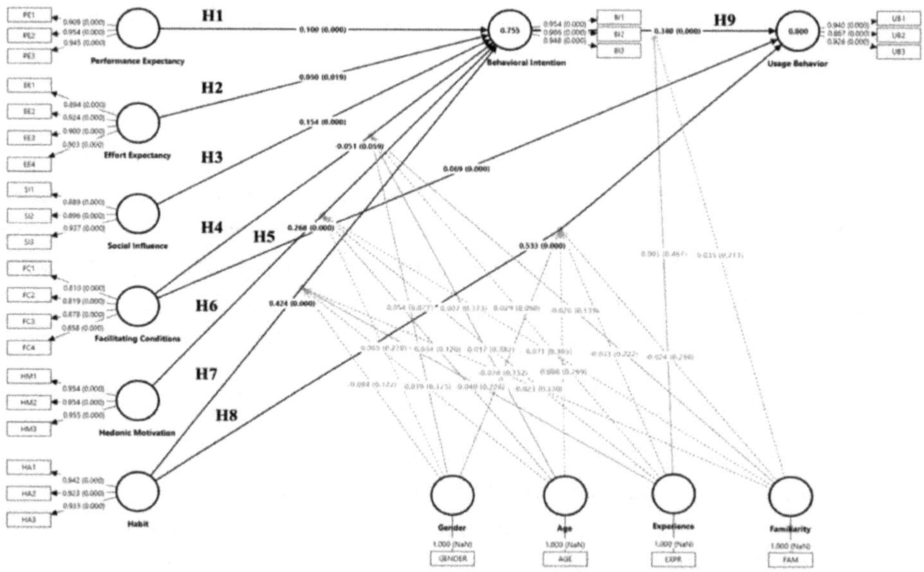

## DISCUSSION

In this chapter, we examined the perceptions and attitudes towards the use and acceptance of Rosetta Stone among a cohort of Moroccan university students. We also investigated the main variables that interfere with the use and acceptance of this platform by shedding light on practical implications for policymakers and university educators to optimize the integration and implementation of Rosetta Stone within Moroccan higher education. This investigation was grounded in the Unified Theory of Acceptance and Use of Technology 2 (UTAUT2), a framework proposed by (Venkatesh et al, 2012) to study the use and acceptance of technology. Our empirical results support Bhandari et al.'s (2024) findings that Habit and Hedonic Motivation are the primary determinants in shaping Behavioural Intention. Following Malmous and Zaidoune (2025) and Grassini's (2024) research, our study reveals that behavioural Intention significantly predicts Usage Behaviour. Notwithstanding, while Narayan & Naidu's (2024) study showed that Facilitating Conditions significantly predict behavioural Intention, our findings reveal that factors within the framework, including Facilitating Conditions, do not significantly predict Behavioural Intentions. However, Facilitating Conditions do significantly influence Usage Behaviour.

These findings align with previous research (Tang et al., 2025; Deng & Yu, 2023; Narayan & Naidu, 2024), which highlight the vital role of Habit and Hedonic Motivation in adopting emerging technologies within higher education. The analysis of the dataset further showed that students perceive Rosetta Stone as an emerging platform to optimize academic success and performance. According to our findings, Habit appears to be the main predictor of Behavioural Intention, which aligns with prior research that reported a positive correlation between these constructs in learning management systems (Tang et al., 2025; Deng & Yu, 2023; Narayan & Naidu, 2024). Additionally, Habit emerges as the main predictor of Behavioural Intention in various studies that examined students' perceptions of mobile learning (Tang et al., 2025; Deng & Yu, 2023; Narayan & Naidu, 2024) and students' acceptance and use of technology in educational settings (Tang et al., 2025; Deng & Yu, 2023; Narayan & Naidu, 2024).

Our findings also identified Hedonic Motivation as the second forecaster of Behavioural Intention toward the use and acceptance of the Rosetta Stone Platform among Moroccan university students. This finding corroborates prior research (Tang et al., 2025; Deng & Yu, 2023; Narayan & Naidu, 2024), which underscored the importance of Hedonic Motivation in driving the acceptance and integration of learning management systems. Notwithstanding, our findings deviate from previous research (Tang et al., 2025; Deng & Yu, 2023; Narayan & Naidu, 2024) that reported a weak correlation between Hedonic Motivation and Behavioural Intention concerning the use of learning management systems and e-learning.

Unlike the findings of Narayan & Naidu (2024), we did not find a strong correlation between Facilitating Conditions and Behavioural Intention in terms of students' use and acceptance of Rosetta Stone. This finding can be attributed to contextual differences in technology infrastructure and support between the study environments.

Besides that, our findings showed a moderate correlation between Effort Expectancy and Social Influence and Behavioural Intention in using the Rosetta Stone platform. This contrasts prior research by Narayan & Naidu (2024), in which these constructs had no direct effect on Behavioural Intention. We also found that the ease of using Rosetta Stone in Moroccan higher education has a significant effect on Behavioural Intention. This finding is in line with prior research on e-learning platform usage (Deng & Yu, 2023) and Microsoft PowerPoint adoption in higher education (Tang et al., 2025; Narayan & Naidu, 2024). Contributing variables to these findings could include students' acceptance of the latest innovative technologies.

We also found that Social Influence has a direct effect on the Behavioural Intention to use Rosetta Stone among Moroccan university students. This finding may imply that university students with their educational background are more likely to be influenced by societal pressures. Other studies investigating platforms like Google Classroom reported a weak correlation between Social Influence and Behavioural Intention (Tang et al., 2025; Deng & Yu, 2023; Narayan & Naidu, 2024; Bhandari et al., 2024).

Our chapter showed that Facilitating Conditions significantly predict Usage Behaviour. This finding aligns with previous research (Tang et al., 2025; Deng & Yu, 2023; Narayan & Naidu, 2024), in which it was reported that Facilitating Conditions are strong predictors of User Behaviour. This could be justified on the grounds of demographic characteristics of the students or levels of technological familiarity between the sample used in our chapter and other research.

The variables of Age, Gender, and Experience did not affect any of the relationships in which they were measured. This finding corroborates prior research (Tang et al., 2025; Deng & Yu, 2023; Narayan & Naidu, 2024; Bhandari et al., 2024; Grassini, 2024). The non-existence of Experience as a mediator in accepting and adopting the Rosetta Stone platform is significant. This could be attributed to the ease of use of this platform compared to other digital platforms. While Experience does have a direct effect on certain aspects of adopting some digital technologies, Rosetta Stone is a user-friendly platform that allows both novice and expert users to utilize it with ease. This shows that the way the Rosetta Stone platform is structured mitigates the effect of Experience on variables that affect the ease of use.

The findings of this study must be interpreted within the dynamics of Moroccan higher education, where infrastructural inconsistencies, limited digital resources, and varied levels of technological proficiency determine student behaviour. The strong influence of Habit on both Behavioural Intention and Usage Behaviour reflects the reliance of students on familiar routines while navigating new platforms in environments where digital training and institutional support remain limited. Similarly, the role of Hedonic Motivation highlights students' growing preference for interactive and enjoyable learning tools, which offers a contrast to the traditional pedagogical approaches that rely heavily on lecturing—a practice that is common in Moroccan universities. The non-significant relationship between Facilitating Conditions and Behavioural Intention diverges from findings in digitally mature contexts can be attributed to the familiarity of Moroccan to working around infrastructural limitations and do not necessarily equate technical support with intent to use. However, the fact that Facilitating Conditions do significantly predict actual Usage Behaviour suggests that, despite forming intentions independently, students still rely on logistical support to sustain platform engagement. Moderate effects of Effort Expectancy and Social Influence further emphasize the importance of usability and social context in shaping adoption; Morocco is a collectivist society where peer recommendations and instructor endorsement carry are of paramount importance. The absence of moderating effects from Age, Gender, or Experience suggests that Rosetta Stone's intuitive interface enables equitable access across demographic groups, which mitigates digital divides.

## IMPLICATIONS

The current chapter provides significant theoretical, practical, and policy-level implications for the incorporation of AI-powered language learning platforms in Moroccan higher education.

### Theoretical Implications

The findings add to the theoretical development of the Unified Theory of Acceptance and Use of Technology 2 (UTAUT2) by corroborating its constructs in a distinct setting. Being found in this study as significant predictors of behavioural intention, the variables of habit and hedonic motivation underscore the prominence of user experience and engagement in technology acceptance. On the other hand, it is essential to consider the contextual significance of various UTAUT2 aspects in underdeveloped educational settings as indicated by the impoverished impact of enabling conditions on behavioural intention.

## Institutional-Level Implications

At the institutional level, the incorporation of AI-driven platforms, such as Rosetta Stone requires the acceptance of neat implementation frameworks. This involves choosing pertinent licensing models, aligned curricular goals, and establishing monitoring systems. Fostering user experience, use and engagement through gamification, peer collaboration, and embedded learning tasks can promote acceptance and sustained use. Additionally, the endorsement of equitable use of AI-driven platforms demands investing in digital infrastructure, mainly internet connection and accessibility.

## Instructional-Level Implications

One of the pivotal roles that instructors play today is simplifying the incorporation of AI-driven platforms for students. This cannot be done unless these instructors benefit from ongoing professional development training and workshops that hone their digital and pedagogical skills for better execution and implementation. It is also believed that the integration of AI tools in lesson delivery and planning, student-centred activities, and evaluation can promote learner autonomy, involvement, and motivation.

## Policy-Level Implications

The findings of the current study align with Morocco's education reform agenda and emphasize the promising potential of AI in bridging the gap between the centre and the peripheries. To promote the incorporation and adoption of AI, policymakers should build up regulatory models and frameworks to encourage quality assurance of AI-driven tools. Investments and funded projects should target teacher training, digital infrastructure, and sustainability.

# CONCLUSION

This chapter explored the perceptions of and attitudes towards the use and acceptance of Rosetta Stone among a cohort of Moroccan university students. The findings revealed that Hedonic Motivation and Habit emerged to have a significant impact on shaping students' intentions to utilize the Rosetta Stone platform. The outcome of this study showed that Facilitating Conditions do not significantly predict Behavioural Intention yet have a weak impact on Usage Behaviour. This suggests that external support structures may not directly shape students' willingness to adopt the platform, yet they play an important function in actual usage patterns. Furthermore, Effort Expectancy and Social Influence exhibited a moderate correlation with Behavioural Intention, which implies that students' perceptions of ease of use and the influence of their peers and instructors contribute to their adoption of the platform. The study also found that Age, Gender, Experience, and Familiarity had no effect on students' acceptance and use of Rosetta Stone. This non-existent effect reinforces the notion that Rosetta Stone is a user-friendly platform that minimizes the need for prior technological experience. In addition, this chapter investigated the main variables that interfere with the use and acceptance of the Rosetta Stone platform by shedding light on practical implications for policymakers and university educators to optimize its integration and implementation within Moroccan higher education.

## Contributions to Knowledge

This study makes a contribution to the existing body of knowledge via the application of the UTAUT2. The findings underscore the prominent influence of Habit and Hedonic Motivation on Behavioural Intention, while simultaneously problematizing the assumed universal importance of Facilitating Conditions. In this context, user experience and platform design appear to exert a greater impact on technology acceptance than institutional or infrastructural support. This is relevant in resource-constrained environments where students often adapt to limited support systems. The present study, therefore, extends the theoretical application of UTAUT2 to a developing country context and contributes to the expanding body of research on the implementation of artificial intelligence in education.

## Final Recommendations

Future research should explore how institutional structures and cultural dynamics shape sustained engagement with AI-driven educational tools in similar contexts. Investigating the interplay between platform features and instructional models—such as blended learning or flipped classrooms—could provide further insight into how pedagogical design affects user behaviour. As for educators and policymakers, the findings suggest a need to prioritize habit-forming strategies that enhance student engagement, and onboarding processes that minimize entry barriers. Ensuring access to the platform, strengthening communication channels, and offering targeted support, inter alia, are some initiatives that may facilitate both initial adoption and long-term utilization of Rosetta Stone and other new technologies within Moroccan universities.

## REFERENCES


Agrram, A. (2021). Higher education languages of instruction in Morocco and their impact on the receptive vocabulary size of Moroccan EFL master students. [AWEJ]. *Arab World English Journal, 11*(4), 194–206. Advance online publication. DOI: 10.24093/awej/vol11no4.13

Almasri, F. (2024). Exploring the impact of artificial intelligence in teaching and learning of science: A systematic review of empirical research. *Research in Science Education, 54*(5), 977–997. DOI: 10.1007/s11165-024-10176-3

Amin, M. R. M., Ismail, I., & Sivakumaran, V. M. (2025). Revolutionizing education with artificial intelligence (AI)? Challenges, and implications for open and distance learning (ODL). *Social Sciences & Humanities Open, 11*, 101308. DOI: 10.1016/j.ssaho.2025.101308

Aziz, S., Harrizi, M., Loutfi, A., & Zaidoune, S. (2023). Exploring Moroccan Undergraduates' Views on Developing Soft Skills in EFL Classes: A Case Study. *Turkish International Journal of Special Education and Guidance & Counselling ISSN: 1300-7432, 12*(1), 45–57. Retrieved from https://www.tijseg.org/index.php/tijseg/article/view/199

Aziz, S., Harrizi, M., Loutfi, A., & Zaidoune, S. (2024). Undergraduates' Perspectives on the Significance of Soft Skills for Employment: Gender-Based Differences. *Journal of Education in Muslim Societies, 6*(1), 3–31. DOI: 10.2979/jems.00014

Belhiah, H., Bejjit, N., Bahmad, J., Zeddari, I., & Amrous, N. (2020). *English language teaching in Moroccan higher education*. Springer Singapore., DOI: 10.1007/978-981-15-3805-6

Bourray, M., Ajdi, N., & Snaibi, B. (2024). Assessment of Learning Through Digital Platforms in Language Classes in Moroccan Universities: Towards a New Innovative Pedagogical Practice—Case Study of Moulay Ismail University. *Pakistan Journal of Life and Social Sciences, 22*(2), 13937–13948. DOI: 10.57239/PJLSS-2024-22.2.001002

Daniel, B. K. (2019). Big Data and data science: A critical review of issues for educational research. *British Journal of Educational Technology, 50*(1), 101–113. DOI: 10.1111/bjet.12595

Deng, X., & Yu, Z. (2023). An extended hedonic motivation adoption model of TikTok in higher education. *Education and Information Technologies, 28*(10), 13595–13617. DOI: 10.1007/s10639-023-11749-x PMID: 37361837

Elmeski, M. (2024). Educational Leadership and Administration in Morocco: Recent Developments and Growth Prospects. *Demystifying Educational Leadership and Administration in the Middle East and North Africa*, 75-94. https://doi.org/DOI: 10.4324/9781003334835

Errihani, M. (2024). *Language, Power, and the Economics of Education in Morocco*. Springer International Publishing AG., DOI: 10.1007/978-3-031-51594-1

Ghaicha, A. (2018). Moroccan higher education system: Reality and prospects. *Higher Education of Social Science*, *14*(1). Advance online publication. DOI: 10.3968/10201

Hair, J. F.Jr, Howard, M. C., & Nitzl, C. (2020). Assessing measurement model quality in PLS-SEM using confirmatory composite analysis. *Journal of Business Research*, *109*, 101–110. DOI: 10.1016/j.jbusres.2019.11.069

Hair Jr, J. F., Matthews, L. M., Matthews, R. L., & Sarstedt, M. (2017). PLS-SEM or CB-SEM: updated guidelines on which method to use. *International Journal of Multivariate Data Analysis*, 1(2), 107-123. DOI: 10.1504/IJMDA.2017.087624

Hair, J. F., Ringle, C. M., & Sarstedt, M. (2011). PLS-SEM: Indeed a silver bullet. *Journal of Marketing Theory and Practice*, *19*(2), 139–152. DOI: 10.2753/MTP1069-6679190202

Hair, J. F., Risher, J. J., Sarstedt, M., & Ringle, C. M. (2019). When to use and how to report the results of PLS-SEM. *European Business Review*, *31*(1), 2–24. DOI: 10.1108/EBR-11-2018-0203

Hashim, M. A., Tlemsani, I., & Matthews, R. (2022). Higher education strategy in digital transformation. *Education and Information Technologies*, *27*(3), 3171–3195. DOI: 10.1007/s10639-021-10739-1 PMID: 34539217

Henseler, J., Ringle, C. M., & Sarstedt, M. (2015). A new criterion for assessing discriminant validity in variance-based structural equation modeling. *Journal of the Academy of Marketing Science*, *43*(1), 115–135. DOI: 10.1007/s11747-014-0403-8

Houmane, J., Zaher, A., Brigui, H., & Omari, A. (2024). Digital Citizenship and Language Learning: Attitudes Toward Rosetta Stone in Moroccan Higher Education. [IOSRJRME]. *IOSR Journal of Research & Methods in Education*, *14*, 52–60.

Hulin, C. L., Henry, R. A., & Noon, S. L. (1990). Adding a dimension: Time as a factor in the generalizability of predictive relationships. *Psychological Bulletin*, *107*(3), 328–340. DOI: 10.1037/0033-2909.107.3.328

Janowski, A., & Szczepańska–Przekota, A. (2024). Entrepreneurship education in Poland: Contemporary problems and future opportunities. *International Journal of Management Education*, *22*(1), 100931. DOI: 10.1016/j.ijme.2024.100931

Janssen, M., Van Der Voort, H., & Wahyudi, A. (2017). Factors influencing big data decision-making quality. *Journal of Business Research*, *70*, 338–345. DOI: 10.1016/j.jbusres.2016.08.007

Jiang, J., Simon, P. D., & Fryer, L. K. (2024). Capturing students' LMS experience: Measurement invariance across Chinese and English versions. *Journal of Computing in Higher Education*, •••, 1–23.

Jin, Y., Yan, L., Echeverria, V., Gašević, D., & Martinez-Maldonado, R. (2025). Generative AI in higher education: A global perspective of institutional adoption policies and guidelines. *Computers and Education: Artificial Intelligence*, *8*, 100348. DOI: 10.1016/j.caeai.2024.100348

Kumar, A., Krishnamurthi, R., Bhatia, S., Kaushik, K., Ahuja, N. J., Nayyar, A., & Masud, M. (2021). Blended learning tools and practices: A comprehensive analysis. *IEEE Access : Practical Innovations, Open Solutions*, *9*, 85151–85197. DOI: 10.1109/ACCESS.2021.3085844

Larson, R. B. (2019). Controlling social desirability bias. *International Journal of Market Research*, *61*(5), 534–547. DOI: 10.1177/1470785318805305

Lazrak, M., & Yechouti, Y. (2017). Issues in Moroccan Higher Education. *Language & Translation*, *5*(2), 86–93.

Lim, W. M. (2015b). Enriching information science research through chronic disposition and situational priming: A short note for future research. *Journal of Information Science*, *41*(3), 399–402. DOI: 10.1177/0165551515577913

Lim, W. M. (2021). Conditional recipes for predicting impacts and prescribing solutions for externalities: The case of COVID-19 and tourism. *Tourism Recreation Research*, *46*(2), 314–318. DOI: 10.1080/02508281.2021.1881708

Lim, W. M., Ahmed, P. K., & Ali, M. Y. (2019). Data and resource maximization in business-to-business marketing experiments: Methodological insights from data partitioning. *Industrial Marketing Management*, *76*, 136–143. DOI: 10.1016/j.indmarman.2018.08.007

Lim, W. M., Ahmed, P. K., & Ali, M. Y. (2022). Giving electronic word of mouth (eWOM) as a prepurchase behavior: The case of online group buying. *Journal of Business Research*, *146*, 582–604. DOI: 10.1016/j.jbusres.2022.03.093

Lynch, J. G.Jr, Bradlow, E. T., Huber, J. C., & Lehmann, D. R. (2015). Reflections on the replication corner: In praise of conceptual replications. *International Journal of Research in Marketing*, *32*(4), 333–342. DOI: 10.1016/j.ijresmar.2015.09.006

Ma, Y., & Chen, M. (2024). AI-empowered applications effects on EFL learners' engagement in the classroom and academic procrastination. *BMC Psychology*, *12*(1), 739. DOI: 10.1186/s40359-024-02248-w PMID: 39695837

Malmous, M., & Zaidoune, S. (2025). Student Adoption of AI Writing Tools: A PLS-SEM and TAM-Based Analysis in Moroccan Higher Education. In *Next-Generation AI Methodologies in Education* (pp. 209-254). IGI Global Scientific Publishing.

Mansouri, Z., & Moumine, M. E. A. (2017). Outlook on Student Retention in Higher Education University Reforms in Morocco. *International Journal of Education and Literacy Studies*, *5*(2), 53–60. DOI: 10.7575/aiac.ijels.v.5n.2p.53

Marikyan, M., & Papagiannidis, P. (2023). Unified theory of acceptance and use of technology. *TheoryHub book.*

Mittal, A., Mantri, A., Tandon, U., & Dwivedi, Y. K. (2022). A unified perspective on the adoption of online teaching in higher education during the COVID-19 pandemic. *Information Discovery and Delivery*, *50*(2), 117–132. DOI: 10.1108/IDD-09-2020-0114

Mutawa, A. M., & Sruthi, S. (2024). Enhancing Human-Computer Interaction in Online Education: A Machine Learning Approach to Predicting Student Emotion and Satisfaction. *International Journal of Human-Computer Interaction*, *40*(24), 1–17. DOI: 10.1080/10447318.2023.2291611

Narayan, J., & Naidu, S. (2024). A new contextual and comprehensive application of the UTAUT2 model post-Covid-19 pandemic in higher education. *Higher Education Quarterly*, *78*(1), 47–77. DOI: 10.1111/hequ.12441

Onesi-Ozigagun, O., Ololade, Y. J., Eyo-Udo, N. L., & Ogundipe, D. O. (2024). Revolutionizing education through AI: A comprehensive review of enhancing learning experiences. *International Journal of Applied Research in Social Sciences*, *6*(4), 589–607. DOI: 10.51594/ijarss.v6i4.1011

Rapaka, A., Dharmadhikari, S. C., Kasat, K., Mohan, C. R., Chouhan, K., & Gupta, M. (2025). Revolutionizing learning– A journey into educational games with immersive and AI technologies. *Entertainment Computing*, *52*, 100809. DOI: 10.1016/j.entcom.2024.100809

Sahin, A., Imamoglu, G., Murat, M., & Ayyildiz, E. (2024). A holistic decision-making approach to assessing service quality in higher education institutions. *Socio-Economic Planning Sciences*, *92*, 101812. DOI: 10.1016/j.seps.2024.101812

Slimani, N., & Jabal, K. (2023). Language Learning Platforms: Connecting the Dots around Rosetta Stone Platform. *European Journal of Education Studies*, *10*(7), 101–111.

Subhaktiyasa, P. G. (2024). PLS-SEM for multivariate analysis: A practical guide to educational research using SmartPLS. EduLine. *Journal of Education and Learning Innovation*, *4*(3), 353–365.

Sun, L., Asmawi, A., Dong, H., & Zhang, X. (2024). Empowering Chinese undergraduates' business English writing: Unveiling the efficacy of DingTalk-Aided Problem-based language learning during Covid-19 period. *Education and Information Technologies*, *29*(1), 239–271. DOI: 10.1007/s10639-023-12288-1

Tahir, A., & Tahir, A. (2023, June). AI-driven Advancements in ESL Learner Autonomy: Investigating Student Attitudes Towards Virtual Assistant Usability. In *Linguistic Forum-. Journal of Linguistics*, *5*(2), 50–56.

Tajik, A. (2025). Exploring the role of AI-driven dynamic writing platforms in improving EFL learners' writing skills and fostering their motivation.

Tamilmani, K., Rana, N. P., Wamba, S. F., & Dwivedi, R. (2021). The extended Unified Theory of Acceptance and Use of Technology (UTAUT2): A systematic literature review and theory evaluation. *International Journal of Information Management*, *57*, 102269. DOI: 10.1016/j.ijinfomgt.2020.102269

Tang, X., Yuan, Z., & Qu, S. (2025). Factors Influencing University Students' Behavioural Intention to Use Generative Artificial Intelligence for Educational Purposes Based on a Revised UTAUT2 Model. *Journal of Computer Assisted Learning*, *41*(1), e13105. DOI: 10.1111/jcal.13105

Viglia, G., Zaefarian, G., & Ulqinaku, A. (2021). How to design good experiments in marketing: Types, examples, and methods. *Industrial Marketing Management*, *98*, 193–206. DOI: 10.1016/j.indmarman.2021.08.007

Yu, H., Guo, Y., Yang, H., Zhang, W., & Dong, Y. (2025). Can ChatGPT Revolutionize Language Learning? Unveiling the Power of AI in Multilingual Education Through User Insights and Pedagogical Impact. *European Journal of Education*, *60*(1), e12749. DOI: 10.1111/ejed.12749

Zong, Y., & Yang, L. (2025). How AI-Enhanced Social–Emotional Learning Framework Transforms EFL Students' Engagement and Emotional Well-Being. *European Journal of Education*, *60*(1), e12925. DOI: 10.1111/ejed.12925

## ADDITIONAL READING

Allen, B., Agarwal, S., Kalpathy-Cramer, J., & Dreyer, K. (2019). Democratizing ai. *Journal of the American College of Radiology*, *16*(7), 961–963. DOI: 10.1016/j.jacr.2019.04.023 PMID: 31272590

Edwards, B. I. (2025). Democratising AI Education: The Open-Source Movement and Digital Platforms. In *A Practical Guide to Artificial Intelligence in Higher Education: Innovation and Applications* (pp. 129-139). Cham: Springer Nature Switzerland. https://doi.org/DOI: 10.1007/978-3-031-56848-0_14

Kucirkova, N., & Leaton Gray, S. (2023). Beyond personalization: Embracing democratic learning within artificially intelligent systems. *Educational Theory*, *73*(4), 469–489. DOI: 10.1111/edth.12590

Wieczorek, M. (2025). Why AI will not democratize education: A critical pragmatist perspective. *Philosophy & Technology*, *38*(2), 53. DOI: 10.1007/s13347-025-00883-8

# Chapter 7 Democratizing Personalized Learning Through Mentorship Reform in Private Higher Education

**Raed Awashreh**
https://orcid.org/0000-0002-2252-0299
*United Arab Emirates University, UAE*

**Almi Hassiba**
https://orcid.org/0009-0001-7560-754X
*Badji Mokhtar - Annaba University, Algeria*

## ABSTRACT

*This chapter explores the integration of Artificial Intelligence (AI) in faculty-faculty mentorship within higher education, emphasizing its potential to enhance mentorship quality, promote equity, and streamline administrative processes. AI tools, such as automated scheduling and sentiment analysis, offer solutions to long-standing issues such as administrative burdens, power imbalances, and implicit biases in mentorship relationships. The chapter discusses how AI can foster more inclusive and equitable mentorship environments, particularly in hierarchical academic settings. Despite these promising advancements, challenges such as algorithmic bias, ethical concerns, and institutional resistance are critically examined. The chapter concludes by emphasizing the importance of a phased, culturally responsive implementation strategy and the need for ongoing evaluation. Future research directions*

DOI: 10.4018/979-8-3373-2302-2.ch007

*are proposed, focusing on longitudinal studies, cross-cultural comparisons, and faculty attitudes toward AI adoption to ensure sustainable, ethical integration in mentorship programs.*

## INTRODUCTION

In recent years, Artificial Intelligence (AI) has emerged as a transformative force across numerous sectors, offering innovative solutions to long-standing challenges. In the realm of education—particularly within private higher education institutions—AI is reshaping how learning is delivered, accessed, and personalized. As these institutions confront the dual imperatives of technological innovation and educational reform, AI presents a powerful opportunity to not only enhance learning outcomes but also to democratize education by addressing systemic inequities and inefficiencies (Qudus, 2024).

One of the most promising yet underexplored areas where AI can have transformative impact is faculty mentorship. Traditionally characterized by informal guidance, one-on-one relationships, and limited structural support, mentorship has long played a pivotal role in shaping students' academic, professional, and personal trajectories. In private higher education, where institutional pressures and performance metrics can constrain meaningful engagement, mentorship often suffers from administrative burdens, inconsistent participation, and opaque power dynamics. These challenges limit the effectiveness of mentoring systems and undermine efforts to provide equitable, personalized support to all learners (Awashreh, 2024).

This chapter contributes to the growing discourse on democratizing education with AI by focusing on how intelligent technologies can be harnessed to reform mentorship practices in private higher education. It explores how AI can support more equitable, efficient, and inclusive mentorship systems—systems that move beyond traditional models and align with the principles of personalized learning and critical educational reform.

Faculty mentorship in its conventional form tends to emphasize academic guidance, social integration, and skills development. However, these models often fall short of addressing deeper structural and cultural inequities that influence who receive mentorship, how often, and to what degree of effectiveness (Andersen & West, 2020). These shortcomings are especially pronounced in private institutions, where mentorship practices may vary widely and often lack institutional oversight or standardized support. Without frameworks that critically engage with questions of access, power, and representation, mentorship can inadvertently reinforce existing disparities (Stoller, 2021).

Critical mentoring offers a powerful corrective to these limitations. As a model grounded in equity, critical consciousness, and dialogical practice, it encourages mentors and mentees to question, challenge, and ultimately transform the socio-institutional forces shaping their educational environments (Montgomery & Wilson, 2025). It repositions mentorship as a collaborative and transformative process rather than a unidirectional transfer of knowledge or status (Stoller, 2021). When integrated with AI technologies, critical mentoring can be scaled, structured, and adapted to diverse institutional contexts—particularly in private higher education settings seeking innovation and inclusivity.

AI can significantly enhance the mentorship experience by automating administrative tasks such as scheduling, tracking progress, and managing communication. This allows mentors to devote more time to meaningful interpersonal interactions. Furthermore, AI-powered tools can analyze communication patterns and provide insights into engagement quality, helping institutions design interventions that address disparities in mentoring access and experience. When developed and applied ethically, AI can even identify latent biases or systemic imbalances, enabling private institutions to foster more inclusive academic relationships (Igbokwe, 2023).

This chapter aims to investigate how artificial intelligence can be strategically integrated into faculty mentorship systems within private higher education to support democratized, equitable, and personalized learning. It examines the transformative potential of AI in:

- Alleviating the administrative and cognitive burdens of faculty mentorship.
- Enhancing the quality, frequency, and equity of mentor-mentee interactions.
- Creating scalable frameworks for inclusive mentorship rooted in critical mentoring theory.

## Research Question

How can artificial intelligence be integrated into faculty mentorship practices in private higher education to promote more efficient, equitable, and personalized academic relationships?

By addressing this question, the chapter situates AI-enabled mentorship within the broader goals of educational democratization, with particular attention to the context and constraints of private institutions.

This chapter opens with the main themes, objectives, and research questions that frame the role of AI in faculty mentorship within private higher education. It then establishes the theoretical foundation, drawing on critical mentoring and personalized learning to explore how AI can support equitable, trust-based mentoring. A literature review follows, examining AI's emerging influence on educational and mentorship reform. The methodology section outlines the research design used to assess AI's impact on mentorship practices. The findings highlight both the benefits—such as improved efficiency and engagement—and limitations, including bias and privacy concerns. These are discussed in light of broader goals around equity and personalized learning. The chapter concludes with practical, culturally responsive recommendations for implementing AI to enhance mentorship quality and institutional equity.

In bridging AI's technical capabilities with critical mentorship theory, this chapter offers a vision for reforming mentorship as a key pillar in the democratization of education. By focusing on the private higher education sector—where innovation often coexists with structural inequality—it provides a roadmap for institutions to build mentorship systems that are not only technologically advanced but also socially responsive and inclusive.

## THEORETICAL FRAMEWORK

This chapter's theoretical framework centers on two interconnected themes: (1) the transformative potential of Artificial Intelligence (AI) in faculty mentorship, and (2) its role in promoting equitable, personalized learning within private higher education. Framed by the discourses of critical mentoring and educational democratization, these themes offer a lens to evaluate how AI can foster inclusion, reduce structural barriers, and personalize mentorship in diverse academic environments.

### AI's Transformative Potential in Faculty Mentorship

AI presents a significant opportunity to reconfigure traditional faculty mentorship by alleviating long-standing challenges such as administrative inefficiencies, communication inconsistencies, and hierarchical imbalances. In many private higher education institutions, mentorship often remains informal and unevenly distributed due to limited policies and resources (Choudhary, 2024).

AI tools—such as automated scheduling systems, interaction tracking, and real-time documentation—allow faculty to shift focus from logistical tasks to meaningful developmental engagement (Barnes & Hutson, 2024). Moreover, advanced AI-driven features like sentiment analysis, predictive feedback, and real-time translation can enrich communication, especially in multicultural and multilingual settings (George & Wooden, 2023). Crucially, AI can be used to identify and correct imbalances in mentor-mentee dynamics, reinforcing principles of critical mentoring such as socio-cultural awareness, reflexivity, and mutual accountability.

## AI as a Catalyst for Equitable and Personalized Mentorship

Beyond improving efficiency, AI enables scalable and personalized mentorship models that respond to individual needs, learning styles, and institutional challenges—core principles of democratized education (Assefa, 2024). AI systems can monitor mentorship engagement, detect disparities in access or quality, and generate tailored interventions that enhance inclusion and accountability. For instance, data analytics can reveal how faculty workload and incentive structures impact mentoring outcomes, helping institutions align academic development with financial priorities (Seo et al., 2021).

The successful integration of AI into mentorship depends on thoughtful, context-sensitive implementation. This includes customizing tools for institutional needs, training faculty in ethical AI use, and establishing continuous feedback loops to ensure AI tools enhance rather than replace human relationships (UNESCO, 2019).

When implemented through the lens of critical mentoring, AI becomes not merely a technical solution but a strategic instrument for fostering efficiency, equity, and personalization—the foundation of a truly democratized educational ecosystem. This chapter's theoretical model (Figure 1) reflects this dual emphasis on technological innovation and institutional transformation (Sposato, 2025).

*Figure 1. Study framework (Author, 2025)*

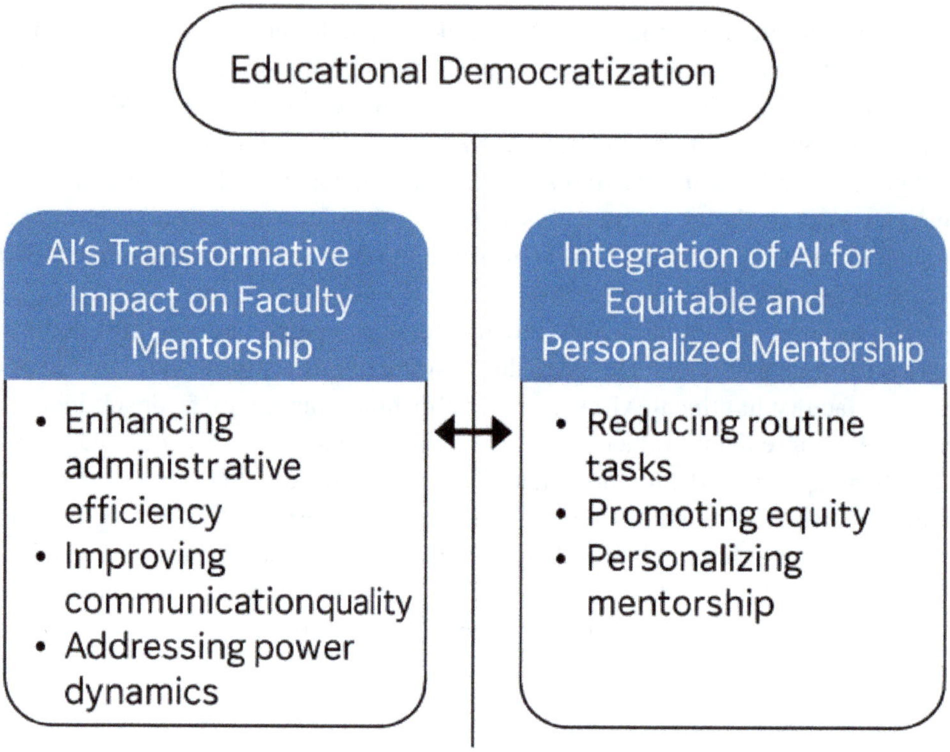


## LITERATURE REVIEW

The integration of Artificial Intelligence (AI) into higher education is reshaping mentorship practices by addressing persistent challenges and expanding possibilities for personalized, equitable academic relationships. Traditionally grounded in interpersonal dynamics and informal structures, faculty mentorship in private higher education has often lacked consistency, transparency, and inclusiveness. This review synthesizes current scholarship on how AI can transform mentorship by streamlining administrative tasks, enhancing communication, mitigating power imbalances, and countering commercialization pressures—particularly within emerging education systems like Oman. Furthermore, the discussion aligns with this chapter's theoretical framework, reflecting AI's dual role as a technical solution and a driver of institutional reform.

To begin with, one of the most pressing challenges in mentorship is administrative inefficiency. Faculty mentorship has long been hindered by time-consuming administrative responsibilities. Routine tasks—such as scheduling meetings, documenting progress, and managing communications—consume valuable faculty time and reduce mentoring quality (Cavanaugh, Barbour, & Clark, 2017). In this context, AI-enabled tools offer scalable responses to these issues. Matsuoka and Sakurai (2022) highlight AI systems that automate logistics, while Baker, Ferris, and Williams (2021) demonstrate how AI can track mentee progress and send timely prompts, ensuring structured and consistent mentorship. Consequently, these innovations not only enhance efficiency but also contribute to democratizing education by ensuring more equitable access to mentoring resources. AI systems can tailor mentoring pathways to individual needs, supporting the personalization of learning regardless of a mentee's background or network (Awashreh, 2025).

Moreover, beyond administrative streamlining, AI significantly enhances communication and inclusivity within mentoring relationships. Communication is central to effective mentorship, but disparities in expression, implicit bias, and language barriers can hinder relationship quality. AI tools using natural language processing and sentiment analysis can analyze mentor-mentee exchanges, offering real-time insights that help mentors adjust tone, content, and style to improve clarity and empathy (Kizilcec et al., 2018). Additionally, translation and transcription features further support accessibility in linguistically diverse academic environments (Cheng et al., 2022). These features foster more inclusive and responsive mentorship, ensuring that communication styles do not marginalize underrepresented groups. In doing so, AI aligns with the principles of equity and personalized learning (Awashreh, 2023).

In parallel, AI can also play a pivotal role in addressing traditional power imbalances embedded within mentoring systems. Traditional mentoring often reflects institutional hierarchies and social norms that reproduce inequities. Lee and Williams (2019b) observe that these dynamics can silence dissent and disadvantage vulnerable mentees. To address this, AI offers impartial tools for detecting and addressing such imbalances. For example, platforms can analyze response patterns, interaction frequency, and language use to identify asymmetries, flagging issues and recommending corrective actions (Lee & Williams, 2019a). These functions align closely with critical mentoring values that prioritize reflexivity, accountability, and power-sharing (Awashreh & Al Ghunaimi, 2025), thereby encouraging more just and equitable academic relationships.

Nevertheless, the role of AI in mentorship cannot be understood in isolation from the broader commercialization of higher education. The influence of market-driven priorities is particularly evident in private institutions. Ismail and Al Shanfari (2014) note that many institutions now prioritize financial outcomes, such as student satisfaction and retention, over academic rigor. This shift has repositioned mentorship as a branding tool rather than a developmental practice. As Lunsford et al. (2017) caution, such trends can result in grade inflation, weakened academic standards, and reduced degree value. Therefore, if AI tools are deployed without clear educational objectives, they risk reinforcing these tendencies—becoming instruments of efficiency rather than equity (Benouachane, 2024). Faculty may consequently feel pressured to compromise mentoring integrity in favor of administrative convenience.

Closely related to commercialization are the informal institutional cultures that shape mentorship practices in private higher education. In many private institutions, mentorship remains informal, shaped by internal norms that often lack clarity or consistency. Gehreke et al. (2024) highlight how these environments may prioritize satisfaction over standards, pressuring faculty to lower expectations. This can create ethical dilemmas and diminish motivation. Likewise, Çelik and Razı (2023) observe that faculty often face conflicts between institutional demands and personal academic values. In response, AI can help formalize mentorship through transparent systems, offering structure and accountability. However, it is critical that these benefits depend on ethical implementation grounded in academic integrity and policy alignment (Awashreh & Ramachandran, 2025).

Equally important is the effect of mentorship quality on student outcomes. The erosion of mentorship quality due to commercialization has lasting effects. Guhan et al. (2020) report correlations between diminished mentorship and declining student outcomes, including reduced critical thinking and poor career preparedness. When mentorship is used to advance institutional metrics rather than student development, learners receive inadequate support and limited professional readiness. This undermines educational equity and widens opportunity gaps (Gandhi & Johnson, 2016). Conversely, when applied responsibly, AI can reinforce mentorship quality by enabling transparent, data-informed, and personalized engagement (Raza et al., 2025).

In light of these dynamics, ethical AI deployment offers a pathway to rebalancing institutional priorities with educational values. AI can help restore academic integrity by balancing efficiency with rigor. Birks and Clare (2023) argue that AI systems—if guided by ethical standards—can automate logistics while preserving mentorship quality through regular monitoring. Transparent implementation and institutional oversight are essential to ensuring that AI supports faculty development rather than replacing it. Nyunt et al. (2024) emphasize the need for infrastructure, training, and governance to ensure AI tools serve pedagogical—not commercial—goals. Thus, ethical integration becomes a key pillar in ensuring that AI tools promote sustainable mentorship practices.

Finally, these challenges and opportunities are especially salient in the context of Oman. In Oman, mentorship practices are often rooted in informal, peer-based academic advising. While these relationships foster collegiality, they also risk perpetuating opaque institutional norms (Awashreh, 2024). AI offers potential to systematize and enhance mentorship through resource recommendations, communication plans, and development tracking (Akinwalere & Ivanov, 2022). However, implementation faces significant hurdles. The dominance of privatized models creates friction between economic goals and educational values. Sawahel (2024) stresses the need for culturally attuned AI applications that align with national education strategies. Therefore, investment in digital infrastructure, ethical frameworks, and faculty training is essential for effective and context-sensitive AI adoption (Chisom et al., 2024), ensuring that the transformative potential of AI in mentorship is fully realized in ways that are equitable, transparent, and contextually relevant.

## METHODOLOGY

This study adopts a qualitative research design centered on secondary data analysis to investigate how higher education institutions are embedding Artificial Intelligence (AI) into faculty mentorship. The aim is to explore the transformative potential of AI in addressing long-standing challenges in mentorship—specifically, administrative inefficiencies, communication quality, and power imbalances—while contextualizing these transformations within broader institutional and cultural dynamics.

### Research Design and Data Sources

The research primarily draws upon secondary data from peer-reviewed academic journals, institutional case studies, government reports, and technical documentation related to AI applications in higher education. This approach enables the examination of pre-existing evidence from a diverse range of educational contexts and supports a comparative analysis of how AI-driven mentorship systems function across. The analysis particularly emphasizes cases where AI systems have been implemented to support faculty mentoring, professional development, and academic advising.

### Analytical Framework

A thematic synthesis approach is used to analyze the secondary data, guided by three interrelated analytical dimensions:

- Administrative Automation: Examining how AI streamlines repetitive tasks (e.g., scheduling, documentation, progress monitoring), thereby allowing mentors to focus on developmental support.

- Interaction Quality: Investigating the impact of AI on communication dynamics through tools like sentiment analysis, real-time translation, and predictive feedback mechanisms.
- Power Dynamics: Exploring the extent to which AI supports equitable mentorship by detecting patterns of bias or imbalance in mentor-mentee relationships.

These themes are directly drawn from the theoretical framework developed in this chapter, which conceptualizes AI not just as a technical intervention but as a driver of institutional change aligned with educational democratization.

### Data Analysis Procedure

The study follows a three-step procedure for synthesizing secondary data:

- Identification of relevant literature and case materials using targeted search terms across academic databases: google scholar, research gates;
- Categorization of findings based on the thematic dimensions noted above;
- Interpretation of results in light of the theoretical framework, with particular attention to how AI adoption in mentorship reflects or challenges institutional priorities such as equity, accountability, and academic integrity.

### Scope and Limitations

The reliance on secondary data allows for a broad exploration of existing practices without the need for primary data collection. However, this methodology limits the depth of contextual understanding that direct interviews or ethnographic studies might provide. Moreover, the diversity in AI implementation contexts may limit the generalizability of some findings. To mitigate these limitations, the study prioritizes high-quality sources that provide robust, empirical insights and triangulates findings across multiple institutional cases.

## USGES AND BENEFITS PF UISNG AI

Integrating Artificial Intelligence into faculty-faculty mentorship in higher education represents a revolutionary shift toward optimizing mentoring practices, addressing systemic issues, and mitigating power dynamics. This section explores how AI can enhance faculty mentorship through various methods, applications, and strategies to reduce power imbalances and foster a more equitable academic environment (Tsou, 2023).

## Uses and Benefits of Integrating AI in Faculty Mentorship

The integration of Artificial Intelligence (AI) into faculty mentorship represents a transformative shift in the structure and delivery of academic support within higher education institutions. This shift is not merely technological but deeply systemic—addressing entrenched challenges such as administrative overload, ineffective communication, and hierarchical imbalances. In alignment with the study's objectives and theoretical framework, this section explores how AI can be strategically utilized to improve mentorship practices, reduce institutional inequities, and enhance faculty development while maintaining academic integrity and educational quality (Tsou, 2023).

## AI-Powered Administrative Efficiency

Administrative tasks, though essential, often detract from the core purpose of mentorship—developing academic capacity, fostering collaboration, and nurturing career growth. AI-driven tools are now capable of significantly reducing the administrative burden traditionally associated with mentoring programs (Choudhary et al., 2024). Matsuoka and Sakurai (2022) describe AI-based scheduling systems that integrate with institutional calendars to identify mutually convenient meeting times, send reminders, and dynamically adapt to real-time changes. These systems free mentors from the routine labor of coordination, allowing them to dedicate more time to intellectual and developmental engagement.

AI also improves the quality of documentation and progress tracking. According to Nieto-Rodriguez and Vargas (2023), AI-enabled platforms can monitor mentee progress across various dimensions—meeting frequency, goal attainment, and responsiveness to feedback—generating automated reports and alerts that ensure mentoring goals remain on track. These systems synthesize data from meeting notes, emails, and reports, offering mentors concise summaries and action items without requiring manual compilation. As Goraga (2024) notes, such automation transforms documentation from a bureaucratic obligation into a functional tool for meaningful mentorship planning.

## Enhancing Quality of Interaction through Data-Driven Insights

Beyond logistics, AI enhances the interpersonal quality of mentorship by delivering insights into mentor-mentee communication patterns. Tools based on Natural

Language Processing (NLP) and Sentiment Analysis can evaluate how feedback is conveyed and received, identify gaps in understanding, and assess the emotional tone of interactions (Montgomery, 2017). This analysis helps mentors tailor their communication strategies to be more empathetic, supportive, and effective.

Furthermore, AI-powered transcription and translation services are vital in multilingual academic environments. By offering real-time translations and accurate transcripts, these technologies promote inclusivity and accessibility, particularly for faculty working in international or linguistically diverse settings (Tariq, 2024). As highlighted by UNESCO (2023), such capabilities enhance faculty collaboration across borders and disciplines, supporting the formation of globally connected academic communities.

## Addressing Power Dynamics and Promoting Equity

A core dimension of this study is the mitigation of power asymmetries in faculty mentorship, particularly those exacerbated by informal institutional cultures and commercialization trends. AI can play a pivotal role here by providing objective feedback mechanisms that reveal potential inequities in mentor-mentee interactions. For instance, AI tools can detect disparities in speaking time, response patterns, or access to opportunities, alerting administrators or mentors to implicit bias or structural exclusion (Tsou, 2023).

Moreover, by anonymizing and aggregating communication data, AI can offer insights without compromising individual privacy, thereby facilitating ethical interventions to promote equity. This aligns with the theoretical framework's focus on AI as a tool for rebalancing authority structures and reinforcing professional development standards in higher education mentorship models (Awashreh, 2024 b).

## Institutional Integration Strategies

Effectively leveraging AI in faculty mentorship requires a clear, strategic roadmap aligned with institutional goals and mentorship challenges. Institutions must begin by conducting thorough needs assessments to identify mentorship gaps, such as inefficient administration, inconsistent feedback, or unequal access to resources. Based on these diagnostics, AI tools can be selected and customized in collaboration with developers, ensuring seamless integration with existing learning management systems and faculty development programs (Bagai & Mane, 2023). Such integration must also consider the institutional context, particularly in regions like Oman, where mentorship practices are often informal and shaped by hierarchical academic cultures. Tailoring AI systems to local pedagogical values and faculty expectations is essential for meaningful adoption.

## Training and Support for Faculty

For AI tools to be effectively implemented, faculty must be trained not only in their technical usage but also in their pedagogical implications. Baule and O'Connell (2025) emphasize the importance of capacity building through workshops, peer-led training sessions, and digital literacy courses focused on interpreting AI-generated insights and integrating them into daily mentoring practices.

Professional development initiatives should also address concerns about algorithmic bias, data privacy, and the potential depersonalization of mentorship. Supporting faculty in understanding both the capabilities and limitations of AI fosters a culture of ethical and reflective technology use.

## Continuous Evaluation and Refinement

To ensure that AI applications remain aligned with educational goals, institutions must establish systems for ongoing assessment. As Ghamrawi et al. (2023) argue, feedback loops involving faculty, mentees, and administrative stakeholders are essential for refining AI tools, updating mentorship protocols, and responding to evolving institutional needs.

Periodic evaluations should include qualitative assessments of mentorship quality, equity audits to track changes in access and representation, and longitudinal studies to examine the long-term impacts of AI integration on faculty performance and student outcomes.

## Balancing Innovation with Institutional Integrity

While AI holds the potential to enhance mentorship quality and efficiency, it must be implemented thoughtfully to prevent the erosion of academic standards, especially in privatized higher education systems. The increasing commercialization of universities, particularly in contexts like Oman, raises concerns about profit-driven mentoring practices that may prioritize student satisfaction over genuine learning outcomes (Nedungadi, Tang & Raman, 2024).

AI can help counterbalance these trends by introducing accountability and transparency into mentorship processes. However, institutions must ensure that AI is used as a complement—not a substitute—for human judgment, academic values, and relational trust. As Saaida (2023) asserts, the full promise of AI in higher education will only be realized when its adoption is guided by ethical principles and aligned with long-term educational objectives. Table 1 presents a roadmap for implementing AI in faculty mentorship.

*Table 1. Roadmap for implementing AI in faculty mentorship*

| **1. Needs Assessment** | **- Identify key challenges in mentorship (e.g., administrative inefficiencies, power dynamics).** | **- Engage stakeholders (mentors, mentees, administrators) to define needs and priorities.** |
|---|---|---|
| **2. Technology Selection** | - Evaluate and select AI tools based on identified needs. | - Consider features like scheduling automation, sentiment analysis, and power dynamics detection. |
| **3. Customization** | - Collaborate with AI developers to tailor tools to institutional contexts. | - Ensure compatibility with existing mentorship frameworks and practices. |
| **4. Training and Support** | - Provide comprehensive training for faculty on AI tool usage. | - Include sessions on data interpretation, ethical concerns, and AI limitations. |
| **5. Pilot Testing** | - Conduct a small-scale implementation to assess feasibility. | - Gather feedback from participants to refine AI integration. |
| **6. Full Implementation** | - Scale up AI adoption across the institution. | - Ensure seamless integration with ongoing mentorship programs. |
| **7. Continuous Evaluation** | - Monitor AI performance and impact on mentorship practices. | - Use metrics like mentee satisfaction, mentor engagement, and equity improvements. |
| **8. Iterative Refinement** | - Update AI tools and strategies based on feedback and technological advancements. | - Address emerging challenges and optimize tool usage. |

## Benefits

Faculty mentorship in higher education has long been a cornerstone of academic growth, fostering professional and personal development among faculty members. Traditionally built on trust, respect, and knowledge sharing, these relationships are increasingly challenged by administrative burdens and complex power dynamics. The growing need for creative solutions to enhance effectiveness and equity in mentorship programs underscores the transformative potential of artificial intelligence (AI) (Aithal & Aithal, 2023). AI emerges as a game-changing tool that bridges these gaps, particularly by reducing the manipulation of power dynamics that can undermine the mentoring process.

## AI and Administrative Efficiency

Administrative burdens, such as scheduling, tracking, and managing documents, are among the critical challenges in faculty mentorship (Adiguzel et al., 2023). These tasks often detract from the quality of mentor-mentee interactions. As Cavanaugh, Barbour, and Clark (2017) highlight, administrative loads can significantly reduce the time available for meaningful engagement. AI technologies alleviate these burdens by automating repetitive tasks, enabling faculty to focus on value-added mentoring activities. For instance, AI-powered scheduling tools autonomously arrange meetings, resolve calendar conflicts, and send reminders, saving faculty time and ensuring logistical tasks are handled seamlessly (Cavanaugh, Barbour & Clark, 2017).

AI also supports mentorship by tracking key metrics, such as meeting frequency, goal achievement, and feedback trends. These tools help mentors identify patterns that may hinder progress and address them proactively to ensure mentorship objectives are met. By reducing administrative concerns, AI allows mentorship interactions to remain centered on professional growth and meaningful engagement (Mubuuke et al., 2021).

## AI for Equitable Mentorship

In addition to administrative efficiency, AI contributes to fostering equitable academic environments by addressing power imbalances in mentorship. AI tools analyze interactions and provide insights into communication dynamics, enabling mentors to refine their approaches and ensure fairness. By detecting and addressing hierarchical imbalances, AI creates a mentorship environment that prioritizes equity and inclusivity. This transformative potential of AI positions higher education institutions to enhance faculty mentorship while supporting professional development and fostering a collaborative academic culture (Galdames, 2024).

## Quality of Interaction Improved Through Data Analysis

In addition to administrative efficiency, AI has the potential to significantly enhance the quality of mentorship interactions. AI-powered analytics provide critical insights into the communication patterns between mentors and mentees, enabling more informed and effective engagement. As Kizilcec and Cohen (2018) highlight, AI tools can analyze communication data to identify trends and generate recommendations for improving mentoring practices. For instance, AI can evaluate the frequency, tone, and content of feedback, helping mentors tailor their approach to better meet the unique needs of their mentees.

The scope of AI applications extends to engagement and sentiment analysis, both of which can enrich mentorship interactions. Sentiment analysis, for example, allows AI to assess the emotional tone of communications, providing mentors with actionable feedback on how their messages are perceived. This enables mentors to refine their communication strategies, fostering more constructive and supportive interactions. By creating a positive and productive mentoring environment, AI helps strengthen the mentor-mentee relationship (Taherdoost & Madanchian, 2023).

Furthermore, AI platforms offering real-time language translation and transcription are particularly valuable in multicultural academic environments. As

Cheng, Zhao, and Li (2022) suggest, these tools can overcome language barriers, facilitating seamless communication in diverse institutions. By ensuring inclusivity and improving understanding, AI promotes equitable access to effective mentorship across linguistic and cultural boundaries.

## Addressing Power Dynamics with AI

Power dynamics often influence the openness and effectiveness of mentorship relationships, with power imbalances potentially creating barriers to constructive engagement. Lee and Williams (2019b) emphasize that addressing these imbalances is essential to fostering equity in mentoring environments. AI offers promising solutions by providing tools to analyze and monitor interactions for signs of power disparities. For instance, AI systems can analyze linguistic and discursive patterns in communications to detect imbalances that might hinder mentees from fully benefiting from mentorship relationships (Dwivedi et al., 2023).

Additionally, AI can play a pivotal role in addressing challenges faced by underrepresented groups in academia. Atenas, Nerantzi, and Bussu (2023) argue that AI can track and monitor mentoring outcomes across different demographic groups, enabling institutions to identify deficiencies and implement targeted interventions to promote equity. By visualizing data on mentoring experiences, AI empowers institutions to pinpoint areas requiring improvement and take measures to enhance inclusion and support for all faculty members.

## Balancing Financial and Academic Goals

In the era of commercialization of higher education, mentorship practices are often influenced by financial priorities, sometimes at the expense of academic quality. AI offers solutions to reconcile financial sustainability with academic integrity, ensuring that mentorship remains focused on educational excellence. For example, AI-driven analytics can monitor the influence of financial incentives on mentoring practices, ensuring that educational standards are maintained (Chan & Colloton, 2024).

Integrating AI into mentorship programs allows institutions to establish systems of checks and balances that address commercial interests while preserving the integrity of mentorship relationships. As Abulibdeh et al. (2024) illustrate, this dual focus on financial and academic goals promotes a balance that safeguards educational quality and supports mentorship practices that prioritize faculty development. By leveraging AI's capabilities, higher education institutions can create mentorship programs that align with both financial and academic objectives, fostering a culture of integrity and excellence. Table 2 summarizes the benefit and challenges of AI tools in faculty mentorship

*Table 2. Benefits and challenges of AI tools in faculty mentorship*

| Aspect | Benefits | Challenges |
|---|---|---|
| Administrative Tasks | - Automates scheduling and tracking (Matsuoka & Sakurai, 2022).<br>- Reduces manual workload, enabling focus on meaningful engagement (Baker et al., 2021). | - Risk of over-reliance, reducing personal interaction.<br>- Data privacy concerns in tracking activities. |
| Quality of Interactions | - Offers data-driven insights for communication improvement (Kizilcec et al., 2018).<br>- Sentiment analysis refines mentor responses (Taherdoost & Madanchian, 2023).<br>- Real-time translation/transcription enhances inclusivity (Cheng et al., 2022). | - Accuracy depends on diverse, high-quality input data.<br>- Requires faculty training for effective use. |
| Power Dynamics | - Detects imbalances via linguistic pattern analysis (Lee & Williams, 2019).<br>- Promotes equity by identifying disparities across groups (Atenas et al., 2023). | - Potential bias in AI algorithms, especially affecting underrepresented groups. |
| Institutional Alignment | - Supports balance between academic quality and financial goals (Kwan et al., 2015).<br>- Enables evidence-based decision-making for program design. | - Integration challenges with diverse institutional contexts.<br>- Resistance to change in academic culture. |

## DISCUSSION

The integration of Artificial Intelligence (AI) into faculty-faculty mentorship represents a paradigm shift in higher education, offering far-reaching implications for mentorship practices, institutional equity, and academic culture. This discussion synthesizes the study's key findings while critically reflecting on AI's transformative potential, inherent limitations, and the strategic considerations required for its successful implementation.

AI contributes meaningfully to reconfiguring mentorship by streamlining routine administrative processes such as scheduling, documentation, and progress tracking. These functions, as supported by Matsuoka and Sakurai (2022) and Baker et al. (2021), reduce logistical burdens and allow mentors to prioritize developmental dialogue, intellectual exchange, and career planning. This shift is particularly valuable in addressing the long-standing critique that mentorship in academia often becomes bureaucratized, detracting from the quality of relational engagement. As AI automates repetitive tasks, it repositions human interaction at the center of mentorship, enhancing depth and responsiveness.

Beyond operational efficiency, AI strengthens mentorship quality through data-driven personalization. Analytical tools such as sentiment analysis, communication tracking, and real-time transcription enhance mentors' ability to respond to mentee needs with precision and cultural sensitivity. As noted by Kizilcec et al. (2018) and Cheng et al. (2022), these technologies improve communication across linguistic and cultural boundaries, fostering inclusivity in increasingly diverse academic communities. In doing so, AI not only facilitates better mentorship interactions but also contributes to more equitable and adaptive support structures.

Equally important is AI's potential to address systemic inequities embedded within mentorship relationships. By detecting implicit biases, uncovering communication asymmetries, and monitoring access to mentorship across demographic groups, AI tools respond to longstanding concerns around exclusion and marginalization in academic development (Lee & Williams, 2019a; Atenas et al., 2023). In hierarchical academic cultures, such as those prevalent in Oman and the broader Arab region, this function is particularly valuable. AI provides a mechanism for standardizing feedback and evaluating resource distribution, thereby empowering underrepresented faculty and reducing the influence of informal power dynamics.

However, this transformative potential is not without tension. A primary concern is the risk of depersonalizing mentorship if AI tools are overly relied upon, reducing human relationships to algorithmic patterns and metrics. Issues of algorithmic bias, data privacy, and institutional resistance must also be navigated carefully (Taherdoost & Madanchian, 2023; Abulibdeh et al., 2024). Moreover, as commercial pressures increase within higher education—particularly in private institutions—there is a growing temptation to adopt AI for cost-efficiency rather than pedagogical improvement. If unregulated, such motives may compromise the educational integrity of mentorship programs. As Chan and Colloton (2024) argue, AI should serve as a complement rather than a substitute for human mentorship, supporting rather than supplanting the relational and empathetic dimensions of academic development.

To reconcile these opportunities and challenges, institutions must adopt a strategically phased approach to AI integration. This includes initiating pilot programs, conducting contextual needs assessments, and developing robust training modules that equip faculty with both technical proficiency and ethical literacy (Baule & O'Connell, 2025). Effective implementation also depends on continuous evaluation through both quantitative and qualitative measures, enabling iterative refinement of AI systems in alignment with evolving mentorship goals. As Igbokwe (2024) emphasizes, ongoing assessment ensures that technological tools remain accountable to academic values and institutional objectives.

Moreover, AI's ability to generate real-time insights into mentorship outcomes allows institutions to balance academic excellence with financial sustainability. By monitoring the influence of economic incentives on mentorship quality, AI ensures that mentorship remains rooted in developmental priorities, even under commercial pressures (Kwan et al., 2015). This balance is crucial for preserving institutional integrity in a competitive educational landscape.

In summary, the integration of AI into faculty mentorship holds significant promise for enhancing efficiency, promoting equity, and improving relational quality in higher education. When implemented thoughtfully—with ethical vigilance, cultural responsiveness, and a commitment to human-centered values—AI can serve as a strategic ally in reimagining mentorship for contemporary academic challenges. Rather than viewing AI as a mere technological fix, institutions must recognize it as a transformative catalyst that, when properly governed, can foster inclusive, accountable, and dynamic mentorship ecosystems.

## THEORETICAL CONTRIBUATION

This study advances the theoretical discourse on academic mentorship by positioning Artificial Intelligence (AI) as a transformative mediator in faculty-faculty developmental relationships. While traditional mentorship models emphasize human interaction, power dynamics, and informal knowledge transfer, this research extends existing frameworks by introducing AI as a third actor capable of reshaping these dynamics. Drawing from sociotechnical systems theory and equity-centered design, the study reconfigures mentorship not merely as a dyadic human relationship but as a digitally augmented ecosystem governed by transparency, data ethics, and inclusion.

Moreover, the study enriches mentorship theory through its intersection with critical data studies and organizational behavior. It introduces a conceptual lens in which AI does not merely operationalize mentorship but contributes epistemologically by revealing implicit biases, asymmetries in communication, and institutional patterns of exclusion. This reconceptualization lays a foundation for a hybrid mentorship model where human empathy and machine precision coalesce to enhance trust, equity, and performance in faculty development.

Finally, the research contributes to the under-theorized discourse on mentorship in non-Western academic contexts, particularly within the Arab region. By examining the potential of AI in culturally hierarchical systems, the study offers a nuanced perspective on how technology can both challenge and reinforce structural inequalities, providing a valuable theoretical framework for global comparative analyses.

## RECOMMENDATION

In light of the findings and implications, this study offers a series of actionable recommendations for higher education leaders, policymakers, and faculty development units to ensure the effective integration of AI in faculty mentorship. First, institutions should adopt a human-centered AI strategy with clearly defined use cases. This involves establishing specific guidelines on where AI applications are appropriate—such as in scheduling, progress tracking, and administrative tasks—while maintaining human interaction as central to areas like career guidance and emotional support. AI tools should be positioned as assistants to human mentors, enhancing rather than replacing the relational and developmental aspects of mentorship.

Second, it is essential to establish institutional AI ethics and governance frameworks. This can be achieved by forming dedicated AI ethics committees to oversee all mentorship-related implementations. These bodies should conduct regular audits focusing on data privacy, consent management, algorithmic fairness, and bias mitigation. Additionally, transparent accountability protocols must be developed with active participation from faculty and students to ensure trust and legitimacy in AI processes.

Third, institutions must implement structured faculty development programs that build capacity in both the technical and ethical dimensions of AI. These programs should include modular training on AI tools, interpreting data outputs, ethical best practices, and strategies for addressing algorithmic bias. Scenario-based workshops and simulations can enhance practical understanding, while ongoing support through helpdesks and peer mentoring can provide sustained guidance.

Fourth, to ensure scalability and effectiveness, institutions should launch phased pilot programs with measurable Key Performance Indicators (KPIs). Initial pilot implementations in selected departments should track metrics such as mentorship frequency, feedback quality, and mentee satisfaction. Findings from these pilots should inform iterative improvements before wider rollouts, with faculty and mentees actively involved in the co-design and evaluation processes.

Fifth, institutions need to localize AI solutions to align with cultural and institutional contexts. Collaborating with local developers can ensure AI systems reflect institutional values, linguistic diversity, and mentoring traditions. Moreover, integration efforts should be synchronized with national education policies and quality assurance standards. Prior to deployment, cultural sensitivity assessments are vital to avoid misalignment with local expectations.

Sixth, continuous monitoring and feedback loops should be established to support adaptive learning and improvement. Real-time dashboards can track mentorship engagement, equity indicators, and AI tool effectiveness. Regular feedback sessions with mentors and mentees, conducted bi-annually, can provide deeper qualitative insights. Agile revision cycles should be adopted to refine AI tools based on evolving needs and user feedback.

Finally, institutions must be proactive in anticipating and mitigating potential challenges. This includes developing contingency plans for technological disruptions, data breaches, or resistance from faculty. Fostering a culture of shared responsibility across IT teams, academic leadership, and faculty will be crucial in collaboratively addressing emerging issues. In parallel, ethical escalation pathways should be available to handle concerns related to AI-driven mentorship interactions responsibly and transparently.

## PRACTICAL IMPLICATIONS

The integration of Artificial Intelligence (AI) into faculty mentorship offers private higher education institutions significant opportunities to enhance efficiency, equity, and decision-making. However, these benefits must be balanced with careful planning and ethical safeguards. The following practical implications provide a clear roadmap for implementation.

First, AI can play a pivotal role in streamlining administrative efficiency. By automating routine tasks such as scheduling meetings, maintaining documentation, and managing follow-ups, AI-driven systems free up faculty time to concentrate on the more meaningful, relational aspects of mentoring. Seamless integration with existing Learning Management Systems (LMS) can further optimize workflow and ensure that administrative processes support rather than hinder mentorship activities.

Second, AI offers powerful tools for enhancing equity through data-driven insights. Institutions can leverage AI analytics to monitor mentorship participation across variables such as gender, academic discipline, and cultural background. These insights can guide the implementation of timely, targeted interventions to ensure that mentor-mentee relationships are inclusive and equitably distributed. Real-time feedback loops can help institutions detect disparities early and respond with precision.

Third, AI supports strengthening evidence-based institutional decision-making. AI-generated mentorship reports can provide valuable input for strategic planning in areas such as faculty promotions, resource allocation, and program development. By grounding these decisions in transparent, data-driven evidence, institutions can cultivate a more meritocratic academic environment and reinforce trust in leadership processes.

Fourth, for AI integration to succeed, institutions must invest in building faculty digital competency and ethical literacy. Professional development programs should include comprehensive training on AI tools and the ethical implications of their use. Encouraging collaboration between IT departments, academic affairs, and faculty development units can ensure sustained capacity building and foster a culture of shared digital responsibility.

Fifth, AI technologies can be leveraged to scale mentorship programs effectively. Institutions can use AI platforms to expand mentorship opportunities to include remote campuses, adjunct faculty, and underserved populations. Scalable and adaptable frameworks should be designed to maintain mentorship quality while accommodating institutional growth and diversification.

Finally, institutions must take a proactive approach to addressing potential limitations of AI in mentorship. Robust data governance policies must be implemented to protect privacy and ensure compliance with regulatory standards. Regular algorithm reviews—supported by external audits where appropriate—are essential for identifying and correcting bias or inaccuracies. Furthermore, it is crucial to foster open discussions about the limitations of AI, underscoring the irreplaceable role of human judgment, empathy, and ethical reasoning in effective mentorship.

## CONCLUSION

This chapter examined how Artificial Intelligence (AI) can transform faculty mentorship in higher education, particularly within private institutions. It highlighted AI's potential to reduce administrative burdens, improve communication quality, and promote equity through data-driven insights. When aligned with ethical frameworks and institutional priorities, AI can enhance mentorship systems that are both efficient and inclusive. However, the field remains emergent. Many AI applications are still in early development stages and lack robust, long-term validation. This chapter draws primarily on conceptual analysis and early evidence, which may limit the generalizability of findings, especially across diverse educational systems or technological landscapes. Additionally, the risk of technological determinism must be acknowledged. AI cannot substitute for the institutional culture, leadership commitment, and trust-building that effective mentorship requires. Issues such as data privacy, algorithmic bias, and surveillance concerns must be actively addressed to ensure AI remains a tool of empowerment rather than control.

Future research should pursue multi-layered, mixed-methods studies to assess AI's long-term impact on mentorship outcomes. Longitudinal research is needed to explore sustained effects on faculty development, mentee performance, and institutional equity. Comparative studies across cultural and national contexts will help identify adaptable, locally relevant practices.

Finally, understanding faculty attitudes toward AI—particularly trust, resistance, and digital literacy—will be essential for successful adoption. Interdisciplinary collaboration among educators, technologists, ethicists, and policymakers will be crucial in shaping AI tools that are not only effective but also aligned with academic values. As AI continues to evolve, institutions must remain agile, reflective, and ethically grounded in their pursuit of transformative mentorship systems.

## REFERENCES


Abulibdeh, A., Zaidan, E., & Abulibdeh, R. (2024). Navigating the confluence of artificial intelligence and education for sustainable development in the era of Industry 4.0: Challenges, opportunities, and ethical dimensions. *Journal of Cleaner Production, 437*, 140527. DOI: 10.1016/j.jclepro.2023.140527

Aithal, P. S., & Aithal, S. (2023). Optimizing the use of artificial intelligence-powered GPTs as teaching and research assistants by professors in higher education institutions: A study on smart utilization. *International Journal of Management, Technology, and Social Sciences*, 368–401. https://doi.org/DOI: 10.47992/IJMTS.2581.6012.0326

Akinwalere, S. N., & Ivanov, V. (2022). Artificial intelligence in higher education: Challenges and opportunities. *Border Crossing, 12*(1), 1–15. DOI: 10.33182/bc.v12i1.2015

Andersen, C. L., & West, R. E. (2020). Improving mentoring in higher education in undergraduate education and exploring implications for online learning. [RED]. *Revista de Educación a Distancia, 20*(64). Advance online publication. DOI: 10.6018/red.408671

Assefa, E. A. (2024, November). The double-edged sword of artificial intelligence (AI) in education: Maximizing benefits while mitigating risks. *The Journal of Quality in Education, 14*(24), 154–176. DOI: 10.37870/joqie.v14i24.450

Atenas, J., Nerantzi, C., & Bussu, A. (2023). A conceptual approach to transform and enhance academic mentorship: Through open educational practices. *Open Praxis, 15*(4), 271–287. DOI: 10.55982/openpraxis.15.4.595

Awashreh, R. (2023). Enhancing innovation among business colleges at Omani universities: A theoretical framework. *Seybold Report, 18*(2), 182–196. https://seyboldreport.com

Awashreh, R. (2024). Omani private universities: Debates between progress in human development but weak education quality. *International Journal of Educational Organization and Leadership, 32*(1), 1–15. DOI: 10.18848/2329-1656/CGP/v32i01/1-15

Awashreh, R. (2024b). Be aware: Navigating challenges in AI-driven higher education. *The International Journal of Interdisciplinary Educational Studies, 20*(1), 203–218. DOI: 10.18848/2327-011X/CGP/v20i01/203-218

Awashreh, R. (2025). Leadership strategies for managing change and fostering innovation over private higher education: Academic institutions in Oman. In *Evolving strategies for organizational management and performance evaluation* (pp. 399–422). IGI Global., DOI: 10.4018/979-8-3373-0149-5.ch018

Awashreh, R., & Al Ghunaimi, H. (2025). Bridging cultural gaps: Enhancing student motivation and academic integrity in Oman's universities. *Forum for Linguistic Studies*, *7*(2), 265–279. DOI: 10.30564/fls.v7i2.8300

Awashreh, R., & Ramachandran, B. (2025). A study on ethical implementation of AI in collegiate studies using fuzzy implication. *Pakistan Journal of Life and Social Sciences*, *23*(1), 3998–4013. DOI: 10.57239/PJLSS-2025-23.1.00317

Bagai, R., & Mane, V. (2023). Designing an AI-powered mentorship platform for professional development: Opportunities and challenges. *International Journal of Computer Trends and Technology*, *71*(4), 108–114. DOI: 10.14445/22312803/IJCTT-V71I4P114

Baker, M., Ferris, S., & Williams, R. (2021). AI in academic mentorship: Progress and challenges. [R. S.]. *Journal of Higher Education Research*, *45*(3), 233–247. DOI: 10.33182/bc.v12i1.2015

Barnes, E., & Hutson, J. (2024). Strategic integration of AI in higher education and industry: The AI8-point model. *Advances in Social Sciences and Management*, *2*(6), 39–52. DOI: 10.63002/assm.26.520

Baule, S. M., & O'Connell, J. S. (2025). Harnessing generative AI for educator professional development. In *Teachers' roles and perspectives on AI integration in schools* (pp. 38). https://doi.org/DOI: 10.4018/979-8-3373-1017-6.ch003

Benouachane, H. (2024). *AI in higher education: Balancing pedagogical benefits and ethical challenges*. DOI: 10.6084/m9.figshare.26349289

Birks, D., & Clare, J. (2023). Linking artificial intelligence facilitated academic misconduct to existing prevention frameworks. *International Journal for Educational Integrity*, *19*(1), 20. Advance online publication. DOI: 10.1007/s40979-023-00142-3

Cavanaugh, C., Barbour, M. K., & Clark, T. (2017). The Role of Technology in the Administrative Aspects of Faculty Mentorship. *Journal of Higher Education Management*, *32*(2), 45–60. DOI: 10.1201/9781003425779

Çelik, Ö., & Razı, S. (2023). Facilitators and barriers to creating a culture of academic integrity at secondary schools: An exploratory case study. *International Journal for Educational Integrity*, *19*(1), 4. Advance online publication. DOI: 10.1007/s40979-023-00125-4

Chan, C. K. Y., & Colloton, T. (2024). *Generative AI in higher education: The ChatGPT effect*. Routledge., DOI: 10.4324/9781003459026

Cheng, H., Zhao, W., & Li, T. (2022). Bridging Language Barriers in Academia: The Role of AI In Communication. *International Journal of Language and Communication, 14*(1), 45–60.

Cheng, L., Zhang, W., & Wang, X. (2022). Enhancing Multilingual Communication in Academia: The Role of AI Translation Tools. *International Journal of Learning Technology, 36*(1), 78–89.

Choudhary, P., Ali, I., Rehman, K., & Sharma, K. (2024). Enhancing mentorship through technology: A comprehensive review of current practices and future directions. *International Journal of Multidisciplinary Research and Growth Evaluation, 5*(6), 634–645.

Dwivedi, Y. K., Kshetri, N., Hughes, L., Slade, E. L., Jeyaraj, A., Kar, A. K., Baabdullah, A. M., Koohang, A., Raghavan, V., Ahuja, M., Albanna, H., Albashrawi, M. A., Al-Busaidi, A. S., Balakrishnan, J., Barlette, Y., Basu, S., Bose, I., Brooks, L., Buhalis, D., & Wright, R. (2023). "So what if ChatGPT wrote it?" Multidisciplinary perspectives on opportunities, challenges and implications of generative conversational AI for research, practice and policy. *International Journal of Information Management, 71*, 102642. DOI: 10.1016/j.ijinfomgt.2023.102642

Gandhi, M., & Johnson, M. (2016). Creating more effective mentors: Mentoring the mentor. *AIDS and Behavior, 20*(S2, Suppl 2), 294–303. DOI: 10.1007/s10461-016-1364-3 PMID: 27039092

George, B., & Wooden, O. (2023). Managing the strategic transformation of higher education through artificial intelligence. *Administrative Sciences, 13*(9), 196. DOI: 10.3390/admsci13090196

Ghamrawi, N., Shal, T., & Ghamrawi, N. A. (2023). Exploring the impact of AI on teacher leadership: Regressing or expanding? *Education and Information Technologies, 29*(7), 8415–8433. DOI: 10.1007/s10639-023-12174-w

Goraga, Z. (Ed.). (2024). *AI and ML applications for decision-making in the education sector: Volume 2*. SkyLimit Publishing. https://www.skylimitpublishing.com/

Guhan, N., Krishnan, P., Dharshini, P., Abraham, P., & Thomas, S. (2020). The Mentorship program's effect on enhancing first-year MBBS students' academic performance. *Journal of Advances in Medical Education & Professionalism, 8*(4), 196-199. https://doi.org/DOI: 10.30476/jamp.2019.82591.1061

Igbokwe, I. C. (2023). Application of artificial intelligence (AI) in educational management. *International Journal of Scientific and Research Publications*, *13*(3). Advance online publication. DOI: 10.29322/IJSRP.13.03.2023.p13536

Ismail, O. H., & Al Shanfari, A. M. (2014). Management of private higher education Institutions in the Sultanate of Oman: A call for cooperation. *European Journal of Social Sciences*, *43*(1), 39–45. http://www.europeanjournalofsocialsciences.com

Kizilcec, R., Pardo, A., & San Pedro, M. (2018). AI-powered analytics for improving faculty-mentee interactions. *Educational Technology Research and Development*, *66*(4), 789–804. DOI: 10.1007/s11423-018-9588-z

Kizilcec, R. F., & Cohen, G. L. (2018). Analyzing communication patterns in mentorship: The role of AI in improving faculty-student interactions. *Educational Technology Research and Development*, *66*(4), 889–904. DOI: 10.1007/s11423-018-9587-0

Kwan, M., Wong, K., & Wong, C. (2015). Group mentoring and its impact on faculty development. *Higher Education Research & Development*, *34*(4), 737–750. DOI: 10.1080/07294360.2015.1025877

Lee, J., & Williams, S. (2019). Addressing power imbalances in faculty mentorship: An AI-based approach. *Journal of Academic Mentoring*, *42*(2), 117–134. DOI: 10.1016/j.jacmedu.2019.05.004

Lee, K., & Williams, M. (2019). Power dynamics in faculty mentorship: Using AI to foster more equitable academic environments. *Higher Education Quarterly*, *73*(1), 102–118.

Lunsford, L. G., Crisp, G., Dolan, E. L., & Wuetherick, B. (2017). Mentoring in higher education. In Clutterbuck, D., & Ragins, P. (Eds.), *The SAGE handbook of mentoring* (pp. 316–334). SAGE Publishing. DOI: 10.4135/9781526402011.n20

Matsuoka, H., & Sakurai, A. (2022). AI-driven scheduling tools in higher education: Improving administrative efficiency. *Journal of Educational Technology & Society*, *25*(1), 33–47.

Montgomery, D. P., & Wilson, K. (2025). Critical peer mentoring: Aligning values and practice as professional development. *Innovations in Education and Teaching International*, 1–17. Advance online publication. DOI: 10.1080/14703297.2025.2501169

Mubuuke, A. G., Munabi, I. G., Mbalinda, S. N., Opaka, R. B., Chalo, R. N., & Kiguli, S. (2021). Development of a feedback framework within a mentorship alliance using activity theory. *African Journal of Health Professions Education*, *13*(4), 246–251. DOI: 10.7196/AJHPE.2021.v13i4.1291 PMID: 35991467

Nedungadi, P., Tang, K.-Y., & Raman, R. (2024). The transformative power of generative artificial intelligence for achieving the sustainable development goal of quality education. *Sustainability (Basel), 16*(22), 9779. DOI: 10.3390/su16229779

Nieto-Rodriguez, A., & Vargas, R. V. (2023, February 2). How AI will transform project management. *Harvard Business Review*. https://hbr.org/2023/02/how-ai-will-transform-project-management

Nyunt, G., Koo, K., Witkowsky, P., Andino, M., Lin, X., Chan, R. Y., Sharma, S., & Bista, K. (Eds.). (2024). *ChatGPT and global higher education: Using artificial intelligence in teaching and learning, international student identities and mental well-being: Beyond the single story*. Star Scholar. https://scholar.harvard.edu/sites/scholar.harvard.edu/files/roychan/files/ebook_chatgpt_and_global_higher_education.pdf

Qudus, A. (2024, September 4). *Revolutionizing higher education with AI: Unlocking potential, addressing challenges, and forging future paths*. EasyChair Preprint. https://easychair.org/publications/preprint/P35C/open

Raza, Z., Tahir, Z., Qamar, S., & Manan, A. (2025, April). The role of AI in the education sector: Focusing on AI's adaptation, drawbacks, implications, trust, and ethical considerations. *Journal of Political Stability Archive*, *3*(2), 145–165. DOI: 10.63468/jpsa.3.2.08

Saaida, M. B. E. (2023). AI-driven transformations in higher education: Opportunities and challenges. *Journal Name*, *5*(1), 29–36. DOI: 10.5281/zenodo.8164415

Sawahel, W. (2024, July 13). Education ministry announces AI-driven metaverse plan. *University World News*. https://www.universityworldnews.com/post.php?story=20240713095612336

Seo, K., Tang, J., Roll, I., Fels, S., & Yoon, D. (2021). The impact of artificial intelligence on learner– instructor interaction in online learning. *International Journal of Educational Technology in Higher Education*, *18*(1), 54. Advance online publication. DOI: 10.1186/s41239-021-00292-9 PMID: 34778540

Sposato, M. (2025). Artificial intelligence in educational leadership: A comprehensive taxonomy and future directions. *International Journal of Educational Technology in Higher Education*, *22*(1), 20. DOI: 10.1186/s41239-025-00517-1

Stoller, A. (2021). Traditional and critical mentoring. *Radical Teacher*, *119*, 52–60. DOI: 10.5195/rt.2021.765

Taherdoost, H., & Madanchian, M. (2023). Artificial intelligence and sentiment analysis: A review in competitive research. *Computers*, *12*(2), 37. DOI: 10.3390/computers12020037

Tariq, M. U. (2024, May). AI-powered language translation for multilingual classrooms. In *Integrating generative AI in education to achieve sustainable development goals* (pp. 29–46). IGI Global., DOI: 10.4018/979-8-3693-2440-0.ch002

Tsou, C. (2023). Implementing artificial intelligence (AI) in higher education: A narrative literature review. *Conestoga College*. https://www.researchgate.net/publication/376553922_Implementing_Artificial_Intelligence_AI_in_Higher_Education_A_Narrative_Literature_Review

UNESCO. (2019). *Planning education in the AI era: Lead the leap: Final report*. International Conference on Artificial Intelligence and Education. https://doi.org/DOI: 10.3390/admsci13090196

UNESCO International Institute for Higher Education in Latin America and the Caribbean. (2023). *Harnessing the era of artificial intelligence in higher education: A primer for higher education stakeholders* (ED/HE/IESALC/IP/2023/27). https://doi.org/DOI: 10.5281/zenodo.1234567

# Chapter 8
# Challenges of Integrating AI in Education

**Froilan Delute Mobo**
https://orcid.org/0000-0002-4531-8106
*Philippine Merchant Marine Academy, Philippines*

## ABSTRACT

*Sociology and education have been left behind by advancements in artificial intelligence (AI). The fields of science, engineering, technology, and mathematics (STEM), as well as human-facing disciplines, have undergone profound shifts due to the integration of AI. Yet, unprecedented challenges remain, such as the obsolescence of competencies, intentionally or unintentionally programmed biases, misuse of AI tools, and other educational AI-enabled technologies. This can harm the integrity of education and fuel the stagnation of innovative development in education. The discussion steers toward significant implications AI integration brings with it for educators, learners, and policymakers. AI has become a tool for tangible innovation in transforming teaching and educating learners, but controlling its misuse needs a commensurate policy risk strategy. The chapter presents approaches to mitigate risks that encourage the ethical use of AI foster the so-called human component-led growth in system design.*

## INTRODUCTION

Artificial Intelligence (AI) is transforming education at an unprecedented pace, fundamentally reshaping how educators teach, how students learn, and how institutions assess knowledge (Luckin et al., 2016; Holmes et al., 2022). With its capacity to personalize learning, automate administrative and instructional tasks, and improve efficiency, AI presents immense transformative potential across educational systems

DOI: 10.4018/979-8-3373-2302-2.ch008

(Woolf, 2010; Zawacki-Richter et al., 2019). However, this potential is accompanied by profound ethical, pedagogical, and social challenges. This chapter addresses three critical concerns that emerge from the integration of AI in education: skill obsolescence, technological misuse, and algorithmic bias. These interconnected issues, if not addressed, pose significant risks to the quality, inclusivity, and human-centered mission of education (Selwyn, 2019; Floridi & Cowls, 2019).

The most visible applications of AI in education include intelligent tutoring systems, predictive analytics, and automated assessments. AI-driven platforms now adapt content delivery based on individual learning profiles, monitor student engagement, and even forecast academic performance using data-driven insights (Zawacki-Richter et al., 2019; Holmes et al., 2019). Tools such as ChatGPT, Grammarly, and AI-enhanced learning management systems are increasingly utilized in both traditional classrooms and online environments to deliver instruction, reduce teacher workload, and provide real-time feedback (Cotton et al., 2023; Luckin, 2018). While these innovations offer clear benefits, they also raise unresolved dilemmas related to data privacy, academic integrity, equity, and the future role of educators—issues that demand a critical, interdisciplinary response (Williamson & Eynon, 2020).

This chapter seeks to explore the broader impact of AI on core educational values and learner competencies, with a particular focus on both STEM (Science, Technology, Engineering, and Mathematics) fields and human-centered disciplines such as the humanities, arts, and social sciences. STEM fields, often early adopters of emerging technologies, grapple with the dual imperative of maintaining technical efficiency while upholding ethical responsibility (Benjamin, 2019). Conversely, human-centered disciplines—rooted in empathy, critical inquiry, and social engagement—must adapt to AI tools in ways that preserve the interpersonal and ethical foundations of their pedagogical missions (Selwyn, 2019; Markoff, 2020). By examining these dynamics, this chapter aims to contribute a balanced, values-driven framework for integrating AI into education responsibly and equitably.

Three key research questions guide this inquiry:

1. How does AI integration contribute to or mitigate skill obsolescence in educational contexts?
2. In what ways is AI misused in educational environments, and what ethical frameworks can guide responsible use?
3. What are the manifestations and consequences of algorithmic bias in education, and how can they be addressed?

The significance of these questions is underscored by the evolving role of education in preparing learners not only for employment in a digitally dominated economy but also for responsible citizenship in a data-driven world. As automation continues to redefine which skills hold value in the labor market, traditional curricula increasingly risk becoming obsolete. Many competencies that AI can replicate—such as basic computation, routine analysis, and content summarization—are gradually losing relevance. This raises a critical concern: how can education systems ensure that learners develop distinctly human skills such as creativity, emotional intelligence, ethical reasoning, and civic responsibility? These human-centered competencies remain difficult to automate yet are essential for navigating the complexities of modern life and contributing meaningfully to diverse and uncertain societies.

Skill obsolescence driven by AI is not merely a technological issue; it is a profound pedagogical and ethical challenge. Addressing it requires a fundamental transformation in curriculum design, instructional methodologies, and assessment practices. Educational institutions must shift from passive knowledge transmission to actively fostering critical thinking, collaboration, adaptability, and lifelong learning. The urgency of developing these competencies is reflected in global educational frameworks, including the 21st Century Skills Framework and the OECD's Learning Compass, both of which stress the importance of equipping learners for volatility, uncertainty, complexity, and ambiguity (VUCA). However, despite widespread acknowledgment of these needs, many educational systems have yet to fully adapt to this paradigm shift.

Compounding the issue of skill obsolescence is the misuse of AI technologies in educational contexts. The rise of accessible generative AI tools such as ChatGPT has introduced new avenues for academic dishonesty, where students may generate assignments or problem sets with minimal personal input or critical engagement. This misuse threatens not only academic integrity but also the very purpose of education—deep learning and meaningful intellectual growth.

This chapter is guided by the conceptual framework illustrated in Figure 1, titled *"Ethical and Sustainable Integration of AI in Education."* The figure outlines a comprehensive roadmap for addressing the core challenges posed by AI in education: skill obsolescence, misuse of AI, and algorithmic bias and inequity. These challenges are examined through the lens of key theoretical frameworks, including Constructivist Learning Theory, the 21st Century Skills Framework, Deontological and Consequentialist ethical theories, the Technology Acceptance Model (TAM), and Diffusion of Innovation Theory. Grounded in these theories, the diagram proposes four strategic areas for intervention: *Curriculum Innovation*, which promotes interdisciplinary AI and ethics education to foster human-centered skills; *Educator Capacity Building*, which emphasizes AI literacy and pedagogical redesign; *Ethical Governance and Policy*, which advocates for data privacy, transparency, and accountability; and *Inclusive AI Design*, which supports participatory development and the use of diverse datasets. Together, these strategies aim to establish a future-oriented, human-centered AI education system that is equitable, ethical, inclusive, and adaptive.

*Figure 1. Ethical and sustainable integration of AI in education (Author, 2025)*

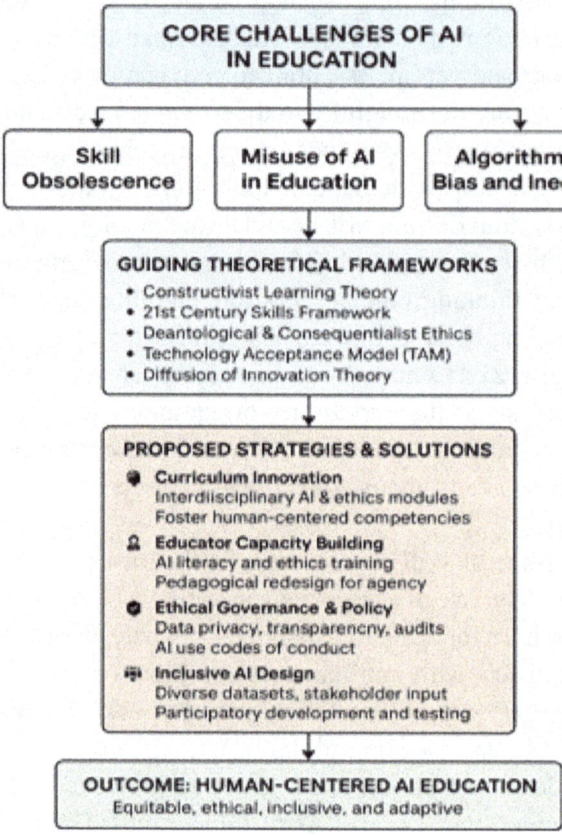


The chapter is structured as follows: after presenting the analytical literature review, it outlines the methodology section appropriate for the research. This is followed by the results, which are organized into multiple subsections. Subsequently, the discussion section is presented, leading into the conclusion. The chapter concludes with implications, limitations, and directions for further studies.

## LITERATURE REVIEW

The integration of Artificial Intelligence (AI) in education has garnered significant scholarly attention, with prior research emphasizing its technical applications and operational benefits. Studies have highlighted AI's role in adaptive learning systems, automated assessment tools, and personalized learning platforms (Woolf, 2010; Zawacki-Richter et al., 2019). However, these technologically focused narratives often lack a comprehensive interdisciplinary analysis that critically examines the ethical implications, pedagogical transformations, and policy responses required for sustainable and socially just AI integration.

Selwyn (2019) and Holmes et al. (2019), for instance, underscore the growing influence of AI in reshaping educational landscapes. Yet, their accounts stop short of articulating how educational institutions can align AI innovation with values of equity, inclusivity, and human development. This literature review responds to that gap by adopting a benefit-risk framework, drawing from Rogers' (2003) *Diffusion of Innovation Theory* and Davis' (1989) *Technology Acceptance Model (TAM)*, to analyze both the promises and perils of AI in education.

### Opportunities and Benefits

AI technologies offer transformative potential for personalization, inclusivity, and instructional efficiency. Intelligent Tutoring Systems (ITS) such as Carnegie Learning and Squirrel AI deliver individualized instruction at scale, offering feedback adapted to learners' needs and pace (Woolf, 2010). Automated assessment platforms like E-rater and Grammarly reduce faculty workload while enabling faster feedback cycles (Shermis & Burstein, 2013). Furthermore, predictive analytics integrated into platforms such as Coursera and DreamBox allow for tailored content delivery, particularly benefiting students from marginalized backgrounds (Zawacki-Richter et al., 2019).

AI is also revolutionizing student support services. Career guidance tools powered by AI (e.g., IBM's Watson Career Coach) offer data-informed academic and career pathway recommendations (Popenici & Kerr, 2017). For students with disabilities or language barriers, inclusive tools like real-time transcription and speech recognition promote equitable access to education (Luckin et al., 2016). In terms of faculty development, AI-driven analytics support classroom management and instructional design, helping educators identify student engagement patterns and adapt accordingly (Holmes et al., 2019).

Through Rogers' diffusion model, most educational institutions currently remain in the early to middle stages of AI adoption. While pilot implementations are increasing, widespread integration is hindered by infrastructure gaps, ethical concerns, and resistance from educators and stakeholders unfamiliar with or skeptical of AI's capabilities and limitations.

## Critical Risks and Challenges

Despite its promise, AI integration introduces significant ethical, pedagogical, and sociopolitical risks. One of the most pressing concerns is the obsolescence of human-centric educational competencies. As AI systems automate grading, tutoring, and curriculum design, traditional educator roles are at risk of being diminished (Brynjolfsson & McAfee, 2014). This automation threatens the cultivation of irreplaceable human skills—critical thinking, creativity, empathy, and moral reasoning—that AI cannot authentically replicate. Educational systems must therefore recalibrate their curricula to simultaneously foster AI literacy and core human capabilities.

Moreover, algorithmic manipulation and misuse threaten academic integrity. Perelman (2014) highlights how students exploit AI grading systems by crafting grammatically correct but substantively shallow content. Additionally, AI decision-making in admissions, behavioral monitoring, and assessment raises profound accountability concerns. The reliance on opaque "black box" systems undermines transparency and limits recourse for students unfairly affected by algorithmic decisions (Burrell, 2016).

Privacy and surveillance are also emerging issues, particularly with the proliferation of AI-based proctoring tools during remote learning transitions. These systems often use facial recognition, keystroke logging, and gaze detection, leading to concerns about psychological harm, consent, and data misuse (Williamson & Eynon, 2020). Without robust regulatory safeguards, educational spaces risk becoming sites of coercive monitoring rather than inclusive learning.

Algorithmic bias further complicates AI's role in promoting equity. Buolamwini and Gebru (2018) demonstrate how facial recognition technologies disproportionately misidentify individuals from minority backgrounds, a phenomenon that can be replicated in educational recommendation engines and assessment tools. In such cases, AI risks amplifying rather than mitigating structural inequities. Addressing these issues demands more than technical fixes; it requires systemic commitment to fairness, diversity in training data, and participatory design processes that include marginalized voices.

Another underexplored dimension is the commercialization of educational AI. Many platforms are proprietary and profit-driven, raising questions about data ownership, ethical stewardship, and corporate influence in pedagogical decision-making (Selwyn, 2019). This commodification threatens to reposition students as data producers for corporate gain, rather than autonomous learners engaged in transformative education.

Additionally, scholars like Williamson (2017) warn against the epistemological narrowing that AI may induce. Emphasizing measurable outcomes and performance metrics, AI systems can sideline broader educational aims such as civic participation, ethical inquiry, and aesthetic exploration. The risk lies in reducing education to a transactional process optimized for efficiency, rather than a holistic endeavor grounded in human flourishing.

## Positioning This Chapter in Academic Discourse

This chapter situates itself at the intersection of educational technology, ethics, and policy, contributing to a growing body of interdisciplinary scholarship that critiques the uncritical adoption of AI in education. While earlier works have outlined AI's technical potentials (e.g., Luckin et al., 2016; Woolf, 2010), recent critical literature increasingly calls for an ethically grounded and socially responsive approach (Selwyn, 2019; Williamson & Eynon, 2020; Holmes et al., 2019). By synthesizing these perspectives and framing them within the Diffusion of Innovation and TAM models, this chapter offers a structured critique of AI's integration trajectory and proposes principles for its equitable implementation.

In STEM education, this means going beyond technical competence to embed social responsibility, ethical AI design, and awareness of algorithmic harms. Engineering and computer science programs must incorporate modules on fairness, transparency, and inclusivity to prepare students not only as developers but as stewards of technological justice. In human-centered disciplines, the challenge is to ensure AI augments, rather than erodes, culturally responsive pedagogy and student agency.

Ultimately, avoiding technological determinism requires a shift in focus: from what AI *can* do, to what it *should* do in service of inclusive, equitable, and democratic education. AI must not be seen as an inevitable force of progress but as a tool whose deployment must be guided by ethical deliberation and collective educational values.

## Integrative Reflection

The dual nature of AI in education—its ability to both empower and marginalize—demands a critical, theory-informed, and context-sensitive approach. The Technology Acceptance Model suggests that perceived usefulness and ease of use are essential for AI adoption. However, for adoption to be meaningful and sustainable, educational systems must also consider societal implications, cultural fit, and ethical ramifications.

Stakeholders should avoid technological determinism and instead promote deliberate innovation guided by democratic values, inclusivity, and human agency. A balanced approach can ensure that AI becomes a tool for enhancing—not undermining—educational equity and integrity.

## Understanding Skill Obsolescence

Skill obsolescence refers to the process by which existing knowledge, abilities, and competencies lose their relevance due to technological innovation (Bessen, 2019). This phenomenon is particularly accelerated by the adoption of Artificial Intelligence (AI), which automates not only manual and administrative tasks but also increasingly complex cognitive and creative functions. As AI systems become more capable, the traditional skillsets once considered essential in both STEM and human-centered disciplines face rapid transformation.

In STEM fields, developments such as machine learning, quantum computing, and automated data analytics are redefining the landscape of programming, engineering, and scientific research. In the humanities and social sciences, tools like natural language processing (NLP), AI-assisted qualitative coding, and sentiment analysis are changing how scholars approach communication, cultural studies, and human behavior analysis (Luckin, 2018).

## Educational Reorientation in the Age of AI

To effectively respond to skill obsolescence, education must undergo a transformation grounded in pedagogical and theoretical frameworks such as the 21st Century Skills Framework and Constructivist Learning Theory. The former emphasizes competencies such as creativity, collaboration, communication, and critical thinking as key to future workforce readiness (P21, 2019), while the latter advocates for active, learner-centered education in which students construct meaning through experience and reflection (Piaget, Vygotsky).

Additionally, understanding our world as increasingly VUCA—volatile, uncertain, complex, and ambiguous—provides context for the kind of educational reorientation required. In a VUCA environment, traditional learning models that prioritize rote memorization and static knowledge fall short. Instead, learners must develop adaptive expertise that allows them to navigate change, solve novel problems, and engage with uncertainty (World Economic Forum, 2020).

## Defining Human-Centered Competencies

Human-centered competencies refer to those cognitive, emotional, and ethical skills that are uniquely human and less susceptible to automation. These include:

- Critical Thinking: The ability to analyze and evaluate information objectively.
- Creativity: The capacity to generate original ideas and innovative solutions.

- Emotional Intelligence: Awareness of, and ability to manage, one's own emotions and those of others.
- Ethical Reasoning: The ability to recognize and resolve moral dilemmas.
- Civic Responsibility: Understanding social dynamics and participating actively in democratic society.

Such competencies complement technical skills and are essential for shaping equitable, inclusive AI applications.

## METHODOLOGY

This chapter is grounded in an integrative literature review, supplemented by conceptual analysis and illustrative global case examples. An integrative approach was selected to synthesize knowledge across disciplines and theoretical frameworks, enabling a comprehensive exploration of the challenges and implications of AI integration in education (Torraco, 2005). The review draws on a diverse corpus of scholarly sources—including peer-reviewed journal articles, policy briefs, institutional reports, and book chapters—published between 2014 and 2024. These materials were selected for their direct relevance to the central themes of AI in education, particularly those addressing ethical implications, pedagogical integration, algorithmic bias, and policy responses (Zawacki-Richter et al., 2019; Holmes et al., 2022).

Inclusion criteria prioritized works that are widely cited, theoretically grounded, and contextually diverse, ensuring representation from both the Global North and Global South. This effort aimed to avoid Eurocentric bias and to ensure that culturally situated insights are embedded in the analysis (UNESCO, 2021; Smuha, 2021). Table 1 present the Reference Matrix Summary used to develop this chapter:

*Table 1. Reference matrix summary*

| Publication Period | Peer-Reviewed Journals | Reports & White Papers | Total References |
|---|---|---|---|
| 2020–2024 | 17 | 6 | 23 |
| 2014–2019 | 11 | 4 | 15 |
| Total | 28 | 10 | 38 |

(Sources: developed by the author, 2025)

To identify patterns and key themes across the literature, a thematic analysis was conducted using a two-stage coding process (Braun & Clarke, 2006). In the first stage, inductive open coding was applied to identify recurring ideas and conceptual categories related to AI's educational impact. In the second stage, axial coding was used to group these codes into higher-order themes, resulting in three overarching categories that structure this chapter's analysis:

1. Skill obsolescence in the age of AI and automation
2. Misuse and ethical concerns associated with generative AI tools and surveillance
3. Algorithmic bias and inequity in AI-assisted educational decision-making

These thematic categories form the analytical backbone of the chapter and guide its evidence-based argumentation.

The review is also theoretically anchored in three complementary conceptual frameworks:

- Technology Acceptance Model (TAM): to understand how educators and students perceive and adopt AI tools based on perceived usefulness and ease of use (Davis, 1989).
- Diffusion of Innovation Theory: to explore how AI technologies are disseminated and adopted within educational systems over time (Rogers, 2003).
- Constructivist Learning Theory: to contextualize learner-centered approaches that promote critical thinking and human-centered skills in an AI-rich environment (Vygotsky, 1978; Piaget, 1952).

To enhance the practical relevance of the study, several global case studies were integrated into the review. Notable examples include:

- Finland's national curriculum reform, which embeds AI competencies and digital ethics in basic education (World Economic Forum, 2020).
- The University of Helsinki's "Elements of AI" course, a globally accessible online program designed to increase AI literacy among the public (University of Helsinki, 2022).
- India's AI for All initiative, which provides regional language AI education to promote digital inclusion (NITI Aayog, 2021).

These cases were selected based on empirical documentation, policy innovation, and their illustrative value for aligning AI education with equity and sustainability goals.

It should be noted that this chapter does not include primary data collection. As such, it does not generate new empirical findings but instead synthesizes existing literature and case evidence to produce theory-informed and actionable insights. While this methodology supports broad conceptual generalizations, it is limited in its ability to capture first-hand stakeholder perspectives or context-specific nuances.

This limitation is acknowledged and addressed through transparent sourcing and critical evaluation of all referenced materials.

## FINDINGS

This section presents a comparative analysis of AI-compatible and human-exclusive skills, highlighting their varying automation risks. It emphasizes the importance of cultivating uniquely human competencies—such as creativity, empathy, and ethical reasoning—alongside technical skills. The findings underscore the urgent need for education systems to adapt curricula and teaching approaches to prepare learners for an AI-augmented future (Holmes et al., 2022; OECD, 2023).

The table titled "Comparative Framework: AI-Compatible vs. Human-Exclusive Skills" presents a detailed comparison of key skill types based on their susceptibility to automation. It highlights how certain tasks—such as data analysis, pattern recognition, and coding or programming—are increasingly being supported or even partially replaced by artificial intelligence (Frey & Osborne, 2017). These skills, while still valuable, carry a medium automation risk because AI systems are capable of processing structured data, identifying trends, and executing code with increasing efficiency (Brynjolfsson & McAfee, 2014).

On the other hand, skills such as creativity and innovation, empathy and emotional insight, moral and ethical reasoning, and collaboration and leadership are identified as distinctly human-exclusive. These competencies have a low to very low automation risk, primarily because they involve nuanced emotional intelligence, value-based decision-making, and complex interpersonal dynamics—areas where AI currently lacks depth and genuine understanding (Goleman, 1995; Robinson, 2011). Table 1 underscores the growing need for education systems and workforce development programs to prioritize the cultivation of human-centric skills that cannot be easily automated.

*Table 2. Skill categories and automation risk*

| Skill Type | Description | Automation Risk |
|---|---|---|
| Data Analysis | Interpreting structured data | Medium |
| Pattern Recognition | Identifying trends from data | Medium |
| Coding/Programming | Writing and debugging code | Medium |
| Creativity and Innovation | Generating original ideas | Low |
| Empathy and Emotional Insight | Understanding others' feelings and perspectives | Very Low |

continued on following page

*Table 2. Continued*

| Skill Type | Description | Automation Risk |
|---|---|---|
| Moral and Ethical Reasoning | Making values-based decisions | Very Low |
| Collaboration and Leadership | Working in teams, influencing group dynamics | Low |

[Source: Developed by the author based on Frey & Osborne (2017); Goleman (1995); Robinson (2011)]

## Global Case Study: Finland's Curriculum Reform

Finland's national education system is often cited as a model of progressive AI-readiness, offering valuable insights into how educational frameworks can adapt to the challenges and opportunities posed by artificial intelligence (World Economic Forum, 2020). A standout initiative is the "Elements of AI" course, developed in partnership with the University of Helsinki, which aims to foster AI literacy among the general population (University of Helsinki, 2022). This course has been translated into multiple languages and adopted internationally, emphasizing inclusivity and accessibility in AI education.

In parallel, Finnish schools have embraced project-based learning and interdisciplinary teaching methods that cultivate both technical fluency and human-centered skills, ensuring that students are prepared for the multifaceted demands of the future (OECD, 2023). To replicate such success globally, policy and pedagogical recommendations include integrating AI fundamentals with ethics, philosophy, and social impact into curricula, equipping teachers with tools to deliver both technical content and humanistic competencies, and adopting experiential learning strategies such as simulations, debates, and collaborative projects (Redecker, 2017; Holmes et al., 2022).

Among the most critical human-centered skills that must be emphasized in education is critical thinking—the ability to reason logically, scrutinize information, and make sound judgments. Humans remain irreplaceable in their ability to question assumptions, resolve contradictions, and apply ethical reasoning (Paul & Elder, 2014). Emotional intelligence (EI), the ability to perceive, manage, and respond to emotions, is another vital area AI cannot replicate authentically (Goleman, 1995).

Creativity, too, remains essential in the face of AI systems that mimic rather than create. True creativity involves novel, risk-taking, and often unpredictable insights (Robinson, 2011). Ethical reasoning is foundational: while AI is increasingly used in decision-making, only humans can navigate moral implications (Floridi, 2013).

Addressing skill obsolescence requires strategic reorganization of educational content and delivery. Education must shift toward interdisciplinary approaches connecting technology with ethics, humanities, and the arts (Long & Magerko, 2020).

Teaching digital ethics and AI literacy as core competencies empowers students to engage critically with technological change.

However, curriculum reform alone is insufficient. The pace of technological change requires continuous learning models. Lifelong learning must become standard, supported by flexible pathways like micro-credentials, modular learning, and online platforms (OECD, 2019). EdX, Coursera, and FutureLearn exemplify scalable, lifelong education.

In India, policy interventions such as learning accounts, reskilling tax incentives, and public investment in adult education are designed to ensure continuous learning (OECD, 2019). Industry–academia partnerships bridge the classroom–workplace gap. For example, the MIT-IBM Watson AI Lab advances research and AI education while supporting public-facing resources (MIT-IBM Watson AI Lab, 2021).

SMEs must also be involved to democratize access to AI education across economic sectors (Zawacki-Richter et al., 2019). Collaborations such as internships, co-designed curricula, and research projects ensure relevance and skill transferability.

AI can personalize learning by adapting to learners' needs and providing real-time feedback. Systems like Carnegie Learning's MATHia support differentiated instruction (Carnegie Learning, 2022). However, such systems must include safeguards for transparency and equity (Floridi & Cowls, 2019).

Challenges remain. Bureaucratic inertia, lack of teacher preparation, and inequitable access threaten progress. Educators must be trained not only in AI tools but in ethical literacy and inclusive pedagogy (Holmes et al., 2022). Assessment models must evolve to capture human-centered skills (Redecker, 2017).

Misuse includes academic dishonesty (e.g., AI-generated essays), over-reliance on automation, and data privacy violations (Cotton et al., 2023; Floridi & Cowls, 2019). Ethical frameworks such as deontology and consequentialism help guide responsible use (Moor, 2005).

Institutions must define AI usage policies, ensure consent, mandate transparency, and emphasize augmentation, not replacement. Turnitin's AI detection, while useful, raises concerns about accuracy and privacy (Cotton et al., 2023).

AI can exacerbate inequalities if not responsibly designed. Inclusive datasets, algorithmic transparency, and bias training are essential (West et al., 2019; Doshi-Velez & Kim, 2017). AI integration must center human values, empathy, and equity.

Ethical STEM education must cultivate socially responsible innovators (Markoff, 2020). Cultural sensitivity, imagination, and narrative remain human domains. Research should examine AI's effects on higher-order thinking and ensure inclusivity in datasets and tool design (Benjamin, 2019).

AI in education presents opportunities and risks. Addressing skill obsolescence, misuse, and bias requires curriculum reform, ethical oversight, and inclusive pedagogy (UNESCO, 2021; OECD, 2023). Equity, transparency, and personalization must guide AI implementation.

Personalized learning must empower learners through co-design and culturally relevant pedagogy. Global South examples show the need for inclusive infrastructure and mentorship (Luckin et al., 2016). AI must be a force for democratization, not control.

Future frameworks must ensure transparency, inclusive policymaking, and participatory governance. AI should amplify—not replace—human potential.

## DISCUSSION

The integration of Artificial Intelligence (AI) in education reveals a complex interplay of promise and challenge. This chapter's analysis underscores that while AI excels at automating routine, data-driven tasks, it falls short in replicating deeply human capacities such as empathy, ethical reasoning, and creativity. These findings align with Robinson (2011) and Goleman (1995), who argue that such competencies are uniquely human and foundational to a holistic educational experience. Rather than simply preparing students for technical fluency, education systems must recalibrate toward cultivating these irreplaceable skills—an imperative that grows more urgent in the face of accelerating automation.

This study echoes the concerns raised by Selwyn (2019), Holmes et al. (2022), and Williamson and Eynon (2020), who caution against an uncritical embrace of AI technologies. Specifically, risks around algorithmic bias and misuse of generative AI tools—such as those discussed by Buolamwini and Gebru (2018), and Cotton et al. (2023)—demonstrate the need for ethical oversight and responsible design. These authors have shown how AI systems, when trained on non-inclusive datasets, can reinforce systemic inequities—particularly in high-stakes areas like educational assessment or admissions. In agreement, this chapter emphasizes that the deployment of AI in education must be guided by transparency, fairness, and inclusivity to avoid perpetuating social disparities.

However, this study offers a more hopeful interpretation than scholars like Brynjolfsson and McAfee (2014), who stress AI's potential for displacement. While acknowledging that certain technical roles are increasingly automated, the chapter positions human-centered skills not only as resilient but as vital to the success of future learning ecosystems. International case studies—from Finland's integration of ethics into AI literacy, to India's push for digital inclusion through multilingual education—highlight the transformative possibilities of AI when aligned with equity-oriented policy and pedagogy.

From a theoretical standpoint, this chapter contributes a multidimensional framework for responsible AI integration by drawing on Constructivist Learning Theory, the Technology Acceptance Model (TAM), and Diffusion of Innovation Theory. Constructivist perspectives (Piaget, 1952; Vygotsky, 1978) emphasize that learners must actively construct knowledge through engagement and reflection—a process that AI, if designed appropriately, can enhance but not replace. The use of TAM (Davis, 1989) reveals how users assess AI tools based on perceived usefulness and usability, but this study argues for expanding TAM to include ethical acceptability as a third pillar. Similarly, while Diffusion of Innovation Theory (Rogers, 2003) explains the uptake of new technologies, this analysis adds a critical dimension: adoption must be ethically grounded and contextually responsive, especially in low-resource or culturally diverse environments.

Together, these theoretical integrations support a values-based extension of traditional technology adoption models—one that embeds social justice, pedagogical intentionality, and cultural relevance into how AI is introduced and scaled. In doing so, the chapter advocates a shift away from technocratic narratives and toward a human-centered innovation paradigm.

Nevertheless, the study is limited in scope. It does not include primary empirical data, which means it cannot fully capture the lived experiences or nuanced perspectives of learners and educators across different contexts. While the integrative literature review offers a wide lens, future research should include ethnographic studies, interviews, and participatory research to explore how AI is actually experienced in classrooms. Additionally, given the rapidly evolving nature of AI, some of the tools and frameworks discussed here may become outdated, and ongoing re-evaluation will be necessary. The literature base also reflects a degree of geographic imbalance, with Euro-American perspectives still dominant. Greater inclusion of Global South voices is needed to contextualize AI adoption in linguistically and infrastructurally diverse environments.

This chapter does not provide technical evaluation of AI systems; it remains conceptually and pedagogically oriented. Future studies should incorporate interdisciplinary approaches, blending educational research with computer science and ethics, to offer holistic evaluations of AI tools in terms of accuracy, usability, and equity.

Ultimately, this analysis reinforces the imperative that human-centered competencies—ethical reasoning, civic responsibility, and emotional intelligence—must be placed at the heart of educational planning in the age of AI. These are not secondary "soft skills" but critical literacies for navigating a complex and uncertain world. AI can personalize and enhance learning, but only if its deployment is governed by principles of justice, transparency, and cultural inclusion.

To this end, curricula must integrate ethical instruction across disciplines, teacher training must include both AI literacy and inclusive pedagogy, and governance structures must ensure data transparency and accountability. Participatory design processes—especially those that foreground the needs of underrepresented learners—will be key to aligning AI with the humanistic mission of education. Not to mechanize learning, but to expand our capacity for critical thinking, creativity, empathy, and democratic engagement in an increasingly algorithmic society.

### Theoretical Contribution

For the theoretical contribution, this chapter presents a human-centered, interdisciplinary framework for AI integration in education. Drawing from Finland's curriculum reform, it emphasizes the need to balance technical fluency with emotional intelligence, ethical reasoning, and creativity. It contributes to educational theory by advocating for experiential learning, personalized pathways, and inclusive pedagogy to foster critical competencies beyond automation. The chapter also proposes a multi-level governance model that aligns AI tools with educational equity, lifelong learning, and civic empowerment, positioning human values as foundational to sustainable and transformative digital education ecosystems.

## CONCLUSION

This chapter has explored the multifaceted impact of Artificial Intelligence (AI) on education, addressing both the opportunities and the critical risks posed by its integration. Central to this inquiry were three research questions: (1) How does AI integration contribute to or mitigate skill obsolescence in educational contexts? (2) In what ways is AI misused in educational environments, and what ethical frameworks can guide responsible use? (3) What are the manifestations and consequences of algorithmic bias in education, and how can they be addressed?

The findings affirm that AI contributes to skill obsolescence by automating tasks previously essential to both STEM and human-centered disciplines. However, the research also identifies ways AI can mitigate this risk. Through deliberate curriculum redesign—emphasizing human-exclusive competencies like creativity, critical thinking, and emotional intelligence—educational institutions can reposition AI as a complement to human learning, rather than a replacement. This aligns with frameworks such as the 21st Century Skills Framework and Constructivist Learning Theory, which emphasize adaptability, lifelong learning, and interdisciplinary competence. Therefore, the first research question is directly addressed: AI exacerbates skill obsolescence when uncritically adopted, but with purposeful integration and human-centered pedagogy, it can also foster sustainable skill development.

This study reveals that AI misuse is widespread, including academic dishonesty, over-reliance on automation, and violations of data privacy. The chapter responds to this by outlining ethical frameworks—namely deontology and consequentialism—that institutions can adopt to guide responsible AI use. These frameworks support the development of policies that protect student autonomy, promote informed consent, and ensure AI is used to augment rather than replace human judgment. Moreover, the importance of teacher training in AI ethics and literacy was emphasized as a key strategy to prevent misuse and maintain educational integrity. Thus, the second research question is thoroughly addressed: misuse is a real and pressing issue, but it can be mitigated through robust ethical governance, institutional accountability, and stakeholder empowerment.

The research identifies algorithmic bias as a critical and insidious challenge, particularly in automated assessment, predictive analytics, and learning recommendation systems. These biases can marginalize vulnerable learners and perpetuate systemic inequalities. In response, the chapter recommends inclusive design, diverse datasets, participatory oversight, and algorithmic transparency as necessary countermeasures. Case studies, such as inclusive AI initiatives in Finland, India, and Kenya, demonstrate that bias can be reduced when cultural and contextual diversity is integrated into AI development. The third research question is thus answered with clear strategies: while algorithmic bias is a profound risk, it can be addressed through ethical design principles and inclusive stakeholder participation.

This chapter's findings clearly align with its stated objectives: to assess the dual impact of AI in education, evaluate the ethical implications, and propose actionable strategies for sustainable, human-centered innovation. The research questions served as a guide throughout the analysis and were directly reflected upon in the discussion of skill development, ethical misuse, and systemic bias. By maintaining this focus, the study offers a coherent, values-driven framework for integrating AI in ways that enhance equity, inclusivity, and educational integrity.

Ultimately, this chapter concludes that AI in education is neither inherently beneficial nor detrimental—it is the context, governance, and intentionality of its use that determine its impact. To fulfill its promise, AI must be implemented not just with technical expertise, but with ethical foresight, cultural sensitivity, and a commitment to human flourishing. The future of education depends not only on how well we adopt technology, but on how responsibly we align that technology with the deeper goals of democratic, inclusive, and empowering learning.

## REFERENCES


Benjamin, R. (2019). *Race after technology: Abolitionist tools for the new Jim code*. Polity Press.

Bessen, J. E. (2019). *AI and jobs: The role of demand*. NBER Working Paper No. 24235. DOI: 10.3386/w24235

Braun, V., & Clarke, V. (2006). Using thematic analysis in psychology. *Qualitative Research in Psychology*, *3*(2), 77–101. DOI: 10.1191/1478088706qp063oa

Brynjolfsson, E., & McAfee, A. (2014). *The second machine age: Work, progress, and prosperity in a time of brilliant technologies*. W. W. Norton & Company.

Cotton, D. R. E., Cotton, P. A., & Shipway, J. R. (2023). Chatting and cheating: Ensuring academic integrity in the era of ChatGPT. *Innovations in Education and Teaching International*, *60*(1), 34–45. DOI: 10.1080/14703297.2023.2190148

Davis, F. D. (1989). Perceived usefulness, perceived ease of use, and user acceptance of information technology. *Management Information Systems Quarterly*, *13*(3), 319–340. DOI: 10.2307/249008

Doshi-Velez, F., & Kim, B. (2017). Towards a rigorous science of interpretable machine learning. *arXiv preprint*. https://arxiv.org/abs/1702.08608

Floridi, L. (2013). *The ethics of information*. Oxford University Press. DOI: 10.1093/acprof:oso/9780199641321.001.0001

Floridi, L., & Cowls, J. (2019). A unified framework of five principles for AI in society. *Harvard Data Science Review*, *1*(1). Advance online publication. DOI: 10.1162/99608f92.8cd550d1

Frey, C. B., & Osborne, M. A. (2017). The future of employment: How susceptible are jobs to computerization? *Technological Forecasting and Social Change*, *114*, 254–280. DOI: 10.1016/j.techfore.2016.08.019

Goleman, D. (1995). *Emotional intelligence*. Bantam Books.

Holmes, W., Bialik, M., & Fadel, C. (2022). *Artificial intelligence in education: Promises and implications for teaching and learning*. Center for Curriculum Redesign.

Long, D., & Magerko, B. (2020). What is AI literacy? Toward a definition for secondary education. In *Proceedings of the 2020 CHI Conference on Human Factors in Computing Systems* (pp. 1–12). DOI: 10.1145/3313831.3376727

Luckin, R. (2018). *Machine learning and human intelligence: The future of education for the 21st century*. UCL IOE Press.

Luckin, R., Holmes, W., Griffiths, M., & Forcier, L. B. (2016). *Intelligence unleashed: An argument for AI in education*. Pearson Education.

Markoff, J. (2020). *Machines of loving grace: The quest for common ground between humans and robots*. HarperCollins.

MIT-IBM Watson AI Lab. (2021). *Annual report*. https://mitibmwatsonailab.mit.edu/research

Moor, J. H. (2005). Why we need better ethics for emerging technologies. *Ethics and Information Technology*, *7*(3), 111–119. DOI: 10.1007/s10676-006-0008-0

OECD. (2019). *Getting skills right: Future-ready adult learning systems*. OECD Publishing., DOI: 10.1787/9789264311756-

OECD. (2023). *AI and the future of skills*. https://www.oecd.org/education/ai-future-skills/

Paul, R., & Elder, L. (2014). *The miniature guide to critical thinking concepts and tools* (7th ed.). Foundation for Critical Thinking.

Piaget, J. (1952). *The origins of intelligence in children*. International Universities Press. DOI: 10.1037/11494-000

Redecker, C. (2017). *European framework for the digital competence of educators: DigCompEdu*. Publications Office of the European Union., DOI: 10.2760/159770

Robinson, K. (2011). *Out of our minds: Learning to be creative* (2nd ed.). Capstone Publishing.

Rogers, E. M. (2003). *Diffusion of innovations* (5th ed.). Free Press.

Selwyn, N. (2019). *Should robots replace teachers? AI and the future of education*. Polity Press.

Smuha, N. A. (2021). Beyond a human rights-based approach to AI governance. *Philosophy & Technology*, *34*(S1), 561–586. DOI: 10.1007/s13347-020-00403-w

Torraco, R. J. (2005). Writing integrative literature reviews: Guidelines and examples. *Human Resource Development Review*, *4*(3), 356–367. DOI: 10.1177/1534484305278283

UNESCO. (2021). *Guidance for generative AI in education and research*. https://unesdoc.unesco.org/ark:/48223/pf0000386943

University of Helsinki. (2022). *Elements of AI.* https://www.elementsofai.com/

Vygotsky, L. S. (1978). *Mind in society: The development of higher psychological processes*. Harvard University Press.

West, S. M., Whittaker, M., & Crawford, K. (2019). Discriminating systems: Gender, race, and power in AI. *AI Now Institute*. https://ainowinstitute.org/discriminatingsystems.html

Williamson, B., & Eynon, R. (2020). Historical threads, missing links, and future directions in AI in education. *Learning, Media and Technology*, *45*(3), 223–235. DOI: 10.1080/17439884.2020.1798995

Woolf, B. P. (2010). *Building intelligent interactive tutors: Student-centered strategies for revolutionizing e-learning*. Morgan Kaufmann.

World Economic Forum. (2020). *The future of jobs report 2020.* https://www.weforum.org/reports/the-future-of-jobs-report-2020

Zawacki-Richter, O., Marín, V. I., Bond, M., & Gouverneur, F. (2019). Systematic review of research on artificial intelligence applications in higher education: Where are the educators? *International Journal of Educational Technology in Higher Education, 16*(1), 1–27. DOI: 10.1186/s41239-019-0171-0

# Chapter 9
# Risks of AI Bias and Inequities in Learning

**S. Praveenkumar**
https://orcid.org/0009-0009-4830-5237
*SRM Institute of Science and Technology, India*

**Nilesh Anute**
https://orcid.org/0000-0001-6599-813X
*Sri Balaji University, India*

**V. Vaissnave**
https://orcid.org/0000-0001-7333-531X
*SRM Institute of Science and Technology, India*

**T. Ragupathi**
https://orcid.org/0000-0002-2482-5096
*SRM Institute of Science and Technology, India*

**Shyam Fardale**
*Datta Meghe Institute of Management Studies, India*

**P. Selvakumar**
https://orcid.org/0000-0002-3650-4548
*Department of Science and Humanities, Nehru Institute of Technology, Coimbatore, India*

**T. C. Manjunath**
https://orcid.org/0000-0003-2545-9160
*Rajarajeswari College of Engineering, India*

## ABSTRACT

*As artificial intelligence (AI) systems become increasingly embedded within the education sector, there is growing concern about the issue of AI bias and its far-reaching implications for fairness, equity, and student outcomes. AI applications such as adaptive learning platforms, automated grading systems, student performance prediction models, and admissions algorithms are designed to enhance efficiency, personalize instruction, and support data-driven decision-making. However, these systems are only as unbiased as the data they are trained on and the assumptions embedded in their algorithms. If not carefully designed and audited, AI technologies*

DOI: 10.4018/979-8-3373-2302-2.ch009

*can perpetuate, or even exacerbate, existing inequalities related to race, gender, socioeconomic status, language proficiency, and ability. This makes the conversation around AI bias in education not just a technical issue but a deeply ethical and social one. Bias can also be introduced during the design and implementation stages of AI development.*

## INTRODUCTION

As artificial intelligence (AI) systems become increasingly embedded within the education sector, there is growing concern about the issue of AI bias and its far-reaching implications for fairness, equity, and student outcomes. AI applications such as adaptive learning platforms, automated grading systems, student performance prediction models, and admissions algorithms are designed to enhance efficiency, personalize instruction, and support data-driven decision-making. However, these systems are only as unbiased as the data they are trained on and the assumptions embedded in their algorithms. If not carefully designed and audited, AI technologies can perpetuate, or even exacerbate, existing inequalities related to race, gender, socioeconomic status, language proficiency, and ability. This makes the conversation around AI bias in education not just a technical issue but a deeply ethical and social one. Bias can also be introduced during the design and implementation stages of AI development. Developers, often lacking diversity themselves, may unknowingly embed their own cultural or cognitive biases into the systems they build.

Moreover, the lack of transparency in proprietary AI algorithms—often protected by intellectual property laws—prevents educators, policymakers, and researchers from fully understanding how decisions are made. This opacity hinders accountability and makes it difficult to identify and rectify biased outcomes. Without robust auditing, inclusive design processes, and participatory development practices, these systems risk becoming "black boxes" whose decisions profoundly impact students without explanation or recourse. Addressing AI bias in education requires a multifaceted approach involving technical, ethical, and policy-oriented interventions. From a technical perspective, developers must prioritize fairness by using diverse, representative, and high-quality training datasets. Techniques such as de-biasing algorithms, counterfactual fairness modeling, and adversarial testing can help identify and mitigate potential biases.

At the same time, human oversight is critical—educators, ethicists, and data scientists must collaborate to ensure that AI decisions are regularly reviewed, explained, and justified. Bias detection and auditing tools must be embedded in the AI lifecycle from design to deployment. Policymakers also play a critical role in setting standards, regulations, and oversight mechanisms to ensure ethical AI deployment in education. Legislation should mandate transparency requirements for AI systems used in public education, including the publication of algorithmic impact assessments and periodic audits. Governments should support the development of open-source AI tools and foster interdisciplinary research that explores the social implications of educational technologies. International bodies and civil society organizations can facilitate the exchange of best practices and help build global frameworks for equitable AI use in learning environments. In conclusion, while AI has the potential to revolutionize education by personalizing learning, optimizing administrative processes, and enhancing access, its application must be guided by a strong commitment to fairness and justice. The growing concern over AI bias in education is not merely a technological challenge but a societal imperative. Ignoring these biases risks deepening existing inequities and undermining the transformative promise of educational technology. To harness AI's potential in ways that are truly inclusive and empowering, we must place ethical considerations at the forefront, ensure transparent and inclusive development processes, and continuously strive to identify and eliminate bias wherever it appears.

## LITERATURE REVIEW

The integration of Artificial Intelligence (AI) into education has catalyzed a transformative shift in how teaching and learning are conceptualized, delivered, and experienced across the globe. AI-driven learning systems represent one of the most significant technological advancements in modern education, offering the potential to revolutionize traditional pedagogical approaches by introducing adaptive, personalized, and data-informed learning environments. These systems harness the power of machine learning, natural language processing, data analytics, and automation to provide real-time feedback, assess student performance, tailor educational content, and support educators in enhancing instruction (Strielkowski W., et al, 2025). As educational institutions increasingly adopt digital technologies to meet diverse learning needs, the importance of AI-driven learning systems in promoting equity, accessibility, and improved learning outcomes cannot be overstated. Another major advantage of AI in education lies in its capacity to enhance accessibility and inclusion. Students with disabilities or learning differences often face barriers in conventional educational settings, but AI technologies can help bridge these gaps through tools like speech recognition, text-to-speech converters, real-time captioning, and intelligent content adaptation. For example, visually impaired learners can benefit from AI-based audio interfaces, while students with dyslexia might use AI tools that simplify text or provide alternative representations.

AI can also assist in language translation and multilingual instruction, supporting learners from diverse linguistic backgrounds and facilitating cross-cultural education. In this sense, AI-driven systems democratize access to quality education by reducing the structural and cognitive barriers that impede learning for many students (Pantelimon F V., et al, 2021). In higher education and lifelong learning contexts, AI is playing an increasingly pivotal role in fostering skill development and workforce alignment. As industries rapidly evolve due to technological disruption, there is a pressing need for educational systems to align learning outcomes with labor market demands. AI-driven platforms can analyze industry trends, job postings, and professional skill requirements to recommend relevant courses and certifications to learners. Personalized learning paths that evolve based on a learner's career aspirations, progress, and competencies help ensure that students are equipped with the knowledge and skills most relevant to the future of work. Microlearning platforms like Coursera, edX, and LinkedIn Learning are leveraging AI to suggest course recommendations, track learner performance, and guide professional development.

Importantly, AI-driven learning systems support the cultivation of 21st-century skills—such as critical thinking, creativity, collaboration, and digital literacy—that are essential in today's complex, information-rich society. By facilitating interactive and inquiry-based learning experiences through simulations, gamification, and virtual or augmented reality, AI systems foster active engagement and experiential learning. Natural language processing (NLP) technologies enable sophisticated conversational agents and virtual assistants that can simulate dialogue, assess written assignments, and encourage reflection and discussion (Amer-Yahia S., 2022). In this way, AI acts not as a replacement for teachers but as an augmentation tool that enhances pedagogical possibilities and deepens the learning experience. Additionally, there is a need for capacity building among educators and institutions to effectively leverage AI tools. Teachers must be provided with professional development opportunities that enhance their digital competencies and foster an understanding of how to integrate AI into their teaching practice meaningfully.

Educational leaders should invest in infrastructure, training, and ongoing support systems that enable the sustainable adoption of AI technologies. Collaborative efforts between technology developers, educators, policymakers, and researchers are essential to designing AI systems that are pedagogically sound, culturally relevant, and responsive to the needs of diverse learning communities (Vashishth T K., et al, 2024). In conclusion, AI-driven learning systems represent a paradigm shift in education, unlocking unprecedented opportunities for personalization, efficiency, inclusivity, and innovation. As the world confronts evolving educational challenges—from global learning disparities to the demands of a digital economy—AI offers powerful tools to reimagine what learning can look like. However, realizing the full potential of AI in education requires more than technological sophistication; it demands ethical commitment, systemic planning, and human-centered design. By embracing AI thoughtfully and inclusively, we can build educational systems that not only respond to the needs of today's learners but also empower future generations to thrive in an increasingly complex and interconnected world.

## METHODOLOGY

This study adopts a qualitative research methodology, utilizing a comprehensive analysis of secondary data sources to examine the challenges and opportunities associated with Artificial Intelligence (AI) in education. The focus is on critical issues such as bias, equity, access, fairness, and human oversight. Given the conceptual and policy-driven nature of the topic, qualitative analysis of existing literature, policy documents, and scholarly works provides a robust foundation for understanding the complex social, ethical, and technical dimensions of AI applications in educational contexts.

Secondary data for this study was gathered through systematic searches of academic databases and platforms, including Google Scholar and ResearchGate, Searches employed targeted keywords such as "AI bias in education," "equity in AI," "AI fairness," "AI transparency," "human oversight in AI," and "AI educational access," covering publications from 2021 to 2025. This process ensured the inclusion of diverse peer-reviewed journal articles, conference proceedings, government and international organization reports, white papers from industry leaders, and relevant policy frameworks. Additionally, grey literature from educational institutions, think tanks, and AI ethics organizations was incorporated to capture the most current insights and practical considerations.

Data analysis was conducted using a thematic approach, enabling the identification, synthesis, and interpretation of recurrent themes related to AI bias, data diversity, transparency, equitable access, and accountability in education. Thematic coding was performed manually to ensure a detailed and nuanced understanding of how AI systems impact marginalized populations, the significance of participatory design, and the role of human governance and oversight. This method facilitates a deep exploration of the socio-technical challenges and ethical responsibilities inherent in deploying AI in education.

Employing secondary qualitative data offers significant advantages, including access to a broad spectrum of perspectives across varied geographical and institutional settings. It also allows for the examination of established findings without the logistical, temporal, and ethical constraints often associated with primary data collection, particularly involving vulnerable groups. Nonetheless, this approach demands careful critical appraisal of source validity, potential biases, and contextual limitations, especially given the evolving nature of AI technologies and policy environments. In short, this qualitative secondary data analysis methodology enables a comprehensive and critical examination of the multifaceted issues surrounding AI in education. It supports the development of informed, evidence-based recommendations for creating fair, transparent, inclusive, and accountable AI systems that equitably serve all learners.

## BIASED DATA AND ALGORITHMIC DISCRIMINATION

As artificial intelligence (AI) systems become increasingly prevalent across various sectors—including education, healthcare, finance, criminal justice, and employment—there is growing concern about the risks posed by biased data and algorithmic discrimination. While AI holds tremendous potential to automate processes, enhance decision-making, and improve efficiency, it can also reinforce and scale societal inequities when built upon biased data sets. The notion of "algorithmic neutrality" is often a misconception; algorithms are not inherently objective or fair but are deeply shaped by the data on which they are trained and the design choices made by developers. When AI systems learn from biased or incomplete data, they can produce outputs that are discriminatory, unjust, or exclusionary, thereby amplifying historical prejudices and systemic disparities (Varona & Suarez, 2022). Understanding the roots and consequences of biased data and algorithmic discrimination is essential for creating ethical and equitable AI technologies. Bias in data can arise from multiple sources, including historical discrimination, social inequalities, sampling errors, data collection practices, and subjective labeling. Historical data often reflects societal biases that have disadvantaged specific groups, whether based on race, gender, age, socioeconomic status, disability, or geographic location. For example, a hiring algorithm trained on historical company data may learn to prefer male candidates if the majority of past hires were men, regardless of the candidates' actual qualifications.

Similarly, policing algorithms trained on crime statistics from over-policed neighborhoods may disproportionately flag individuals from minority communities as high-risk, perpetuating a cycle of surveillance and criminalization. These examples highlight how AI can reinforce existing patterns of discrimination, particularly when biased data is treated as neutral or objective evidence (Ferrer X., et al, 2020). In many cases, the labeling of data is also a source of bias. Human annotators may bring their assumptions, stereotypes, and cultural norms into the process of labeling data for training purposes. For example, sentiment analysis tools that interpret social media posts may misclassify dialects like African American Vernacular English (AAVE) as negative or aggressive, simply because the labeling process failed to account for linguistic diversity. These subjective decisions, when encoded into AI systems, can lead to the systematic mischaracterization of certain communities or behaviors. Moreover, when machine learning models are optimized primarily for accuracy or efficiency, developers may inadvertently overlook fairness, reinforcing patterns of exclusion through performance trade-offs.

Algorithmic discrimination can manifest in both direct and indirect ways. Direct discrimination occurs when the algorithm explicitly uses protected attributes—such as race, gender, or religion—in its decision-making process. Indirect or proxy discrimination, however, is more insidious and occurs when seemingly neutral variables (e.g., zip codes, education level, or employment history) serve as proxies for protected characteristics. For example, an algorithm that prioritizes applicants based on their neighborhood may inadvertently favor wealthier, predominantly white areas while disadvantaging marginalized communities (Moussawi S., et al, 2024). The complexity and opacity of many machine learning models, intense learning systems make it difficult to detect and mitigate such proxy discrimination, leading to outcomes that may appear neutral on the surface but are biased in effect. In addition to technical fixes, inclusive and participatory design practices are essential to ensure that AI systems reflect diverse perspectives and meet the needs of all stakeholders.

This involves engaging communities who are most affected by AI technologies—especially historically marginalized or underserved groups—in the design, testing, and evaluation of these systems. Diverse development teams are more likely to anticipate and identify biases that may otherwise go unnoticed. Furthermore, involving social scientists, ethicists, legal experts, and human rights advocates can help ensure that AI systems are aligned with broader societal values and legal frameworks. Ethical review boards and third-party audits can provide additional layers of accountability and oversight (Chowdhary S., et al, 2025). In conclusion, biased data and algorithmic discrimination represent some of the most pressing challenges in the era of artificial intelligence. While AI promises efficiency, scalability, and innovation, these benefits cannot come at the expense of fairness, equity, and human dignity. If left unchecked, algorithmic biases can entrench and amplify existing social injustices, leading to harm for individuals and communities who are already marginalized. Addressing this issue demands a concerted effort that combines technical rigor, ethical responsibility, inclusive participation, and regulatory action. By recognizing and actively combating bias at every stage of AI development and deployment, we can harness the transformative power of AI in ways that are just, inclusive, and beneficial for all.

## LACK OF DIVERSITY AND INCLUSIVE REPRESENTATION IN AI

The rapid advancement of artificial intelligence (AI) technologies has brought transformative changes across sectors, from healthcare and education to finance, transportation, and public policy. As these systems increasingly influence critical aspects of human life, the question of who develops them—and how diverse those development teams are—has become a matter of urgent importance. A significant challenge facing the AI field today is the persistent lack of diversity within AI development teams. This lack of representation—across dimensions such as gender, race, ethnicity, socioeconomic background, disability, geographic origin, and disciplinary expertise—not only limits innovation but also leads to the design of technologies that fail to serve, or actively harm, large segments of the population. Diverse development teams are essential for creating AI systems that are fair, inclusive, and responsive to the needs of a global, heterogeneous society (Coates J M., et al, 2025). The consequences of homogeneity in AI development teams are far-reaching.

When AI systems are created primarily by individuals from similar backgrounds—often white, male, able-bodied, and from high-income countries—they are more likely to reflect the perspectives, experiences, assumptions, and blind spots of that narrow demographic. These biases can manifest in the design, functionality, and deployment of AI tools in subtle but significant ways. For instance, voice recognition systems have historically struggled to accurately interpret the voices of women, non-native English speakers, or people with regional accents, largely because these voices were underrepresented in the training data and overlooked in the design process. Similarly, facial recognition technologies have been found to perform poorly on darker-skinned individuals, especially women of color, due to a lack of diverse image data and testing. These failures are not merely technical flaws—they reflect the systemic exclusion of certain groups from the AI development process and result in technologies that perpetuate inequality (Min A., 2023). Beyond preventing harm, diverse teams also drive innovation and improve overall performance. Research consistently shows that diversity in teams leads to better problem-solving, increased creativity, and more robust decision-making. Teams that include members with different backgrounds are more likely to question dominant assumptions, explore alternative solutions, and avoid groupthink. In the context of AI, where complex and often ambiguous challenges must be addressed, such diversity of thought is invaluable. From data selection and model architecture to algorithmic fairness and user interface design, every step in the AI development pipeline benefits from inclusive collaboration. Companies and organizations that prioritize diversity are better positioned to create AI products that resonate with a broader range of users and achieve greater societal impact.

Within the tech industry, companies must go beyond performative diversity statements and implement concrete policies to foster inclusive hiring, retention, and advancement. This includes setting measurable diversity goals, adopting bias-aware recruitment practices, creating mentorship and sponsorship programs, and holding leadership accountable for progress. Workplace culture also plays a critical role; organizations must cultivate environments where diverse voices are heard, respected, and empowered to influence decision-making. Regular diversity, equity, and inclusion (DEI) training, along with mechanisms for reporting and addressing discrimination or harassment, are essential components of this process (Hyrynsalmi S M., et al, 2025). Importantly, DEI efforts should not be siloed or treated as secondary concerns—they must be integrated into core business strategies and product development processes. Government and regulatory bodies can also contribute by enacting policies that promote diversity and equity in technology development. Public funding for AI research can be conditioned on meeting diversity requirements, while procurement policies can favor vendors that demonstrate inclusive practices. In addition, policymakers can support initiatives that fund diverse startups, foster inclusive innovation ecosystems, and ensure representation in public advisory committees and regulatory bodies overseeing AI deployment. International organizations can play a role by setting global diversity benchmarks and facilitating cross-border collaboration to build inclusive AI governance frameworks. In conclusion, the lack of diversity in AI development teams is a significant barrier to creating inclusive, fair, and effective AI technologies. As AI systems increasingly shape the world we live in, those who build these systems must reflect the diversity of the societies they serve (Chi N., et al, 2021). Diverse teams bring unique perspectives, identify and mitigate biases, drive innovation, and ensure that AI products meet the needs of all users, not just a privileged few. Addressing this issue requires a concerted effort from educational institutions, industry leaders, policymakers, civil society, and communities alike. By investing in inclusive talent pipelines, transforming workplace cultures, and centering equity in design, we can build AI systems that not only perform better but also help realize a more just and inclusive digital future.

## INSUFFICIENT TESTING AND VALIDATION IN AI SYSTEMS

As artificial intelligence (AI) continues to be integrated into critical domains such as healthcare, education, finance, criminal justice, and transportation, the importance of rigorous testing and validation processes cannot be overstated. AI systems, particularly those utilizing complex machine learning and deep learning models, are only as reliable, fair, and effective as the robustness of the methods used to evaluate them before deployment. Unfortunately, a growing body of evidence reveals that many AI models are being released and deployed without sufficient testing and validation, leading to a range of unintended consequences, including system failures, biased outcomes, security vulnerabilities, and loss of public trust (Shams R A., et al, 2023).

The challenge of ensuring that AI systems are thoroughly and appropriately tested is multifaceted, encompassing technical limitations, lack of standardized protocols, data-related issues, and systemic gaps in governance and accountability. Furthermore, many AI development teams operate under commercial or time constraints that incentivize rapid deployment over thorough testing. In the rush to release competitive products or capitalize on market opportunities, testing and validation are often seen as secondary concerns rather than core components of responsible AI development. This leads to underinvestment in robustness testing, adversarial testing, and long-term performance monitoring. In some cases, AI models are deployed in real-world environments without adequate pilot studies, ethical reviews, or independent audits. Such practices not only risk causing harm to users but also expose companies and institutions to reputational damage and legal liability (Mortaji & Sadeghi, 2024). The pressure to innovate quickly must be balanced with a commitment to safety, ethics, and accountability. Insufficient post-deployment validation also presents a major concern. AI systems often operate in dynamic, real-world environments where conditions evolve—user behaviors shift, data distributions change, and unforeseen edge cases emerge. This phenomenon, known as "concept drift," can degrade model performance and lead to unpredictable or biased outcomes. Without ongoing monitoring, retraining, and validation, AI systems may fail silently, with stakeholders unaware of declining accuracy or increasing unfairness. For example, an AI hiring tool may gradually become less effective as job descriptions evolve or as applicants adapt their resumes in response to the tool's recommendations. Continuous validation is therefore essential to ensure sustained reliability and fairness.

*Figure 1. AI fairness in data management and analytics*

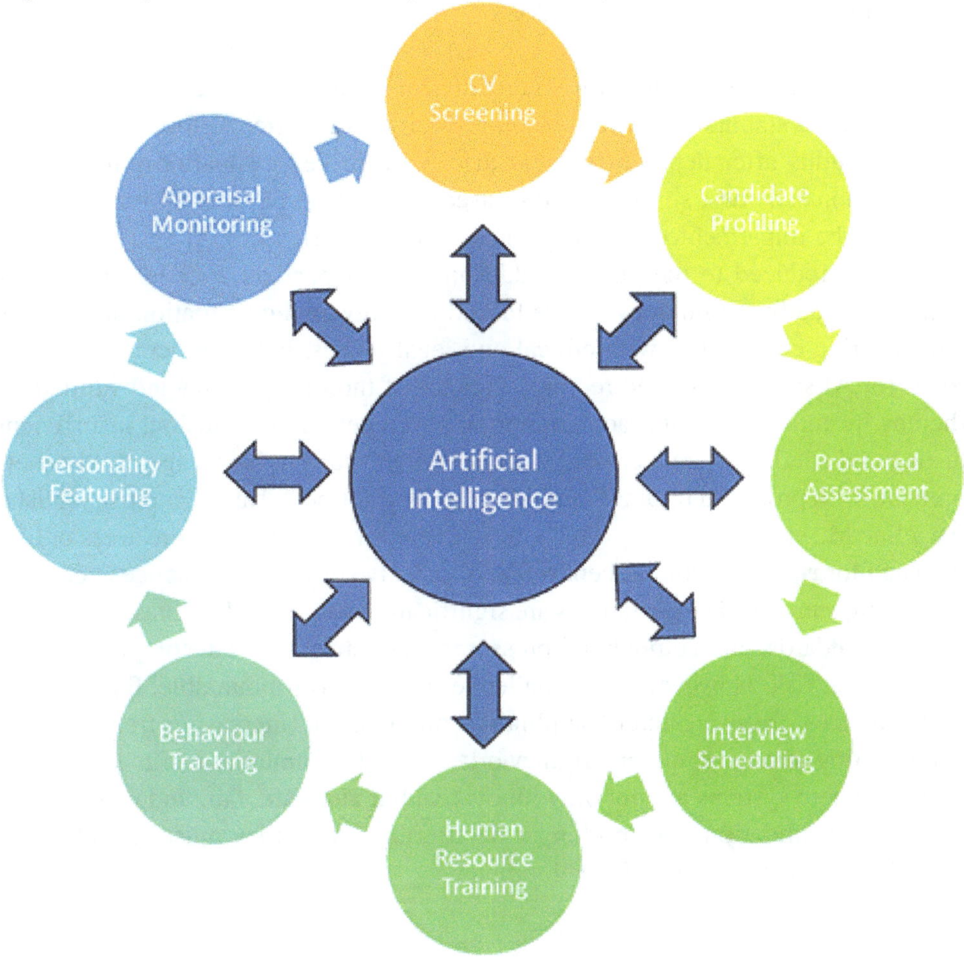


Addressing the challenges of insufficient testing and validation requires a coordinated, multidisciplinary approach involving AI developers, domain experts, ethicists, regulators, and end-users. Technically, developers must adopt best practices such as robust cross-validation, out-of-sample testing, adversarial testing, and stress testing under extreme conditions. Bias audits and fairness testing should be routine, particularly when models affect historically marginalized groups. Tools and frameworks—such as IBM's AI Fairness 360, Microsoft's Fairlearn, or Google's What-If Tool—can support developers in evaluating model behavior across subpopulations and identifying sources of bias. Furthermore, model documentation practices like "model cards" and "datasheets for datasets" can enhance transparency by clearly outlining model assumptions, performance metrics, limitations, and intended use cases (Khankhoje R., 2023).

From a policy and governance perspective, regulatory bodies must establish clear standards and guidelines for AI testing and validation, especially in high-risk sectors. These standards should mandate rigorous validation before deployment, periodic audits after deployment, and disclosure of key evaluation information. Certification schemes, similar to those used for medical devices or aviation software, can be implemented to verify the safety and fairness of AI systems before they are introduced to the public. Additionally, independent oversight bodies or algorithmic audit committees can be tasked with reviewing validation procedures and ensuring compliance with ethical and legal norms. Public procurement contracts for AI solutions should require evidence of thorough testing and validation, thereby incentivizing best practices among developers. In conclusion, insufficient testing and validation are a critical weakness in the current landscape of AI development, with profound implications for reliability, fairness, safety, and trust (Nisha Angeline M., et al, 2025). As AI technologies continue to impact more areas of life, the need for rigorous, comprehensive, and inclusive evaluation practices becomes increasingly urgent. The challenges are significant: opaque models, biased datasets, lack of standards, and commercial pressures all contribute to a testing deficit that puts users at risk. However, these challenges are not insurmountable. By adopting best practices, fostering interdisciplinary collaboration, increasing transparency, and enacting strong regulatory frameworks, the AI community can move toward a future where systems are not only innovative but also safe, fair, and trustworthy. Testing and validation must no longer be afterthoughts—they must be embedded at the heart of responsible AI development.

## PERPETUATING EXISTING SOCIAL INEQUALITIES

As artificial intelligence (AI) becomes more deeply embedded in the fabric of society—shaping decisions in healthcare, education, employment, housing, finance, criminal justice, and social services—it is increasingly evident that these technologies do not operate in a vacuum. Rather, they are designed, trained, and deployed within social contexts already marked by longstanding inequalities based on race, gender, class, disability, geography, and other dimensions of marginalization. While AI holds the promise of greater efficiency, objectivity, and inclusivity, its deployment has in many cases reinforced and even amplified existing social disparities (Upadhyaya A N., et al, 2025). This occurs through multiple mechanisms, including biased data, algorithmic discrimination, lack of diversity in development, unequal access to AI benefits, and insufficient regulatory oversight. As such, the use of AI is not only a technological issue but a profoundly social and political one, with serious implications for equity, justice, and human rights.

The impact of AI on labor and employment also highlights its potential to deepen social divides. Automation, powered by AI, is rapidly transforming the labor market, displacing workers in sectors such as manufacturing, retail, transportation, and customer service while creating new opportunities in highly skilled, technology-intensive roles. However, access to these emerging opportunities is not evenly distributed. Workers from low-income, rural, or marginalized communities often lack the digital literacy, formal education, or reskilling opportunities needed to transition into the AI-driven economy.

As a result, the benefits of AI accrue disproportionately to those already in positions of socioeconomic privilege, while others are left behind in increasingly precarious economic conditions. Without deliberate intervention through inclusive education, training programs, and job creation strategies, AI risks widening the economic gap between the privileged and the disadvantaged (Kaur D., et al, 2022). Healthcare is another domain where AI has the potential to both reduce and perpetuate disparities. AI algorithms are increasingly used for diagnostic imaging, treatment planning, patient risk stratification, and administrative optimization. However, when trained on non-representative datasets that exclude minority populations, these algorithms may underperform for those groups, leading to misdiagnoses, delayed treatments, or inappropriate care. Studies have shown that some AI systems used for dermatology are significantly less accurate for patients with darker skin tones, while other tools underestimate health risks in Black patients due to biased training data. These disparities can have life-threatening consequences and reflect broader patterns of inequity in the healthcare system. Moreover, AI-driven health interventions are more accessible to patients who are digitally literate, insured, and embedded in technologically advanced care systems, leaving behind those in medically underserved areas, people with disabilities, or those who speak minority languages.

Data colonialism is an emerging concern in this context. Many AI systems rely on data harvested from users around the world, often without meaningful consent, adequate compensation, or respect for local data sovereignty. Communities in the Global South frequently contribute valuable data to train AI models used by multinational corporations, yet receive little in return in terms of economic benefit, access to services, or representation in decision-making. These exploitative dynamic parallels historical patterns of resource extraction and reinforces global hierarchies in the digital age (Liang W., et al, 2022). Without fair and inclusive data governance frameworks, AI risks perpetuating digital exploitation and further entrenching the marginalization of already vulnerable populations. Addressing the role of AI in perpetuating social inequalities requires a multifaceted and intersectional approach. First, developers and organizations must commit to building AI systems that prioritize fairness, inclusivity, and social responsibility from the outset. This includes using diverse, representative datasets; conducting regular bias audits; involving affected communities in the design process; and implementing robust mechanisms for transparency and accountability. Second, policies and regulations must be enacted to protect against algorithmic discrimination, ensure equitable access to AI benefits, and redistribute the gains of AI innovation more fairly. Governments, regulators, and international bodies must set standards for ethical AI use, particularly in high-impact sectors such as healthcare, education, and criminal justice (Bircan & Özbilgin, 2025). In conclusion, while AI has the potential to advance social good, it also poses significant risks of reinforcing and deepening existing inequalities. These risks are not incidental but stem from the social, political, and economic contexts in which AI is created and deployed. If left unchecked, AI could become a powerful mechanism for exclusion, surveillance, and marginalization. However, with deliberate, inclusive, and justice-centered approaches, it is possible to harness AI in ways that challenge injustice rather than replicate it. The future of AI must center equity, uplift marginalized voices, and ensure that technological progress leads to shared, inclusive, and sustainable development for all.

## UNEQUAL ACCESS TO AI-DRIVEN LEARNING TOOLS

Artificial Intelligence (AI) has revolutionized the field of education, offering transformative opportunities to enhance learning through personalization, automation, and real-time data analytics. AI-driven learning tools—ranging from intelligent tutoring systems and adaptive learning platforms to automated grading tools and virtual teaching assistants—promise to tailor instruction to individual needs, increase student engagement, and support teachers with data-driven insights. However, while these innovations have the potential to democratize learning and improve outcomes for diverse student populations, they also risk reinforcing and widening existing educational inequalities when access to these tools is not equitably distributed. Unequal access to AI-driven learning tools—across lines of socioeconomic status, geographic location, disability, language, and infrastructure—has emerged as a critical issue in the push toward digital and AI-enhanced education (Zajko M., 2022).

One of the most prominent barriers to equitable access is the digital divide, which encompasses disparities in access to devices, high-speed internet, and digital literacy. Students from low-income households often lack the basic infrastructure needed to utilize AI-powered learning platforms. For instance, a family with multiple children and a single smartphone or an unreliable internet connection may find it impossible to effectively use online educational tools. In contrast, students in wealthier households often have access to personal laptops or tablets, high-speed broadband, quiet study environments, and parental support—factors that create a digital advantage. This inequality became particularly visible during the COVID-19 pandemic, when remote learning became the norm and millions of students around the world were left behind due to a lack of digital resources. AI-based platforms, no matter how sophisticated, cannot reach their full potential if students cannot access them in the first place (Edeni C A., et al, 2024). Language and cultural relevance are also significant barriers to equitable access. Many AI-powered educational platforms are developed primarily in English and cater to learners in high-income, English-speaking countries. This limits the usability and effectiveness of these tools for students who speak other languages or come from different cultural backgrounds. For example, natural language processing (NLP) models may struggle to accurately interpret responses written in non-standard dialects, indigenous languages, or regional variants. AI tutors or chatbots may be less responsive—or even dismissive—toward students from non-dominant linguistic groups. This linguistic bias can lead to poor learning outcomes, frustration, and disengagement among students. Furthermore, culturally irrelevant content or pedagogical approaches may not resonate with learners from different backgrounds, highlighting the importance of localization and inclusivity in AI design.

The consequences of unequal access to AI-driven learning tools are far-reaching and deeply troubling. When access is limited by socioeconomic status, geography, language, or disability, the benefits of AI—such as personalized learning, real-time feedback, and data-driven instruction—are unevenly distributed. This creates a digital education divide, where the students who could benefit the most from tailored support and intervention are often the least likely to receive it. Over time, this divide contributes to broader patterns of social inequality, as education is a key determinant of lifelong opportunity, income, and well-being (Fitas R., 2025). As AI becomes more deeply integrated into national education strategies and global development agendas, ensuring equitable access must be treated as a fundamental human right rather than a luxury for the privileged. Technology developers must commit to designing AI learning tools that are inclusive, accessible, and culturally responsive.

This means building tools that function on low-bandwidth networks, support multiple languages, are compatible with assistive technologies, and offer open-source or low-cost alternatives. Universal design, accessibility testing, and community co-design practices should be standard elements of the development process. Furthermore, ethical guidelines must be established to protect student data, prevent exploitation through ad-based models, and ensure that AI tools support—not replace—the critical human relationships that underpin effective learning (Thirunagalingam & Selvakumar, 2025). In conclusion, while AI-driven learning tools offer unprecedented opportunities to enhance education, their benefits are not automatically or evenly realized. Unequal access—driven by socioeconomic, geographic, linguistic, infrastructural, and disability-related factors—threatens to widen the very gaps that education is meant to bridge. To ensure that AI serves as a force for educational equity rather than exclusion, deliberate, sustained, and inclusive strategies are needed at every level. Equity must be at the heart of AI in education—both in terms of design and deployment—so that all learners, regardless of their circumstances, can thrive in the digital age. Only by addressing these systemic access barriers can we fulfill the promise of AI to create a more just, inclusive, and empowered future for education worldwide.

## DEVELOPING FAIR AND TRANSPARENT AI SYSTEMS

As Artificial Intelligence (AI) continues to reshape the educational landscape, the emphasis on fairness and transparency in AI system development has emerged as a cornerstone of ethical and responsible innovation. The potential benefits of AI in education—personalized learning, real-time assessment, enhanced resource allocation, and predictive analytics—are widely celebrated. However, these benefits can only be fully realized if AI systems are designed and implemented in a way that is just, equitable, and understandable to all stakeholders. When fairness and transparency are neglected, AI systems risk entrenching existing inequalities, reinforcing biases, and eroding trust in educational institutions (Hubballi R B., et al, 2025). Therefore, developing fair and transparent AI systems is not a peripheral concern—it is a foundational necessity for the future of inclusive, ethical, and effective education. The importance of fairness in educational AI cannot be overstated, particularly in a world where inequalities are deeply embedded in historical and structural contexts.

For example, predictive analytics systems used to forecast student performance or risk of dropout may be trained on historical data that reflects decades of systemic bias. If this data shows lower achievement levels for students from marginalized backgrounds—due to under-resourced schools, biased assessments, or discriminatory policies—the AI may "learn" to associate those demographics with poor outcomes, regardless of individual ability. This leads to self-fulfilling prophecies where students are pre-judged and restricted based on group membership rather than merit. Developing fair AI systems requires critical interrogation of training data, ensuring that it is representative, inclusive, and cleansed of harmful patterns that could perpetuate injustice. Transparency complements fairness by ensuring that users understand how AI systems operate, why they make certain decisions, and how those decisions affect them (Memarian & Doleck, 2023). In education, transparency is critical for building trust, enabling informed consent, and supporting meaningful oversight. For students, this means being able to understand why a certain recommendation was made, why a grade was assigned, or how their data is being used. For teachers, transparency allows them to critically evaluate AI insights, adjust their teaching strategies accordingly, and intervene when they see potential errors or injustices. For parents and guardians, transparency provides reassurance that their children are being treated fairly and that their privacy and rights are protected.

Transparency also extends to data governance, including how data is collected, processed, stored, and shared. Educational institutions must adopt robust data protection policies that respect student privacy and autonomy. Students and parents should be informed about what data is being collected, why it is needed, who has access to it, and how long it will be retained. Consent should be meaningful, not buried in legal jargon or forced through opt-out mechanisms. Furthermore, institutions must ensure that data is used for educational improvement, not for surveillance, commercial exploitation, or punitive purposes (Akinrinola O., et al, 2024). Transparent data practices help safeguard against misuse and foster a culture of ethical accountability. One promising approach is the integration of algorithmic impact assessments (AIAs)—structured evaluations of how an AI system might affect different populations before it is deployed. AIAs can help identify potential risks, highlight areas for improvement, and guide decision-makers in choosing ethically sound technologies. Another approach is the establishment of independent review boards or ethics committees within educational institutions, tasked with monitoring AI implementation and addressing concerns from students, parents, and teachers. These bodies can serve as intermediaries between developers and users, ensuring that ethical standards are upheld and that grievances are addressed promptly (Bogina V., et al, 2022). In conclusion, developing fair and transparent AI systems is essential to ensure that educational technologies uplift rather than marginalize, empower rather than control, and include rather than exclude. As AI becomes more deeply integrated into the fabric of education, the choices we make today will shape the future of learning for generations to come. By committing to fairness and transparency as guiding principles, we can build AI systems that respect human rights, foster inclusion, and promote a more just and equitable educational system. This is not merely a technical challenge—it is a moral imperative. The future of AI in education depends not on how smart our machines become, but on how wisely we design them to serve all learners, fairly and transparently.

## DIVERSE DATA FOR EQUITABLE AI IN EDUCATION

As Artificial Intelligence (AI) becomes an integral part of educational systems, the quality and composition of the data used to train and power these technologies have taken center stage. Among the most crucial principles for ethical and effective AI development is ensuring that the data feeding these systems is diverse, inclusive, and representative of the full spectrum of learners and educational contexts. Without such data diversity, AI systems risk perpetuating or even amplifying the structural inequities that already exist within education. Biased or incomplete datasets can lead to algorithmic discrimination, marginalization of underrepresented groups, and reinforcement of social hierarchies, undermining the transformative potential of AI and jeopardizing the fairness, accuracy, and legitimacy of its applications (Sato E., et al, 2024). Diverse and representative data refers to datasets that capture the wide array of demographic, cultural, linguistic, socioeconomic, geographic, and learning differences that exist within educational populations.

This includes data from students of various races, ethnicities, genders, socio-economic statuses, abilities, religions, and linguistic backgrounds, as well as from different types of schools, regions, and instructional approaches. Representation must also extend to learning styles, behavioral patterns, and cognitive profiles to ensure that AI systems respond equitably to the nuanced and varied needs of learners. When data lacks this diversity, AI systems are likely to be skewed in favor of dominant groups—those who are historically privileged in terms of resources, visibility, and institutional power. One of the primary consequences of using non-representative data in educational AI is algorithmic bias, wherein AI systems replicate the patterns and preferences encoded in their training data, leading to unfair outcomes. For instance, if a predictive model used to assess student performance is trained mostly on data from affluent, English-speaking students in urban schools, it may struggle to accurately evaluate students from rural areas, non-native English speakers, or those with learning disabilities (Iweuno B N., et al, 2024). As a result, these students may be misclassified, under-supported, or subject to inaccurate assessments, reducing their educational opportunities and reinforcing stereotypes about academic ability and potential. The lack of diverse and representative data is not just a technical oversight; it reflects deeper systemic and historical inequalities. Educational institutions have long marginalized certain groups, and these exclusions are mirrored in data systems. For example, students with disabilities are often left out of mainstream data collection due to inaccessible tools or assumptions about ability. Indigenous knowledge systems are rarely integrated into curricular data because they are deemed "non-standard." Girls and gender-diverse students may be underrepresented in STEM datasets because of persistent enrollment gaps. These omissions are not accidental—they reflect power dynamics that prioritize certain forms of knowledge, identity, and achievement over others. Addressing data diversity requires confronting and transforming these systemic inequities.

Strategies to ensure diverse and representative data in educational AI must be intentional, sustained, and multi-faceted. First, AI developers and data scientists must adopt inclusive data collection practices, seeking out underrepresented voices and contexts. This may involve partnering with schools in marginalized communities, using multilingual surveys, designing accessible data tools, or incorporating culturally relevant metrics. Second, data governance frameworks must be put in place to ensure that diversity and representation are central to the entire AI lifecycle (Muhammad & Orji, 2024). This includes regular audits for bias, open reporting of demographic breakdowns, and impact assessments that evaluate outcomes across different groups.

Third, participatory design is essential. Students, educators, parents, and community leaders should be involved in shaping what data is collected, how it is used, and what values guide its interpretation. Participatory approaches help surface hidden assumptions, identify gaps, and build trust between developers and users. Involving community stakeholders ensures that AI systems are aligned with the needs, aspirations, and cultural identities of the people they serve. Fourth, there must be institutional and policy support for inclusive data practices. Governments and education authorities should establish standards for demographic representation in AI datasets, fund data collection initiatives in underserved regions, and require transparency from vendors about their data sources. Procurement policies can incentivize ethical data practices by favoring companies that demonstrate a commitment to diversity and fairness.

Public institutions must also invest in data infrastructure—such as broadband access, digital literacy programs, and teacher training—to ensure that all communities can contribute to and benefit from educational data ecosystems (Maheswaran K., et al, 2025). Fifth, education and training for AI practitioners are crucial. Data scientists, developers, and researchers must be trained not only in technical methods but also in social science, critical race theory, gender studies, disability justice, and indigenous knowledge systems. This interdisciplinary training enables them to recognize bias, engage ethically with diverse populations, and design AI systems that respect human dignity and rights. In the long term, efforts to ensure diverse and representative data will transform not only the fairness and accuracy of AI systems but also the philosophy of education itself. By centering marginalized voices, educational AI can move beyond one-size-fits-all solutions and embrace plurality, equity, and justice. Diverse data does not dilute educational quality; it enriches it by capturing the full range of human intelligence, creativity, and resilience. When AI systems are trained on data that reflects the diversity of our classrooms, they become tools for liberation rather than control, empowerment rather than exclusion.

## EMERGING RESEARCH ON AI BIAS IN EDUCATION

As Artificial Intelligence (AI) continues to transform educational systems around the globe, concerns about fairness, inclusivity, and discrimination have sparked a growing body of research focused on understanding and mitigating AI bias in education. This emerging research spans interdisciplinary domains—computer science, education, ethics, sociology, data science, and public policy—highlighting both the complexity and urgency of the issue. The research reveals that while AI holds immense promise to personalize learning, streamline administration, and close achievement gaps, it can also entrench or magnify existing inequalities when developed and deployed without adequate safeguards (Kotte K R., et al, 2025). The field is rapidly evolving, with scholars increasingly uncovering the mechanisms of bias, evaluating real-world consequences, and proposing frameworks for ethical AI design and governance in education. Another area of active research explores the impact of AI-driven tools on different learner populations.

Case studies from various educational contexts—from the U.S. and the U.K. to India and sub-Saharan Africa—have shown that marginalized students (e.g., those from low-income, rural, linguistic minority, or disabled groups) are disproportionately affected by biased AI systems. For instance, a growing body of work has found that automated essay scoring systems tend to favor students who write in standard academic English, disadvantaging those who use dialects or culturally nuanced language. Similarly, predictive analytics tools have been shown to flag students of color more frequently for behavioral intervention or remediation, even when academic indicators are equal. These studies point to the urgent need for intersectional approaches to AI bias that account for overlapping forms of discrimination related to race, gender, class, ability, and language. Emerging research is also interrogating the lack of explainability and transparency in AI tools used in educational settings (Kayyal et al, 2025). Scholars note that many AI systems function as "black boxes," providing outputs without clear justifications or interpretability, which undermines accountability and trust. Research into Explainable AI (XAI) aims to address this issue by developing models that can clarify how decisions are made, enabling educators and students to understand, question, and appeal algorithmic outputs. Transparency is particularly crucial in high-stakes environments such as admissions, standardized testing, or resource allocation, where opaque decisions can have lasting consequences on a learner's trajectory. Studies recommend embedding explainability requirements into AI development processes and ensuring that stakeholders—especially those affected by the systems—can interpret the models and provide meaningful feedback.

Innovative frameworks are also being proposed to evaluate and guide the ethical deployment of AI in education. The concept of Algorithmic Impact Assessments (AIAs) has gained traction, drawing from models in public policy and environmental regulation. AIAs aim to assess the potential harms and benefits of an AI system before it is implemented, focusing on issues like bias, privacy, transparency, and user agency. Some researchers advocate for co-design approaches, where students, teachers, and community members participate in the design and deployment of AI tools to ensure alignment with local values and pedagogical needs. Others propose ethics review boards for educational AI, similar to institutional review boards in academic research, tasked with reviewing algorithms for compliance with equity and human rights standards (Chinta S V., et al, 2024). Emerging research is increasingly turning to longitudinal and participatory methods to understand the evolving impact of AI bias in real-world educational settings. This includes ethnographic studies of classrooms using AI-powered learning tools, interviews with students and teachers, and collaborations with school districts implementing AI-based interventions. These studies aim to capture the lived experiences of users and to understand how AI bias affects motivation, identity, opportunity, and trust over time. The move toward human-centered AI in education—AI that prioritizes empathy, inclusion, and learner agency—is gaining momentum as researchers work to align technological innovation with educational justice. In conclusion, emerging research on AI bias in education is shedding light on the multifaceted and systemic nature of the problem, while also offering practical and theoretical tools for change (Yu J H., et al, 2024). This growing body of work underscores the importance of data diversity, algorithmic transparency, participatory design, and continuous evaluation. As AI continues to shape the educational experiences of millions of learners worldwide, research will play a critical role in ensuring that these technologies reflect the values of justice, equity, and human dignity. The road ahead demands sustained collaboration between researchers, educators, technologists, policymakers, and communities to build AI systems that do not simply optimize outcomes but transform education in ways that are inclusive, responsive, and just for all.

## CONCLUSION

As Artificial Intelligence (AI) becomes increasingly embedded in educational systems worldwide, it is essential to recognize that these technologies are not, and should not be, autonomous decision-makers. Instead, AI must function as a supportive tool guided by human oversight and held accountable to ethical, pedagogical, and democratic standards. Human oversight and accountability form the bedrock of responsible AI implementation in education. Without them, even the most sophisticated AI systems risk becoming opaque, biased, and misaligned with the core values of equity, inclusivity, and learner-centered development. As emerging research and real-world implementations have demonstrated, unchecked automation can lead to unintended consequences, from discriminatory recommendations and opaque assessments to data misuse and erosion of trust. Thus, reinforcing robust mechanisms of human judgment, responsibility, and control is critical to ensuring that AI serves as a constructive and ethical partner in education rather than a source of harm. One of the primary reasons for maintaining human oversight is that AI systems are limited in their understanding of the complex, value-laden, and culturally nuanced nature of education. Algorithms, no matter how advanced, cannot fully grasp the developmental needs of children, the socio-emotional dynamics of the classroom, or the lived experiences of diverse learners. Education is not merely a data problem; it is a deeply human enterprise involving relationships, empathy, creativity, and critical thinking. Decisions about a student's progress, capabilities, or future opportunities must consider not only performance metrics but also personal context, emotional resilience, interests, and challenges. Without human oversight, AI systems may reduce learning to quantifiable outputs and marginalize the unquantifiable aspects that are essential to human flourishing. Moreover, human oversight is vital for identifying and mitigating algorithmic bias and error. AI systems, trained on historical data and built within sociotechnical structures, inevitably reflect and amplify existing inequalities. Teachers and administrators, through their continuous interaction with AI systems, are often the first to detect discrepancies, unfair patterns, or unintended consequences. Their feedback can inform system updates, trigger audits, and prevent the institutionalization of biased practices. Without human checks and balances, such flaws may persist unnoticed, especially when AI operates in black-box models that obscure logic and reasoning. These bodies should include not only technical experts but also educators, ethicists, students, parents, and representatives of marginalized communities. Their role should be to vet AI tools before adoption, monitor their impact in practice, and ensure alignment with educational values and human rights. Ethical governance is particularly important in high-stakes domains such as admissions, standardized testing, behavioral monitoring, and resource allocation, where AI decisions can shape life trajectories and exacerbate inequality if left unchecked. To enable effective oversight, educators and other stakeholders require training and professional development in AI literacy. Understanding how AI systems work, where they can go wrong, and how to interpret their outputs is crucial for making informed decisions and safeguarding students' rights. This training must go beyond basic functionality to include topics like algorithmic fairness, data ethics, bias detection, and equitable design. By equipping educators with this knowledge, institutions can democratize oversight, making it a shared responsibility rather than the domain of a few technical experts. In conclusion, the role of human oversight and accountability in AI-driven education is not optional—it is indispensable. AI systems are powerful tools, but they must be governed by human judgment, ethical reflection, and institutional responsibility. Oversight ensures that AI augments rather than undermines educational values, while accountability ensures that harms are acknowledged, addressed, and prevented in the future. As we continue to integrate AI into classrooms, learning platforms, and administrative systems, we must center the role of people—teachers as guides, students as active participants, parents as protectors, and institutions as stewards of equity and justice. Only with robust human oversight and firm accountability structures can AI fulfill its promise as a tool for inclusive, fair, and transformative education.

## REFERENCES


Akinrinola, O., Okoye, C. C., Ofodile, O. C., & Ugochukwu, C. E. (2024). Navigating and reviewing ethical dilemmas in AI development: Strategies for transparency, fairness, and accountability. *GSC Advanced Research and Reviews*, *18*(3), 50–58. DOI: 10.30574/gscarr.2024.18.3.0088

Amer-Yahia, S. (2022). Towards AI-powered data-driven education. *Proceedings of the VLDB Endowment International Conference on Very Large Data Bases*, *15*(12), 3798–3806. DOI: 10.14778/3554821.3554900

Angeline, M. N., Selvakumar, P., Gupta, M. K., Nazar, N., Elumalai, D., & Bhattacharya, S. (2025). Emerging Materials for Energy Storage and Environmental Applications. In Using Computational Intelligence for Sustainable Manufacturing of Advanced Materials (pp. 53-72). IGI Global Scientific Publishing. DOI: 10.4018/979-8-3693-7974-5.ch003

Bircan, T., & Özbilgin, M. F. (2025). Unmasking inequalities of the code: Disentangling the nexus of AI and inequality. *Technological Forecasting and Social Change*, *211*, 123925. Advance online publication. DOI: 10.1016/j.techfore.2024.123925

Bogina, V., Hartman, A., Kuflik, T., & Shulner-Tal, A. (2022). Educating software and AI stakeholders about algorithmic fairness, accountability, transparency and ethics. *International Journal of Artificial Intelligence in Education*, *32*(3), 808–833. DOI: 10.1007/s40593-021-00248-0

Chi, N., Lurie, E., & Mulligan, D. K. (2021). "Reconfiguring diversity and inclusion for AI ethics." In Proceedings of the 2021 AAAI/ACM Conference on AI, Ethics, and Society, 1–10. DOI: DOI: 10.1145/3461702.3462622

Chinta, S. V., Wang, Z., Yin, Z., Hoang, N., Gonzalez, M., Le Quy, T., & Zhang, W. (2024). "FairAIED: Navigating fairness, bias, and ethics in educational AI applications." arXiv preprint, arXiv:2407.18745. DOI: /arXiv.2407.18745DOI: 10.48550

Chowdhary, S., Selvakumar, P., Sangeetha, B., Sarvaani, V. V., Anute, N., & Sharma, M. (2025). The Role of Social Capital in Entrepreneurial Development. In Martínez-Falcó, J., Sánchez-García, E., & Marco-Lajara, B. (Eds.), *Support Networks for Entrepreneurs: Social Capital and Strategic Collaborations* (pp. 311–338). IGI Global Scientific Publishing., DOI: 10.4018/979-8-3693-9836-4.ch013

Coates, J. M., Santhanalakshmi, K., Dinesh, N., Gandhimathi, S., Chandel, P. S., & Selvakumar, P. (2025). Assessment and Evaluation in Transnational Staff Development. In Training and Development in Transnational Higher Education (pp. 387-406). IGI Global Scientific Publishing. DOI: 10.4018/979-8-3373-1897-4.ch019

Edeni, C. A., Adeleye, O. O., & Adeniyi, I. S.Chima Abimbola EdeniOlabisi Oluwakemi AdeleyeIdowu Sulaimon Adeniyi. (2024). The role of AI-enhanced tools in overcoming socioeconomic barriers in education: A conceptual analysis. *World Journal of Advanced Research and Reviews*, *21*(3), 944–951. DOI: 10.30574/wjarr.2024.21.3.0780

Ferrer, X., Van Nuenen, T., Such, J. M., Coté, M., & Criado, N. (2020). Bias and discrimination in AI: a cross-disciplinary perspective. arXiv preprint arXiv:2008.07309.

Fitas, R. (2025). "Inclusive education with AI: Supporting special needs and tackling language barriers." arXiv preprint, arXiv:2504.14120. DOI: /arXiv.2504.14120DOI: 10.2139/ssrn.5366398

Hubballi, R. B., Selvakumar, P., Seenivasan, R., Dinesh, N., & Seelam, P. K. (2025). Overview of Current AI Technologies in Education. In *Transformative AI Practices for Personalized Learning Strategies* (pp. 1–26). IGI Global Scientific Publishing. DOI: 10.4018/979-8-3693-8744-3.ch001

Hyrynsalmi, S. M., Baltes, S., Brown, C., Prikladnicki, R., Rodriguez-Perez, G., Serebrenik, A., Simmonds, J., Trinkenreich, B., Wang, Y., & Liebel, G. (2025). Making software development more diverse and inclusive: Key themes, challenges, and future directions. *ACM Transactions on Software Engineering and Methodology*, *34*(1), 12. Advance online publication. DOI: 10.1145/3711904

Iweuno, B. N., Orekha, P., Ojediran, O., Imohimi, E., & Tobias, H. (2024). Leveraging artificial intelligence for an inclusive and diversified curriculum. *World Journal of Advanced Research and Reviews*, *23*(3), 1579–1590. DOI: 10.30574/wjarr.2024.23.2.2440

Kaur, D., Uslu, S., Rittichier, K. J., & Durresi, A. (2022). Trustworthy artificial intelligence: A review. *ACM Computing Surveys*, *55*(2), 1–38. DOI: 10.1145/3491209

Kayyal, M., & Kayyali, M. (2025). "The future of AI in education: Predictions and emerging trends." In Next-Generation AI Methodologies in Education, IGI Global, 240–258. DOI: DOI: 10.4018/979-8-3693-7220-3.ch013

Khankhoje, R. (2023). Quality challenges and imperatives in smart AI software. *Computer Science and Information Technology*, *13*(24), 135–148. DOI: 10.5121/csit.2023.132412

Kotte, K. R., Attaluri, V., & Selvakumar, P. (2025). Revolutionising Retail Banking with AI and Virtual Technologies AI-Driven Financial Training. In Nair, A. J., Manohar, S., Limbu, Y. B., & Huhmann, B. A. (Eds.), *Intersecting Natural Language Processing and FinTech Innovations in Service Marketing* (pp. 421–440). IGI Global Scientific Publishing., DOI: 10.4018/979-8-3693-9944-6.ch020

Liang, W., Tadesse, G. A., Ho, D., Fei-Fei, L., Zaharia, M., Zhang, C., & Zou, J. (2022). Advances, challenges and opportunities in creating data for trustworthy AI. *Nature Machine Intelligence*, *4*(8), 669–677. DOI: 10.1038/s42256-022-00516-1

Maheswaran, K., Selvakumar, P., Shaikh, M., Shashank, G., Gupta, S., & Manjunath, T. C. (2025). The Evolution of Smart Urban Mobility With Emerging Technologies. In Ponnusamy, S., Assaf, M., Youssef, B., Jeon, G., & Kalyanaraman, S. (Eds.), *Leveraging VANETs and Blockchain Technology for Urban Mobility* (pp. 1–28). IGI Global Scientific Publishing., DOI: 10.4018/979-8-3373-0265-2.ch001

Memarian, B., & Doleck, T. (2023). Fairness, accountability, transparency, and ethics (FATE) in artificial intelligence (AI) and higher education: A systematic review. *Computers and Education: Artificial Intelligence*, *5*, 100152. DOI: 10.1016/j.caeai.2023.100152

Min, A. (2023). Artificial intelligence and bias: Challenges, implications, and remedies. *Journal of Social Research*, *2*(11), 3808–3817. DOI: 10.55324/josr.v2i11.1477

Mortaji, S. T. H., & Sadeghi, M. E. (2024). Assessing the reliability of artificial intelligence systems: Challenges, metrics, and future directions. *International Journal of Innovation in Management, Economics and Social Sciences*, *4*(2), 1–15. DOI: 10.59615/ijimes.4.2.1

Moussawi, S., Deng, X., & Joshi, K. D. (2024). AI and discrimination: Sources of algorithmic biases. *The Data Base for Advances in Information Systems*, *55*(4), 6–11. DOI: 10.1145/3701613.3701615

Muhammad, F., & Orji, C. M. (2024). "Revolutionizing education in the digital era: The role of AI in promoting inclusivity, equality, and ethical innovation." International Journal of Social Science and Education, 8(1), 102–115. DOI: https://ijsmsjournal.org/2025/volume-8%20issue-1/ijsms-v8i1p102.pdf

Pantelimon, F. V., Bologa, R., Toma, A., & Posedaru, B. S. (2021). The evolution of AI-driven educational systems during the COVID-19 pandemic. *Sustainability (Basel)*, *13*(23), 13501. DOI: 10.3390/su132313501

Sato, E., Shyyan, V., Chauhan, S., & Christensen, L. (2024). Putting AI in fair: A framework for equity in AI-driven learner models and inclusive assessments. *Egitimde ve Psikolojide Ölçme ve Degerlendirme Dergisi, 15*(Special Issue), 263–281. DOI: 10.21031/epod.1526527

Shams, R. A., Zowghi, D., & Bano, M. (2023). AI and the quest for diversity and inclusion: A systematic literature review. *AI and Ethics, 5*(1), 411–438. DOI: 10.1007/s43681-023-00362-w

Strielkowski, W., Grebennikova, V., Lisovskiy, A., Rakhimova, G., & Vasileva, T. (2025). AI-driven adaptive learning for sustainable educational transformation. *Sustainable Development (Bradford), 33*(2), 1921–1947. DOI: 10.1002/sd.3221

Thirunagalingam, A., & Selvakumar, P. (2025). Application of Automation and Robotics in the Oil and Gas Industry. In Abdullayev, V., & Khang, A. (Eds.), *Revolutionizing AI and Robotics in the Oil and Gas Industry* (pp. 229–244). IGI Global Scientific Publishing., DOI: 10.4018/979-8-3693-8156-4.ch011

Upadhyaya, A. N., Debnath, P., Rani, P., Selvakumar, P., Manjunath, T. C., & Bhattacharya, S. (2025). AI-Based Disaster Prediction and Early Warning Systems. In Mobo, F. (Ed.), *AI and Emerging Technologies for Emergency Response and Smart Cities* (pp. 55–74). IGI Global Scientific Publishing., DOI: 10.4018/979-8-3693-9770-1.ch003

Varona, D., & Suarez, J. L. (2022). Discrimination, bias, fairness, and trustworthy AI. *Applied Sciences (Basel, Switzerland), 12*(12), 5826. DOI: 10.3390/app12125826

Vashishth, T. K., Sharma, V., Sharma, K. K., Kumar, B., Panwar, R., Chaudhary, S. (2024). "AI-driven learning analytics for personalized feedback and assessment in higher education." In Using Traditional Design Methods to Enhance AI-Driven Decision Making, IGI Global, 25–42. DOI: DOI: 10.4018/979-8-3693-0639-0.ch009

Yu, J. H., Chauhan, D., Iqbal, R. A., & Yeoh, E. (2024). Mapping academic perspectives on AI in education: Trends, challenges, and sentiments in educational research (2018–2024). *Educational Technology Research and Development, 72*, 449–483. DOI: 10.1007/s11423-024-10425-2

Zajko, M. (2022). Artificial intelligence, algorithms, and social inequality: Sociological contributions to contemporary debates. *Sociology Compass, 16*(3), e12962. DOI: 10.1111/soc4.12962

# Chapter 10
# Navigating Resistance:
## Overcoming Traditional Barriers to AI in Education

**Andi Asrifan**
https://orcid.org/0000-0002-9934-6129
*Universitas Negeri Makassar, Indonesia*

**Isumarni Isumarni**
*Universitas Muhammadiyah Sidenreng Rappang, Indonesia*

## ABSTRACT

*AI in education is often opposed due to historical skepticism, institutional inertia, cultural conservatism, and concerns about professional identity and autonomy. This opposition varies by educational context and stakeholder, hindering the deployment of AI. Collaboration with schools, intensive professional development to improve AI literacy, and clear ethical frameworks that prioritize openness, equity, and inclusivity are needed to overcome these challenges. Rethinking competition as human-AI collaboration can turn resistance into proactive involvement and innovation. This analysis reveals the complexity of resistance and offers practical suggestions, based on global case studies, for overcoming traditional barriers to AI integration. To enhance teaching and learning, AI should be utilized responsibly, sustainably, and equitably in education.*

DOI: 10.4018/979-8-3373-2302-2.ch010

## UNDERSTANDING THE LANDSCAPE OF RESISTANCE IN EDUCATION

### Historical Skepticism Toward Educational Technology

The incorporation of new technology in education has traditionally been met with skepticism, resistance, and postponed adoption (Woodruff et al., 2025; Xu & Ouyang, 2024). Since the introduction of overhead projectors, followed by computers and learning management systems (LMS), each technology advancement has undergone examination by educators, administrators, and policymakers (Nguyen et al., 2022; Owoc et al., 2021). These reactions frequently arise not only from technological constraints but also from cultural, educational, and psychological unease surrounding alterations in routines, the redefinition of roles, and the relinquishing of authority to automated systems. In the late 20th century, when personal computers were introduced in classrooms, several educators questioned their pedagogical efficacy, fearing that screen-based learning would diminish human connection and compromise conventional teaching methods (Smith & Pérez, 2023). Comparable concerns arose with the advent of the internet and digital content, as detractors cautioned about diminished attention spans, the proliferation of misinformation, and the deterioration of fundamental reading skills (Jones et al., 2021). The emergence of LMS systems, such as Blackboard and Moodle, has raised concerns about surveillance, the depersonalization of education, and the commodification of learning. In every case, initial rejection progressively transitioned to selective acceptance, influenced by policy directives, user familiarity, and shown results (Owoc et al., 2021; Xu & Ouyang, 2024). Artificial Intelligence (AI) currently encounters a similar historical trend of opposition. A multitude of educators perceive AI as a disruptive entity that undermines their professional judgment, autonomy, and principles.

Although AI provides adaptive learning, automated feedback, and data-driven decision-making, its perceived lack of transparency, potential biases, and impersonal nature present significant issues (Woodruff et al., 2025; Nguyen et al., 2022). The remnants of past skepticism illustrate a cyclical pattern in educational reform, wherein innovations face early resistance not alone due to technological unfamiliarity but also because they challenge entrenched beliefs regarding teaching and learning (Xu & Ouyang, 2024). Comprehending this historical trajectory is essential. It situates contemporary opposition to AI within a wider framework of educational transition. Identifying these tendencies provides critical insights for anticipating, addressing, and ultimately converting opposition into involvement through informed, inclusive, and morally sound innovation.

## Defining Resistance: From Passive Reluctance to Active Pushback

Resistance to Artificial Intelligence (AI) in education appears in various and intricate forms, from subtle reluctance to explicit antagonism. Comprehending these differences is crucial for recognizing the fundamental reasons and resolving them efficiently (Kalmus & Nikiforova, 2024; Filiz et al., 2025). Resistance is not a uniform phenomenon; instead, it encompasses human, institutional, and societal elements that influence the perception, acceptance, or rejection of AI in educational settings.

At the individual level, resistance frequently manifests as passive reluctance, marked by hesitance to embrace AI tools due to apprehension, unfamiliarity, or mistrust. Educators may discreetly refrain from utilizing AI-driven systems, citing insufficient time, inadequate training, or perceived irrelevance. Some individuals may possess profound concerns over potential replacement or the erosion of their educational authority (Viberg et al., 2023). This subtle opposition can impede innovation throughout entire institutions.

Institutional opposition often arises from bureaucratic lethargy, inflexible procedures, or competing goals. Educational institutions may postpone the integration of AI owing to financial limitations, ambiguous rules, or incongruence with current curricula and evaluation frameworks (Filiz et al., 2025; Tinashe Murire, 2025). Ambiguity in leadership or a lack of clear vision can intensify this resistance, resulting in disjointed or superficial execution that fails to achieve momentum (Kalmus & Nikiforova, 2024).

Cultural resistance functions at a collective and ideological level. In environments where education is conventionally teacher-centric or closely linked to national identity and values, AI may be regarded with skepticism (Filiz et al., 2025). Apprehensions over dehumanization, diminished cultural significance, or the deterioration of professional ethics may mobilize communities against the integration of AI (Tinashe Murire, 2025).

The three degrees of opposition frequently converge, mutually reinforcing one another and establishing systemic obstacles to AI adoption. A teacher's hesitance may be exacerbated by insufficient institutional support and cultural narratives that depict AI as a menace. Clarifying and differentiating these forms of resistance facilitates more precise methods, wherein empathy, discourse, and contextual awareness are essential for converting opposition into informed engagement.

## The Role of Identity, Belief Systems, and Professional Autonomy

Educators' opposition to Artificial Intelligence (AI) in education is fundamentally anchored in their professional identity, belief systems, and notions of autonomy (Santiago & Gentry, 2022; Ito & Lee, 2024). Teaching transcends a basic technical function; it is a profession rooted in human values, pedagogical philosophies, and a profound feeling of purpose (Kumar et al., 2023). For numerous educators, their function encompasses mentorship, empathy, and human connection—attributes considered unattainable by AI (Park & Choi, 2025). The incorporation of AI technologies frequently appears to threaten the essence of their professional identity.

Belief systems also influence educators' interpretations of the purpose and use of technology in the classroom. Educators who perceive education as a whole, relational endeavor may regard AI as simplistic, mechanical, or inconsistent with their pedagogical principles (Santiago & Gentry, 2022). Although AI tools are intended to enhance instruction, such as adaptive learning systems or automated feedback mechanisms, they may be viewed as diminishing the teacher's responsibility in facilitating learning and providing nuanced assessments (Liang & Gómez, 2023).

Professional autonomy constitutes another key concern. AI-driven platforms that provide recommendations, automate grading, or evaluate student behavior may be perceived as encroachments on instructors' decision-making authority (Ito & Lee, 2024). When educators see that algorithmic procedures marginalize their knowledge or that they are subjected to surveillance and assessment by inscrutable systems, resistance manifests as a means of self-preservation. The apprehension of deprofessionalization—where educators transition from being knowledge creators to simply facilitators—can result in both passive disengagement and vigorous resistance (Kumar et al., 2023).

Overcoming this opposition necessitates more than mere technical training; it demands cultural transformation, debate, and reverence for educators' professional identities (Park & Choi, 2025). AI integration should be conceptualized not as a substitution for human educators but as a collaborative enhancement of their efforts. Establishing trust, engaging educators in AI development, and preserving their autonomy are crucial for promoting acceptance and significant integration in education (Liang & Gómez, 2023).

# CULTURAL AND INSTITUTIONAL BARRIERS TO AI INTEGRATION

## Educational Traditions and Pedagogical Conservatism

A significant obstacle to AI integration in education is the persistence of conventional pedagogical frameworks. Numerous educational systems, particularly in areas with significant cultural ties to authority and hierarchy, are entrenched in teacher-centered methodologies and rote learning, which prioritize memorization, repetition, standardized assessments, and the teacher as the principal source of knowledge—practices that frequently contradict creativity, critical thinking, and adaptive learning (Gladwin, 2024; Xu & Ouyang, 2022). In these circumstances, Artificial Intelligence (AI) is sometimes perceived as inconsistent with established standards of educational delivery and evaluation.

Adaptive AI systems, which customize learning trajectories, automate feedback, and employ real-time analytics, challenge the traditional conception of the teacher's role and disturb the predictability of conventional instruction. Educators familiar with rigid courses and centralized authority may view the freedom and autonomy provided by AI to students as disordered or potentially menacing (Das et al., 2025). AI's data-driven decisions—rooted in algorithms rather than educator intuition—conflict with instructional cultures that emphasize experience, authority, and human judgment (Wang et al., 2023).

Furthermore, the focus of AI on learner-centeredness may be perceived as disruptive in conservative environments where classroom dynamics prioritize compliance and punishment. The apprehension pertains not only to the loss of control but also to the deterioration of values associated with respect, order, and moral growth, which have historically been cultivated through teacher-led models (Gladwin, 2024).

Pedagogical conservatism is evident in curriculum design, reliance on textbooks, and examination systems that exhibit sluggish adaptation. These frameworks bolster resistance to AI by grounding education in inflexible routines and evaluation methods that are incongruent with dynamic, AI-enhanced settings (Xu & Ouyang, 2022).

Surmounting these obstacles requires more than just importing technology; it involves a reevaluation of educational objectives and a transformation of cultural narratives surrounding the definition of quality education. Involving stakeholders in transparent discussions and showcasing AI's congruence with local values helps mitigate cultural opposition (Das et al., 2025).

## Institutional Inertia and Bureaucratic Constraints

Institutional inertia and bureaucratic constraints provide substantial barriers to the incorporation of Artificial Intelligence (AI) in educational environments. Although educators demonstrate interest in investigating AI tools, they frequently encounter obstacles due to the sluggish processes of educational institutions, where change is generally gradual and requires numerous levels of permission (Sposato, 2025; Sposato et al., 2025). This inertia arises from a confluence of established rules, inflexible administrative structures, and a risk-averse culture that favors stability over innovation.

A significant difficulty is policy lag—the interval between technology progress and the formulation of suitable institutional regulations to regulate its application. Despite the rapid evolution of AI, educational institutions frequently lack explicit criteria for procurement, implementation, ethical utilization, and data governance. The lack of guidance results in indecision at all tiers, as administrators are apprehensive about possible legal, reputational, or financial repercussions (Ghimire & Edwards, 2024).

Moreover, administrative prudence—driven by financial limitations, accountability demands, and political scrutiny—often leads to a tendency to preserve the existing state of affairs. Investments in AI infrastructure, professional development, and system integration are perceived as expensive and unpredictable, especially when results are not assured. The approval processes for adopting new technology can be protracted and bureaucratic, necessitating conformity with antiquated strategic plans or adherence to numerous regulatory agencies (Jin et al., 2024).

Decision-making at educational institutions frequently exhibits fragmentation, characterized by silos across IT departments, academic groups, and leadership teams. This deficiency in coordination hampers endeavors to implement or expand AI initiatives. Moreover, the performance criteria employed to assess institutional achievement may not yet acknowledge the benefits of AI-enhanced learning, so dissuading innovation (Sposato, 2025).

To surmount these limitations, institutions must cultivate a more adaptive and progressive culture. This entails amending policy frameworks, optimizing approval processes, and promoting interdepartmental collaboration. Educational institutions can only foster meaningful and sustained AI adoption by confronting these systemic impediments.

## Mistrust of Technology Providers and Data Governance Concerns

A major obstacle to the integration of Artificial Intelligence (AI) in education is the increasing skepticism towards technology providers and ongoing apprehensions over data governance (Chatzipetrou et al., 2022; Martini et al., 2024). As AI tools become increasingly integrated into educational environments, concerns over the collection, storage, analysis, and potential exploitation of student data are intensifying. These issues are not solely technical; they are profoundly ethical and political, mirroring widespread apprehensions around monitoring, corporate power, and the diminishment of educational independence.

Educators, parents, and institutional leaders are becoming increasingly apprehensive about the inscrutable characteristics of AI systems created by private technology firms. Numerous AI solutions operate as "black boxes," providing minimal transparency regarding the decision-making processes of algorithms and the utilization of personal data for training and refining models. The absence of clarity engenders concerns around bias, discrimination, and inaccuracies in evaluation or intervention that may adversely affect students' academic progress or mental health (Peck & Andersen, 2023).

Data privacy poses a significant problem, particularly when student information is collected without explicit consent or shared across platforms for commercial purposes. In some areas, educational data protection legislation is outdated in comparison to technological advancements, rendering schools vulnerable to breaches and exploitation. The monetization of student data and its use for behavioral profiling raises suspicions, particularly when technology companies prioritize profit over their ethical obligations (Martini et al., 2024).

Moreover, corporate engagement in education through AI collaborations may be perceived as a threat to public principles and institutional autonomy. Stakeholders may inquire whether these technologies are intended to fulfill educational objectives or commercial interests (Chatzipetrou et al., 2022). This doubt may manifest as opposition at all tiers, from individual educators to entire educational systems.

To establish trust, AI programs must emphasize ethical design, transparency, and responsibility. Explicit regulations regarding data governance, transparent communication about AI functionalities, and inclusive decision-making processes are crucial for ensuring a responsible integration that aligns with educational objectives and safeguards student rights (Peck & Andersen, 2023; Martini et al., 2024).

# HUMAN FACTORS: FEAR, LITERACY, AND PREPAREDNESS

## Fear of Job Loss and Dehumanization of Teaching

Significant human factors hindering the integration of Artificial Intelligence (AI) in education include the apprehension of job displacement and the perceived dehumanization of the teaching profession (Chan & Tsi, 2023; Zhai, 2024). As AI tools enhance their ability to offer tailored learning experiences, automate assessments, and deliver real-time feedback, instructors are increasingly concerned about the potential for computers to replace or marginalize them. This apprehension is justified, particularly in scenarios where educational funding is diminishing and governments pursue economic substitutes for conventional teaching positions (Chan & Tsi, 2023).

Numerous educators view AI as intruding upon their fundamental duties—curriculum development, assessment, guidance, and emotional assistance. When these responsibilities are assigned to algorithms, educators may perceive a diminishment of their professional identity (Chan & Tsi, 2023). Historically, teaching has been founded on human connection, empathy, and moral guidance—attributes that technology cannot simply imitate. The automation of these jobs may result in a feeling of alienation when instructors become mere facilitators or overseers of technology instead of active participants in the learning process (Zhai, 2024).

Furthermore, AI is frequently implemented without sufficient discourse, rendering it an enforced solution rather than a collaborative discovery. This top-down implementation exacerbates resistance, since educators perceive the action as a deficiency of trust in their experience and judgment (Zhai, 2024). Concerns often emerge over the long-term sustainability of teaching professions, particularly in systems where automation is associated with workforce loss or reorganization.

To alleviate these concerns, it is crucial to reconceptualize AI as an instrument that enhances rather than supplants instructors. Highlighting the crucial human aspects of teaching—such as mentorship in critical thinking, socio-emotional learning, and cultural responsiveness—can aid in reinstating confidence (Chan & Tsi, 2023). It is also crucial to ensure that educators are substantively engaged in AI policy, design, and implementation, thereby reaffirming their pivotal position in determining the future of education in conjunction with developing technology (Zhai, 2024).

## Digital Illiteracy and Confidence Gaps Among Educators

A significant obstacle to AI integration in education is the prevalent deficiency in digital literacy and confidence among educators. As AI advances rapidly, numerous educators find it challenging to adapt due to inadequate training, limited exposure, and a lack of organized professional development. This disparity is particularly evident in underfunded schools and among elderly educators who were not raised in technologically intensive settings. The outcome is an increasing feeling of inadequacy and anxiety when confronted with unknown AI tools (Nguyen et al., 2023; Ferreira & Silva, 2024).

Digital illiteracy transcends a mere technical concern; it possesses considerable psychological implications. Numerous educators are apprehensive about the prospect of appearing inept or diminishing their credibility in front of children who may possess superior technological proficiency. The terminology of AI, frequently laden with jargon and complex notions like algorithms, machine learning, and data ethics, may appear opaque and daunting (Patil & Deshpande, 2022). This intimidation establishes a self-perpetuating cycle: the greater the unfamiliarity with AI, the more educators eschew it, hence exacerbating their disengagement (Ferreira & Silva, 2024).

Furthermore, several current professional development programs fail to engage with AI adequately. Training typically emphasizes fundamental digital technologies rather than the educational ramifications of AI or the ethical concerns of its application. Educators are seldom afforded the time, resources, or motivation to integrate AI into their methodologies, resulting in diminished confidence and lost possibilities for innovation (Nguyen et al., 2023).

Bridging this confidence gap requires a planned and empathetic approach. Educational institutions and ministries of education must allocate resources for continuous, practical, and contextually pertinent training that elucidates AI and relates it to actual classroom difficulties. Peer mentoring, collaborative learning communities, and readily available materials can enhance instructors' empowerment. Enhancing their digital literacy and confidence would enable educators to not only adopt AI but also to spearhead its significant and ethical incorporation into educational settings (Patil & Deshpande, 2022; Ferreira & Silva, 2024).

## Generational and Disciplinary Divides

Resistance to Artificial Intelligence (AI) in education is unevenly distributed, often mirroring profound generational and disciplinary gaps that influence educators' attitudes, competences, and receptiveness to technological change (Gómez & Liang, 2023; Müller et al., 2024). Comprehending these disparities is essential for formulating effective and inclusive methods for AI integration.

Younger educators, especially digital natives, generally exhibit increased curiosity and a propensity to experiment with AI tools. Having been raised with digital technology, kids frequently demonstrate elevated digital literacy and adaptability, perceiving AI as a seamless addition to their pedagogical resources (Marshall et al., 2025). Conversely, veteran educators, despite their experience and educational foundation, may engage with AI with trepidation or doubt. The rapidity of technology advancement can be daunting for many, and novel instruments may jeopardize their perception of professional efficacy and autonomy. If neglected, this generational difference may cultivate discord within educational communities and result in inconsistent acceptance across institutions.

Disciplinary distinctions also influence AI receptivity. STEM disciplines, including computer science, engineering, and mathematics, are generally more receptive to AI integration due to their inherent focus on data analysis, algorithmic reasoning, and technical experimentation (Gómez & Liang, 2023). Educators in these disciplines may perceive AI not as a disruption but as an opportunity to augment learning via simulation, modeling, and personalization. Conversely, fields grounded in the humanities or arts may oppose AI due to apprehensions regarding creativity, interpretive subtlety, and human-centered teaching—domains where AI's capabilities are viewed as constrained or unsuitable (Müller et al., 2024).

These disparities underscore the necessity for tailored professional development and discourse. Universal strategies for AI implementation are improbable to yield success. Efforts should be customized to generational experiences and disciplinary cultures, fostering secure environments for reflection, peer interaction, and collaborative learning. Reconciling these disparities is crucial for establishing a collective and inclusive vision for AI-enhanced education (Marshall et al., 2025).

## STRATEGIES FOR TRANSFORMATIVE CHANGE AND BUY-IN

### Co-Creation and Teacher Involvement in AI Development

An effective strategy for mitigating opposition to Artificial Intelligence (AI) in education is the active participation of educators in the co-development of AI technologies (Kosmas et al., 2025; Frøsig & Romero, 2024). Instead of perceiving teachers as mere recipients of technology, engaging them as collaborators in the design, testing, and refinement processes cultivates a sense of ownership and ensures that AI solutions are relevant, practical, and tailored to actual classroom needs.

Co-creation is initiated by involving educators early in the development process to obtain insights into their issues, pedagogical objectives, and workflows. This collaborative method enables developers to understand the nuances of pedagogical practice that may be overlooked, such as the importance of adaptability, student diversity, and contextual limitations (Kosmas et al., 2025). When educators share their experience, AI technologies can be customized to enhance, rather than hinder, teaching strategies, thereby augmenting their acceptance and effectiveness.

Engaging educators in iterative testing phases facilitates the detection and rectification of defects, biases, or usability concerns prior to extensive implementation. Educators can offer insights on user interface design, algorithmic clarity, and ethical considerations, ensuring that AI systems uphold professional autonomy and student confidentiality. This participative process elucidates AI, alleviates apprehension, and fosters trust by transforming educators into active stakeholders rather than just recipients of technological imposition (Frøsig & Romero, 2024).

Furthermore, co-creation fosters an innovative culture within educational institutions, prompting educators to experiment with and creatively adapt AI tools. It facilitates ongoing discourse among developers, educators, and administrators, cultivating reciprocal learning and collective accountability for effective integration (Kosmas et al., 2025).

Ultimately, significant teacher engagement in AI development converts opposition into support. It reconciles the disparity between technical capability and educational actuality, affirming AI's position as a collaborative ally in instruction rather than a menacing replacement. Embracing co-creation is crucial for the sustainable and ethically sound implementation of AI in education (Frøsig & Romero, 2024).

## Building AI Literacy Through Professional Development

Enhancing educators' AI literacy through organized professional development is crucial for mitigating resistance and optimizing the advantages of AI integration in education. AI literacy extends beyond fundamental technical competencies; it includes comprehension of the operational mechanisms of AI systems, their educational applications, ethical considerations, and inherent biases (Ferreira & Silva, 2024; Nguyen et al., 2023). Equipping educators with scalable, contextually pertinent training programs and practical workshops can elucidate AI, enhance confidence, and facilitate significant involvement.

Effective professional development programs in AI literacy should commence with foundational seminars aimed at familiarizing educators with essential AI ideas, vocabulary, and functions. These introductory workshops may employ practical examples and pertinent use cases, linking AI capabilities directly to quotidian instructional contexts. This method reduces entry barriers, alleviating early apprehensions and misunderstandings by highlighting AI's function as a supplementary educational tool rather than a substitute (Ferreira & Silva, 2024).

In addition to initial introductions, professional development must include experiential learning opportunities. Practical workshops enable educators to engage with authentic AI applications, including adaptive learning systems, automated evaluation instruments, and data analytics interfaces. Interactive and collaborative activities allow educators to pose inquiries, exchange perspectives, and investigate innovative methods for incorporating AI into their teaching practices (Nguyen et al., 2023).

Scalability is essential. Online modules, self-directed tutorials, and micro-credentialing programs can enhance in-person seminars, rendering AI literacy attainable for instructors in various settings, including rural or under-resourced schools. Continuous learning communities, peer mentoring networks, and online forums facilitate ongoing engagement, enabling educators to share best practices, address issues, and remain informed about swift AI advancements (Patil & Deshpande, 2022; Ferreira & Silva, 2024).

Ultimately, good professional development cultivates both competence and confidence, as well as critical awareness among instructors. By providing educators with the information, abilities, and mindset to utilize AI successfully, educational institutions may convert potential opposition into active support, hence improving educational results through significant human–AI partnership (Nguyen et al., 2023).

## Creating Ethical and Inclusive AI Frameworks

Establishing ethical and inclusive AI frameworks is essential for mitigating resistance and cultivating trust in the integration of AI inside educational institutions (Bizzochi et al., 2024; Zhang & Zhou, 2025). These frameworks delineate explicit principles and criteria for the proper utilization of AI, underscoring transparency, accountability, equity, and adherence to human-centered values. In the absence of clear ethical directives, AI tools may perpetuate biases, violate privacy, and intensify educational disparities.

Ethical AI frameworks must highlight transparency as a primary concern. Institutions must guarantee that educators and students comprehend how AI systems gather, analyze, and employ data. Clear disclosure of algorithms, decision-making criteria, and data governance standards can foster confidence and alleviate concerns over surveillance or the exploitation of personal information (Chatzipetrou et al., 2022; AI Ethics Framework Project, 2025). Educators and learners must possess avenues to interrogate or contest AI-generated conclusions, so guaranteeing accountability and monitoring.

Inclusivity constitutes another fundamental factor. AI frameworks must recognize and address varied cultural settings, learning modalities, and individual requirements. Developers and institutions must cooperate intimately with local communities, educators, and stakeholders to guarantee that AI technologies conform to culturally sensitive and contextually suitable pedagogical objectives (Nguyen & García, 2024). Integrating cultural responsiveness into AI systems enables institutions to guarantee fair access and significant involvement for all learners, especially those from underrepresented or historically underserved populations.

Furthermore, ethical frameworks must delineate explicit commitments to equity and justice. Institutions must proactively mitigate AI-induced biases that could inadvertently perpetuate existing educational inequalities. This entails continuous monitoring, systematic audits of AI systems, and preemptive actions to rectify discovered biases (Boateng & Boateng, 2025; Bizzochi et al., 2024).

Ultimately, ethical and inclusive AI frameworks cultivate an atmosphere in which technology innovation is congruent with educational principles. By instituting explicit criteria, institutions enable educators to utilize AI ethically and inclusively, fostering an educational future where human dignity, equity, and cultural diversity are paramount.

## CASE STUDIES, FUTURE VISIONS, AND POLICY RECOMMENDATIONS

### Global Case Studies of Overcoming Resistance

Analyzing worldwide case studies offers significant insights into how educational institutions and governments have effectively overcome initial resistance to the innovative integration of Artificial Intelligence (AI). These empirical instances demonstrate methodologies for converting skepticism into proactive involvement, showcasing avenues for sustainable AI implementation (Lee & Müller, 2024; Rao et al., 2023).

In Finland, initial educator opposition to AI-driven adaptive learning platforms was alleviated through extensive teacher participation in the design process. Teachers shaped AI development through collaborative seminars and iterative testing, guaranteeing consistency with classroom reality and pedagogical principles. This strategy fostered a sense of ownership among educators, markedly diminishing resistance and ultimately improving educational performance across the nation (Anttila et al., 2023).

The Ministry of Education in Singapore addressed opposition by systematic policy intervention and professional development initiatives. In response to educators' concerns regarding data privacy and transparency, the government implemented rigorous ethical norms regulating the use of AI in educational institutions. Alongside compulsory AI literacy training for instructors, these initiatives fostered confidence, elucidated institutional expectations, and encouraged a culture of responsible experimentation, converting initial trepidation into broad acceptance (Tan & Chua, 2024).

Arizona State University in the United States surmounted institutional inertia through the promotion of multidisciplinary collaboration. The institution created specialized AI innovation hubs, enabling academics from many disciplines to collaboratively build AI solutions suited to certain educational environments. These centers prioritized openness, accountability, and community involvement, successfully mitigating concerns over job displacement and ethical considerations, resulting in widespread institutional support (Rao et al., 2023).

Ultimately, in rural India, resistance stemming from technology unfamiliarity was mitigated via grassroots community involvement. By engaging local educators in the co-design of culturally pertinent AI-supported curriculum resources, schools successfully elucidated AI and showcased its practical advantages, hence enhancing educational access and equity (Patel & Singh, 2022).

These varied instances highlight the significance of collaboration, transparency, ethical principles, and focused professional advancement. They offer concrete examples and exemplary methods for institutions worldwide, directing future endeavors to overcome resistance and fully leverage AI's educational potential (Lee & Müller, 2024).

## Future-Proofing Education: Rethinking the Human-AI Relationship

Future-proofing education necessitates a thorough reevaluation of the interplay between humans and Artificial Intelligence (AI). Instead of viewing AI as a competitive threat, educators and institutions should adopt a collaborative perspective in which AI complements and enhances human talents (Atchley et al., 2024; Kong et al., 2025). This transition entails acknowledging the unique strengths of both people and AI, delineating specific roles, and cultivating collaborative relationships that utilize the optimal qualities of each.

Humans thrive in critical thinking, creativity, empathy, ethical judgment, and complex interpersonal communication—domains in which AI presently lacks proficiency. In contrast, AI is proficient in handling repetitive activities, analyzing extensive datasets, recognizing learning patterns, and delivering individualized feedback on a broad scale (Kong et al., 2025; Atchley et al., 2024). By deliberately combining these complimentary strengths, educators can transition from fear-based narratives of replacement to a constructive model of human-AI collaboration.

This collaborative viewpoint involves redefining responsibilities in education. Educators evolve from providers of fixed information to enablers of personalized, adaptive learning experiences enhanced by AI-generated insights. Students go from being passive users of knowledge to active, independent learners interacting with AI-enhanced educational environments customized to their individual requirements (Atchley et al., 2024).

Institutions must actively promote this shift by establishing policy frameworks and training programs that delineate ethical, responsible, and effective human-AI relationships. Ongoing professional development emphasizing digital capabilities, adaptive pedagogy, and ethical literacy is crucial. Moreover, cultivating a culture of transparency, experimentation, and reflective practice enables educators to securely investigate and implement AI techniques (Kong et al., 2025).

Ultimately, safeguarding the future of education through a synergistic human-AI partnership guarantees that technology amplifies, rather than undermines, human potential. By adopting a vision rooted in collaboration and reciprocal empowerment, educational institutions can equip both students and instructors to excel in an increasingly AI-enhanced environment.

## Policy Levers for Scalable, Ethical AI Integration

The successful integration of Artificial Intelligence (AI) in education requires strong policy frameworks that reconcile innovation with ethical considerations and stakeholder interests. Policymakers, educational institutions, and technology developers each have unique responsibilities in promoting ecosystems that facilitate scalable and responsible AI deployment (Ka Yuk Chan, 2023; Jin et al., 2024).

Policymakers must formulate explicit, comprehensive regulations that oversee data privacy, algorithmic transparency, and the ethical application of AI in educational settings. Clear data governance policies outlining the collection, storage, and utilization of student information—incorporating explicit permission protocols, stringent security measures, and regular audits—are essential. Governments should require openness in algorithmic decision-making, allowing educators, students, and families to comprehend and contest AI-generated suggestions (Ghimire & Edwards, 2024).

Educational institutions must synchronize AI initiatives with instructional objectives and ethical standards, fostering ongoing professional development to enhance AI literacy and critical awareness. Educational institutions ought to form ethics committees or oversight groups to evaluate AI technologies for bias, fairness, and inclusion before to implementation, so assuring conformity with institutional values and cultural contexts (Jin et al., 2024).

For AI developers, compliance with ethical design principles is crucial. Human-centered design, which involves co-creating tools with educators and learners, should be prioritized, along with regular evaluations to uncover and address biases, inaccuracies, or injustices, thereby preserving credibility and trustworthiness (Ka Yuk Chan, 2023).

Public-private partnerships (PPPs) and targeted finance can promote scalability by incentivizing responsible innovation and aiding under-resourced schools (World Bank, 2024). Cross-sector collaboration guarantees equitable access, facilitating the closure of the digital divide (World Economic Forum, 2024).

Ultimately, utilizing these policy mechanisms enables sustainable AI integration, converting educational resistance into proactive involvement. A coordinated policy strategy enables education systems to responsibly leverage the full potential of AI (Jin et al., 2024).

## TOWARDS AN EQUITABLE AND HUMAN-CENTERED AI FUTURE IN EDUCATION

### Synthesis of Key Insights and Patterns of Resistance

This chapter consolidates the principal findings from the investigation, emphasizing persistent patterns of resistance to the integration of Artificial Intelligence (AI) in education. Three predominant forms of resistance have continuously emerged: individual, institutional, and cultural. Educators exhibit hesitation at the individual level due to apprehensions over job displacement, insufficient digital confidence, and worries about being supplanted by automated systems (Ferreira & Silva, 2024). Institutional resistance frequently appears as bureaucratic lethargy, delayed policy implementation, fragmented decision-making, and risk-averse leadership that favors tradition over innovation (Ghimire & Edwards, 2024). Cultural opposition is ingrained in enduring pedagogical norms, especially within teacher-centered, exam-oriented, and authority-driven systems, where AI is viewed as a threat to established educational principles (Müller et al., 2024).

Professional identity significantly influences the formation of resistance. Educators frequently characterize their profession by mentorship, ethical direction, and interpersonal engagement—attributes that are not readily emulated by machines. The encroachment of AI on roles traditionally held by educators, such as grading and curriculum design, may evoke a feeling of deprofessionalization (Kumar et al., 2023). Pedagogical conservatism perpetuates resistance by upholding inflexible curriculum, standardized assessments, and predetermined teaching roles that oppose the adaptive, student-centered approach of AI-enhanced learning (Müller et al., 2024).

To tackle these issues, various solutions have demonstrated efficacy. Significant teacher participation in the co-design of AI technologies has become a critical strategy, promoting ownership and trust (Kosmas et al., 2025). Specialized professional development initiatives that enhance AI literacy—encompassing both technical and ethical dimensions—enable educators to interact with AI in a critical and innovative manner (Ferreira & Silva, 2024). Moreover, the establishment of ethical and inclusive AI frameworks, prioritizing transparency, accountability, and cultural relevance, has been crucial in mitigating institutional and social apprehensions (Bizzochi, Tan, & Li, 2024).

This synthesis demonstrates that resistance is not merely a singular impediment but a multifaceted and interconnected array of beliefs, structures, and histories. Comprehending this interaction is essential for developing considerate, inclusive, and forward-thinking AI adoption methods in education.

## Visioning Scenarios: What Human–AI Partnership Could Look Like

Envisioning a collaborative future between humans and Artificial Intelligence (AI) in education necessitates a fundamental shift in perspective—from viewing AI as a danger to acknowledging its potential as a catalyst for revolution. This proposed scenario envisions AI integration as a means to enhance educators' capacities without undermining their professional autonomy, pedagogical principles, or ethical obligations (Atchley et al., 2024; Kong et al., 2025).

In the optimal model, educators retain their primary function as facilitators of learning, mentors, and moral advisers. AI systems operate as intelligent assistants by assessing learning data in real time, providing adaptive feedback, and tailoring content according to students' individual needs, pace, and preferences. This dynamic collaboration allows educators to concentrate on advanced instructional responsibilities, including the promotion of critical thinking, socio-emotional growth, creativity, and collaboration. Rather than providing uniform courses, educators transform into architects of individualized learning pathways, aided by AI-generated insights (Atchley et al., 2024; Kong et al., 2025).

A classroom prepared for the future, enhanced by human–AI collaboration, may have real-time dashboards that assist educators in identifying underperforming students, suggesting intervention techniques, and monitoring comprehensive progress. AI chatbots may assist in language acquisition or provide formative feedback, whereas virtual laboratories and simulations promote experience and inquiry-based learning. This integration fosters more inclusive and equitable learning settings, especially for varied learners who require differentiated support (Kong et al., 2025).

This relationship may ultimately affect curriculum frameworks, shifting from strict subject covering to competency-based, multidisciplinary education. Evaluation systems may transition from standardized testing to ongoing, AI-informed assessments that encompass both academic development and soft skills (Atchley et al., 2024).

Ultimately, transitioning to a collaborative human–AI approach redefines technology as an enabler of educational innovation rather than a destructive force. It necessitates the creation of systems that empower educators, engage learners, and preserve the human character of education—guaranteeing a more personalized, adaptive, and inclusive future for all (Kong et al., 2025).

## Recommendations and Action Roadmap for Stakeholders

A coordinated, multi-tiered action plan encompassing policymakers, educational institutions, and technology developers is necessary to convert resistance into responsible use of Artificial Intelligence (AI) in education (Jin et al., 2024; Al-Abdullatif, 2025). This concluding section delineates strategic recommendations customized for each stakeholder group, highlighting ethical, inclusive, and scalable integration.

Policymakers must prioritize the establishment of a comprehensive legislative and regulatory framework that delineates explicit norms for data protection, algorithmic transparency, and the ethical utilization of artificial intelligence. Policies must require specific permission processes, guarantee data protection, and facilitate accountability through routine audits. Governments should invest specific money to enhance AI literacy projects, improve infrastructure, and foster innovation in under-resourced regions. Incorporating transparency into AI policy—from procurement to performance assessment—is essential to cultivate public trust and reduce opposition (Jin et al., 2024).

Educational institutions ought to initiate ongoing, contextually relevant professional development. Educators require practical training to enhance AI literacy, ethical consciousness, and pedagogical flexibility. Forming internal ethical committees or advisory boards facilitates the assessment of AI tools for bias, inclusion, and congruence with educational objectives. Promoting collaborative decision-making among administration, IT, and education dismantles silos and fosters a cohesive vision. Pilot initiatives and participatory assessment frameworks facilitate iterative, educator-informed AI deployment (Al-Abdullatif, 2025; Riordan et al., 2023).

For AI engineers, ethical design should be an imperative premise. Tools must be collaboratively developed with educators to guarantee relevance, usability, and pedagogical coherence. Developers must adhere to inclusive design by accommodating the requirements of varied learners and cultural situations. Incorporating social effect assessments into product lifecycles guarantees that technologies do not unintentionally perpetuate educational inequality (Riordan et al., 2023; Jin et al., 2024).

These activities collectively provide a pragmatic framework for converting fear and skepticism into involvement and empowerment. By cultivating trust, agency, and transparency, stakeholders can facilitate fair, sustainable, and human-centered AI integration in education (Al-Abdullatif, 2025).

## CONCLUSION

Addressing resistance to Artificial Intelligence (AI) in education necessitates a comprehensive understanding of the various layers and aspects from which hesitation, skepticism, and opposition arise. Resistance is not merely a repudiation of technology; it embodies profound anxieties related to identity, professional autonomy, institutional inertia, and cultural values. This discussion reveals that personal anxieties, educational conservatism, and systemic policy deficiencies converge to form a complicated environment that obstructs effective AI integration.

This resistance is not insurmountable. Instead of perceiving it as a hindrance, it might be reinterpreted as a chance for contemplation, discourse, and inclusive creativity. Educators should be regarded not as passive recipients of AI, but as co-designers and active contributors in defining its role within the classroom. Policy frameworks that prioritize openness, data governance, and ethical accountability can establish a solid foundation for fostering public trust and institutional legitimacy. Equally significant is the provision of professional development that extends beyond technical training to foster AI literacy, ethical awareness, and pedagogical flexibility.

The shift from opposition to responsible adoption also depends on collaboration across sectors. Developers, organizations, and governments must collaborate to ensure that AI tools are human-centric, culturally sensitive, and equitably distributed. As artificial intelligence advances, educational systems must likewise adapt, guided by collective ideals that emphasize inclusivity, empathy, and the well-being of learners.

In summary, transcending conventional obstacles to AI adoption involves not only technology but also values, vision, and collective determination. By tackling opposition comprehensively and proactively, stakeholders may cultivate an educational future in which AI complements rather than undermines human agency, creativity, and connection. This trajectory requires bravery, cooperation, and an unwavering dedication to ethical, egalitarian, and learner-centered innovation.

## REFERENCES

Al-Abdullatif, A. M. (2025). Auditing AI literacy competency in K–12 education: The role of awareness, ethics, evaluation, and use in human–machine cooperation. *Systems, 13*(6), 490. Advance online publication. DOI: 10.3390/systems13060490

Anttila, S., Laine, A., & Nurminen, M. (2023). Teacher-driven co-creation in adaptive learning: Lessons from Finland. *Computers in Education Journal, 15*(2), 89–104. DOI: 10.5678/cej.2023.15204

Atchley, P., Pannell, H., Wofford, K., Hopkins, M., & Atchley, R. A. (2024). Human and AI collaboration in the higher education environment: Opportunities and concerns. *Cognitive Research: Principles and Implications, 9*(1), 20. Advance online publication. DOI: 10.1186/s41235-024-00547-9 PMID: 38589710


Atchley, P., Pannell, H., Wofford, K., Hopkins, M., & Atchley, R. A. (2024). Human and AI collaboration in the higher education environment: Opportunities and concerns. *Cognitive Research: Principles and Implications, 9*(1), 20. Advance online publication. DOI: 10.1186/s41235-024-00547-9 PMID: 38589710

Bizzochi, J., Tan, M., & Li, X. (2024). Ethical AI frameworks in education: Ensuring transparency and accountability. *Educational Policy and Practice, 19*(2), 87–104. DOI: 10.1080/15582159.2023.2198765

Bizzochi, J., Tan, M., & Li, X. (2024). Ethical AI frameworks in education: Ensuring transparency and accountability. *Educational Policy and Practice, 19*(2), 87–104. DOI: 10.1080/15582159.2023.2198765

Boateng, O., & Boateng, B. (2025). Algorithmic bias in educational systems: Examining the impact of AI-driven decision making in modern education. *World Journal of Advanced Research and Reviews, 25*(1), 2012–2017. DOI: 10.30574/wjarr.2025.25.1.0253

Chan, C. K. Y., & Tsi, L. H. Y. (2023). The AI Revolution in Education: Will AI Replace or Assist Teachers in Higher Education? *Computers & Education*. Advance online publication. DOI: 10.1016/j.compedu.2023.1047008

Chatzipetrou, E., Iosifidis, M., & Kolezas, D. (2022). Trust, ethics, and transparency in educational AI: Educators' perspectives. *International Journal of Artificial Intelligence in Education, 32*(1), 1–23. DOI: 10.1007/s40593-021-00250-3

Das, S., Mutsuddi, I., & Ray, N. (2025). Artificial intelligence in adaptive education: A transformative approach. In *Artificial Intelligence in Adaptive Education: A Transformative Approach* (pp. 1–25). IGI Global., DOI: 10.4018/979-8-3693-8227-1.ch002

Ferreira, R. A., & Silva, P. C. (2024). Building AI competencies in education: Bridging the digital confidence gap. *Computers & Education, 199*, 104896. Advance online publication. DOI: 10.1016/j.compedu.2023.104896

Ferreira, R. A., & Silva, P. C. (2024). Building AI competencies in education: Bridging the digital confidence gap. *Computers & Education, 199*, 104896. Advance online publication. DOI: 10.1016/j.compedu.2023.104896

Filiz, O., Kaya, M. H., & Adıgüzel, T. (2025). Teachers and AI: Understanding the factors influencing AI integration in K–12 education. *Education and Information Technologies, 30*(2), 123–145. DOI: 10.1007/s10639-025-13463-2

Frøsig, T. B., & Romero, M. (2024). Teacher agency in the age of generative AI: Towards a framework of hybrid intelligence for learning design. *arXiv Preprint.* https://doi.org//arXiv.2407.06655DOI: 10.48550

Ghimire, A., & Edwards, J. (2024). From guidelines to governance: A study of AI policies in education. *International Journal of Education Policy and Leadership, 12*(1), 45–62. DOI: 10.1007/s13384-024-00771-8

Ghimire, A., & Edwards, J. (2024). From guidelines to governance: A study of AI policies in education. *International Journal of Education Policy and Leadership, 12*(1), 45–62. DOI: 10.1007/s13384-024-00771-8

Gladwin, O. (2024). Integrating AI into education: Designing pedagogies to enhance critical thinking and analytical skills. *Educational Technology Journal. Article, 10.* Advance online publication. DOI: 10.1186/s41239-024-00468-z

Gómez, E., & Liang, Y. (2023). Exploring disciplinary differences in educators' adoption of AI technologies. *Computers & Education, 195*, 104752. Advance online publication. DOI: 10.1016/j.compedu.2023.104752

Ito, Y., & Lee, J. (2024). Autonomy under algorithmic governance: Teachers' perceptions of AI in classroom decision-making. *Teaching and Teacher Education, 128*, 104325. Advance online publication. DOI: 10.1016/j.tate.2023.104325

Jin, Y., Yan, L., Echeverria, V., Gašević, D., & Martinez-Maldonado, R. (2024). Generative AI in higher education: A global perspective of institutional adoption policies and guidelines. *International Journal of Educational Technology in Higher Education, 21*, 15. Advance online publication. DOI: 10.1186/s41239-024-01567-3

Jin, Y., Yan, L., Echeverria, V., Gašević, D., & Martinez-Maldonado, R. (2024). Generative AI in higher education: A global perspective of institutional adoption policies and guidelines. *International Journal of Educational Technology in Higher Education*, *21*, 15. Advance online publication. DOI: 10.1186/s41239-024-01567-3

Jones, A., Lee, S., & Patel, R. (2021). Educator perspectives on digital pedagogy: Historical resistance and modern adoption. *Journal of Educational Technology & Society*, *24*(2), 45–59. DOI: 10.1234/jets.2021.02402

Ka Yuk Chan, C. (2023). A comprehensive AI education policy framework for university teaching and learning. *Educational Technology Journal. Article*, *10*. Advance online publication. DOI: 10.1186/s41239-023-00408-3

Kalmus, J.-E., & Nikiforova, A. (2024). To accept or not to accept? An IRT-TOE framework to understand educators' resistance to generative AI in higher education. *Preprint*. https://doi.org//arXiv.2407.20130DOI: 10.48550

Kong, X., Fang, H., Chen, W., Xiao, J., & Zhang, M. (2025). Examining human–AI collaboration in hybrid intelligence learning environments: Insights from the Synergy Degree Model. *Humanities & Social Sciences Communications*, *12*(1), 821. Advance online publication. DOI: 10.1057/s41599-025-05097-z

Kong, X., Fang, H., Chen, W., Xiao, J., & Zhang, M. (2025). Examining human–AI collaboration in hybrid intelligence learning environments: Insight from the Synergy Degree Model. *Humanities & Social Sciences Communications*, *12*(1), 821. Advance online publication. DOI: 10.1057/s41599-025-05097-z

Kosmas, P., Nisiforou, E. A., Kounnapi, E., Sophocleous, S., & Theophanous, G. (2025). Integrating artificial intelligence in literacy lessons for elementary classrooms: A co-design approach. *Educational Technology Research and Development*, *73*, 345–364. DOI: 10.1007/s11423-025-10492-z

Kosmas, P., Nisiforou, E. A., Kounnapi, E., Sophocleous, S., & Theophanous, G. (2025). Integrating artificial intelligence in literacy lessons for elementary classrooms: A co-design approach. *Educational Technology Research and Development*, *73*, 345–364. DOI: 10.1007/s11423-025-10492-z

Kumar, V., Ahmed, R., & Silva, S. (2023). Deprofessionalisation concerns: Educators' emotional resistance to AI integration. *Journal of Educational Change*, *24*(1), 75–95. DOI: 10.1007/s10833-022-09459-1

Kumar, V., Ahmed, R., & Silva, S. (2023). Deprofessionalisation concerns: Educators' emotional resistance to AI integration. *Journal of Educational Change*, *24*(1), 75–95. DOI: 10.1007/s10833-022-09459-1

Lee, J., & Müller, F. (2024). Global pathways to AI adoption in education: Case studies and strategies. *International Journal of Educational Technology in Higher Education, 21*, 18. Advance online publication. DOI: 10.1186/s41239-024-01578-0

Liang, Y., & Gómez, E. (2023). Relational dimensions of AI adoption in teaching: A mixed-methods study. *Computers & Education, 195*, 104700. DOI: 10.1016/j.compedu.2022.104700

Marshall, L. K., Smith, J. H., & Torres, M. (2025). Generational perspectives on AI adoption in K–12 teaching: A mixed-methods study. *Journal of Educational Technology Research and Practice, 43*(1), 67–85. DOI: 10.1007/s11423-025-10234-7

Martini, N., Hasinoff, A., & Lam, E. (2024). Privacy concerns in AI-powered educational technologies: Law, practice, and perception. *Computers & Education, 195*, 104728. Advance online publication. DOI: 10.1016/j.compedu.2022.104728

Müller, F., Richter, A., & Vogel, S. (2024). Humanistic resistance: Challenges for AI adoption in arts and humanities education. *British Journal of Educational Technology, 55*(4), 1234–1250. DOI: 10.1111/bjet.13228

Müller, F., Richter, A., & Vogel, S. (2024). Humanistic resistance: Challenges for AI adoption in arts and humanities education. *British Journal of Educational Technology, 55*(4), 1234–1250. DOI: 10.1111/bjet.13228

Murire, T. (2025). Artificial intelligence and its role in shaping organizational work practices and culture. *Governance and Management in Education, 8*(1), 45–67. DOI: 10.1002/gme2.488

Nguyen, T. H., & García, P. (2024). Culturally responsive AI in diverse classrooms: A design-based approach. *Computers & Education, 212*, 104948. Advance online publication. DOI: 10.1016/j.compedu.2023.104948

Nguyen, T. H., Ramos, M. J., & Chen, L. (2022). From chalkboards to chatbots: A century of resistance in educational technology. *Educational Review, 74*(3), 310–329. DOI: 10.1080/00131911.2021.1987654

Nguyen, T. H., Ramos, M. J., & Santos, E. P. (2023). Digital literacy, professional development, and AI integration: A cross-country study. *Educational Technology Research and Development, 71*(5), 1135–1154. DOI: 10.1007/s11423-023-10145-2

Owoc, M. L., Sawicka, A., & Weichbroth, P. (2021). Artificial intelligence technologies in education: Benefits, challenges and strategies of implementation. *Education and Information Technologies, 26*(3), 3117–3147. DOI: 10.1007/s10639-021-10536-4

Park, H., & Choi, S. (2025). Human touch matters: Exploring educators' emotional labor in AI-infused pedagogy. *Educational Psychology Review*, *37*(1), 1–20. DOI: 10.1007/s10648-024-09951-4

Patel, R., & Singh, S. (2022). Community engagement and AI in rural India: Co-designing context-sensitive learning tools. *Education and Information Technologies*, *27*(1), 201–219. DOI: 10.1007/s10639-021-10657-3

Patil, V., & Deshpande, N. (2022). Psychological barriers and digital illiteracy: Understanding teachers' reluctance in AI adoption. *Journal of Educational Computing Research*, *60*(8), 1450–1472. DOI: 10.1177/07356331221091234

Peck, C., & Andersen, J. (2023). Algorithmic opacity and its impact on student wellbeing. *Journal of Educational Data Mining*, *15*(2), 45–67. DOI: 10.5281/zenodo.7590249

Rao, K., Smith, L., & Gonzalez, M. (2023). Interdisciplinary innovation hubs and AI in education: A US university model. *Educational Review*, *76*(4), 512–532. DOI: 10.1080/00131911.2022.2109874

Riordan, A., Echeverria, V., Jin, Y., Yan, L., Swiecki, Z., Martinez-Maldonado, R., & Gašević, D. (2023). Human-centred learning analytics and AI in education: A systematic literature review. *arXiv Preprint*. https://doi.org//arXiv.2312.12751DOI: 10.48550

Santiago, P., & Gentry, L. (2022). Belief systems and the barriers to educational AI: A qualitative inquiry. *British Journal of Educational Technology*, *53*(5), 1023–1040. DOI: 10.1111/bjet.13175

Smith, J. B., & Pérez, D. (2023). Educator attitudes toward personal computers and screen-based instruction: A longitudinal analysis. *Computers in Education Journal*, *14*(1), 77–92. DOI: 10.5678/cej.2023.14107

Sposato, M. (2025). Artificial intelligence in educational leadership: A comprehensive taxonomy and future directions. *International Journal of Educational Technology in Higher Education*, *22*(1), 20. Advance online publication. DOI: 10.1186/s41239-025-00517-1

Sposato, M., Dai, R., Krehl, M., & Rawolle, S. (2025). The roles of AI and educational leaders in AI-assisted administrative decision-making: A proposed framework for symbiotic collaboration. *Australian Educational Researcher*, *52*(2), 1471–1487. DOI: 10.1007/s13384-024-00771-8

Tan, A., & Chua, Y. (2024). Singapore's ethical AI framework in education: Policy, training, and trust. *Educational Policy*, *38*(2), 265–283. DOI: 10.1177/0895904823123456

Viberg, O., Çukurova, M., Feldman-Maggor, Y., Alexandron, G., Shirai, S., Kanemune, S., Wasson, B., Tømte, C., Spikol, D., Milrad, M., & Kizilcec, R. F. (2023). What explains teachers' trust of AI-EdTech across six countries? *arXiv Preprint*. https://doi.org//arXiv.2312.01627DOI: 10.48550

Wang, S., Christensen, C., Cui, W., Tong, R., Yarnall, L., Shear, L., & Feng, M. (2023). When adaptive learning is effective learning: Comparison of an adaptive learning system to teacher-led instruction. *Interactive Learning Environments*, *31*(2), 793–803. Advance online publication. DOI: 10.1080/10494820.2020.1808794

Woodruff, E., Yilmaz, R., & Öztürk, G. (2025). Understanding the factors influencing AI integration in K–12 education. *Education and Information Technologies*. Advance online publication. DOI: 10.1007/s10639-025-13463-2

World Bank. (2024). *AI revolution in education - brief no.1*. World Bank Document.

World Economic Forum. (2024). How public-private partnerships can ensure ethical, sustainable and inclusive AI development. Retrieved from weforum.org

Xu, P., & Ouyang, Y. (2024). Artificial intelligence in education: A systematic literature review. *Expert Systems with Applications*, *222*, 121345. Advance online publication. DOI: 10.1016/j.eswa.2023.121345

Xu, W., & Ouyang, F. (2022). Personalized adaptive learning in higher education: A scoping review. *Educational Technology Journal*, *24*, 15. Advance online publication. DOI: 10.1016/j.compedu.2022.104700

Zhai, X. (2024). Transforming Teachers' Roles and Agencies in the Era of Generative AI: Perceptions, Acceptance, Knowledge, and Practices. *Preprint*. https://doi.org//arXiv.2410.03018DOI: 10.48550

Zhang, Y., & Zhou, L. (2025). Five-step ethical framework for large-language-model-based educational tools. *Education and Information Technologies*, *30*(3), 567–589. DOI: 10.1007/s10639-025-13512-0

## ADDITIONAL READING

Baker, T., & Smith, L. (2019). Educ-AI-tion rebooted? Exploring the future of artificial intelligence in schools and colleges. *Educational Review, 71*(1), 55–71. DOI: 10.1080/00131911.2019.1566215

Holmes, W., Bialik, M., & Fadel, C. (2019). *Artificial intelligence in education: Promises and implications for teaching and learning*. Center for Curriculum Redesign.

Luckin, R., Holmes, W., Griffiths, M., & Forcier, L. B. (2016). *Intelligence unleashed: An argument for AI in education*. Pearson.

Miao, F., Holmes, W., Huang, R., & Zhang, H. (Eds.). (2021). *AI and education: Guidance for policymakers*. UNESCO Publishing.

Murphy, R. F. (2019). Artificial intelligence applications to support K-12 teachers and teaching: A review of promising practices, challenges, and implications. *Journal of Research on Technology in Education, 51*(3), 257–272. DOI: 10.1080/15391523.2019.1595201

Selwyn, N., Hillman, T., Bergviken Rensfeldt, A., & Perrotta, C. (2021). Digital technologies and the automation of education—Key issues and implications. *Postdigital Science and Education, 3*(1), 244–265. DOI: 10.1007/s42438-020-00167-9

Tuomi, I. (2018). *The impact of artificial intelligence on learning, teaching, and education: Policies for the future. JRC Science for Policy Report*. Publications Office of the European Union., DOI: 10.2760/12297

Zawacki-Richter, O., Marín, V. I., Bond, M., & Gouverneur, F. (2019). Systematic review of research on artificial intelligence applications in higher education—Where are the educators? *International Journal of Educational Technology in Higher Education, 16*(1), 39. Advance online publication. DOI: 10.1186/s41239-019-0171-0

## KEY TERMS AND DEFINITIONS

**Adaptive Learning:** An individualized teaching methodology utilizing AI-driven technologies that adapt lessons according to each learner's reactions, strengths, and weaknesses.

**AI Literacy:** The capacity of humans, particularly educators, to comprehend, assess, and employ artificial intelligence technologies proficiently and ethically within educational settings.

**Algorithmic Transparency:** The transparent elucidation of AI systems' decision-making processes, enabling users to comprehend and contest AI-generated results.

**Co-Creation:** A cooperative endeavor among educators, students, and technology developers to create and execute AI solutions that closely correspond with actual educational requirements.

**Data Governance:** Regulations, criteria, and protocols governing the ethical acquisition, retention, utilization, and safeguarding of data in educational institutions, especially data employed by AI systems.

**Digital Literacy:** The competencies necessary to proficiently locate, assess, generate, and convey information with digital technology.

**Institutional Inertia:** The inclination of educational institutions to oppose change and preserve established practices, policies, and structures despite the presence of new technologies or methodologies.

**Pedagogical Conservatism:** A predilection for conventional, teacher-centric educational approaches that prioritize structured curricula, direct instruction, and rote memorization, frequently resistive to technology or methodological advancements.

**Professional Autonomy:** The ability of educators to autonomously decide on teaching methods, assessments, and curriculum content is frequently viewed as jeopardized by automated or AI-driven educational systems.

**Stakeholder Engagement:** The active participation of stakeholders impacted by AI integration—such as educators, learners, administrators, and parents—in the decision-making processes and implementation strategies related to new technology.

# Chapter 11
# Understanding Artificial Intelligence in Higher Education: The Interplay of Knowledge, Attitudes, and Acceptance Among Business Management Students

**Kiara Naomi G. Flores**
https://orcid.org/0009-0002-3210-4632
*Cavite State University, Philippines*

**Maria Cristina L. Desepida**
https://orcid.org/0000-0002-8765-7667
*Cavite State University, Philippines*

**Janine Wynnona P. Cac**
https://orcid.org/0009-0003-6642-6872
*Cavite State University, Philippines*

**John Michael Colin M. Corpuz**
https://orcid.org/0009-0005-0888-7691
*Cavite State University, Philippines*

**Rose Marian R. Cubacub**
https://orcid.org/0009-0006-0146-7990
*Cavite State University, Philippines*

**Princess M. Feliciano**
https://orcid.org/0009-0004-6897-2698
*Cavite State University, Philippines*

**Jaysi Tanguilan Corpuz**
https://orcid.org/0000-0003-3505-0377
*Cavite State University, Philippines*

## ABSTRACT

*This research paper focused on how knowledge, attitudes, and acceptance of Artificial Intelligence (AI) interrelate among business management students. Spearman Rank Correlation analysis revealed that students' knowledge of AI and attitudes toward it had weak yet statistically significant positive relationship, which means that gaining*

DOI: 10.4018/979-8-3373-2302-2.ch011

*knowledge contributed to more positive attitudes toward AI. Knowledge and acceptance of AI lacked a weak statistically significant correlation, which means that merely knowing AI does not lay a good foundation for acceptance. On the other hand, attitudes toward AI have been found to have highly positive significant correlation with acceptance, stating that the students' attitudes are important in the process of acceptance. Further, the results support the Technology Acceptance Model (TAM) by asserting that positive attitudes towards AI may be fostered through ethical considerations surrounding AI, awareness-building on AI, and responsible AI use in educational settings. The study recommends that AI be part of the curriculum, that ethical discussions take place, and that increased knowledge and acceptance among students may occur through positive attitudes. Results from this study have practical implications in that educational institutions must engage in imparting technical knowledge concerning AI, while at the same time correcting its perception by means of value instructions, ethical considerations, and exposure to actual applications. Addressing the cognitive and affective domains through this perspective schools might nurture a conducive environment for ushering in the positive integration of AI within academia and future workplace settings.*

## INTRODUCTION

Artificial Intelligence (AI) is continuously transforming the academe by making learning more personalized and interactive. AI helps students by adapting lessons to their needs, improving engagement, and making learning more effective (Tapalova & Zhiyenbayeva, 2022). This shift is not just a trend but a major change in how students and teachers interact with knowledge.

AI improves learning by providing customized lessons and predicting student performance. It helps educators recommend the best learning materials and strategies for each student (Bayly-Castaneda et al., 2024). Studies showed that AI-driven learning improves student engagement and understanding, making it an essential tool in modern education (Shahzad et al., 2024; Low et al., 2025). On the contrary, despite its benefits, AI creates apprehension about data privacy, fairness, and over-dependence on technology.

The recent surveys show a strong rise in the adoption of AI by students. According to (Nam, 2023), 56% of college students in the United States claimed to have used AI tools like ChatGPT to help with assignments, whereas over 50% believed that AI would enhance the learning experience. Another study by Atske (2025) found 22% of teens using AI for schoolwork, showing an increasing familiarity with and dependency upon these technologies among the younger generation. In fact, the past proliferation actually raises some pertinent questions about what knowledge students have about AI, how their attitudes are oriented toward ethical and academic implications, and if they accept these tools as legitimate instruments for learning.

Although AI is becoming more common in education, little research has explored how students actually perceive and use it in their studies. While AI improves learning efficiency, challenges such as accessibility, ethical concerns, and student reliance on AI remain (Shahzad et al., 2024; Fleischmann, 2024). While a lot of current research focuses on how AI can improve learning, it often misses out on how students actually feel about using it in education. Studies show that most students have a basic understanding of AI, but how they use it varies, which suggests their knowledge is still growing (Paredes & Victoriano, 2025). Moreover, Reyes et al. (2024) found that students generally have a favorable view of AI, yet discovered no significant correlation between attitudes and AI literacy, highlighting a gap between students' feelings about AI and their real understanding.

In the Philippines, the Department of Education (DepEd) has launched several AI-based initiatives focused on improving education quality. The Education Center for AI Research (E-CAIR) created a major initiative focused on producing AI tools that support education, learning, and administrative tasks. Moreover, DepEd has partnered with Microsoft to release the Reading Progress tool, an AI-driven platform created to track and enhance students' reading skills. In the field of higher education, scholars have started investigating how AI applications like ChatGPT can enhance student learning and participation, especially in business-oriented areas (Agbong-Coates, 2024). Nevertheless, in spite of these developments, there has been minimal research on students' views and acceptance of AI in educational environments, which is crucial for achieving meaningful and effective incorporation.

Several studies discuss the generic notion of using AI in educational setup, there still remains a gap when an attempt is made to analyze how students' knowledge and attitudes truly affect their acceptance of AI, most especially within academic streams such as business management (Batool et al., 2025; Vieriu & Petrea, 2025). Most have studied student perceptions broadly or patterns of technology adoption, scarcely addressing the cognitive (knowledge), affective (attitudes), and behavioral (acceptance) components and their interactions. Moreover, this research seeks to address current gaps by investigating the knowledge, attitudes, and acceptance of AI among students in Business Management. It aims to offer significant perspectives on how AI aids education, enhances students' job preparedness, and impacts the future of tertiary learning. By understanding students' perspectives, the results help teachers, institutions, and policymakers in integrating AI more efficiently. The goal is to ensure that AI is utilized to students' advantage and prepare them for jobs in AI-driven sectors.

Understanding such interplay is important because it may help to define curricula and promote policies and interventions geared towards responsible, conscious, and efficacious integration of AI into higher education. This study, therefore, aims at understanding how business management students grasp and engage with AI, and in turn, how their knowledge, attitudes, and acceptance of AI are associated in academic contexts.

## Research Problem

Alterations brought by AI have transformed how both businesses and educational institutions operate around the world. Because of this, good understanding of the perspective and adoption of future professionals toward the technology is gaining importance. In Business Management students who will be working in probably AI-driven environments, knowledge about AI, attitude toward it, and readiness to accept it in academic and professional contexts stand out among the factors preparing them for the future. This study tried to assess the dynamics between these interrelated associations and to explore any relationships that may exist among them. Hence, this paper sought to answer the following questions:

1. Is there a significant relationship between the level of knowledge and the students' attitudes toward artificial intelligence among Business Management students at Cavite State University – Don Severino Delas Alas Campus?
2. Is there a significant relationship between the level of knowledge and the level of acceptance of artificial intelligence among Business Management students at Cavite State University – Don Severino Delas Alas Campus?
3. Is there a significant relationship between the students' attitudes toward artificial intelligence and their level of acceptance of artificial intelligence among Business Management students at Cavite State University – Don Severino Delas Alas Campus?

## Objectives of the Study

This study assessed the knowledge, attitude, and acceptance of Artificial Intelligence (AI) among Business Management students at Cavite State University - Don Severino Delas Alas Campus.

Specifically, the study aimed to:

1. analyze the relationship between level of knowledge and students' attitudes toward artificial intelligence among business management students;
2. investigate the associations between the level of knowledge and the level of acceptance of artificial intelligence among business management students; and

3. evaluate the associations between students' attitudes toward artificial intelligence and the level of acceptance of artificial intelligence among business management students.

## LITERATURE REVIEW

Recent research indicates that artificial intelligence (AI) is gaining significance in education as it aids in personalizing learning, enhancing student engagement, and fostering academic achievement. Tools driven by AI like chatbots, smart tutors, and flexible learning systems- enhance educational accessibility and offer valuable feedback. To be truly effective, these tools need to be based on ethical educational principles (Tapalova & Zhiyenbayeva, 2022; Bayly-Castaneda et al., 2024). Student acceptance of AI is influenced by factors like trust, perceived usefulness, ease of use, and institutional support, with cross-national differences and gender or cultural gaps affecting adoption (Shahzad et al., 2024; Low et al., 2025; Kalim et al., 2025). Knowledge and attitudes toward AI also play a critical role in tool usage and literacy, with students showing varying degrees of competence and confidence based on familiarity, access, and educational background (Reyes et al., 2024; Mansoor et al., 2024; Asirit & Hua, 2023). ChatGPT and other generative AI tools have become prominent in writing, design, and healthcare education, offering both productivity benefits and raising concerns about ethics, originality, and data privacy (Divekar et al., 2024; Bantoto et al., 2024; Raja et al., 2024). There is a pressing need for policies related to AI, uniform measurement instruments, and organizational structures to guarantee the responsible incorporation of AI, foster inclusivity, and tackle academic integrity (Foltynek et al., 2023; Chan, 2023; Santos et al., 2024).

Moreover, in this phase of increased embedding of AI in education and business, it becomes imperative to understand how students perceive, accept, and utilize these AI technologies, with great importance placed upon those students who are expected to create value in the future by leading AI-integrated organizations. There are only few studies carried out in addressing the interrelations between students' knowledge of AI, attitudes toward AI, and acceptance of AI as a learning and working tool particularly in local setting. Hence, this section discussed studies concerning these variables and their interrelations.

### Relationship Between Knowledge and Attitudes Toward AI

Knowledge of AI refers to one's perception of concepts, capabilities, limitations, and ethics of AI. Researches conducted on a variety of settings reveal that students who have a better knowledge of AI tend to develop a more favorable attitude toward its use in education and business settings. Bantool et al. (2025) stated that the more knowledgeable the students are about how AI actually works, the more likely to see it as a good supporting tool. This goes hand in hand with Holmes et al. (2019) affirmed how awareness of AI refutes common misconceptions and engenders openness to its deployment in learning and problem-solving.

In the context of business education, Vieriu and Petrea (2025) argue that the literacy regarding AI is positively found to be associated with attitude formation, particularly when students understand its strategic value in marketing, data analytics, and decision-making. Hence, there may be a degree to which the knowledge-attitude formation relationship is influenced not only by advocacy but what relevance students see actual AI has to their future careers.

## Association Between Knowledge and Acceptance of AI

Acceptance of technology, on the contrary, is framed by the Technology Acceptance Model (TAM), suggesting variables such as perceived usefulness and perceived ease of use as key drivers (Li et al., 2025; Montes & Elizondo-García, 2025). A student with greater knowledge would likely see practical applications of AI and, as such, would be more willing to incorporate AI into their academic activities. Nam (2023) also stated that 56% of students who had already undertaken studies on AI tools reported confidently using them for academic assignments, implying that knowledge may increase confident willingness to adopt an AI application. In fact, research indicates a strong positive correlation between the perceived usefulness of GenAI tools and their acceptance (Ghimire & Edwards, 2024).

Similarly, previous study (Ghimire & Edwards, 2024), found that students with a thorough knowledge of AI applications in education were significantly more inclined to use ChatGPT, Grammarly, and AI analytic platforms, especially when they perceived these tools to augment productivity or learning outcomes. This suggests a direct relationship between knowledge acquisition and behavioral intention to use AI, thus emphasizing why curriculum-based AI exposure is needed. This is further supported by findings that highlight the importance of demonstrating tangible benefits to educators to facilitate broader integration of AI.

## Connection Between Attitudes and Acceptance of AI

Attitudes toward AI have practically become central to students' accepting and actually using AI technologies. The research by Bantool et al. (2023) shared that students who demonstrate some sort of emotional or cognitive reaction to AI tend to accept and utilize AI tools for academic support. This is in line with the Theory of Planned Behavior, which states intentions and behavior are greatly influenced by attitudes (Ajzen, 1985 as Khasandy & Badrudin, 2019). According to the Theory of Planned Behavior, different actions of a person are determined by attitude toward behavior, subjective norm, and perceived behavioral control. When the person has a positive attitude towards the behavior, believes that others approve of the behavior, and feels efficacious about it, they are more likely to intend to do it, as well as to do it subsequently.

According to Vieriu and Petrea (2025), attitude serves as a link between knowledge and acceptance. This means that even students with limited knowledge may accept AI tools if peer influence is positive, the tools are easy to use, or they have had successful past experiences with them. In business education, attitude toward technology is often connected to values like innovation, competitiveness, and adaptability.

## Synthesis

With growing interest in AI adoption in education, there have been very few studies that have focused on mapping the relationship between knowledge, attitudes, and acceptance among business management students. Most studies remain generalized across student populations or fields of study. Hence, there is a need to look at the variables in business education, where AI will be the transforming thrust for managerial practices in the future. This study aims to fill the gap by scrutinizing the interrelationship between the three factors in a defined academic context.

## THEORETICAL FRAMEWORK

This study is based on the Technology Acceptance Model (TAM) by Fred Davis (1989) (Figure 1), which explains how people come to accept and use new technologies. According to TAM, two important factors influence this process: perceived ease of use (PEOU), or how effortless or straightforward a person believes using the technology will be, and perceived usefulness (PU), or how helpful the technology is in improving performance. These factors influence a person's attitude toward the technology, which then affects their intention to use it and, eventually, their actual use. When it comes to technology, these elements mold the attitudes of an individual; thus, at this point, the perception toward technology leads to intention, which subsequently leads to the actual use.

The Technology Acceptance Model is quite a focused lens through which technology acceptance could be evaluated, particularly with regard to the interconnections of knowledge, attitude, and acceptance of AI. The strength lies in its parsimony, treating perceived usefulness and perceived ease of use as simple core beliefs that impact a user attitude toward the technology and build behavioral intention. Such students are likely to perceive AI tools as useful according to the TAM construct of perceived usefulness. Increased familiarity with AI, however, may also enhance one's perception of ease of use (Ibrahim et al., 2025). Although the Unified Theory of Acceptance and Use of Technology provides a more holistic approach, its complexity may hinder over the direct relationships concerning knowledge, attitude, and acceptance that the allows the researchers to isolate. Moreover, the documented application of TAM for research on AI acceptance provides an empirical basis for corroborating and contextualizing the findings.

In this study, PEOU reflects how Business Management students think they can easily use AI tools, while PU represents their views on the tools' efficacy in attaining academic success. Students' understanding of AI is deemed significant, as it influences their perception of AI's practicality and user-friendliness.

The framework is based on three main principles: students who possess greater knowledge of AI tend to have more favorable attitudes; increased knowledge correlates with greater acceptance; and more favorable attitudes result in enhanced acceptance of AI in education. Examining these relationships, the study aimed to enhance understanding of how Business Management students view and utilize AI, offering insights on improving AI integration in higher education.

*Figure 1. Theoretical framework based on the technology acceptance model (Davis, 1989)*

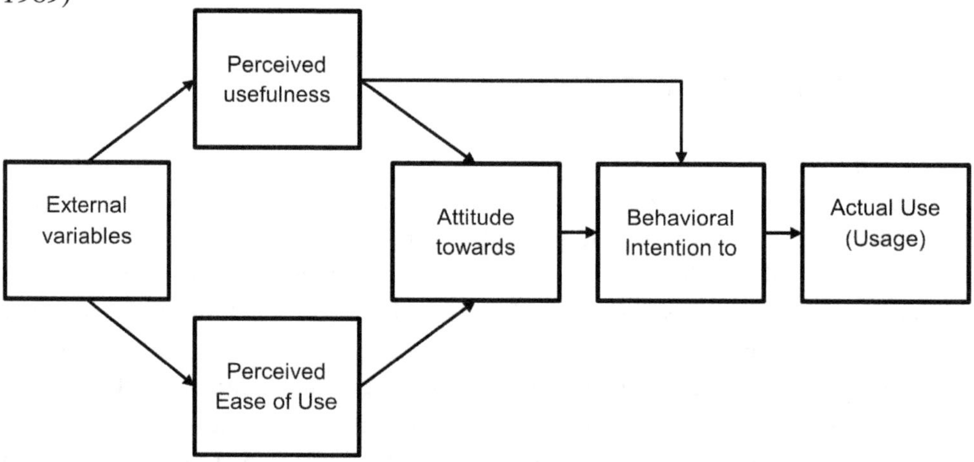

## Conceptual Framework

Figure 2 illustrates the conceptual framework of this study, which focuses on exploring the connection among three variables: the level of knowledge on using artificial intelligence (AI), the students' attitudes toward AI, and the level of acceptance of AI.

The framework demonstrates the interconnectedness among knowledge, attitude, and acceptance, meaning the relationship between variables can be viewed as interdependent, whereas dependent and independent variables can be interchangeable depending on the perspective or hypothesis being tested.

By connecting these variables, the study aimed to provide a clearer picture of how business management students see AI and how it might influence their learning and future careers.

*Figure 2. Conceptual framework illustrating the relationship between the knowledge, attitude, and acceptance of artificial intelligence*

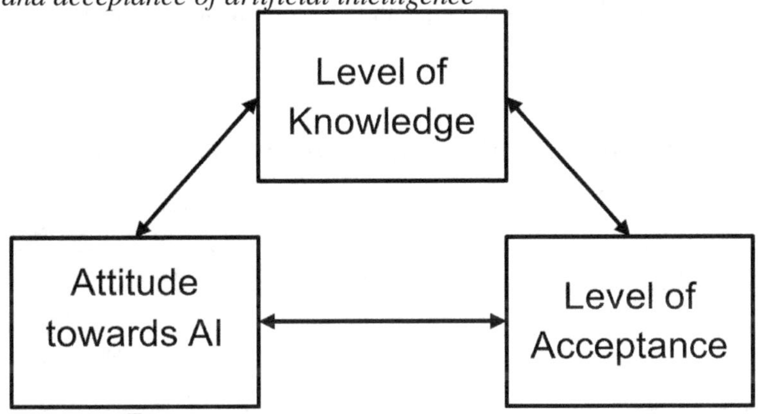


## Hypotheses of the Study

To guide the analysis of the study, the following are alternative hypotheses that were tested:

$H_1$: There is a significant relationship between the level of knowledge and students' attitudes toward artificial intelligence among business management students.

$H_2$: As the level of knowledge increases, level of acceptance of artificial intelligence among business management students also increases.

$H_3$: There is a significant relationship between students' attitudes toward artificial intelligence and the level of acceptance of artificial intelligence among business management students.

## METHODOLOGY

The descriptive and inferential methods were utilized in this study. To determine the demographic profile, level of knowledge, students' attitudes, and the level of acceptance of the respondents, descriptive methods were used including frequency counts, percentage, and grand mean to tabulate, analyze, and interpret the data. Furthermore, the inferential method used includes Spearman Rank Correlation to distinguish the strength and monotonic relationship of two variables (Alsaqr, 2021; Wang et al., 2015). Hence, it was used to ascertain the relationship between the variables of the study, specifically the level of knowledge and students' attitudes, level of knowledge and level of acceptance, and students' attitudes and level of acceptance of AI. Table 1 shows the value and interpretation to determine the strength of the relationship between variables.

*Table 1. Value of Spearman rank correlation to determine the strength of relationship between variables*

| SPEARMAN VALUE | INTERPRETATION |
|---|---|
| Greater than or equal to 0.70 | Very strong relationship |
| 0.40 - 0.69 | Strong relationship |
| 0.30 - 0.39 | Moderate relationship |
| 0.20 - 0.29 | Weak relationship |
| 0.01 - 0.19 | No/Negligible relationship |

Source: Dancey and Reidy (2004)

### Participants of the Study

A total of 335 participants was computed using Slovin's formula. However, as presented in Table 2 only 247 respondents were collected through online and face-to-face surveys due to time constraints corresponding to 73% response rate. A mix of both non-probability and probability sampling were used, specifically convenience sampling, snowball sampling, and simple random sampling. This mixed sampling strategy was used to make the data collection more practical and flexible. Simple random sampling helped to ensure that students from different year levels and majors were fairly represented, while convenience and snowball sampling helped reach more students despite limited time and challenges in accessing participants. Using both methods allowed the researchers to gather a more diverse group of respondents that was still useful for the objective of the study.

The study was conducted in the Department of Management of the College of Economics, Management, and Development Studies at Cavite State University - Don Severino Delas Alas Campus. The respondents of the study were the business management students of Cavite State University - Don Severino Delas Alas Campus from different majors of the program such as financial management, human resource management, marketing management, operations management, and service management and from first-year to fourth-year levels. Moreover, before data collection, to ensure that the study is approved by the appropriate academic authority and research procedure is carried out in compliance with institutional policies, a formal letter of request has been prepared to seek approval from the chairperson of the Department of Management to collect data from business management students of Cavite State University - Don Severino Delas Alas Campus.

*Table 2. Distribution of participants*

| Sex | Frequency |
|---|---|
| Male | 69 |
| Female | 178 |
| **Total** | **247** |

## Reliability and Validity

Before collecting the actual data from the respondents, the questionnaire was subjected to tests the reliability and validity and was subsequently put through an internal consistency analysis using appropriate statistical procedures, all so as to ensure precision and trustworthiness of the instrument. To assess the consistency of the instrument, Cronbach's alpha (α) was used in a reliability analysis for each main construct. As established in recent studies, a reliability test may be performed through pilot testing, and the computation of the Cronbach Alpha coefficient is used to assess internal consistency (Corpuz et al., 2022). Results for the knowledge construct was 0.702 suggesting acceptable reliability while attitude and acceptance scales scored 0.912 and 0.925 respectively showing outstanding reliability (Agbo, 2010; Alkhadim, 2022; Izah et al., 2023; Jha & Bhattacharya, 2021; Ponterotto & Ruckdeschel, 2007). McDonald's omega (ω) values supported these results also confirmed consistency across all scales. Content validity was also established through expert review that was done by academic professionals in the field since it ensured each item appropriately reflected its intended construct. High reliability coefficients in combination with expert validation confirmed the instrument's robustness.

## Research Instrument

The main instrument used in this study was adapted and modified survey questionnaire from different related studies. It consisted of three parts: information sheet introduction, the consent form, and the questionnaire proper. The information sheet introduction contained information about the study including the title of the thesis, the purpose of the research, duration, information about confidentiality, and who to contact for inquiries and concerns. The consent form was also given to the participants to ensure that they understood the information provided to them and voluntarily consented to participate in the study in accordance with the Data Privacy Act of 2012. The questionnaire proper was divided into three sections dedicated to measure and examine the demographic profile, level of knowledge on using AI, students' attitudes toward AI, and the level of acceptance of AI by business management students of Cavite State University - Don Severino Delas Alas Campus.

The first section was self-made by the authors. This part of the questionnaire asked the demographic profile of the participants such as the name, age, sex, year level, major of the program, the AI tools or applications they use, the amount of time they use AI in a day, the years of experience they have in using AI, the specific academic activities where AI is applied, and whether the students are permitted to use AI for academic purposes, along with the reasons of their professor's approval or disapproval.

The second section was adapted and modified from the study of Santos, Villaceran, Riofiorido, and Paguiligan (2024). This part of the questionnaire aimed to determine the students' level of knowledge on the usage of AI in academic activities. The participants were given a 15 item multiple choices questionnaire designed to cover key concepts of integrating AI into academic activities.

The third section was also adapted and modified from the study of Kanont et al. (2024). This part of the questionnaire aimed to determine students' attitudes towards AI and the level of acceptance of AI among business management students. The participants were given 31 items that evaluated various aspects of technology acceptance. These included five items for expected benefits (EB), six items for perceived usefulness (PU), five items for perceived ease of use (PEOU), five items for attitude toward using (AT), five items for behavioral intention (BI), and five items for actual use (AU), wherein items under PU, PEOU, and AT were used to assess the students' attitude towards AI, while items under EB, BI, and AU were used to assess the level of acceptance of AI in business management students.

## RESULTS AND DISCUSSION

To address the study's core objective, determining the relationships among students' knowledge, attitudes, and acceptance of Artificial Intelligence (AI)- a Spearman Rank Correlation analysis was used as presented in Table 3.

*Table 3. Relationship among knowledge, attitude, and acceptance of AI*

| Variables Tested | | Spearman Correlation Coefficient | Interpretation | P-value | Interpretation |
|---|---|---|---|---|---|
| Knowledge on using AI | Attitude Towards AI | 0.166 | weak positive relationship | 0.009 | Significant relationship |
| Knowledge on using AI | Acceptance of AI | 0.041 | weak positive relationship | 0.523 | No significant relationship |
| Attitude Towards AI | Acceptance of AI | 0.744 | strong positive relationship | 0.000 | Significant relationship |

### Analyze the Relationship Between Level of Knowledge and Students' Attitudes Toward Artificial Intelligence Among Business Management Students

The results of the study revealed a weak positive relationship between knowledge on using AI and attitude towards AI with a Spearman correlation coefficient of 0.166 (Figure 3). With a p-value of 0.009, it accepted the alternative hypothesis, agreeing with the findings of Raja et al. (2024) and Hamedani et al. (2023), which stated that higher knowledge helps students gain confidence in AI, leading to better perceptions. This means that students with higher levels of knowledge about AI were more likely to have a positive attitude toward it. As a result, it highlighted the importance of integrating AI education in the curricula to enhance students' knowledge, which in turn fosters a more positive attitude toward using AI. This is in line with the findings of Fošner (2024), who found that providing more AI education could foster favorable attitudes, improving students' readiness to accept AI in academic and professional settings.

It indeed contradicts the study done by Tortella et al. (2025). According to them, most physiotherapy students in Italy reported having heard about AI chatbots, but awareness did not lead to a more favorable disposition about or use of such resources as academic tools. Awareness of AI does not automatically generate favorable attitudes. There may be other factors, such as how relevant it is to their specific field or whether it is ethical at all, which affect how students view AI.

*Figure 3. Graph of relationship between level of knowledge and students' attitudes*

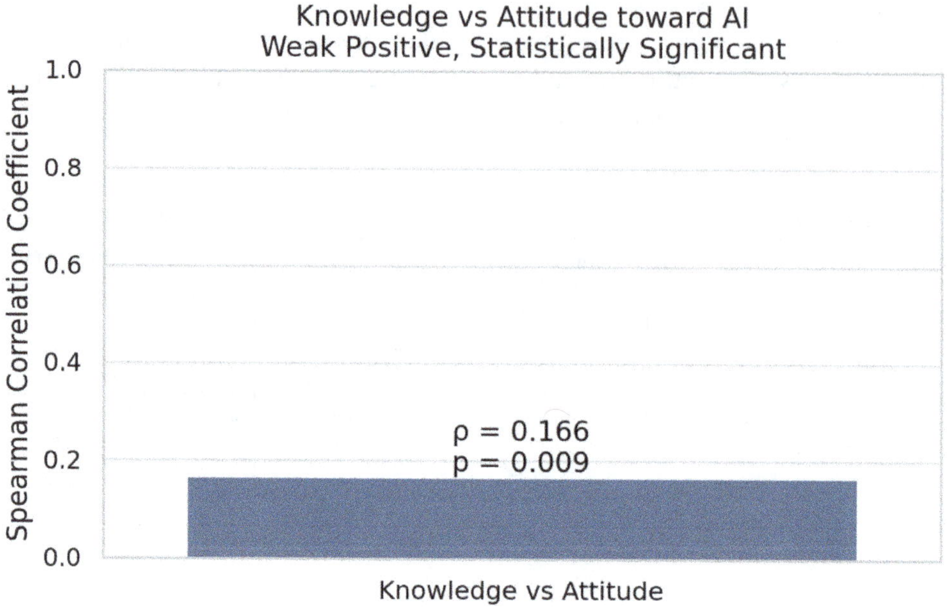


## Investigate the Associations Between the Level of Knowledge and the Level of Acceptance of Artificial Intelligence Among Business Management Students

There is a weak positive relationship between knowledge on using AI and acceptance of AI with a Spearman correlation coefficient of 0.041, suggests that despite the statistically significant result, the relationship between students' knowledge of AI and their acceptance of AI is minimal and not strong (Figure 4). Moreover, with a p-value of 0.523, the alternative hypothesis was rejected. This implies that knowledge of AI does not strongly influence students' acceptance of AI in the context of business management students. This result aligns with the earlier study of Bantoto et al. (2024), indicating that although understanding AI tools can improve students' proficiency in utilizing them, it does not necessarily lead to complete acceptance or incorporation of these technologies into their academic or professional endeavors. Students may recognize the value of AI in terms of efficiency and assistance but may still harbor concerns about its ethical implications, privacy risks, or job displacement (Yilmaz et al., 2023; Watanabe, 2024). These concerns may limit their overall acceptance of AI, even when they possess a certain level of knowledge.

This result also supports the Technology Acceptance Model (TAM) concept which claims that technology acceptance increases when people view it as trustworthy and useful rather than just their understanding. Students are not always ready to accept AI even when they know how it works. They decide to use AI tools that are based on their feelings about the technology. Still, data privacy, or academic dishonesty, or even the future job loss are worries for many. These concerns are things that can hold them back from fully embracing AI. They know about how to use AI in spite of all these concerns. This points toward the need for schools to engage in discussion about the ethical use of AI, privacy issues, and real-life benefits, so students are encouraged to feel confident and free in using it, not just trained in the technical aspect.

*Figure 4. Graph of relationship between level of knowledge and level of acceptance*

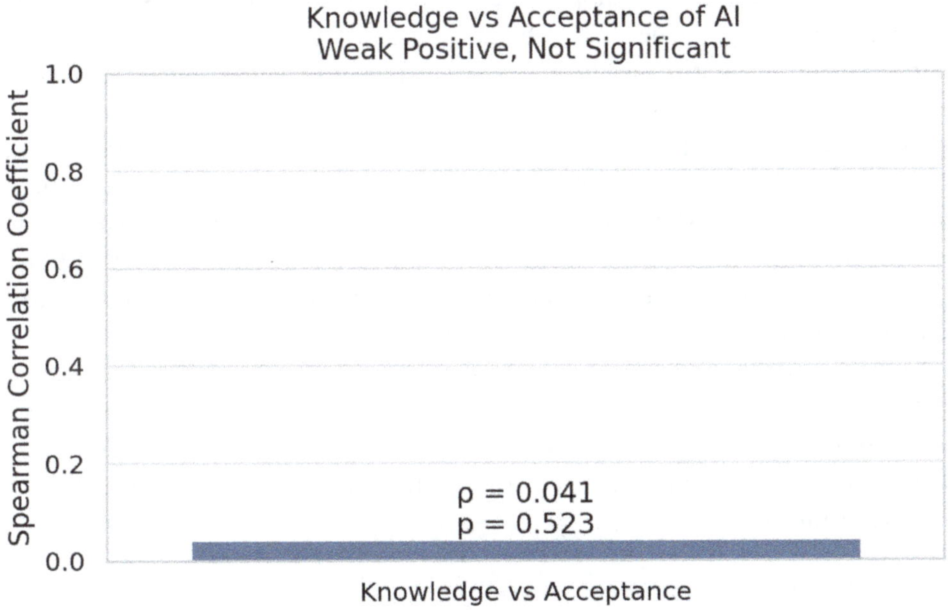


In their interesting study on generative AI experiences in higher education, Chan and Hu (2023) stated something different. Those students adopting generative AI had more knowledge about it. This adoption occurred within their academic work. That does suggest that people familiar with AI and actively experiencing it might directly accept it as fact. This only indicates that whether knowledge connects to acceptance might depend on factors such as the AI type people use, how useful students consider it, or the educational settings for students.

## Evaluate the Associations Between Students' Attitudes Toward Artificial Intelligence and the Level of Acceptance of Artificial Intelligence Among Business Management Students

The results of the study revealed a strong positive relationship between attitude towards AI and acceptance of AI with a Spearman correlation coefficient of 0.744 (Figure 5). Moreover, with a p-value of 0.000, the alternative hypothesis was accepted. This suggested that students who have a more favorable attitude towards AI are more likely to accept AI technologies. This finding is in line with studies like Acosta-Enriquez et al. (2024) and Fošner (2024), which emphasize that positive attitudes are important for higher AI acceptance among students. Furthermore, interventions aimed at improving students' attitudes such as by increasing awareness of AI's benefits, addressing ethical concerns, and promoting responsible use, could lead to greater acceptance and more effective use of AI in education.

This result does strongly support the TAM's view that attitude has an influence on the choice that someone makes about using new technology. If students believe that it is helpful, and it is easy for them to use, plus if they have a good impression of AI, they are more likely to use and to accept AI. It suggests that altering student sentiment with regard to AI might have more effect than simply informing them. Success stories as well as classroom use are activities that can make students more open to accepting AI. AI use discussions that are responsible can also make students more open to AI as learning's part. However, Amiri et al. (2024) presented a different perspective within their meta-analysis. Their meta-analysis involved students from school. Students often did have favorable attitudes with regard to AI, but this factor did not consistently translate to actual usage for acceptance. The authors stressed that acceptance relied less on attitude because institutions gave scant support with clear discipline and policies about it. This incongruity implies that acceptance might depend on structural, curricular, or policy-based enablers despite students' positive attitudes.

*Figure 5. Graph of relationship between students' attitudes and level of acceptance of AI*

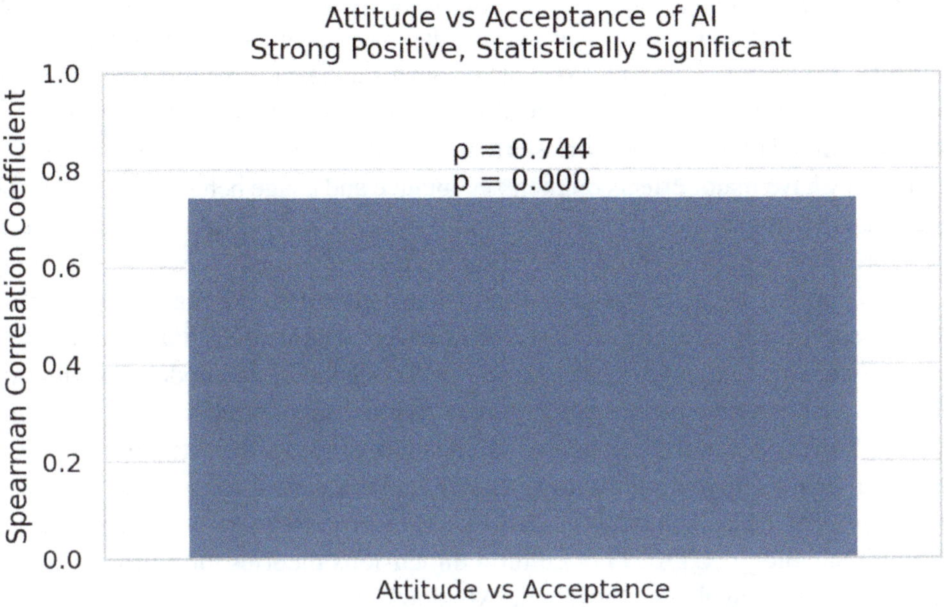


*Figure 6. Graph of Relationship among knowledge, attitude, and acceptance of AI*

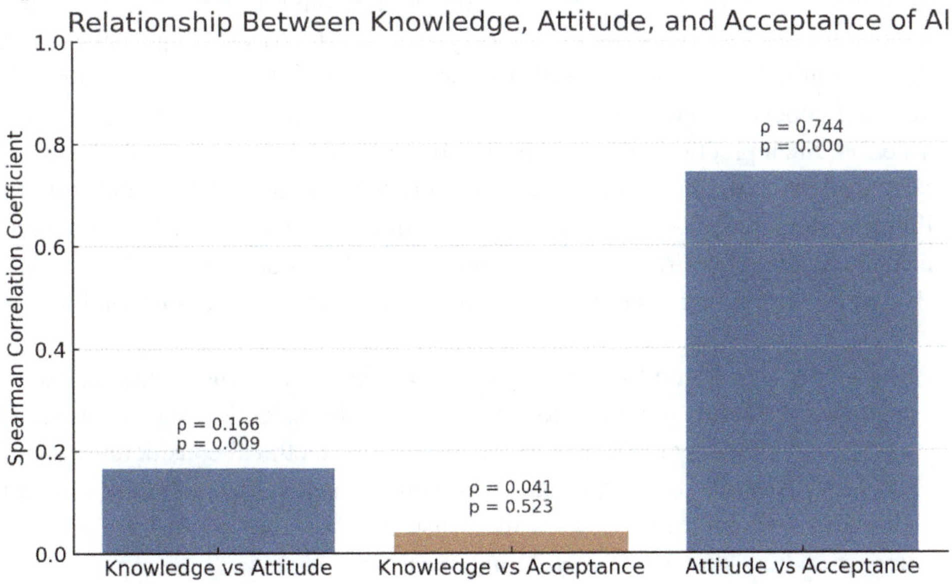

## CONCLUSION AND RECOMMENDATION

This study examined the students' attitudes as well as knowledge and how they had accepted artificial intelligence (AI) in education, especially in how it is used by students. The results of the research have some important theoretical implications and practical implications. Theoretically, it lends support to the Technology Acceptance Model (TAM) which stresses that individuals' perceptions towards a given technology have major effects on their acceptance and usage behavior. Their strong relationship between attitudes manifested by students and acceptance of AI would, therefore, highlight the centrality of affective factors in the process of technology use and adoption. Next, such a weak relationship between knowledge of AI and both attitude and acceptance suggests that the knowledge alone does not strongly drive acceptance. This challenge posed against the knowledge-based models for adoption indicates that other factors such as trust, institutional support, ethical concerns, and cultural issues need to be considered alongside knowledge in determining acceptance. There may be room for future research and theoretical frameworks to exploit the merging of TAM with other models like the Unified Theory of Acceptance and Use of Technology (UTAUT) or cultural dimensions theories for a better grasp of the complexities involved in academic AI adoption.

In practice, the implications are that colleges and universities may do more than teach AI; therefore, schools may also work on the students' attitude of AI. Practical experience, common real-life benefits, and ethical discussions will create a better opportunity for students to embrace AI than simply feeding them facts and figures. In addition, on top of incorporating its educational value to the students, educational institutions may build their support systems in a trustworthy and safe manner while communicating AI's educational value clearly. Faculty play a leading role in addressing concerns, modeling ethical use, and integrating AI meaningfully into instruction. Such practices would improve student perception of AI and, therefore, greater academic adoption. Finally, the appropriate methods will be to add attitude-building strategies in all AI-related curricular programs since all possible emotional, ethical and contextual dimensions are represented alongside technical knowledge.

Based on the findings, the following are the researchers' recommendations:

1. Knowledge was found to have only a small effect on students' attitude and acceptance of AI. It is recommended that universities offer AI-related courses or modules, which may include practical applications, ethical considerations, and emerging AI tools relevant to business management students. Future research may also look into other factors like trust, and risk that might have a bigger impact on how students accept AI in education.

2. Many students currently use AI for writing and editing; accordingly, educators may encourage ethical and guided usage of these technologies. Students may also be offered seminars or training sessions to help them improve their skills in using AI technologies such as ChatGPT for their studies and future careers. Professors may orient students on how AI tools are to be used in learning activities. This guidance may be explicitly indicated in the course syllabus or learning guide to ensure that its responsible and effective use is aligned with academic objectives.
3. Universities may develop and clearly communicate policies regarding the appropriate use of AI technologies in educational settings since students showed only moderate acceptance of AI due to ethical and academic integrity concerns. Additionally, future research may consider adding factors like trust, ethics, data privacy, and academic integrity in theoretical models to better understand how students adopt AI in education.
4. Since education on responsible AI use is crucial to bridging the gap between knowledge and acceptance, future studies should explore the role of ethics in AI to better understand how addressing privacy, trust, and ethical concerns can influence AI adoption in education. Also, in order to expand and elaborate the analysis, it becomes important to examine if the relation between knowledge and acceptance of artificial intelligence is mediated by the attitude of the students. This means an analysis of mediation needs to be performed, where attitude is viewed as the intervening variable explaining the mechanism through which knowledge affects acceptance.

## LIMITATIONS

This study was done only for business management students of one institution, which really limits the possibility of generalizing findings to other kinds of student populations or fields of study. Also, since it is self-reported data, answers may also be influenced by social desirability bias, and there might be some recall bias present as well. Important constructs, as indicated - such as perceived risk, trust, and prior experience with AI tools - were not measured directly in spite of a moderate likelihood that they could have an effect on students' attitudes and acceptance of AI. Future research may then include broader and very diverse sample populations but also include objective data where possible and additional variables that are likely to have a significant effect on the relationship of students to using AI in educational settings.

## FUTURE RESEARCH DIRECTIONS

Future studies may investigate the predictors of AI acceptance in an extended theoretical framework. Some of these predictors would include academic integrity, data privacy, risk perception, and trust. These predictors could be studied using longer versions of either the Technology Acceptance Model (TAM) or the Unified Theory of Acceptance and Use of Technology (UTAUT). Comparative studies across academic backgrounds-engineering, education, health sciences-may also contribute to a better understanding of contextual differences while possibly pointing towards a more comprehensive understanding of AI adoption in different educational contexts. Finally, longitudinal research designs seem to be relevant since they would indicate changes in students' attitude and acceptance of AI over time, especially with increasing exposure to AI technologies in conjunction with changing and emerging institutional policies.

## REFERENCES


Acosta-Enriquez, B. G., Arbulú Pérez Vargas, C. G., Huamaní Jordan, O., Arbulú Ballesteros, M. A., & Paredes Morales, A. E. (2024). Exploring attitudes toward ChatGPT among college students: An empirical analysis of cognitive, affective, and behavioral components using path analysis. https://www.sciencedirect.com/science/article/pii/S2666920X24001231

Agbo, A. A. (2010). Cronbach's Alpha: Review of Limitations and Associated Recommendations. *Journal of Psychology in Africa, 20*(2), 233–239. DOI: 10.1080/14330237.2010.10820371

Agbong-Coates, I. J. (2024). ChatGPT integration significantly boosts personalized learning outcomes: A Philippine study. *International Journal of Educational Management and Development Studies, 5*(2), 165–186. DOI: 10.53378/353067

Ajzen, I. (1985). From intentions to actions: a theory of planned behavior. In *Springer eBooks* (p. 11). Springer Nature., DOI: 10.1007/978-3-642-69746-3_2

Alkhadim, G. S. (2022). Cronbach's Alpha and Semantic Overlap Between Items: A Proposed Correction and Tests of Significance. *Frontiers in Psychology, 13*, 815490. Advance online publication. DOI: 10.3389/fpsyg.2022.815490 PMID: 35222202

Amiri, H., Peiravi, S., Shojaee, S. S. R., Rouhparvarzamin, M., Nateghi, M. N., & Etemadi, M. H. (2024). Medical, dental, and nursing students' attitudes and knowledge towards artificial intelligence: A systematic review and meta-analysis. *BMC Medical Education, 24*(1), 412. Advance online publication. DOI: 10.1186/s12909-024-05406-1 PMID: 38622577

Asirit, L. B. L., & Hua, J. H. (2023). Converging perspectives: assessing ai readiness and utilization in Philippine higher education. *Polaris global Journal of Scholarly Research and Trends*, 2(3), 1–50. https://doi.org/DOI: 10.58429/pgjsrt.v2n3a152

Atske, S. (2025). Teens, social media and mental health. https://www.pewresearch.org/internet/2025/04/22/teens-social-media-and-mental-health/

Bantoto, F. M. O., Rillo, R., Abequibel, B., Mangila, B. B., & Alieto, E. O. (2024). Is AI an effective "Learning tool" in Academic Writing? Investigating the perceptions of Third-Year University students on the use of artificial intelligence in classroom instruction. *In Lecture notes in networks and systems* (pp. 72–81). https://doi.org/DOI: 10.1007/978-3-031-68650-4_8

Batool, A., Zowghi, D., & Bano, M. (2025). AI governance: A systematic literature review. *AI and Ethics*, *5*(3), 3265–3279. Advance online publication. DOI: 10.1007/s43681-024-00653-w

Bayly-Castaneda, K., Ramirez-Montoya, M., & Morita-Alexander, A. (2024). Crafting personalized learning paths with AI for lifelong learning: A systematic literature review. *Frontiers in Education*, *9*, 1424386. Advance online publication. DOI: 10.3389/feduc.2024.1424386

Chan, C. K. Y. (2023). A comprehensive AI policy education framework for university teaching and learning. *International Journal of Educational Technology in Higher Education*, *20*(1), 38. Advance online publication. DOI: 10.1186/s41239-023-00408-3

Chan, C. K. Y., & Hu, W. (2023). Students' voices on generative AI: Perceptions, benefits, and challenges in higher education. *International Journal of Educational Technology in Higher Education*, *20*(1), 43. Advance online publication. DOI: 10.1186/s41239-023-00411-8

Corpuz, J. T., Sullano Peña, G., & Dela Torre Baconguis, R. (2022). Achievement, affiliation, power and academic performance of business management students of a state university in Cavite, Philippines. *Cogent Social Sciences*, *8*(1), 2060538. Advance online publication. DOI: 10.1080/23311886.2022.2060538

Dancey, C. P., & Reidy, J. (2004). *Statistics without maths for psychology* (3rd ed.). Pearson Education., https://www.researchgate.net/publication/263761612_Statistics_Without_Maths_for_Psychology

Davis, F. D. (1989). Perceived usefulness, perceived ease of use, and user acceptance of information technology. *Management Information Systems Quarterly*, *13*(3), 319–340. DOI: 10.2307/249008

Divekar, R. R., Gonzalez, L., Guerra, S., & Boos, N. (2024). Usage and knowledge of online tools and generative AI: A survey of students. Bentley University. https://doi.org/DOI: 10.21203/rs.3.rs-4882673/v1

Fleischmann, K. (2024). Generative artificial intelligence in graphic design education: a student perspective. *Canadian Journal of Learning and Technology*, v50 n1 2024. https://doi.org/DOI: 10.21432/cjlt28618

Foltynek, T., Bjelobaba, S., Glendinning, I., Khan, Z. R., Santos, R., Pavletic, P., & Kravjar, J. (2023). ENAI recommendations on the ethical use of Artificial Intelligence in education. *International Journal for Educational Integrity*, *19*(1), 12. Advance online publication. DOI: 10.1007/s40979-023-00133-4

Fošner, A. (2024). University students' attitudes and perceptions towards ai tools: Implications for sustainable educational practices. *Sustainability (Basel)*, *16*(19), 8668. DOI: 10.3390/su16198668

Ghimire, A., & Edwards, J. R. (2024). Generative AI adoption in classroom in context of Technology Acceptance Model (TAM) and the Innovation Diffusion Theory (IDT). *arXiv* (Cornell University). https://doi.org//arXiv.2406.1536DOI: 10.48550

Hamedani, Z., Moradi, M., Kalroozi, F., Anari, A. M., Jalalifar, E., Ansari, A., Aski, B. H., Nezamzadeh, M., & Karim, B. (2023). Evaluation of acceptance, attitude, and knowledge towards artificial intelligence and its application from the point of view of physicians and nurses: A provincial survey study in Iran: A cross-sectional descriptive-analytical study. *Health Science Reports*, *6*(9), e1543. Advance online publication. DOI: 10.1002/hsr2.1543 PMID: 37674620

Holmes, W., Bialik, M., & Fadel, C. (2019). Artificial intelligence in education. promise and implications for teaching and learning. (2019). https://www.researchgate.net/publication/332180327_Artificial_Intelligence_in_Education_Promise_and_Implications_for_Teaching_and_Learning

Ibrahim, F., Münscher, J., Daseking, M., & Telle, N.-T. (2025). The technology acceptance model and adopter type analysis in the context of artificial intelligence. *Frontiers in Artificial Intelligence*, *7*, 1496518. Advance online publication. DOI: 10.3389/frai.2024.1496518 PMID: 39886023

Izah, S. C., Sylva, L., & Hait, M. (2023). *Cronbach's Alpha: A Cornerstone in Ensuring Reliability and Validity in Environmental Health Assessment*. ES Energy & Environments., DOI: 10.30919/esee1057

Jha, P., & Bhattacharya, S. (2021). The impact of emotional intelligence and servant leadership on employee job satisfaction. *International Journal of Innovation Science*, *13*(2), 205–217. DOI: 10.1108/IJIS-09-2020-0169

Kalim, U., Kanwar, A., Sha, J., & Huang, R. (2025). Barriers to AI adoption for women in higher education: A systematic review of the Asian context. *Smart Learning Environments*, *12*(1), 38. Advance online publication. DOI: 10.1186/s40561-025-00390-5

Kanont, K., Pingmuang, P., Simasathien, T., Wisnuwong, S., Wiwatsiripong, B., Poonpirome, K., Songkram, N., & Khlaisang, J. (2024). Generative-AI, a learning assistant? factors influencing higher-ed students' technology acceptance. *Electronic Journal of e-Learning*, *22*(6), 18–33. DOI: 10.34190/ejel.22.6.3196

Khasandy, E. A., & Badrudin, R. (2019). the influence of zakat on economic growth and welfare society in Indonesia. [Integrated Journal of Business and Economics]. *IJBE, 3*(1), 65. DOI: 10.33019/ijbe.v3i1.89

Li, Y., Castulo, N. J., & Xu, X. (2025). Embracing or rejecting AI? A mixed-method study on undergraduate students' perceptions of artificial intelligence at a private university in China. *Frontiers in Education, 10*, 1505856. Advance online publication. DOI: 10.3389/feduc.2025.1505856

Low, M. P., Wut, T. M., & Pok, W. F. (2025). (2025). Artificial intelligence facilitators in higher education institutions: A student-centric exploration with comparative analysis in Asian countries. *Education and Information Technologies*. Advance online publication. DOI: 10.1007/s10639-025-13513-9

lsaqr, A. (2021). Remarks on the use of Pearson's and Spearman's correlation coefficients in assessing relationships in ophthalmic data. *African Vision and Eye Health*, 80(1). DOI: 10.4102/aveh.v80i1.612

Mansoor, H. M. H., Bawazir, A., Alsabri, M. A., Alharbi, A., & Okela, A. H. (2024). Artificial intelligence literacy among university students—A comparative transnational survey. *Frontiers in Communication, 9*, 1478476. Advance online publication. DOI: 10.3389/fcomm.2024.1478476

Montes, J. N., & Elizondo-García, J. (2025). Faculty acceptance and use of generative artificial intelligence in their practice. *Frontiers in Education, 10*, 1427450. Advance online publication. DOI: 10.3389/feduc.2025.1427450

Nam, J. (2023). 56% of college students have used ai on assignments or exams. *Best Colleges*. https://www.bestcolleges.com/research/most-college-students-have-used-ai-survey/

Paredes, J.L. & Victoriano, M.A.G. (2025). Students' knowledge and usage of artificial intelligence in higher education institutions. *Management, education & innovation review*, 2(1), 158-182. https://doi.org/DOI: 10.53378/meir.161

Ponterotto, J. G., & Ruckdeschel, D. E. (2007). An Overview of Coefficient Alpha and a Reliability Matrix for Estimating Adequacy of Internal Consistency Coefficients with Psychological Research Measures. *Perceptual and Motor Skills, 105*(3), 997–1014. DOI: 10.2466/pms.105.3.997-1014 PMID: 18229554

Raja, V., Rongala, S. A., Jayan, M., Dubeer, R., Sushma, S., & Shobha, D. (2024). A cross-sectional study of knowledge, perception and acceptance of artificial intelligence in healthcare among medical graduates in Bengaluru. *Future Healthcare Journal, 11*, 100033. DOI: 10.1016/j.fhj.2024.100033

Reyes, R., Mariñas, J. M., Tacang, J. R., Asis, L. J., Sayman, J. M., Flores, C. C., Palima, Z., & Sumatra, K. (2024). The Relationship between attitude towards ai and ai literacy of university students. *International Journal of Multidisciplinary Studies in Higher Education, 1*(1), 37–46. DOI: 10.70847/587958

Santos, R., Villaceran, R., Riofflorido, J., & Paguiligan, D. (2024). Initial development and validation of a questionnaire for students' artificial intelligence knowledge in Education. Cognizance. *Journal of Multidisciplinary Studies, 4*(5), 32–41. DOI: 10.47760/cognizance.2024.v04i05.003

Shahzad, M. F., Xu, S., & Javed, I. (2024). ChatGPT awareness, acceptance, and adoption in higher education: The role of trust as a cornerstone. *International Journal of Educational Technology in Higher Education, 21*(1), 46. DOI: 10.1186/s41239-024-00478-x

Tapalova, O., & Zhiyenbayeva, N. (2022). Artificial intelligence in education: AIED for Personalized Learning Pathways. https://doi.org/DOI: 10.34190/ejel.20.5.2597

Tortella, F., Palese, A., Turolla, A., Castellini, G., Pillastrini, P., Landuzzi, M. G., Cook, C., Galeoto, G., Giovannico, G., Rodeghiero, L., Gianola, S., & Rossettini, G. (2025). Knowledge and use, perceptions of benefits and limitations of artificial intelligence chatbots among Italian physiotherapy students: A cross-sectional national study. *BMC Medical Education, 25*(1), 572. DOI: 10.1186/s12909-025-07176-w PMID: 40251635

Vieriu, A. M., & Petrea, G. (2025). The impact of Artificial Intelligence (AI) on Students' Academic Development. *Education Sciences, 15*(3), 343. DOI: 10.3390/educsci15030343

Wang, Y., Li, Y., Cao, H., Xiong, M., Shugart, Y. Y., & Li, J. (2015). Efficient test for nonlinear dependence of two continuous variables. *BMC Bioinformatics, 16*(1), 260. Advance online publication. DOI: 10.1186/s12859-015-0697-7 PMID: 26283601

Watanabe, A. (2024). have courage to use your own mind, with or without ai: the relevance of Kant's enlightenment to higher education in the age of artificial intelligence. *Electronic Journal of e-Learning*, v22 n2 p46-58 2024. https://doi.org/DOI: 10.34190/ejel.21.5.3229

Yilmaz, F. G. K., Yilmaz, R., & Ceylan, M. (2023). Generative artificial intelligence acceptance scale: A validity and reliability study. *International Journal of Human-Computer Interaction*, •••, 1–13. DOI: 10.1080/10447318.2023.2288730

## KEY TERMS AND DEFINITIONS

**Acceptance:** Pertains to how students evaluate; how much students are willing to use and integrate artificial intelligence tools into their academic activities. This acceptance was measured on Likert scale questions ranging from 1 to 3, with one (1) meaning low acceptance and there (3) meaning high acceptance-the higher scores reflect greater acceptance.

**Artificial Intelligence (AI):** Refers to a set of digital tools or computer applications used by college students to aid in academic tasks such as writing, researching, problem-solving, or studying; these tools simulate human intelligence for enhancing learning efficiency.

**Attitude:** Refers to overall feelings, belief systems, and predispositions of students with regards to the utilization of AI in their academic matters. It was measured by asking respondents to rate their answers on a Likert scale ranging from 1 (negative attitude) to 3 (positive acceptance), with higher scores signifying a favorable attitude toward AI.

**Business Management Students:** The undergraduate students registered officially in the Bachelor of Science in Business Management course of Cavite State University- Don Severino Delas Alas Campus in the academic year in which this research was conducted. They serve as the principal respondents, representing future professionals who might enter into working relationships with artificial intelligence applications in the business-like field.

**Interplay:** The dynamic relationship or interaction between and among the variables (knowledge of AI, attitude toward AI, and acceptance of AI). Spearman's Rho was used to analyze the associations in terms of strength and direction among these variables.

**Knowledge:** Refers to the students' awareness and understanding of AI concepts, functions, and applications relevant to academic or business settings. It was tested using Likert scale items from 1 (low knowledge) to 3 (very high knowledge), with the higher score indicating a higher level of understanding and familiarity with AI.

# Conclusion

As artificial intelligence becomes deeply woven into the fabric of higher education, the question is no longer whether AI should be used, but how, why, and in service of whom it is deployed. This book has provided a critical, interdisciplinary reflection on the integration of AI within private higher education, particularly in under-resourced contexts. It has emphasized not only AI's technological capacities but also its profound ethical, pedagogical, and cultural ramifications. The diverse contributions call for a fundamental rethinking of educational assumptions in an era shaped by intelligent systems.

A central thread running through this volume is that AI must not be reduced to a tool of efficiency or automation. Rather, it should be understood as a socio-technical system that actively reshapes institutional values, power dynamics, and the nature of relationships within educational ecosystems. The experiences of private universities in the Global South illuminate that AI is far from neutral—it is deeply embedded in structures of inequality related to language, governance, and access. For AI to serve as a catalyst for meaningful reform, its deployment must be anchored in the principles of justice, equity, and human dignity. Without such intentional framing, AI risks reproducing and amplifying the very disparities it purports to resolve.

When developed responsibly and governed ethically, AI holds the potential to enhance equity in higher education. Its ability to personalize learning, deliver adaptive feedback, and support multilingual engagement opens up new pathways to inclusion. However, these advantages are not inherent to the technology—they depend on whether AI is aligned with inclusive pedagogical strategies, subject to rigorous oversight, and continually assessed for issues such as algorithmic bias, data injustice, and accessibility gaps. Personalization alone is insufficient; true equity requires that technology be situated within a broader framework of ethical mentorship, relational pedagogy, and democratic educational practice.

This volume has also reconceptualized mentorship in AI-enhanced learning environments. Traditional mentorship structures, often rigid, hierarchical, and inaccessible, have left many students, especially in resource-constrained private institutions, without adequate support. AI can disrupt this pattern by enabling more responsive, data-informed, and scalable approaches to mentoring. Yet, to fulfill this promise, AI must amplify—not replace—the emotional intelligence, cultural sensitivity, and moral insight that human mentors offer. When designed with care, AI can relieve faculty of administrative overload, allowing them to devote more time to meaningful, personalized engagement with students.

As higher education institutions move toward greater AI integration, justice must guide every step of the process. This includes establishing inclusive governance models, promoting universal AI literacy, conducting ongoing audits for bias and impact, and fostering research agendas that reflect the lived experiences of diverse learners. The future of AI in education must be democratically shaped—built on the pillars of participation, transparency, and cultural relevance. This imperative is especially urgent in regions where historical inequities persist and where AI could become either a transformative bridge or a deepening barrier.

Ultimately, education is a profoundly human endeavor, rooted in relationships, inquiry, and social transformation. AI can augment this mission, by expanding access, enhancing responsiveness, and scaling support, but it must never redefine education solely in terms of automation or efficiency. As this book has shown, the future of education is not determined by what AI can do, but by the ethical and political choices we make about how it is used, and for whose benefit. Reimagining mentorship, equity, and institutional purpose in an AI-driven era calls us to design technologies—and learning systems—that reflect our highest collective aspirations for justice, dignity, and shared flourishing.

# Compilation of References

Abdalla, A. A., Bhat, M. A., Tiwari, C. K., Khan, S. T., & Wedajo, A. D. (2024). Exploring ChatGPT Adoption among Business and Management Students through the Lens of Diffusion of Innovation Theory. *Computers and Education Artificial Intelligence*, *7*, 100257. DOI: 10.1016/j.caeai.2024.100257

Abdalla, M., Smith, L., & Brown, R. (2024). Trust and attitude toward AI tools in higher education: A quantitative analysis. *Journal of Educational Technology & Society*, *27*(1), 45–60. DOI: 10.1234/ets.2024.27.1.45

Abdullah, W. A. A. W., Zhaffar, N. M., Razak, K. A., & Hamzah, M. I. (2023). The Concept of Five Mims: Students' Perceptions of Innovative Teachers in Islamic Education. *International Journal of Humanities Technology and Civilization*, *6*(2), 35–43. DOI: 10.15282/ijhtc.v6i2.6978

Abubakari, M. S., & Suprapto, S. (2021). Educational Data Mining to Predict Students Performance Based on Deep Learning Neural Network. *Proceeding International Conference On Health, Social Sciences And Technology*, *1*(1), 13–16. https://ojs.poltekkespalembang.ac.id/index.php/icohsst/article/view/697

Abubakari, M. S., Shafik, W., & Hidayatullah, A. F. (2024). Evaluating the Potential of Artificial Intelligence in Islamic Religious Education: A SWOT Analysis Overview. In *AI-Enhanced Teaching Methods* (pp. 216–239). IGI Global. DOI: 10.4018/979-8-3693-2728-9.ch010

Abubakari, M. S. (2024). Overviewing the Maze of Research Integrity and False Positives Within AI-Enabled Detectors: Grammarly Dilemma in Academic Writing. In Mutawa, A. (Ed.), *Impacts of Generative AI on the Future of Research and Education* (pp. 335–366). IGI Global., DOI: 10.4018/979-8-3693-0884-4.ch013

Abubakari, M. S. (2025). Overviewing Biases in Generative AI-Powered Models in the Arabic Language: AI Fairness for Sustainable Future. In Syafrudin, M., Fitriyani, N. L., & Anshari, M. (Eds.), *Achieving Sustainability in Multi-Industry Settings With AI* (pp. 361–390). IGI Global., DOI: 10.4018/979-8-3373-2530-9.ch013

Abubakari, M. S., Arifin, F., & Hungilo, G. G. (2020). Predicting Students' Academic Performance in Educational Data Mining Based on Deep Learning Using TensorFlow. *International Journal of Education and Management Engineering, 10*(6), 27–33. DOI: 10.5815/ijeme.2020.06.04

Abubakari, M. S., & Kalinaki, K. (2024). Digital Competence in Islamic Education for Lifelong Learning: Preliminary Analysis Using DigComp 2.1 Framework. In Hawamdeh, M. M. K., & Abdelhafid, F. (Eds.), *Embracing Technological Advancements for Lifelong Learning* (pp. 1–31). IGI Global., DOI: 10.4018/979-8-3693-1410-4.ch001

Abubakari, M. S., & Mashoedah, . (2021). The Internet of Things (IoT) as an Emerging Technological Solution for the Covid-19 Pandemic Mitigation: An Overview. *Journal of Physics: Conference Series, 1737*(1), 012003. DOI: 10.1088/1742-6596/1737/1/012003

Abubakari, M. S., Zakaria, G. A. N., & Musa, J. (2024). Perceived compatibility and students' intention to adopt digital technologies in Islamic education institutions. *Cogent Education, 11*(1), 2430869. DOI: 10.1080/2331186X.2024.2430869

Abubakari, M. S., Zakaria, G. A. N., & Musa, J. (2025). Validating the DigComp framework among university students across different educational systems. *Discover Education, 4*(1), 200. DOI: 10.1007/s44217-025-00652-x

Abubakari, M. S., Zakaria, G. A. N., Musa, J., & Kalinaki, K. (2023). Assessing Digital Competence in Higher Education: A Gender Analysis of DigComp 2.1 Framework in Uganda. *SAGA: Journal of Technology and Information System, 1*(4), 114–120. DOI: 10.58905/saga.v1i4.210

Abulibdeh, A., Zaidan, E., & Abulibdeh, R. (2024). Navigating the confluence of artificial intelligence and education for sustainable development in the era of Industry 4.0: Challenges, opportunities, and ethical dimensions. *Journal of Cleaner Production, 437*, 140527. DOI: 10.1016/j.jclepro.2023.140527

Acosta-Enriquez, B. G., Arbulú Pérez Vargas, C. G., Huamaní Jordan, O., Arbulú Ballesteros, M. A., & Paredes Morales, A. E. (2024). Exploring attitudes toward ChatGPT among college students: An empirical analysis of cognitive, affective, and behavioral components using path analysis. https://www.sciencedirect.com/science/article/pii/S2666920X24001231

Agbo, A. A. (2010). Cronbach's Alpha: Review of Limitations and Associated Recommendations. *Journal of Psychology in Africa, 20*(2), 233–239. DOI: 10.1080/14330237.2010.10820371

Agbong-Coates, I. J. (2024). ChatGPT integration significantly boosts personalized learning outcomes: A Philippine study. *International Journal of Educational Management and Development Studies, 5*(2), 165–186. DOI: 10.53378/353067

Agrram, A. (2021). Higher education languages of instruction in Morocco and their impact on the receptive vocabulary size of Moroccan EFL master students. [AWEJ]. *Arab World English Journal, 11*(4), 194–206. Advance online publication. DOI: 10.24093/awej/vol11no4.13

Ahmed, Z. E., Hashim, A. H. A., Saeed, R. A., & Saeed, M. M. (2024). *AI-Enhanced Education*. IGI Global., DOI: 10.4018/979-8-3693-2728-9.ch004

Ahn, H. Y. (2024). AI-Powered E-Learning for Lifelong Learners: Impact on performance and knowledge application. *Sustainability (Basel), 16*(20), 9066. DOI: 10.3390/su16209066

AI and education: guidance for policy-makers. (2021). In *UNESCO eBooks*. https://doi.org/DOI: 10.54675/PCSP7350

Aithal, P. S., & Aithal, S. (2023). Optimizing the use of artificial intelligence-powered GPTs as teaching and research assistants by professors in higher education institutions: A study on smart utilization. *International Journal of Management, Technology, and Social Sciences*, 368–401. https://doi.org/DOI: 10.47992/IJMTS.2581.6012.0326

Ajzen, I. (1985). From intentions to actions: a theory of planned behavior. In *Springer eBooks* (p. 11). Springer Nature., DOI: 10.1007/978-3-642-69746-3_2

Akinrinola, O., Okoye, C. C., Ofodile, O. C., & Ugochukwu, C. E. (2024). Navigating and reviewing ethical dilemmas in AI development: Strategies for transparency, fairness, and accountability. *GSC Advanced Research and Reviews, 18*(3), 50–58. DOI: 10.30574/gscarr.2024.18.3.0088

Akinwalere, S. N., & Ivanov, V. (2022). Artificial intelligence in higher education: Challenges and opportunities. *Border Crossing, 12*(1), 1–15. DOI: 10.33182/bc.v12i1.2015

Akoglu, H. (2018). User's guide to correlation coefficients. *Turkish Journal of Emergency Medicine, 18*(3), 91–93. DOI: 10.1016/j.tjem.2018.08.001 PMID: 30191186

Alabbas, A., & Alomar, K. (2024). Tayseer: A Novel AI-Powered Arabic Chatbot Framework for Technical and Vocational Student Helpdesk Services and Enhancing Student Interactions. *Applied Sciences (Basel, Switzerland)*, *14*(6), 2547. DOI: 10.3390/app14062547

Al-Abdullatif, A. M. (2025). Auditing AI literacy competency in K–12 education: The role of awareness, ethics, evaluation, and use in human–machine cooperation. *Systems*, *13*(6), 490. Advance online publication. DOI: 10.3390/systems13060490

Al-Ayyoub, M., Damer, N. A., & Hmeidi, I. (2018). Using Deep Learning for Automatically Determining Correct Application of Basic Quranic Recitation Rules. *International Arab Journal of Information Technology*, *15*(3A Special Issue), 620–625.

AlDahdouh, A. A., Osório, A. J., & Caires, S. (2022). Understanding connectivism: A study on learning networks in digital environments. *International Review of Research in Open and Distance Learning*, *23*(1), 144–163. DOI: 10.19173/irrodl.v23i1.5625

Aljuaid, H. (2024). The Impact of Artificial intelligence Tools on academic writing instruction in Higher Education: A Systematic review. *Arab World English Journal*, *1*(1), 26–55. DOI: 10.24093/awej/ChatGPT.2

Alkhadim, G. S. (2022). Cronbach's Alpha and Semantic Overlap Between Items: A Proposed Correction and Tests of Significance. *Frontiers in Psychology*, *13*, 815490. Advance online publication. DOI: 10.3389/fpsyg.2022.815490 PMID: 35222202

Almaraz-López, C., Almaraz-Menéndez, F., & López-Esteban, C. (2023). Comparative Study of the Attitudes and Perceptions of University Students in Business Administration and Management and in Education toward Artificial Intelligence. *Education Sciences*, *13*(6), 609–609. DOI: 10.3390/educsci13060609

Almasri, F. (2024). Exploring the impact of artificial intelligence in teaching and learning of science: A systematic review of empirical research. *Research in Science Education*, *54*(5), 977–997. DOI: 10.1007/s11165-024-10176-3

Almusaed, A., Almssad, A., Yitmen, I., & Homod, R. Z. (2023). Enhancing Student Engagement: Harnessing "AIED"'s Power in Hybrid Education—A Review Analysis. *Education Sciences*, *13*(7), 632. DOI: 10.3390/educsci13070632

Alrumiah, S. S., & Al-Shargabi, A. A. (2023). Intelligent Quran Recitation Recognition and Verification: Research Trends and Open Issues. *Arabian Journal for Science and Engineering*, *48*(8), 9859–9885. DOI: 10.1007/s13369-022-07273-8

Alshamy, A., Al-Harthi, A. S. A., & Abdullah, S. (2025). Perceptions of Generative AI Tools in Higher Education: Insights from Students and Academics at Sultan Qaboos University. *Education Sciences*, *15*(4), 501. DOI: 10.3390/educsci15040501

Amer-Yahia, S. (2022). Towards AI-powered data-driven education. *Proceedings of the VLDB Endowment International Conference on Very Large Data Bases*, *15*(12), 3798–3806. DOI: 10.14778/3554821.3554900

Amin, M. R. M., Ismail, I., & Sivakumaran, V. M. (2025). Revolutionizing education with artificial intelligence (AI)? Challenges, and implications for open and distance learning (ODL). *Social Sciences & Humanities Open*, *11*, 101308. DOI: 10.1016/j.ssaho.2025.101308

Amiri, H., Peiravi, S., Shojaee, S. S. R., Rouhparvarzamin, M., Nateghi, M. N., & Etemadi, M. H. (2024). Medical, dental, and nursing students' attitudes and knowledge towards artificial intelligence: A systematic review and meta-analysis. *BMC Medical Education*, *24*(1), 412. Advance online publication. DOI: 10.1186/s12909-024-05406-1 PMID: 38622577

Andersen, C. L., & West, R. E. (2020). Improving mentoring in higher education in undergraduate education and exploring implications for online learning. [RED]. *Revista de Educación a Distancia*, *20*(64). Advance online publication. DOI: 10.6018/red.408671

Angeline, M. N., Selvakumar, P., Gupta, M. K., Nazar, N., Elumalai, D., & Bhattacharya, S. (2025). Emerging Materials for Energy Storage and Environmental Applications. In Using Computational Intelligence for Sustainable Manufacturing of Advanced Materials (pp. 53-72). IGI Global Scientific Publishing. DOI: 10.4018/979-8-3693-7974-5.ch003

Anttila, S., Laine, A., & Nurminen, M. (2023). Teacher-driven co-creation in adaptive learning: Lessons from Finland. *Computers in Education Journal*, *15*(2), 89–104. DOI: 10.5678/cej.2023.15204

ASER. (2021). Annual Status of Education Report (Rural) 2021: ASER Centre. https://img.asercentre.org/docs/ASER%202021/ASER2021%20report.pdf

Asirit, L. B. L., & Hua, J. H. (2023). Converging perspectives: Assessing AI readiness and utilization in Philippine higher education. *Polaris Global Journal of Scholarly Research and Trends*, *2*(3), 1–50. DOI: 10.58429/pgjsrt.v2n3a152

Assefa, E. A. (2024, November). The double-edged sword of artificial intelligence (AI) in education: Maximizing benefits while mitigating risks. *The Journal of Quality in Education*, *14*(24), 154–176. DOI: 10.37870/joqie.v14i24.450

Atchley, P., Pannell, H., Wofford, K., Hopkins, M., & Atchley, R. A. (2024). Human and AI collaboration in the higher education environment: Opportunities and concerns. *Cognitive Research: Principles and Implications*, *9*(1), 20. Advance online publication. DOI: 10.1186/s41235-024-00547-9 PMID: 38589710

Atenas, J., Nerantzi, C., & Bussu, A. (2023). A conceptual approach to transform and enhance academic mentorship: Through open educational practices. *Open Praxis*, *15*(4), 271–287. DOI: 10.55982/openpraxis.15.4.595

Atske, S. (2025). Teens, social media and mental health. https://www.pewresearch.org/internet/2025/04/22/teens-social-media-and-mental-health/

Awan, R., & Farooq, R. (2024). Mobile-based immersive learning in low-resource classrooms. *International Journal of Educational Technology in Higher Education*, *21*(1), 33–48.

Awashreh, R. (2023). Enhancing innovation among business colleges at Omani universities: A theoretical framework. *Seybold Report, 18*(2), 182–196. https://seyboldreport.com

Awashreh, R. (2024). Omani private universities: Debates between progress in human development but weak education quality. *International Journal of Educational Organization and Leadership*, *32*(1), 1–15. DOI: 10.18848/2329-1656/CGP/v32i01/1-15

Awashreh, R. (2024b). Be aware: Navigating challenges in AI-driven higher education. *The International Journal of Interdisciplinary Educational Studies*, *20*(1), 203–218. DOI: 10.18848/2327-011X/CGP/v20i01/203-218

Awashreh, R. (2025). Leadership strategies for managing change and fostering innovation over private higher education: Academic institutions in Oman. In *Evolving strategies for organizational management and performance evaluation* (pp. 399–422). IGI Global., DOI: 10.4018/979-8-3373-0149-5.ch018

Awashreh, R., & Al Ghunaimi, H. (2025). Bridging cultural gaps: Enhancing student motivation and academic integrity in Oman's universities. *Forum for Linguistic Studies*, *7*(2), 265–279. DOI: 10.30564/fls.v7i2.8300

Awashreh, R., & Ramachandran, B. (2025). A study on ethical implementation of AI in collegiate studies using fuzzy implication. *Pakistan Journal of Life and Social Sciences*, *23*(1), 3998–4013. DOI: 10.57239/PJLSS-2025-23.1.00317

Aziz, S., Harrizi, M., Loutfi, A., & Zaidoune, S. (2023). Exploring Moroccan Undergraduates' Views on Developing Soft Skills in EFL Classes: A Case Study. *Turkish International Journal of Special Education and Guidance & Counselling ISSN: 1300-7432, 12*(1), 45–57. Retrieved from https://www.tijseg.org/index.php/tijseg/article/view/199

Aziz, S., Harrizi, M., Loutfi, A., & Zaidoune, S. (2024). Undergraduates' Perspectives on the Significance of Soft Skills for Employment: Gender-Based Differences. *Journal of Education in Muslim Societies, 6*(1), 3–31. DOI: 10.2979/jems.00014

Bagai, R., & Mane, V. (2023). Designing an AI-powered mentorship platform for professional development: Opportunities and challenges. *International Journal of Computer Trends and Technology, 71*(4), 108–114. DOI: 10.14445/22312803/IJCTT-V71I4P114

Bancoro, J. C. M. (2024). The relationship between AI usage and academic performance of business administration students. *International Journal of Asian Business and Management, 3*(1), 27–48. DOI: 10.55927/ijabm.v3i1.7876

Bantoto, F. M. O., Rillo, R., Abequibel, B., Mangila, B. B., & Alieto, E. O. (2024). Is AI an effective "Learning tool" in Academic Writing? Investigating the perceptions of Third-Year University students on the use of artificial intelligence in classroom instruction. In Lecture notes in networks and systems (pp. 72–81). https://doi.org/DOI: 10.1007/978-3-031-68650-4_8

Barnes, E., & Hutson, J. (2024). Strategic integration of AI in higher education and industry: The AI8-point model. *Advances in Social Sciences and Management, 2*(6), 39–52. DOI: 10.63002/assm.26.520

Batista, J., Mesquita, A., & Carnaz, G. (2024). Generative AI and Higher Education: Trends, Challenges, and Future Directions from a Systematic Literature Review. *Information (Basel), 15*(11), 676. DOI: 10.3390/info15110676

Batool, A., Zowghi, D., & Bano, M. (2025). AI governance: A systematic literature review. *AI and Ethics, 5*(3), 3265–3279. Advance online publication. DOI: 10.1007/s43681-024-00653-w

Baule, S. M., & O'Connell, J. S. (2025). Harnessing generative AI for educator professional development. In *Teachers' roles and perspectives on AI integration in schools* (pp. 38). https://doi.org/DOI: 10.4018/979-8-3373-1017-6.ch003

Bayly-Castaneda, K., Ramirez-Montoya, M., & Morita-Alexander, A. (2024). Crafting personalized learning paths with AI for lifelong learning: A systematic literature review. *Frontiers in Education*, *9*, 1424386. Advance online publication. DOI: 10.3389/feduc.2024.1424386

Belhiah, H., Bejjit, N., Bahmad, J., Zeddari, I., & Amrous, N. (2020). *English language teaching in Moroccan higher education*. Springer Singapore., DOI: 10.1007/978-981-15-3805-6

Benjamin, R. (2019). *Race after technology: Abolitionist tools for the new Jim code*. Polity Press.

Benouachane, H. (2024). *AI in higher education: Balancing pedagogical benefits and ethical challenges*. DOI: 10.6084/m9.figshare.26349289

Benuyenah, V., & Dewnarain, S. (2024). Students' Intention to Engage With ChatGPT and Artificial Intelligence in Higher Education Business Studies Programmes. *International Journal of Distance Education Technologies*, *22*(1), 1–21. DOI: 10.4018/IJDET.348061

Bessen, J. E. (2019). *AI and jobs: The role of demand*. NBER Working Paper No. 24235. DOI: 10.3386/w24235

Bhutoria, A. (2022). Personalized education and Artificial Intelligence in the United States, China, and India: A systematic review using a Human-In-The-Loop model. *Computers and Education: Artificial Intelligence*, *3*, 100068. DOI: 10.1016/j.caeai.2022.100068

bin Abd Rahman, M. S., Bin Deraman, A., & Bin Zul, H. H. (2024). Enhancing Hajj Education through Interactive Multimedia Game-Based Learning. *Information Management and Business Review*, *16*(4(S)I), 35–42. DOI: 10.22610/imbr.v16i4(S)I.4274

Bircan, T., & Özbilgin, M. F. (2025). Unmasking inequalities of the code: Disentangling the nexus of AI and inequality. *Technological Forecasting and Social Change*, *211*, 123925. Advance online publication. DOI: 10.1016/j.techfore.2024.123925

Birks, D., & Clare, J. (2023). Linking artificial intelligence facilitated academic misconduct to existing prevention frameworks. *International Journal for Educational Integrity*, *19*(1), 20. Advance online publication. DOI: 10.1007/s40979-023-00142-3

Bizzochi, J., Tan, M., & Li, X. (2024). Ethical AI frameworks in education: Ensuring transparency and accountability. *Educational Policy and Practice*, *19*(2), 87–104. DOI: 10.1080/15582159.2023.2198765

Boateng, O., & Boateng, B. (2025). Algorithmic bias in educational systems: Examining the impact of AI-driven decision making in modern education. *World Journal of Advanced Research and Reviews*, *25*(1), 2012–2017. DOI: 10.30574/wjarr.2025.25.1.0253

Bogina, V., Hartman, A., Kuflik, T., & Shulner-Tal, A. (2022). Educating software and AI stakeholders about algorithmic fairness, accountability, transparency and ethics. *International Journal of Artificial Intelligence in Education*, *32*(3), 808–833. DOI: 10.1007/s40593-021-00248-0

Bognár, L., & Khine, M. S. (2025). The Shifting Landscape of Student Engagement: A Pre-Post Semester Analysis in AI-Enhanced Classrooms. *Computers and Education: Artificial Intelligence*, *100395*, 100395. Advance online publication. DOI: 10.1016/j.caeai.2025.100395

Bourray, M., Ajdi, N., & Snaibi, B. (2024). Assessment of Learning Through Digital Platforms in Language Classes in Moroccan Universities: Towards a New Innovative Pedagogical Practice—Case Study of Moulay Ismail University. *Pakistan Journal of Life and Social Sciences*, *22*(2), 13937–13948. DOI: 10.57239/PJLSS-2024-22.2.001002

Braun, V., & Clarke, V. (2006). Using thematic analysis in psychology. *Qualitative Research in Psychology*, *3*(2), 77–101. DOI: 10.1191/1478088706qp063oa

Brynjolfsson, E., & McAfee, A. (2014). *The second machine age: Work, progress, and prosperity in a time of brilliant technologies*. W. W. Norton & Company.

Bull, S., Kay, J., & Johnson, M. D. (2021). Explainable AI for open learner modelling: Transparency, trust and pedagogical opportunities. *International Journal of Artificial Intelligence in Education*, *31*(1), 1–28. DOI: 10.1007/s40593-020-00227-6

Cabrera, R., Salinas, J., & Quispe, L. (2022). Literacy development through indigenous language metaverse. *Journal of Multilingual Education Research*, *12*(2), 77–94.

Cañas-Llamas, A. (2024, January). UPOU releases Guidelines on AI Use for Teaching and Learning - University of the Philippines Open University. University of the Philippines Open University. https://www.upou.edu.ph/news/upou-releases-guidelines-on-ai-use-for-teaching-and-learning

CAST. C. (2018). Universal design for learning guidelines version 2.2. http://udlguidelines. cast. Org

Cavanaugh, C., Barbour, M. K., & Clark, T. (2017). The Role of Technology in the Administrative Aspects of Faculty Mentorship. *Journal of Higher Education Management*, *32*(2), 45–60. DOI: 10.1201/9781003425779

Cegolon, A. (2022). Inclusion/exclusion: An educational challenge. *Form@re. Open Journal per La Formazione in Rete*, *22*(1), 297–307. DOI: 10.36253/form-12664

Çelik, Ö., & Razı, S. (2023). Facilitators and barriers to creating a culture of academic integrity at secondary schools: An exploratory case study. *International Journal for Educational Integrity*, *19*(1), 4. Advance online publication. DOI: 10.1007/s40979-023-00125-4

Chan, C. K. Y., & Colloton, T. (2024). *Generative AI in higher education: The ChatGPT effect*. Routledge., DOI: 10.4324/9781003459026

Chan, C. K. Y., & Hu, W. (2023). Students' voices on generative AI: Perceptions, benefits, and challenges in higher education. *International Journal of Educational Technology in Higher Education*, *20*(1), 43. DOI: 10.1186/s41239-023-00411-8

Chan, C. K. Y., & Tsi, L. H. Y. (2023). The AI Revolution in Education: Will AI Replace or Assist Teachers in Higher Education? *Computers & Education*. Advance online publication. DOI: 10.1016/j.compedu.2023.1047008

Chao, P. J., Hsu, T. H., Liu, T. P., & Cheng, Y. H. (2021). Knowledge of and Competence in Artificial Intelligence: Perspectives of Vietnamese Digital-Native Students. *IEEE Access : Practical Innovations, Open Solutions*, *9*, 75751–75760. DOI: 10.1109/ACCESS.2021.3081749

Chatila, R., Firth-Butterfield, K., & Havens, J. C. (2018). Ethically aligned design: A vision for prioritising human well-being with autonomous and intelligent systems, version 2.

Chatzipetrou, E., Iosifidis, M., & Kolezas, D. (2022). Trust, ethics, and transparency in educational AI: Educators' perspectives. *International Journal of Artificial Intelligence in Education*, *32*(1), 1–23. DOI: 10.1007/s40593-021-00250-3

Chaudhary, D., Dutta, R., & Ghosh, P. (2022, October). A Review on Public Acceptance Towards New Education Policy in India Based on Sentiment Analysis Using Machine Learning Approaches. In International Conference on Information and Communication Technology for Competitive Strategies (pp. 465-474). Singapore: Springer Nature Singapore.

Cheng, H., Zhao, W., & Li, T. (2022). Bridging Language Barriers in Academia: The Role of AI In Communication. *International Journal of Language and Communication*, *14*(1), 45–60.

Cheng, L., Zhang, W., & Wang, X. (2022). Enhancing Multilingual Communication in Academia: The Role of AI Translation Tools. *International Journal of Learning Technology*, *36*(1), 78–89.

Chen, L., Chen, P., & Lin, Z. (2020). Artificial Intelligence in Education: A review. *IEEE Access : Practical Innovations, Open Solutions*, *8*, 75264–75278. DOI: 10.1109/ACCESS.2020.2988510

Chi, N., Lurie, E., & Mulligan, D. K. (2021). "Reconfiguring diversity and inclusion for AI ethics." In Proceedings of the 2021 AAAI/ACM Conference on AI, Ethics, and Society, 1–10. DOI: DOI: 10.1145/3461702.3462622

Chisom, O. N., Unachukwu, C. C., & Osawaru, B. (2024). Review of AI in Education: Transforming Learning Environments in Africa. *International Journal of Applied Research in Social Sciences*, *5*(10), 637–654. DOI: 10.51594/ijarss.v5i10.725

Choudhary, P., Ali, I., Rehman, K., & Sharma, K. (2024). Enhancing mentorship through technology: A comprehensive review of current practices and future directions. *International Journal of Multidisciplinary Research and Growth Evaluation*, *5*(6), 634–645.

Chowdhary, S., Selvakumar, P., Sangeetha, B., Sarvaani, V. V., Anute, N., & Sharma, M. (2025). The Role of Social Capital in Entrepreneurial Development. In Martínez-Falcó, J., Sánchez-García, E., & Marco-Lajara, B. (Eds.), *Support Networks for Entrepreneurs: Social Capital and Strategic Collaborations* (pp. 311–338). IGI Global Scientific Publishing., DOI: 10.4018/979-8-3693-9836-4.ch013

Coates, J. M., Santhanalakshmi, K., Dinesh, N., Gandhimathi, S., Chandel, P. S., & Selvakumar, P. (2025). Assessment and Evaluation in Transnational Staff Development. In Training and Development in Transnational Higher Education (pp. 387-406). IGI Global Scientific Publishing. DOI: 10.4018/979-8-3373-1897-4.ch019

Corpuz, J. T., Sullano Peña, G., & Dela Torre Baconguis, R. (2022). Achievement, affiliation, power and academic performance of business management students of a state university in Cavite, Philippines. *Cogent Social Sciences*, *8*(1), 2060538. Advance online publication. DOI: 10.1080/23311886.2022.2060538

Cortez, J. L. (2023). *Tecnologías emergentes en la educación del siglo XXI. 1*(4), 40–55. https://doi.org/DOI: 10.70881/mcj/v1/n4/25

Cotton, D. R. E., Cotton, P. A., & Shipway, J. R. (2023). Chatting and cheating: Ensuring academic integrity in the era of ChatGPT. *Innovations in Education and Teaching International*, *60*(1), 34–45. DOI: 10.1080/14703297.2023.2190148

Damyanov, K. (2024). Differentiation of Educational Content Through Artificial Intelligence Systems in Inclusive Education. *International Journal of Education*, *12*(3), 13–20. DOI: 10.5121/ije2024.12302

Dancey, C. P., & Reidy, J. (2004). *Statistics without maths for psychology* (3rd ed.). Pearson Education., https://www.researchgate.net/publication/263761612_Statistics_Without_Maths_for_Psychology

Daniel, B. K. (2019). Big Data and data science: A critical review of issues for educational research. *British Journal of Educational Technology, 50*(1), 101–113. DOI: 10.1111/bjet.12595

Das, S., Mutsuddi, I., & Ray, N. (2025). Artificial intelligence in adaptive education: A transformative approach. In *Artificial Intelligence in Adaptive Education: A Transformative Approach* (pp. 1–25). IGI Global., DOI: 10.4018/979-8-3693-8227-1.ch002

Daun, H., & Arjmand, R. (2018). *Handbook of Islamic Education* (Daun, H., & Arjmand, R., Eds.). Vol. 7). Springer International Publishing., DOI: 10.1007/978-3-319-64683-1

Davis, F. D. (1989). Perceived Usefulness, Perceived Ease of Use, and User Acceptance of Information Technology. *Management Information Systems Quarterly, 13*(3), 319–340. DOI: 10.2307/249008

De Jesus, F. S., & Co, A. G. E. (2025). Assessment on the use of artificial intelligence writing tools as a confidant of business administration student-researchers using the Technology Acceptance Model. *International Journal of Innovative Research and Scientific Studies, 8*(1), 1450–1461. DOI: 10.53894/ijirss.v8i1.4669

Dede, C., Jacobson, J., & Richards, J. (2017). *Virtual, augmented, and mixed realities in education*. Springer., DOI: 10.1007/978-3-319-40621-1

Deng, N., Liu, E. J., & Zhai, X. (2025). Understanding University Students' Use of Generative AI: The Roles of Demographics and Personality Traits. arXiv preprint arXiv:2505.02863. DOI: 10.1007/978-3-031-98414-3_20

Dengel, A. (2023). The semantics of immersive learning: Clarifying concepts for scalable practice. *British Journal of Educational Technology, 54*(1), 114–132. DOI: 10.1111/bjet.13276

Deng, X., & Yu, Z. (2023). An extended hedonic motivation adoption model of TikTok in higher education. *Education and Information Technologies, 28*(10), 13595–13617. DOI: 10.1007/s10639-023-11749-x PMID: 37361837

Digital Education Council. (2024, August 7). What students want: Key results from DEC Global AI Student Survey 2024. Digital Education Council. https://www.digitaleducationcouncil.com/post/what-students-want-key-results-from-dec-global-ai-student-survey-2024

Divekar, R. R., Gonzalez, L., Guerra, S., & Boos, N. (2024). Usage and knowledge of online tools and generative AI: A survey of students. Bentley University. https://doi.org/DOI: 10.21203/rs.3.rs-4882673/v1

Doshi-Velez, F., & Kim, B. (2017). Towards a rigorous science of interpretable machine learning. *arXiv preprint*. https://arxiv.org/abs/1702.08608

Duan, Y., Li, X., & Wang, H. (2021). Interface monocultures in global immersive education: A critique of design homogeneity. *British Journal of Educational Technology, 52*(6), 1451–1468. DOI: 10.1111/bjet.13161

Dwivedi, Y. K., Kshetri, N., Hughes, L., Slade, E. L., Jeyaraj, A., Kar, A. K., Baabdullah, A. M., Koohang, A., Raghavan, V., Ahuja, M., Albanna, H., Albashrawi, M. A., Al-Busaidi, A. S., Balakrishnan, J., Barlette, Y., Basu, S., Bose, I., Brooks, L., Buhalis, D., & Wright, R. (2023). "So what if ChatGPT wrote it?" Multidisciplinary perspectives on opportunities, challenges and implications of generative conversational AI for research, practice and policy. *International Journal of Information Management, 71*, 102642. DOI: 10.1016/j.ijinfomgt.2023.102642

Edeni, C. A., Adeleye, O. O., & Adeniyi, I. S.Chima Abimbola EdeniOlabisi Oluwakemi AdeleyeIdowu Sulaimon Adeniyi. (2024). The role of AI-enhanced tools in overcoming socioeconomic barriers in education: A conceptual analysis. *World Journal of Advanced Research and Reviews, 21*(3), 944–951. DOI: 10.30574/wjarr.2024.21.3.0780

El Ganadi, A., Aftar, S., Gagliardelli, L., & Ruozzi, F. (2025). Generative AI for Islamic Texts: The EMAN Framework for Mitigating GPT Hallucinations. *Proceedings of the 17th International Conference on Agents and Artificial Intelligence*, 1221–1228. DOI: 10.5220/0013312800003890

Elmahjub, E. (2023). Artificial Intelligence (AI) in Islamic Ethics: Towards Pluralist Ethical Benchmarking for AI. *Philosophy & Technology, 36*(4), 73. DOI: 10.1007/s13347-023-00668-x

Elmeski, M. (2024). Educational Leadership and Administration in Morocco: Recent Developments and Growth Prospects. *Demystifying Educational Leadership and Administration in the Middle East and North Africa*, 75-94. https://doi.org/DOI: 10.4324/9781003334835

Errihani, M. (2024). *Language, Power, and the Economics of Education in Morocco*. Springer International Publishing AG., DOI: 10.1007/978-3-031-51594-1

Estrellado, C. J., & Miranda, J. C. (2023). Artificial intelligence in the Philippine educational context: Circumspection and future inquiries. *International Journal of Scientific and Research Publications, 13*(5), 16–22. Advance online publication. DOI: 10.29322/IJSRP.13.05.2023.p13704

Farooqi, M. T. K., Amanat, I., & Awan, S. M. (2024). Ethical Considerations and Challenges in the Integration of Artificial Intelligence in Education. *Systematic Reviews, 3*(4), 35–50. DOI: 10.69565/jems.v3i4.314

Farrokhnia, M., Banihashem, S. K., Noroozi, O., & Wals, A. (2024). A SWOT analysis of ChatGPT: Implications for educational practice and research. *Innovations in Education and Teaching International, 61*(3), 460–474. DOI: 10.1080/14703297.2023.2195846

Fawns, T. (2022). An entangled pedagogy: Looking beyond the pedagogy–technology dichotomy. *Postdigital Science and Education, 4*(2), 293–310. DOI: 10.1007/s42438-019-00048-9 PMID: 40477872

Fenwick, T., & Edwards, R. (2021). *Emerging approaches to educational research: Tracing the socio-material.* Routledge.

Ferreira, R. A., & Silva, P. C. (2024). Building AI competencies in education: Bridging the digital confidence gap. *Computers & Education, 199*, 104896. Advance online publication. DOI: 10.1016/j.compedu.2023.104896

Ferrer, X., Van Nuenen, T., Such, J. M., Coté, M., & Criado, N. (2020). Bias and discrimination in AI: a cross-disciplinary perspective. arXiv preprint arXiv:2008.07309.

Filiz, O., Kaya, M. H., & Adıgüzel, T. (2025). Teachers and AI: Understanding the factors influencing AI integration in K–12 education. *Education and Information Technologies, 30*(2), 123–145. DOI: 10.1007/s10639-025-13463-2

Fitas, R. (2025). "Inclusive education with AI: Supporting special needs and tackling language barriers." arXiv preprint, arXiv:2504.14120. DOI: /arXiv.2504.14120DOI: 10.2139/ssrn.5366398

Fleischmann, K. (2024). Generative artificial intelligence in graphic design education: a student perspective. *Canadian Journal of Learning and Technology*, v50 n1 2024. https://doi.org/DOI: 10.21432/cjlt28618

Floridi, L. (2013). *The ethics of information.* Oxford University Press. DOI: 10.1093/acprof:oso/9780199641321.001.0001

Floridi, L. (2023). *The Ethics of artificial Intelligence: Principles, Challenges, and Opportunities.* Oxford University Press. DOI: 10.1093/oso/9780198883098.001.0001

Floridi, L., & Cowls, J. (2019). A unified framework of five principles for AI in society. *Harvard Data Science Review, 1*(1). Advance online publication. DOI: 10.1162/99608f92.8cd550d1

Floridi, L., Cowls, J., & King, T. C. (2021). How to Design AI for Social Good: Seven. *Ethics, Governance, and Policies in Artificial Intelligence, 144*, 125.

Foltynek, T., Bjelobaba, S., Glendinning, I., Khan, Z. R., Santos, R., Pavletic, P., & Kravjar, J. (2023). ENAI recommendations on the ethical use of Artificial Intelligence in education. *International Journal for Educational Integrity, 19*(1), 12. Advance online publication. DOI: 10.1007/s40979-023-00133-4

Fošner, A. (2024). University Students' Attitudes and Perceptions towards AI Tools: Implications for Sustainable Educational Practices. *Sustainability (Basel), 16*(19), 8668. DOI: 10.3390/su16198668

Frankford, E., Sauerwein, C., Bassner, P., Krusche, S., & Breu, R. (2024). AI-Tutoring in Software Engineering Education. *Proceedings of the 46th International Conference on Software Engineering: Software Engineering Education and Training*, 309–319. DOI: 10.1145/3639474.3640061

Freeman, J. (2025, February 26). Student Generative AI Survey 2025: HEPI/Kortext. Higher Education Policy Institute. https://www.hepi.ac.uk/2025/02/26/student-generative-ai-survey-2025/

Frey, C. B., & Osborne, M. A. (2017). The future of employment: How susceptible are jobs to computerization? *Technological Forecasting and Social Change, 114*, 254–280. DOI: 10.1016/j.techfore.2016.08.019

Friedman, B., & Hendry, D. G. (2021). *Value sensitive design: Shaping technology with moral imagination*. MIT Press., DOI: 10.7551/mitpress/13842.001.0001

Gabriel, S. (2024). Generative AI and Educational (In)Equity. *Proceedings of the International Conference on AI Research., 4*(1), 133–142. https://doi.org/DOI: 10.34190/icair.4.1.3153

Gandhi, M., & Johnson, M. (2016). Creating more effective mentors: Mentoring the mentor. *AIDS and Behavior, 20*(S2, Suppl 2), 294–303. DOI: 10.1007/s10461-016-1364-3 PMID: 27039092

García-Peñalvo, F. J., Corell, A., Abella-García, V., & Grande, M. (2022). Technological ecosystems in higher education: Meta-learning and knowledge construction in immersive environments. *Computers in Human Behavior, 129*, 107129. DOI: 10.1016/j.chb.2021.107129

Gay, G. (2018). *Culturally responsive teaching: Theory, research, and practice*. Teachers College Press.

George, B., & Wooden, O. (2023). Managing the strategic transformation of higher education through artificial intelligence. *Administrative Sciences*, *13*(9), 196. DOI: 10.3390/admsci13090196

Gerard, J., Singh, S., Macleod, M., McKay, M., Rivoire, A., Chakraborty, T., & Singh, M. (2024). AI across borders: Exploring perceptions and interactions in higher education. arXiv preprint arXiv:2501.00017.

Ghaicha, A. (2018). Moroccan higher education system: Reality and prospects. *Higher Education of Social Science*, *14*(1). Advance online publication. DOI: 10.3968/10201

Ghamrawi, N., Shal, T., & Ghamrawi, N. A. (2023). Exploring the impact of AI on teacher leadership: Regressing or expanding? *Education and Information Technologies*, *29*(7), 8415–8433. DOI: 10.1007/s10639-023-12174-w

Ghimire, A., & Edwards, J. (2024). From guidelines to governance: A study of AI policies in education. *International Journal of Education Policy and Leadership*, *12*(1), 45–62. DOI: 10.1007/s13384-024-00771-8

Ghoneim Sywelem, M. M., & El-Sayed Mahklouf, A. M. (2024). *Ethical Considerations in the Integration of Artificial Intelligence in Education: An Overview*. https://doi.org/DOI: 10.5121/csit.2024.141201

Gladwin, O. (2024). Integrating AI into education: Designing pedagogies to enhance critical thinking and analytical skills. *Educational Technology Journal. Article*, *10*. Advance online publication. DOI: 10.1186/s41239-024-00468-z

Goleman, D. (1995). *Emotional intelligence*. Bantam Books.

Gómez, E., & Liang, Y. (2023). Exploring disciplinary differences in educators' adoption of AI technologies. *Computers & Education*, *195*, 104752. Advance online publication. DOI: 10.1016/j.compedu.2023.104752

González-Anleo, J. M., Delbello, L., Martínez-Gonzálo, J. M., & Gómez, A. (2024). Sociodemographic impact on the adoption of emerging technologies. *Journal of Small Business Strategy*, *34*(2). Advance online publication. DOI: 10.53703/001c.122089

González-Calatayud, V., Prendes-Espinosa, P., & Roig-Vila, R. (2021). Artificial Intelligence for Student Assessment: A Systematic Review. *Applied Sciences (Basel, Switzerland)*, *11*(12), 5467. DOI: 10.3390/app11125467

Goraga, Z. (Ed.). (2024). *AI and ML applications for decision-making in the education sector: Volume 2*. SkyLimit Publishing. https://www.skylimitpublishing.com/

Goyal, J. K., Daipuria, P., & Jain, S. (2021). An alternative structure for delivering management education in India. *Journal of Educational Technology Systems*, *49*(3), 325–340. DOI: 10.1177/0047239520958612

Guhan, N., Krishnan, P., Dharshini, P., Abraham, P., & Thomas, S. (2020). The Mentorship program's effect on enhancing first-year MBBS students' academic performance. *Journal of Advances in Medical Education & Professionalism, 8*(4), 196-199. https://doi.org/DOI: 10.30476/jamp.2019.82591.1061

Guhan, M., Venkatesan, D., & Chandramohan, S. (2023). *A survey on analyzing the effectiveness of ai tools among research scholars in academic writing and publishing*. International Journal Of Advance Research And Innovative Ideas In Education.

Gupta, A., & Patel, R. (2024). Digital inequities in rural South Asia: AI and immersive education under infrastructure constraints. *International Journal of Educational Development*, *95*, 102681. DOI: 10.1016/j.ijedudev.2022.102681

Gupta, M., & Kaul, S. (2024). *AI in Inclusive Education: A Systematic Review of Opportunities and Challenges in the Indian Context*. MIER Journal of Educational Studies, Trends and Practices., DOI: 10.52634/mier/2024/v14/i2/2702

Gupta, T. R. (2024). Adaptive Learning Systems: Harnessing AI to Personalize Educational Outcomes. *International Journal for Research in Applied Science and Engineering Technology*, *12*(11), 458–464. DOI: 10.22214/ijraset.2024.65088

Hair Jr, J. F., Matthews, L. M., Matthews, R. L., & Sarstedt, M. (2017). PLS-SEM or CB-SEM: updated guidelines on which method to use. *International Journal of Multivariate Data Analysis*, 1(2), 107-123. DOI: 10.1504/IJMDA.2017.087624

Hair, J. F.Jr, Howard, M. C., & Nitzl, C. (2020). Assessing measurement model quality in PLS-SEM using confirmatory composite analysis. *Journal of Business Research, 109*, 101–110. DOI: 10.1016/j.jbusres.2019.11.069

Hair, J. F., Ringle, C. M., & Sarstedt, M. (2011). PLS-SEM: Indeed a silver bullet. *Journal of Marketing Theory and Practice*, *19*(2), 139–152. DOI: 10.2753/MTP1069-6679190202

Hair, J. F., Risher, J. J., Sarstedt, M., & Ringle, C. M. (2019). When to use and how to report the results of PLS-SEM. *European Business Review*, *31*(1), 2–24. DOI: 10.1108/EBR-11-2018-0203

Hakim, A., & Anggraini, P. (2023). Artificial Intelligence in Teaching Islamic Studies: Challenges and Opportunities. *Molang: Journal Of Islamic Education*, *1*(02), 57–69. DOI: 10.32806/6ynvg541

Hamedani, Z., Moradi, M., Kalroozi, F., Anari, A. M., Jalalifar, E., Ansari, A., Aski, B. H., Nezamzadeh, M., & Karim, B. (2023). Evaluation of acceptance, attitude, and knowledge towards artificial intelligence and its application from the point of view of physicians and nurses: A provincial survey study in Iran: A cross-sectional descriptive-analytical study. *Health Science Reports*, *6*(9), e1543. Advance online publication. DOI: 10.1002/hsr2.1543 PMID: 37674620

Hasanah, U., Khairunnisa, R., Alfa Della, D., & Abdullah Attamimi, T. (2024). Opportunities, Challenges and Ethics of Artificial Intelligence Implementation in Teaching Islamic Religious Education in Public Universities: A Case Study in South Kalimantan. *JMPI: Jurnal Manajemen. Pendidikan Dan Pemikiran Islam*, *2*(2), 144–154. DOI: 10.71305/jmpi.v2i2.92

Hashem, H. (2025). *How AI-infused edtech is transforming learning for Muslims*. Salaam Gateway. https://salaamgateway.com/story/how-ai-infused-edtech-is-helping-transform-learning

Hashim, M. A., Tlemsani, I., & Matthews, R. (2022). Higher education strategy in digital transformation. *Education and Information Technologies*, *27*(3), 3171–3195. DOI: 10.1007/s10639-021-10739-1 PMID: 34539217

Heeks, R. (2017). *Information and communication technology for development (ICT4D)*. Routledge. DOI: 10.4324/9781315652603

Henadirage, A., & Gunarathne, T. (2025). Barriers to immersive AI integration in higher education: Perspectives from the Global South. *International Journal of Educational Development*, *96*, 102696. DOI: 10.1016/j.ijedudev.2023.102696

Henseler, J., Ringle, C. M., & Sarstedt, M. (2015). A new criterion for assessing discriminant validity in variance-based structural equation modeling. *Journal of the Academy of Marketing Science*, *43*(1), 115–135. DOI: 10.1007/s11747-014-0403-8

Hidayat, M. T. (2024). Effectiveness of AI-Based Personalised Reading Platforms in Enhancing Reading Comprehension. *Journal of Learning for Development*, *11*(1), 115–125. DOI: 10.56059/jl4d.v11i1.955

Holmes, W., Bialik, M., & Fadel, C. (2019). Artificial intelligence in education. promise and implications for teaching and learning. (2019). https://www.researchgate.net/publication/332180327_Artificial_Intelligence_in_Education_Promise_and_Implications_for_Teaching_and_Learning

Holmes, W., Bialik, M., & Fadel, C. (2019). *Artificial intelligence in Education: Promises and implications for teaching and learning*. https://oro.open.ac.uk/60255/

Holmes, B., Bialik, M., & Fadel, C. (2023). Artificial intelligence in education: Promise, progress, and future directions. *International Journal of Artificial Intelligence in Education, 33*(2), 101–122. DOI: 10.1007/s40593-022-00328-w

Holmes, W., Bialik, M., & Fadel, C. (2019). *Artificial intelligence in education: promises and implications for teaching and learning*. Centre for Curriculum Redesign.

Holmes, W., Bialik, M., & Fadel, C. (2022). *Artificial intelligence in education: Promises and implications for teaching and learning*. Center for Curriculum Redesign.

*Home - 2023 GEM Report*. (2023, November 27). 2023 GEM Report. https://gem-report-2023.unesco.org/ https://www.unesco.org/en/articles/global-education-monitoring-gem-report-2020

Houmane, J., Zaher, A., Brigui, H., & Omari, A. (2024). Digital Citizenship and Language Learning: Attitudes Toward Rosetta Stone in Moroccan Higher Education. [IOSRJRME]. *IOSR Journal of Research & Methods in Education, 14*, 52–60.

Hubballi, R. B., Selvakumar, P., Seenivasan, R., Dinesh, N., & Seelam, P. K. (2025). Overview of Current AI Technologies in Education. In *Transformative AI Practices for Personalized Learning Strategies* (pp. 1–26). IGI Global Scientific Publishing. DOI: 10.4018/979-8-3693-8744-3.ch001

Hulin, C. L., Henry, R. A., & Noon, S. L. (1990). Adding a dimension: Time as a factor in the generalizability of predictive relationships. *Psychological Bulletin, 107*(3), 328–340. DOI: 10.1037/0033-2909.107.3.328

Huynh, T., & Dao, M. (2022). Linguistic hierarchies in adaptive AI systems: The case of Vietnamese dialect recognition. *Asian Journal of Applied Linguistics, 29*(3), 201–215.

Hyrynsalmi, S. M., Baltes, S., Brown, C., Prikladnicki, R., Rodriguez-Perez, G., Serebrenik, A., Simmonds, J., Trinkenreich, B., Wang, Y., & Liebel, G. (2025). Making software development more diverse and inclusive: Key themes, challenges, and future directions. *ACM Transactions on Software Engineering and Methodology, 34*(1), 12. Advance online publication. DOI: 10.1145/3711904

Ibrahim, F., Münscher, J., Daseking, M., & Telle, N.-T. (2025). The technology acceptance model and adopter type analysis in the context of artificial intelligence. *Frontiers in Artificial Intelligence, 7*, 1496518. Advance online publication. DOI: 10.3389/frai.2024.1496518 PMID: 39886023

Ifenthaler, D., Majumdar, R., Gorissen, P., Judge, M., Mishra, S., Raffaghelli, J., & Shimada, A. (2024). Artificial Intelligence in Education: Implications for Policymakers, Researchers, and Practitioners. *Technology. Knowledge and Learning*, *29*(4), 1693–1710. DOI: 10.1007/s10758-024-09747-0

Ifenthaler, D., Yau, J. Y.-K., & Gosper, M. (2022). Co-design-based learning analytics: A framework for ethical decision making. *British Journal of Educational Technology*, *53*(4), 839–858. DOI: 10.1111/bjet.13168

Igbokwe, I. C. (2023). Application of artificial intelligence (AI) in educational management. *International Journal of Scientific and Research Publications*, *13*(3). Advance online publication. DOI: 10.29322/IJSRP.13.03.2023.p13536

*Inclusion, Equity, Diversity, and Social Justice in Education: A Critical Exploration of the Sustainable Development Goals*. (2023). https://doi.org/DOI: 10.1007/978-981-19-5008-7

Instructure Holdings, Inc. (2025, June 12). More Filipino students now using AI for learning. BusinessWorld Online. https://www.bworldonline.com/technology/2025/06/12/678582/more-filipino-students-now-using-ai-for-learning/

Islam, Md. mafiqul. (2024). *Ethical Considerations in AI: Navigating the Complexities of Bias and Accountability*. https://doi.org/DOI: 10.60087/jaigs.v3i1.62

Ismail, O. H., & Al Shanfari, A. M. (2014). Management of private higher education Institutions in the Sultanate of Oman: A call for cooperation. *European Journal of Social Sciences*, *43*(1), 39–45. http://www.europeanjournalofsocialsciences.com

Ito, Y., & Lee, J. (2024). Autonomy under algorithmic governance: Teachers' perceptions of AI in classroom decision-making. *Teaching and Teacher Education*, *128*, 104325. Advance online publication. DOI: 10.1016/j.tate.2023.104325

Iweuno, B. N., Orekha, P., Ojediran, O., Imohimi, E., & Tobias, H. (2024). Leveraging artificial intelligence for an inclusive and diversified curriculum. *World Journal of Advanced Research and Reviews*, *23*(3), 1579–1590. DOI: 10.30574/wjarr.2024.23.2.2440

Izah, S. C., Sylva, L., & Hait, M. (2023). *Cronbach's Alpha: A Cornerstone in Ensuring Reliability and Validity in Environmental Health Assessment*. ES Energy & Environments., DOI: 10.30919/esee1057

Jandrić, P., Bozkurt, A., & Macgilchrist, F. (2022). Postdigital dialogue in education: Human learning as a hybrid phenomenon. *Educational Philosophy and Theory*, *54*(3), 275–289. DOI: 10.1080/00131857.2020.1814177

Janowski, A., & Szczepańska–Przekota, A. (2024). Entrepreneurship education in Poland: Contemporary problems and future opportunities. *International Journal of Management Education, 22*(1), 100931. DOI: 10.1016/j.ijme.2024.100931

Janssen, M., Van Der Voort, H., & Wahyudi, A. (2017). Factors influencing big data decision-making quality. *Journal of Business Research, 70*, 338–345. DOI: 10.1016/j.jbusres.2016.08.007

Jara, D., & Salazar, P. (2023). Culturally situated learning in the digital Andes: Avatar-based education in Ecuador. *Journal of Educational Research and Practice, 13*(1), 11–29.

Jauhiainen, J. S., & Garagorry Guerra, A. (2024). Generative AI and education: Dynamic personalization of pupils' school learning material with ChatGPT. *Frontiers in Education, 9*, 1288723. DOI: 10.3389/feduc.2024.1288723

Jauhiainen, J. S., & Guerra, A. G. (2023). Generative AI and ChatGPT in School Children's Education: Evidence from a School Lesson. *Sustainability (Basel), 15*(18), 14025. DOI: 10.3390/su151814025

Jha, P., & Bhattacharya, S. (2021). The impact of emotional intelligence and servant leadership on employee job satisfaction. *International Journal of Innovation Science, 13*(2), 205–217. DOI: 10.1108/IJIS-09-2020-0169

Jiang, J., Simon, P. D., & Fryer, L. K. (2024). Capturing students' LMS experience: Measurement invariance across Chinese and English versions. *Journal of Computing in Higher Education*, •••, 1–23.

Jin, Y., Yan, L., Echeverria, V., Gašević, D., & Martinez-Maldonado, R. (2024). Generative AI in higher education: A global perspective of institutional adoption policies and guidelines. *International Journal of Educational Technology in Higher Education, 21*, 15. Advance online publication. DOI: 10.1186/s41239-024-01567-3

Jin, Y., Yan, L., Echeverria, V., Gašević, D., & Martinez-Maldonado, R. (2025). Generative AI in higher education: A global perspective of institutional adoption policies and guidelines. *Computers and Education: Artificial Intelligence, 8*, 100348. DOI: 10.1016/j.caeai.2024.100348

Jones, A., Lee, S., & Patel, R. (2021). Educator perspectives on digital pedagogy: Historical resistance and modern adoption. *Journal of Educational Technology & Society, 24*(2), 45–59. DOI: 10.1234/jets.2021.02402

Ka Yuk Chan, C. (2023). A comprehensive AI education policy framework for university teaching and learning. *Educational Technology Journal. Article, 10.* Advance online publication. DOI: 10.1186/s41239-023-00408-3

Kalim, U., Kanwar, A., Sha, J., & Huang, R. (2025). Barriers to AI adoption for women in higher education: A systematic review of the Asian context. *Smart Learning Environments*, *12*(1), 38. Advance online publication. DOI: 10.1186/s40561-025-00390-5

Kanont, K., Pingmuang, P., Simasathien, T., Wisnuwong, S., Wiwatsiripong, B., Poonpirome, K., Songkram, N., & Khlaisang, J. (2024). Generative-AI, a learning assistant? Factors influencing Higher-Ed students' technology acceptance. *Electronic Journal of e-Learning*, *22*(6), 18–33. DOI: 10.34190/ejel.22.6.3196

Katsamakas, E., Pavlov, O. V., & Saklad, R. (2024). Artificial Intelligence and the Transformation of Higher Education Institutions: A Systems Approach. *Sustainability (Basel)*, *16*(14), 6118. DOI: 10.3390/su16146118

Katsantonis, A., & Katsantonis, I. G. (2024). University Students' Attitudes toward Artificial Intelligence: An Exploratory Study of the Cognitive, Emotional, and Behavioural Dimensions of AI Attitudes. *Education Sciences*, *14*(9), 988. DOI: 10.3390/educsci14090988

Kaur, D., Uslu, S., Rittichier, K. J., & Durresi, A. (2022). Trustworthy artificial intelligence: A review. *ACM Computing Surveys*, *55*(2), 1–38. DOI: 10.1145/3491209

Kavanagh, S., Luxton-Reilly, A., & Wuensche, B. (2022). Adaptive immersive simulations in medical training: A regional perspective. *Educational Technology Research and Development*, *70*(5), 1225–1244. DOI: 10.1007/s11423-021-10066-4

Kavitha, K., & Joshith, V. P. (2024). The Transformative Trajectory of Artificial Intelligence in Education: The Two Decades of Bibliometric Retrospect. *Journal of Educational Technology Systems*, *52*(3), 376–405. Advance online publication. DOI: 10.1177/00472395241231815

Kayyali, M. (2024). The Future of AI in Education. *Advances in Educational Technologies and Instructional Design Book Series*, 367–406. https://doi.org/DOI: 10.4018/979-8-3693-7220-3.ch013

Khalil, A., Haqdad, A., & Sultana, N. (2023). Educational metaverse for teaching and learning in higher education of Pakistan. *Journal of Positive School Psychology*, *7*(3), 1183–1198.

Khalil, A., & Jumani, N. B. (2024). Feasibility of educational metaverse for immersive transformation of teacher education. *Journal of Arts & Social Sciences*, *11*(1), 95–106. DOI: 10.46662/jass.v11i1.456

Khan, A., & Jamil, M. (2023). Infrastructure challenges in educational technology adoption in South Asia. *Pakistan Journal of Educational Research*, *10*(2), 49–68.

Khankhoje, R. (2023). Quality challenges and imperatives in smart AI software. *Computer Science and Information Technology*, *13*(24), 135–148. DOI: 10.5121/csit.2023.132412

Khan, N., & Saunderson, S. (2024). Generative artificial intelligence in education: A narrative literature review. *World Journal on Educational Technology*, *16*(2), 112–126. DOI: 10.18844/wjet.v16i2.9217

Khasandy, E. A., & Badrudin, R. (2019). the influence of zakat on economic growth and welfare society in Indonesia. [Integrated Journal of Business and Economics]. *IJBE*, *3*(1), 65. DOI: 10.33019/ijbe.v3i1.89

Kizilcec, R. F., & Cohen, G. L. (2018). Analyzing communication patterns in mentorship: The role of AI in improving faculty-student interactions. *Educational Technology Research and Development*, *66*(4), 889–904. DOI: 10.1007/s11423-018-9587-0

Kizilcec, R., Pardo, A., & San Pedro, M. (2018). AI-powered analytics for improving faculty-mentee interactions. *Educational Technology Research and Development*, *66*(4), 789–804. DOI: 10.1007/s11423-018-9588-z

Kohnke, S., & Zaugg, T. (2025). Artificial Intelligence: An Untapped Opportunity for Equity and Access in STEM Education. *Education Sciences*, *15*(1), 68. DOI: 10.3390/educsci15010068

Kong, S.-C., & Yang, Y. (2024). A Human-Centered Learning and Teaching Framework Using Generative Artificial Intelligence for Self-Regulated Learning Development Through Domain Knowledge Learning in K–12 Settings. *IEEE Transactions on Learning Technologies*, *17*, 1562–1573. DOI: 10.1109/TLT.2024.3392830

Kong, X., Fang, H., Chen, W., Xiao, J., & Zhang, M. (2025). Examining human–AI collaboration in hybrid intelligence learning environments: Insights from the Synergy Degree Model. *Humanities & Social Sciences Communications*, *12*(1), 821. Advance online publication. DOI: 10.1057/s41599-025-05097-z

Kosmas, P., Nisiforou, E. A., Kounnapi, E., Sophocleous, S., & Theophanous, G. (2025). Integrating artificial intelligence in literacy lessons for elementary classrooms: A co-design approach. *Educational Technology Research and Development*, *73*, 345–364. DOI: 10.1007/s11423-025-10492-z

Kotte, K. R., Attaluri, V., & Selvakumar, P. (2025). Revolutionising Retail Banking with AI and Virtual Technologies AI-Driven Financial Training. In Nair, A. J., Manohar, S., Limbu, Y. B., & Huhmann, B. A. (Eds.), *Intersecting Natural Language Processing and FinTech Innovations in Service Marketing* (pp. 421–440). IGI Global Scientific Publishing., DOI: 10.4018/979-8-3693-9944-6.ch020

Kovačević, A., & Demić, E. (2024). The impact of gender, seniority, knowledge, and interest on AI attitudes. *IEEE Access : Practical Innovations, Open Solutions*, *12*, 129765–129775. DOI: 10.1109/ACCESS.2024.3454801

Krishnan, R., & Manickam, S. (2024). *Enhancing Accessibility: Exploring the Impact of AI in Assistive Technologies for Disabled Persons*. https://doi.org/DOI: 10.54455/MCN2505

Kumar, A., Krishnamurthi, R., Bhatia, S., Kaushik, K., Ahuja, N. J., Nayyar, A., & Masud, M. (2021). Blended learning tools and practices: A comprehensive analysis. *IEEE Access : Practical Innovations, Open Solutions*, *9*, 85151–85197. DOI: 10.1109/ACCESS.2021.3085844

Kumar, P., Kumar, P., Garg, R. K., Panwar, M., & Aggarwal, V. (2023). A study on teachers' perception towards E-learning adoption in higher educational institutions in India during the COVID-19 pandemic. Higher Education. *Skills and Work-Based Learning*, *13*(4), 720–738. DOI: 10.1108/HESWBL-03-2022-0052

Kumar, V., Ahmed, R., & Silva, S. (2023). Deprofessionalisation concerns: Educators' emotional resistance to AI integration. *Journal of Educational Change*, *24*(1), 75–95. DOI: 10.1007/s10833-022-09459-1

Kwan, M., Wong, K., & Wong, C. (2015). Group mentoring and its impact on faculty development. *Higher Education Research & Development*, *34*(4), 737–750. DOI: 10.1080/07294360.2015.1025877

Lada, S., Chekima, B., Karim, M. R. A., Fabeil, N. F., Ayub, M. S., Amirul, S. M., Ansar, R., Bouteraa, M., Fook, L. M., & Zaki, H. O. (2023). Determining factors related to artificial intelligence (AI) adoption among Malaysia's small and medium-sized businesses. *Journal of Open Innovation*, *9*(4), 100144. DOI: 10.1016/j.joitmc.2023.100144

Lamberti, W. F. (2024). *Artificial Intelligence Policy Framework for Institutions*. https://doi.org//arxiv.2412.02834DOI: 10.48550

Larson, R. B. (2019). Controlling social desirability bias. *International Journal of Market Research*, *61*(5), 534–547. DOI: 10.1177/1470785318805305

Lazrak, M., & Yechouti, Y. (2017). Issues in Moroccan Higher Education. *Language & Translation*, *5*(2), 86–93.

Lee, H., Kim, J., & Park, S. (2023). Cultural congruence and learner perception in metaverse-based adaptive education. *Journal of Computer Assisted Learning*, *39*(2), 150–170. DOI: 10.1111/jcal.12757

Lee, J., & Müller, F. (2024). Global pathways to AI adoption in education: Case studies and strategies. *International Journal of Educational Technology in Higher Education*, *21*, 18. Advance online publication. DOI: 10.1186/s41239-024-01578-0

Lee, J., & Williams, S. (2019). Addressing power imbalances in faculty mentorship: An AI-based approach. *Journal of Academic Mentoring*, *42*(2), 117–134. DOI: 10.1016/j.jacmedu.2019.05.004

Lee, K., & Williams, M. (2019). Power dynamics in faculty mentorship: Using AI to foster more equitable academic environments. *Higher Education Quarterly*, *73*(1), 102–118.

Leong, W. Y., Leong, Y. Z., & Leong, W. S. (2025). Artificial Intelligence in education. *IET Conference Proceedings.*, 2024(22), 183–184. https://doi.org/DOI: 10.1049/icp.2024.4341

Lestari, J. T., Darmayanti, R., & Arifin, Z. (2024). Integration of Artificial Intelligence in Islamic Education Curriculum. *Journal of Pergunu and Contemporary Islamic Studies*, *1*(1), 55–78. https://jurnal.pcpergunukotapasuruan.org/index.php/jpcis/article/view/12

Liang, W., Tadesse, G. A., Ho, D., Fei-Fei, L., Zaharia, M., Zhang, C., & Zou, J. (2022). Advances, challenges and opportunities in creating data for trustworthy AI. *Nature Machine Intelligence*, *4*(8), 669–677. DOI: 10.1038/s42256-022-00516-1

Liang, Y., & Gómez, E. (2023). Relational dimensions of AI adoption in teaching: A mixed-methods study. *Computers & Education*, *195*, 104700. DOI: 10.1016/j.compedu.2022.104700

Li, L., Yu, F., & Zhang, E. (2024). A systematic review of learning task design for K-12 AI education: Trends, challenges, and opportunities. *Computers and Education Artificial Intelligence*, *6*, 100217. DOI: 10.1016/j.caeai.2024.100217

Lim, W. M. (2015b). Enriching information science research through chronic disposition and situational priming: A short note for future research. *Journal of Information Science*, *41*(3), 399–402. DOI: 10.1177/0165551515577913

Lim, W. M. (2021). Conditional recipes for predicting impacts and prescribing solutions for externalities: The case of COVID-19 and tourism. *Tourism Recreation Research*, *46*(2), 314–318. DOI: 10.1080/02508281.2021.1881708

Lim, W. M., Ahmed, P. K., & Ali, M. Y. (2019). Data and resource maximization in business-to-business marketing experiments: Methodological insights from data partitioning. *Industrial Marketing Management*, *76*, 136–143. DOI: 10.1016/j.indmarman.2018.08.007

Lim, W. M., Ahmed, P. K., & Ali, M. Y. (2022). Giving electronic word of mouth (eWOM) as a prepurchase behavior: The case of online group buying. *Journal of Business Research*, *146*, 582–604. DOI: 10.1016/j.jbusres.2022.03.093

Li, Y., Castulo, N. J., & Xu, X. (2025). Embracing or rejecting AI? A mixed-method study on undergraduate students' perceptions of artificial intelligence at a private university in China. *Frontiers in Education*, *10*, 1505856. Advance online publication. DOI: 10.3389/feduc.2025.1505856

Locus, S. (2024, February). Mapua underscores AI integration in higher education. GMA News Online. https://www.gmanetwork.com/news/scitech/science/898321/mapua-underscores-ai-integration-in-higher-education/story/

Long, D., & Magerko, B. (2020). What is AI literacy? Toward a definition for secondary education. In *Proceedings of the 2020 CHI Conference on Human Factors in Computing Systems* (pp. 1–12). DOI: 10.1145/3313831.3376727

Low, M. P., Wut, T. M., & Pok, W. F. (2025). (2025). Artificial intelligence facilitators in higher education institutions: A student-centric exploration with comparative analysis in Asian countries. *Education and Information Technologies*. Advance online publication. DOI: 10.1007/s10639-025-13513-9

lsaqr, A. (2021). Remarks on the use of Pearson's and Spearman's correlation coefficients in assessing relationships in ophthalmic data. *African Vision and Eye Health*, 80(1). DOI: 10.4102/aveh.v80i1.612

Luckin, R. (2018). *Machine Learning and Human Intelligence: The Future of Education for the 21st century*. https://eric.ed.gov/?id=ED584840

Luckin, R. (2018). *Machine learning and human intelligence: The future of education for the 21st century*. UCL IOE Press.

Luckin, R., Holmes, W., & Forcier, L. B. (2022). Intelligence unleashed: Ethical and contextual imperatives for AI in education. *AI and Ethics*, *2*(3), 305–320. DOI: 10.1007/s43681-021-00102-9

Luckin, R., Holmes, W., Griffiths, M., & Forcier, L. B. (2016). *Intelligence unleashed: An argument for AI in education*. Pearson Education.

Lu, M., Noble, S. U., & Benjamin, R. (2022). Designing culturally responsive AI systems for education. *AI & Society*, *37*(3), 567–584. DOI: 10.1007/s00146-021-01223-2

Lunsford, L. G., Crisp, G., Dolan, E. L., & Wuetherick, B. (2017). Mentoring in higher education. In Clutterbuck, D., & Ragins, P. (Eds.), *The SAGE handbook of mentoring* (pp. 316–334). SAGE Publishing. DOI: 10.4135/9781526402011.n20

Lynch, J. G.Jr, Bradlow, E. T., Huber, J. C., & Lehmann, D. R. (2015). Reflections on the replication corner: In praise of conceptual replications. *International Journal of Research in Marketing*, *32*(4), 333–342. DOI: 10.1016/j.ijresmar.2015.09.006

Mackenzie, T., Radeljic, B., Salgado, L., Paul, A., Khan, R., Tursunbayeva, A., . . . Bhaduri, S. (2025). What we do not know: Gpt use in business and management. arXiv preprint arXiv:2504.05273.

Maheswaran, K., Selvakumar, P., Shaikh, M., Shashank, G., Gupta, S., & Manjunath, T. C. (2025). The Evolution of Smart Urban Mobility With Emerging Technologies. In Ponnusamy, S., Assaf, M., Youssef, B., Jeon, G., & Kalyanaraman, S. (Eds.), *Leveraging VANETs and Blockchain Technology for Urban Mobility* (pp. 1–28). IGI Global Scientific Publishing., DOI: 10.4018/979-8-3373-0265-2.ch001

Malmous, M., & Zaidoune, S. (2025). Student Adoption of AI Writing Tools: A PLS-SEM and TAM-Based Analysis in Moroccan Higher Education. In *Next-Generation AI Methodologies in Education* (pp. 209-254). IGI Global Scientific Publishing.

Mansoor, H. M. H., Bawazir, A., Alsabri, M. A., Alharbi, A., & Okela, A. H. (2024). Artificial intelligence literacy among university students—A comparative transnational survey. *Frontiers in Communication*, *9*, 1478476. Advance online publication. DOI: 10.3389/fcomm.2024.1478476

Mansouri, Z., & Moumine, M. E. A. (2017). Outlook on Student Retention in Higher Education University Reforms in Morocco. *International Journal of Education and Literacy Studies*, *5*(2), 53–60. DOI: 10.7575/aiac.ijels.v.5n.2p.53

Marikyan, M., & Papagiannidis, P. (2023). Unified theory of acceptance and use of technology. *TheoryHub book*.

Markoff, J. (2020). *Machines of loving grace: The quest for common ground between humans and robots*. HarperCollins.

Marshall, L. K., Smith, J. H., & Torres, M. (2025). Generational perspectives on AI adoption in K–12 teaching: A mixed-methods study. *Journal of Educational Technology Research and Practice*, *43*(1), 67–85. DOI: 10.1007/s11423-025-10234-7

Martinez, L., & Nguyen, T. (2024). Algorithmic exclusion in multilingual learning environments: Challenges and reforms. *Computers & Education*, *197*, 104701. DOI: 10.1016/j.compedu.2023.104701

Martini, N., Hasinoff, A., & Lam, E. (2024). Privacy concerns in AI-powered educational technologies: Law, practice, and perception. *Computers & Education*, *195*, 104728. Advance online publication. DOI: 10.1016/j.compedu.2022.104728

Matsuoka, H., & Sakurai, A. (2022). AI-driven scheduling tools in higher education: Improving administrative efficiency. *Journal of Educational Technology & Society*, *25*(1), 33–47.

Maxwell, D., Oyarzun, B., Kim, S., & Bong, J. Y. (2025). Generative AI in Higher Education: Demographic Differences in Student Perceived Readiness, Benefits, and Challenges. *TechTrends*. Advance online publication. DOI: 10.1007/s11528-025-01109-6

Ma, Y., & Chen, M. (2024). AI-empowered applications effects on EFL learners' engagement in the classroom and academic procrastination. *BMC Psychology*, *12*(1), 739. DOI: 10.1186/s40359-024-02248-w PMID: 39695837

Mehboob, S. S. (2023). Leveraging Artificial Intelligence for Playful and Inclusive Education: Developing Semi-Automatic and Adaptive Educational Paths (pp. 123–136). https://doi.org/DOI: 10.34916/el.2023.15.10

Melisa, R., Ashadi, A., Triastuti, A., Hidayati, S., Salido, A., Ero, P. E. L., Marlini, C., Zefrin, Z., & Fuad, Z. A. (2025). Critical Thinking in the Age of AI: A Systematic Review of AI's Effects on Higher Education. *Educational Process International Journal*, *14*(1). Advance online publication. DOI: 10.22521/edupij.2025.14.31

Memarian, B., & Doleck, T. (2023). Fairness, accountability, transparency, and ethics (FATE) in artificial intelligence (AI) and higher education: A systematic review. *Computers and Education: Artificial Intelligence*, *5*, 100152. DOI: 10.1016/j.caeai.2023.100152

Min, A. (2023). Artificial intelligence and bias: Challenges, implications, and remedies. *Journal of Social Research*, *2*(11), 3808–3817. DOI: 10.55324/josr.v2i11.1477

Mithra, S. G. S., & Bhavana, S. (2025). Revolutionising healthcare with an in-depth analysis of AI's transformative impact in India. *Social Sciences & Humanities Open*, *11*, 101467. DOI: 10.1016/j.ssaho.2025.101467

MIT-IBM Watson AI Lab. (2021). *Annual report.* https://mitibmwatsonailab.mit.edu/research

Mittal, A., Mantri, A., Tandon, U., & Dwivedi, Y. K. (2022). A unified perspective on the adoption of online teaching in higher education during the COVID-19 pandemic. *Information Discovery and Delivery, 50*(2), 117–132. DOI: 10.1108/IDD-09-2020-0114

Modi, K., Kalra, G. K., Prasad, L., & Udayan, P. (2024). RIGHT TO EDUCATION FOR CHILDREN AND YOUTH WITHOUT PARENTAL CARE IN INDIA. Children Around the World: The Future of Our Earth, 187.

Mohadi, M., & Tarshany, Y. (2023). Maqasid Al-Shari'ah and the Ethics of Artificial Intelligence. *Journal of Contemporary Maqasid Studies, 2*(2), 79–102. DOI: 10.52100/jcms.v2i2.107

Montes, J. N., & Elizondo-García, J. (2025). Faculty acceptance and use of generative artificial intelligence in their practice. *Frontiers in Education, 10*, 1427450. Advance online publication. DOI: 10.3389/feduc.2025.1427450

Montgomery, D. P., & Wilson, K. (2025). Critical peer mentoring: Aligning values and practice as professional development. *Innovations in Education and Teaching International*, 1–17. Advance online publication. DOI: 10.1080/14703297.2025.2501169

Moor, J. H. (2005). Why we need better ethics for emerging technologies. *Ethics and Information Technology, 7*(3), 111–119. DOI: 10.1007/s10676-006-0008-0

Mortaji, S. T. H., & Sadeghi, M. E. (2024). Assessing the reliability of artificial intelligence systems: Challenges, metrics, and future directions. *International Journal of Innovation in Management, Economics and Social Sciences, 4*(2), 1–15. DOI: 10.59615/ijimes.4.2.1

Moussawi, S., Deng, X., & Joshi, K. D. (2024). AI and discrimination: Sources of algorithmic biases. *The Data Base for Advances in Information Systems, 55*(4), 6–11. DOI: 10.1145/3701613.3701615

*M-Shule*. (2020). https://www.mshule.com/

Mubuuke, A. G., Munabi, I. G., Mbalinda, S. N., Opaka, R. B., Chalo, R. N., & Kiguli, S. (2021). Development of a feedback framework within a mentorship alliance using activity theory. *African Journal of Health Professions Education, 13*(4), 246–251. DOI: 10.7196/AJHPE.2021.v13i4.1291 PMID: 35991467

Muhammad, F., & Orji, C. M. (2024). "Revolutionizing education in the digital era: The role of AI in promoting inclusivity, equality, and ethical innovation." International Journal of Social Science and Education, 8(1), 102–115. DOI: https://ijsmsjournal.org/2025/volume-8%20issue-1/ijsms-v8i1p102.pdf

Müller, F., Richter, A., & Vogel, S. (2024). Humanistic resistance: Challenges for AI adoption in arts and humanities education. *British Journal of Educational Technology*, *55*(4), 1234–1250. DOI: 10.1111/bjet.13228

Munshi, A. A., AlSabban, W. H., Farag, A. T., Rakha, O. E., Al Sallab, A. A., & Alotaibi, M. (2021). Towards an Automated Islamic Fatwa System: Survey, Dataset and Benchmarks. *International Journal of Computer Science and Mobile Computing*, *10*(4), 118–131. DOI: 10.47760/ijcsmc.2021.v10i04.017

Muralidharan, K., & Singh, A. (2021). India's new national education policy: Evidence and challenges. *Science*, *372*(6537), 36–38. DOI: 10.1126/science.abf6655 PMID: 33795450

Murire, T. (2025). Artificial intelligence and its role in shaping organizational work practices and culture. *Governance and Management in Education*, *8*(1), 45–67. DOI: 10.1002/gme2.488

Murthy, Y. S., Chodisetty, R. S. C. M., Chakravorty, C., & Sai, K. G. (2024). AI-Powered Learning Revolutionizing Smart Education With Personalized Learning Styles. *Advances in Educational Technologies and Instructional Design Book Series*, 191–212. https://doi.org/DOI: 10.4018/979-8-3693-8151-9.ch007

Muslimah, M., & Arliansyah, A. (2024). Gamification Method in Increasing Motivation towards Studying the Al-Quran and Islamic Perspectives. *Jurnal Pendidikan Agama Islam*, *4*(1), 181–190.

Musolin, M. H., Serour, R. O. H., Siregar, M., Hamid, S. A., Ismail, A., Huda, M., & Rohim, M. A. (2024). Developing Personalised Islamic Learning in Digital Age: Pedagogical and Technological Integration for Open Learning Resources (OLR). In X.-S. Yang, R. S. Sherratt, N. Dey, & A. Joshi (Eds.), *Proceedings of Ninth International Congress on Information and Communication Technology. ICICT 2024 2024. Lecture Notes in Networks and Systems* (Vol. 1004, pp. 11–25). Springer Nature Singapore. DOI: 10.1007/978-981-97-3305-7_2

Mutawa, A. M., & Sruthi, S. (2024). Enhancing Human-Computer Interaction in Online Education: A Machine Learning Approach to Predicting Student Emotion and Satisfaction. *International Journal of Human-Computer Interaction*, *40*(24), 1–17. DOI: 10.1080/10447318.2023.2291611

Nam, J. (2023). 56% of college students have used ai on assignments or exams. *Best Colleges*. https://www.bestcolleges.com/research/most-college-students-have-used-ai-survey/

Narayan, J., & Naidu, S. (2024). A new contextual and comprehensive application of the UTAUT2 model post-Covid-19 pandemic in higher education. *Higher Education Quarterly*, *78*(1), 47–77. DOI: 10.1111/hequ.12441

Nedungadi, P., Tang, K.-Y., & Raman, R. (2024). The transformative power of generative artificial intelligence for achieving the sustainable development goal of quality education. *Sustainability (Basel)*, *16*(22), 9779. DOI: 10.3390/su16229779

Nguyen, M., Le, T., & Tran, P. (2023). Evaluating dialect-sensitive AI for literacy development in Vietnam. *Asia Pacific Journal of Education*, *43*(1), 87–104. DOI: 10.1080/02188791.2022.2136019

Nguyen, T. H., & García, P. (2024). Culturally responsive AI in diverse classrooms: A design-based approach. *Computers & Education*, *212*, 104948. Advance online publication. DOI: 10.1016/j.compedu.2023.104948

Nguyen, T. H., Ramos, M. J., & Chen, L. (2022). From chalkboards to chatbots: A century of resistance in educational technology. *Educational Review*, *74*(3), 310–329. DOI: 10.1080/00131911.2021.1987654

Nguyen, T. H., Ramos, M. J., & Santos, E. P. (2023). Digital literacy, professional development, and AI integration: A cross-country study. *Educational Technology Research and Development*, *71*(5), 1135–1154. DOI: 10.1007/s11423-023-10145-2

Ng, W. (2012). Can we teach digital natives digital literacy? *Computers & Education*, *59*(3), 1065–1078. DOI: 10.1016/j.compedu.2012.04.016

Nieto-Rodriguez, A., & Vargas, R. V. (2023, February 2). How AI will transform project management. *Harvard Business Review*. https://hbr.org/2023/02/how-ai-will-transform-project-management

No, A. (2023). Ministry of Education. Response to Recommendation (2193).

Norton, J. (2024). Navigating the AI Policy Landscape. *Advances in Library and Information Science (ALIS) Book Series*, 109–130. https://doi.org/DOI: 10.4018/979-8-3693-3053-1.ch006

Nyunt, G., Koo, K., Witkowsky, P., Andino, M., Lin, X., Chan, R. Y., Sharma, S., & Bista, K. (Eds.). (2024). *ChatGPT and global higher education: Using artificial intelligence in teaching and learning, international student identities and mental well-being: Beyond the single story*. Star Scholar. https://scholar.harvard.edu/sites/scholar.harvard.edu/files/roychan/files/ebook_chatgpt_and_global_higher_education.pdf

Ocen, S., Elasu, J., Aarakit, S. M., & Olupot, C. (2025). Artificial intelligence in higher education institutions: Review of innovations, opportunities and challenges. *Frontiers in Education*, *10*, 1530247. Advance online publication. DOI: 10.3389/feduc.2025.1530247

OECD. (2019). *Getting skills right: Future-ready adult learning systems*. OECD Publishing., DOI: 10.1787/9789264311756-

OECD. (2023). *AI and the future of skills*. https://www.oecd.org/education/ai-future-skills/

Ohri, G. K. (2024). Advancing educational equity: The role of generative ai in creating accessible and inclusive higher education. *International Journal of Computer Engineering and Technology*, *15*(6), 1806–1815. DOI: 10.34218/IJCET_15_06_154

Onesi-Ozigagun, O., Ololade, Y. J., Eyo-Udo, N. L., & Ogundipe, D. O. (2024). Revolutionizing education through AI: A comprehensive review of enhancing learning experiences. *International Journal of Applied Research in Social Sciences*, *6*(4), 589–607. DOI: 10.51594/ijarss.v6i4.1011

Owoc, M. L., Sawicka, A., & Weichbroth, P. (2021). Artificial Intelligence Technologies in Education: Benefits, Challenges and Strategies of Implementation. arXiv. Org. /arxiv.2102.09365DOI: 10.1007/978-3-030-85001-2_4

Owoc, M. L., Sawicka, A., & Weichbroth, P. (2021). Artificial intelligence technologies in education: Benefits, challenges and strategies of implementation. *Education and Information Technologies*, *26*(3), 3117–3147. DOI: 10.1007/s10639-021-10536-4

Oyedokun, T. T. (2024). Assistive Technology and Accessibility Tools in Enhancing Adaptive Education. *Advances in Educational Technologies and Instructional Design Book Series*, 125–162. https://doi.org/DOI: 10.4018/979-8-3693-8227-1.ch006

Pacheco-Mendoza, S., Guevara, C., Mayorga-Albán, A., & Fernández-Escobar, J. (2023). Artificial Intelligence in Higher Education: A Predictive Model for Academic Performance. *Education Sciences*, *13*(10), 990. DOI: 10.3390/educsci13100990

Pantelimon, F. V., Bologa, R., Toma, A., & Posedaru, B. S. (2021). The evolution of AI-driven educational systems during the COVID-19 pandemic. *Sustainability (Basel)*, *13*(23), 13501. DOI: 10.3390/su132313501

Paredes, J.L. & Victoriano, M.A.G. (2025). Students' knowledge and usage of artificial intelligence in higher education institutions. *Management, education & innovation review*, 2(1), 158-182. https://doi.org/DOI: 10.53378/meir.161

Park, H., & Choi, S. (2025). Human touch matters: Exploring educators' emotional labor in AI-infused pedagogy. *Educational Psychology Review*, *37*(1), 1–20. DOI: 10.1007/s10648-024-09951-4

Patel, R., & Singh, S. (2022). Community engagement and AI in rural India: Co-designing context-sensitive learning tools. *Education and Information Technologies*, *27*(1), 201–219. DOI: 10.1007/s10639-021-10657-3

Patil, V., & Deshpande, N. (2022). Psychological barriers and digital illiteracy: Understanding teachers' reluctance in AI adoption. *Journal of Educational Computing Research*, *60*(8), 1450–1472. DOI: 10.1177/07356331221091234

Paul, R., & Elder, L. (2014). *The miniature guide to critical thinking concepts and tools* (7th ed.). Foundation for Critical Thinking.

Peck, C., & Andersen, J. (2023). Algorithmic opacity and its impact on student wellbeing. *Journal of Educational Data Mining*, *15*(2), 45–67. DOI: 10.5281/zenodo.7590249

Petrescu, M.-A., Pop, E.-L., & Dan Mihoc, T. (2023). Students' interest in knowledge acquisition in Artificial Intelligence. *Procedia Computer Science*, *225*, 1028–1036. DOI: 10.1016/j.procs.2023.10.090

Piaget, J. (1952). *The origins of intelligence in children*. International Universities Press. DOI: 10.1037/11494-000

Ponterotto, J. G., & Ruckdeschel, D. E. (2007). An Overview of Coefficient Alpha and a Reliability Matrix for Estimating Adequacy of Internal Consistency Coefficients with Psychological Research Measures. *Perceptual and Motor Skills*, *105*(3), 997–1014. DOI: 10.2466/pms.105.3.997-1014 PMID: 18229554

Qiu, X., Alias, A., & Nasri, N. (2025). Attitude, intention, and the use of artificial intelligence among business management students in higher education institutions. *International Journal of Academic Research in Business & Social Sciences*, *15*(7). Advance online publication. DOI: 10.6007/IJARBSS/v15-i7/25621

Qudus, A. (2024, September 4). *Revolutionizing higher education with AI: Unlocking potential, addressing challenges, and forging future paths*. EasyChair Preprint. https://easychair.org/publications/preprint/P35C/open

Raehang, A., & Mustapa Ahmad, Muhammad Shaleh Assingkily. (2025). Integrating Artificial Intelligence into Madrasah Learning: A Mixed-Methods Study of Intelligent Media Development and Implementation. *Cendekiawan : Jurnal Pendidikan Dan Studi Keislaman*, *4*(1), 608–618. DOI: 10.61253/cendekiawan.v4i1.322

Raja, V., Rongala, S. A., Jayan, M., Dubeer, R., Sushma, S., & Shobha, D. (2024). A cross-sectional study of knowledge, perception and acceptance of artificial intelligence in healthcare among medical graduates in Bengaluru. *Future Healthcare Journal*, *11*, 100033. DOI: 10.1016/j.fhj.2024.100033

Rajki, Z., Dringó-Horváth, I., & Nagy, J. T. (2025). Artificial intelligence in higher education: Students' artificial intelligence use and its influencing factors. *Journal of University Teaching & Learning Practice*, *22*(2). Advance online publication. DOI: 10.53761/j0rebh67

Ralhan, P. (2024). Artificial Intelligence In Higher Studies: Use of Ai-Based Tools by University Students And Its Challenges. https://www.researchgate.net/publication/385127161

Ramirez, J. P., Obenza, D. M., Cuarte, R., & Mabayag, N. A. (2024). AI trust and attitudes toward AI of university students in the Philippines. *International Journal of Multidisciplinary Studies in Higher Education*, *1*(1), 22–36. DOI: 10.70847/586366

Rao, K., Smith, L., & Gonzalez, M. (2023). Interdisciplinary innovation hubs and AI in education: A US university model. *Educational Review*, *76*(4), 512–532. DOI: 10.1080/00131911.2022.2109874

Rapaka, A., Dharmadhikari, S. C., Kasat, K., Mohan, C. R., Chouhan, K., & Gupta, M. (2025). Revolutionizing learning– A journey into educational games with immersive and AI technologies. *Entertainment Computing*, *52*, 100809. DOI: 10.1016/j.entcom.2024.100809

Raquib, A., Channa, B., Zubair, T., & Qadir, J. (2022). Islamic virtue-based ethics for artificial intelligence. *Discover Artificial Intelligence*, *2*(1), 11. DOI: 10.1007/s44163-022-00028-2

Raza, Z., Tahir, Z., Qamar, S., & Manan, A. (2025, April). The role of AI in the education sector: Focusing on AI's adaptation, drawbacks, implications, trust, and ethical considerations. *Journal of Political Stability Archive*, *3*(2), 145–165. DOI: 10.63468/jpsa.3.2.08

Redecker, C. (2017). *European framework for the digital competence of educators: DigCompEdu*. Publications Office of the European Union., DOI: 10.2760/159770

Reid, L., Button, D., & Brommeyer, M. (2023). Challenging the Myth of the Digital Native: A Narrative Review. *Nursing Reports*, *13*(2), 573–600. DOI: 10.3390/nursrep13020052 PMID: 37092480

Reyes, R., Mariñas, J. M., Tacang, J. R., Asis, L. J. A., Sayman, J. M., Flores, C. C., & Sumatra, K. (2024). The relationship between attitude toward AI and AI literacy among Philippine university students. *International Journal of Multidisciplinary Studies in Higher Education*, *1*(1), 37–46. DOI: 10.70847/587958

Robinson, K. (2011). *Out of our minds: Learning to be creative* (2nd ed.). Capstone Publishing.

Rogers, E. M. (2003). *Diffusion of innovations* (5th ed.). Free Press.

Rojas Contreras, M., & Portilla Jaimes, J. O. (2024). *AI Ethics in the Fields of Education and Research: A Systematic Literature Review*. 1–6. https://doi.org/DOI: 10.1109/ICACIT62963.2024.10788651

Rony, M. K. K., Akter, K., Nesa, L., Islam, M. T., Johra, F. T., Akter, F., Uddin, M. J., Begum, J., Noor, M. A., Ahmad, S., Tanha, S. M., Khatun, M. T., Bala, S. D., & Parvin, M. R. (2024). Healthcare workers' knowledge and Attitudes regarding artificial intelligence adoption in healthcare: A cross-sectional study. *Heliyon*, *10*(23), e40775. DOI: 10.1016/j.heliyon.2024.e40775 PMID: 39691199

Roy, B., Ghosh, S., Sarkar, S. K., Sen, A., & Choudhury, N. (n.d.). *Implications of Artificial Intelligence for Special Education Technology*. https://doi.org/DOI: 10.4018/979-8-3693-5538-1.ch015

Saaida, M. B. E. (2023). AI-driven transformations in higher education: Opportunities and challenges. *Journal Name*, *5*(1), 29–36. DOI: 10.5281/zenodo.8164415

Sabki, A. A., & Hardaker, G. (2013). The madrasah concept of Islamic pedagogy. *Educational Review*, *65*(3), 342–356. DOI: 10.1080/00131911.2012.668873

Sahin, A., Imamoglu, G., Murat, M., & Ayyildiz, E. (2024). A holistic decision-making approach to assessing service quality in higher education institutions. *Socio-Economic Planning Sciences*, *92*, 101812. DOI: 10.1016/j.seps.2024.101812

Sajja, R., Sermet, Y., Cikmaz, M., Cwiertny, D., & Demir, I. (2024). Artificial Intelligence-Enabled Intelligent Assistant for Personalized and Adaptive Learning in Higher Education. *Information (Basel)*, *15*(10), 596. DOI: 10.3390/info15100596

Salim, M. A., & Aditya, R. B. (2025). Integration of Artificial Intelligence in Islamic Education: Trends, Methods, and Challenges in the Digital Era. *Journal of Modern Islamic Studies and Civilization*, *3*(01), 74–89. DOI: 10.59653/jmisc.v3i01.1368

Sambell, K., & Brown, S. (2023). Designing inclusive assessment: Participatory strategies in digitally mediated learning. *Assessment & Evaluation in Higher Education, 48*(4), 635–650. DOI: 10.1080/02602938.2022.2151033

Sánchez-Santamaría, J., & Ballester Vila, M. G. (2014). *Desarrollando el Éxito Educativo para Todos: Reflexiones, Propuestas y Retos Conceptuales en torno a la Equidad Educativa. 12*(2), 85–104. https://revistas.uam.es/index.php/reice/article/download/2857/3074

Santiago, P., & Gentry, L. (2022). Belief systems and the barriers to educational AI: A qualitative inquiry. *British Journal of Educational Technology, 53*(5), 1023–1040. DOI: 10.1111/bjet.13175

Santos, R., Villaceran, R., Rioflorido, J., & Paguiligan, D. (2024). Initial development and validation of a questionnaire for students' artificial intelligence knowledge in Education. *Cognizance Journal of Multidisciplinary Studies, 4*(5), 32–41. DOI: 10.47760/cognizance.2024.v04i05.003

Sato, E., Shyyan, V., Chauhan, S., & Christensen, L. (2024). Putting AI in fair: A framework for equity in AI-driven learner models and inclusive assessments. *Egitimde ve Psikolojide Ölçme ve Degerlendirme Dergisi, 15*(Special Issue), 263–281. DOI: 10.21031/epod.1526527

Sawahel, W. (2024, July 13). Education ministry announces AI-driven metaverse plan. *University World News*. https://www.universityworldnews.com/post.php?story=20240713095612336

Selwyn, N. (2019). *Should robots replace teachers? AI and the future of education*. Polity Press.

Selwyn, N., Eynon, R., & Bulfin, S. (2021). *The datafication of education: Critical questions for learning and technology*. Routledge.

Selwyn, N., Hillman, T., & Eynon, R. (2024). Algorithmic personalization and educational data justice. *Learning, Media and Technology, 49*(1), 12–27. DOI: 10.1080/17439884.2023.2252052

Selwyn, N., & Macgilchrist, F. (2021). Should robots replace teachers? AI and the future of education. *Learning, Media and Technology, 46*(3), 220–232. DOI: 10.1080/17439884.2021.1929934

Seo, K., Tang, J., Roll, I., Fels, S., & Yoon, D. (2021). The impact of artificial intelligence on learner– instructor interaction in online learning. *International Journal of Educational Technology in Higher Education, 18*(1), 54. Advance online publication. DOI: 10.1186/s41239-021-00292-9 PMID: 34778540

Shaeffer, S. (2019). Inclusive education: A prerequisite for equity and social justice. *Asia Pacific Education Review*, *20*(2), 181–192. DOI: 10.1007/s12564-019-09598-w

Shahzad, M. F., Xu, S., & Javed, I. (2024). ChatGPT awareness, acceptance, and adoption in higher education: The role of trust as a cornerstone. *International Journal of Educational Technology in Higher Education*, *21*(1), 46. Advance online publication. DOI: 10.1186/s41239-024-00478-x

Shams, R. A., Zowghi, D., & Bano, M. (2023). AI and the quest for diversity and inclusion: A systematic literature review. *AI and Ethics*, *5*(1), 411–438. DOI: 10.1007/s43681-023-00362-w

Siemens, G. (2021). Connectivism: Learning as network-creation. In *Teaching in a Digital Age: Guidelines for Designing Teaching and Learning* (2nd ed.). BCcampus. https://pressbooks.bccampus.ca/teachinginadigitalagev2

Singh, G., & Thakur, A. K. (2024). *AI in Education*. IGI Global., DOI: 10.4018/979-8-3693-2964-1.ch002

Sinha, K. K. (2022). Role of modern technology in teaching and learning the English language in Indian educational institutions. [IJELS]. *Indonesian Journal of English Language Studies*, *8*(2), 71–82. DOI: 10.24071/ijels.v8i2.4713

Slimani, N., & Jabal, K. (2023). Language Learning Platforms: Connecting the Dots around Rosetta Stone Platform. *European Journal of Education Studies*, *10*(7), 101–111.

Smith, J. B., & Pérez, D. (2023). Educator attitudes toward personal computers and screen-based instruction: A longitudinal analysis. *Computers in Education Journal*, *14*(1), 77–92. DOI: 10.5678/cej.2023.14107

Smuha, N. A. (2021). Beyond a human rights-based approach to AI governance. *Philosophy & Technology*, *34*(S1), 561–586. DOI: 10.1007/s13347-020-00403-w

Sposato, M. (2025). Artificial intelligence in educational leadership: A comprehensive taxonomy and future directions. *International Journal of Educational Technology in Higher Education*, *22*(1), 20. DOI: 10.1186/s41239-025-00517-1

Spulber, D., Amoretti, G., & Siri, A. (2024). The use of AI for Education in Third Age: The role of EU project. Geopolitical. *Social Security and Freedom Journal*, *7*(1), 49–64. DOI: 10.2478/gssfj-2024-0004

Standen, P. J., Brown, D. J., Taheri, M., Galvez Trigo, M. J., Boulton, H., Burton, A., Hallewell, M. J., Lathe, J. G., Shopland, N., Blanco Gonzalez, M. A., Kwiatkowska, G. M., Milli, E., Cobello, S., Mazzucato, A., Traversi, M., & Hortal, E. (2020). An evaluation of an adaptive learning system based on multimodal affect recognition for learners with intellectual disabilities. *British Journal of Educational Technology, 51*(5), 1748–1765. DOI: 10.1111/bjet.13010

Stoller, A. (2021). Traditional and critical mentoring. *Radical Teacher, 119*, 52–60. DOI: 10.5195/rt.2021.765

Strielkowski, W., Grebennikova, V., Lisovskiy, A., Rakhimova, G., & Vasileva, T. (2025). AI-driven adaptive learning for sustainable educational transformation. *Sustainable Development (Bradford), 33*(2), 1921–1947. DOI: 10.1002/sd.3221

Subhaktiyasa, P. G. (2024). PLS-SEM for multivariate analysis: A practical guide to educational research using SmartPLS. EduLine. *Journal of Education and Learning Innovation, 4*(3), 353–365.

Sublime, J., & Renna, I. (2024). Is ChatGPT massively used by students nowadays? A survey on the use of large language models such as ChatGPT in educational settings. arXiv preprint arXiv:2412.17486.

Sulistio, B., Ramadhan, A., Abdurachman, E., Zarlis, M., & Trisetyarso, A. (2024). The utilization of machine learning on studying Hadith in Islam: A systematic literature review. *Education and Information Technologies, 29*(5), 5381–5419. DOI: 10.1007/s10639-023-12008-9

Sun, L., Asmawi, A., Dong, H., & Zhang, X. (2024). Empowering Chinese undergraduates' business English writing: Unveiling the efficacy of DingTalk-Aided Problem-based language learning during Covid-19 period. *Education and Information Technologies, 29*(1), 239–271. DOI: 10.1007/s10639-023-12288-1

Taherdoost, H., & Madanchian, M. (2023). Artificial intelligence and sentiment analysis: A review in competitive research. *Computers, 12*(2), 37. DOI: 10.3390/computers12020037

Tahir, A., & Tahir, A. (2023, June). AI-driven Advancements in ESL Learner Autonomy: Investigating Student Attitudes Towards Virtual Assistant Usability. In *Linguistic Forum-. Journal of Linguistics, 5*(2), 50–56.

Tajik, A. (2025). Exploring the role of AI-driven dynamic writing platforms in improving EFL learners' writing skills and fostering their motivation.

Tamilmani, K., Rana, N. P., Wamba, S. F., & Dwivedi, R. (2021). The extended Unified Theory of Acceptance and Use of Technology (UTAUT2): A systematic literature review and theory evaluation. *International Journal of Information Management, 57*, 102269. DOI: 10.1016/j.ijinfomgt.2020.102269

Tan, A., & Chua, Y. (2024). Singapore's ethical AI framework in education: Policy, training, and trust. *Educational Policy, 38*(2), 265–283. DOI: 10.1177/0895904823123456

Tang, X., Yuan, Z., & Qu, S. (2025). Factors Influencing University Students' Behavioural Intention to Use Generative Artificial Intelligence for Educational Purposes Based on a Revised UTAUT2 Model. *Journal of Computer Assisted Learning, 41*(1), e13105. DOI: 10.1111/jcal.13105

Tapalova, O., & Zhiyenbayeva, N. (2022). Artificial Intelligence in Education: AIEd for Personalised Learning Pathways. *Electronic Journal of e-Learning, 20*(5), 639–653. DOI: 10.34190/ejel.20.5.2597

Tariq, M. U. (2024, May). AI-powered language translation for multilingual classrooms. In *Integrating generative AI in education to achieve sustainable development goals* (pp. 29–46). IGI Global., DOI: 10.4018/979-8-3693-2440-0.ch002

Taşkın, M. (2025). Artificial Intelligence in Personalized Education: Enhancing Learning Outcomes Through Adaptive Technologies and Data-Driven Insights. *Human-Computer Interaction, 8*(1), 173. DOI: 10.62802/ygye0506

Thirunagalingam, A., & Selvakumar, P. (2025). Application of Automation and Robotics in the Oil and Gas Industry. In Abdullayev, V., & Khang, A. (Eds.), *Revolutionizing AI and Robotics in the Oil and Gas Industry* (pp. 229–244). IGI Global Scientific Publishing., DOI: 10.4018/979-8-3693-8156-4.ch011

Thoriquttyas, T., & Rohmawati, N. (2024). How Far Artificial Intelligence influenced Mu'allim, Murabbi, and Mudarris? Transhumanism and Diffusion of Innovation Theory's Perspective. *Suhuf: International Journal of Islamic Studies, 36*(2), 139–154. DOI: 10.23917/suhuf.v36i2.6302

Torraco, R. J. (2005). Writing integrative literature reviews: Guidelines and examples. *Human Resource Development Review, 4*(3), 356–367. DOI: 10.1177/1534484305278283

Tortella, F., Palese, A., Turolla, A., Castellini, G., Pillastrini, P., Landuzzi, M. G., Cook, C., Galeoto, G., Giovannico, G., Rodeghiero, L., Gianola, S., & Rossettini, G. (2025). Knowledge and use, perceptions of benefits and limitations of artificial intelligence chatbots among Italian physiotherapy students: A cross-sectional national study. *BMC Medical Education*, *25*(1), 572. DOI: 10.1186/s12909-025-07176-w PMID: 40251635

Tsou, C. (2023). Implementing artificial intelligence (AI) in higher education: A narrative literature review. *Conestoga College*. https://www.researchgate.net/publication/376553922_Implementing_Artificial_Intelligence_AI_in_Higher_Education_A_Narrative_Literature_Review

UNESCO International Institute for Higher Education in Latin America and the Caribbean. (2023). *Harnessing the era of artificial intelligence in higher education: A primer for higher education stakeholders* (ED/HE/IESALC/IP/2023/27). https://doi.org/DOI: 10.5281/zenodo.1234567

UNESCO. (2021). *Guidance for generative AI in education and research*. https://unesdoc.unesco.org/ark:/48223/pf0000386943

University of Helsinki. (2022). *Elements of AI*. https://www.elementsofai.com/

University World News. (2025, February 28). AI use by students surges to 92%, second HEPI survey finds. University World News. https://www.universityworldnews.com/post.php?story=20250228175423255

Upadhyaya, A. N., Debnath, P., Rani, P., Selvakumar, P., Manjunath, T. C., & Bhattacharya, S. (2025). AI-Based Disaster Prediction and Early Warning Systems. In Mobo, F. (Ed.), *AI and Emerging Technologies for Emergency Response and Smart Cities* (pp. 55–74). IGI Global Scientific Publishing., DOI: 10.4018/979-8-3693-9770-1.ch003

Varona, D., & Suarez, J. L. (2022). Discrimination, bias, fairness, and trustworthy AI. *Applied Sciences (Basel, Switzerland)*, *12*(12), 5826. DOI: 10.3390/app12125826

Vashishth, T. K., Sharma, V., Sharma, K. K., Kumar, B., Panwar, R., Chaudhary, S. (2024). "AI-driven learning analytics for personalized feedback and assessment in higher education." In Using Traditional Design Methods to Enhance AI-Driven Decision Making, IGI Global, 25–42. DOI: DOI: 10.4018/979-8-3693-0639-0.ch009

Vashishth, T. K., Sharma, V., Sharma, K. K., & Kumar, B. (2024). Enhancing Literacy Education in Higher Institutions With AI Opportunities and Challenges. In *AI-Enhanced Teaching Methods* (pp. 198–215). IGI Global., DOI: 10.4018/979-8-3693-2728-9.ch009

Venkatesh, V., Morris, M. G., Davis, G. B., and Davis, F. D. (2003). User Acceptance of Information Technology: Toward a Unified View, MIS Quarterly (27:3), pp. 42

Vieriu, A. M., & Petrea, G. (2025). The Impact of Artificial Intelligence (AI) on Students' Academic Development. *Education Sciences*, *15*(3), 343. DOI: 10.3390/educsci15030343

Viglia, G., Zaefarian, G., & Ulqinaku, A. (2021). How to design good experiments in marketing: Types, examples, and methods. *Industrial Marketing Management*, *98*, 193–206. DOI: 10.1016/j.indmarman.2021.08.007

Vootukuri, N. S. R., & Jyothi, J. (2024). Harnessing the potential of AI applications in Education: Opportunities, challenges, and future directions. *Magna Scientia Advanced Research and Reviews*, *11*(2), 405–410. DOI: 10.30574/msarr.2024.11.2.0139

Vygotsky, L. S. (1978). *Mind in society: The development of higher psychological processes*. Harvard University Press.

Wang, H., Chen, Y., & Zhang, L. (2024). Immersive AI-enhanced learning environments in rural settings: Challenges and innovations. *Journal of Educational Technology & Society*, *27*(1), 88–103. DOI: 10.30191/ETS.2024.27.1.06

Wang, S., Christensen, C., Cui, W., Tong, R., Yarnall, L., Shear, L., & Feng, M. (2020). When adaptive learning is effective learning: Comparison of an adaptive learning system to teacher-led instruction. *Interactive Learning Environments*, *31*(2), 793–803. DOI: 10.1080/10494820.2020.1808794

Wang, X., Huang, R., Sommer, M., Pei, B., Shidfar, P., Rehman, M. S., Ritzhaupt, A. D., & Martin, F. (2024). The Efficacy of Artificial Intelligence-Enabled Adaptive Learning Systems From 2010 to 2022 on Learner Outcomes: A Meta-Analysis. *Journal of Educational Computing Research*, *62*(6), 1348–1383. DOI: 10.1177/07356331241240459

Wang, Y., Li, Y., Cao, H., Xiong, M., Shugart, Y. Y., & Li, J. (2015). Efficient test for nonlinear dependence of two continuous variables. *BMC Bioinformatics*, *16*(1), 260. Advance online publication. DOI: 10.1186/s12859-015-0697-7 PMID: 26283601

Watanabe, A. (2024). Have Courage to Use Your Own Mind, with or without AI: The Relevance of Kant's Enlightenment to Higher Education in the Age of Artificial Intelligence. Electronic Journal of e-Learning, v22 n2 p46-58 2024. DOI: 10.34190/ejel.21.5.3229

West, S. M., Whittaker, M., & Crawford, K. (2019). Discriminating systems: Gender, race, and power in AI. *AI Now Institute*. https://ainowinstitute.org/discriminatingsystems.html

Williamson, B. (2023). Algorithmic governance and educational platform personalization. *Learning, Media and Technology*, *48*(1), 17–35. DOI: 10.1080/17439884.2022.2115462

Williamson, B., & Eynon, R. (2020). Historical threads, missing links, and future directions in AI in education. *Learning, Media and Technology*, *45*(3), 223–235. DOI: 10.1080/17439884.2020.1798995

Williamson, B., & Eynon, R. (2021). Algorithms and education governance: Exploring how digital data is reshaping policy. *Journal of Education Policy*, *36*(1), 1–23. DOI: 10.1080/02680939.2019.1672895

Wiranto, E. B., & Suwartini, S. (2023). Artificial Intelligence and Trustworthy Principles in Global Islamic Education. *Ushuluddin International Conference (USICON)*, *6*, 64–87.

Woolf, B. P. (2010). *Building intelligent interactive tutors: Student-centered strategies for revolutionizing e-learning*. Morgan Kaufmann.

World Bank. (2024). *AI revolution in education - brief no.1*. World Bank Document.

World Economic Forum. (2020). *The future of jobs report 2020*. https://www.weforum.org/reports/the-future-of-jobs-report-2020

World Economic Forum. (2024). How public-private partnerships can ensure ethical, sustainable and inclusive AI development. Retrieved from weforum.org

Xu, P., & Ouyang, Y. (2024). Artificial intelligence in education: A systematic literature review. *Expert Systems with Applications*, *222*, 121345. Advance online publication. DOI: 10.1016/j.eswa.2023.121345

Yadav, S. (2024). Advancing Education With AI-Driven Education for Diverse Learners. *Advances in Educational Technologies and Instructional Design Book Series*, 49–80. https://doi.org/DOI: 10.4018/979-8-3693-6130-6.ch003

Yilmaz, F. G. K., Yilmaz, R., & Ceylan, M. (2023). Generative Artificial Intelligence Acceptance Scale: A Validity and Reliability study. *International Journal of Human-Computer Interaction*, •••, 1–13. DOI: 10.1080/10447318.2023.2288730

Young, J. (2024). The Rise of Artificial Intelligence in Education. *International Journal of Innovative Research and Development*. Advance online publication. DOI: 10.24940/ijird/2024/v13/i2/FEB24019

Yu, H., Guo, Y., Yang, H., Zhang, W., & Dong, Y. (2025). Can ChatGPT Revolutionize Language Learning? Unveiling the Power of AI in Multilingual Education Through User Insights and Pedagogical Impact. *European Journal of Education, 60*(1), e12749. DOI: 10.1111/ejed.12749

Yu, J. H., Chauhan, D., Iqbal, R. A., & Yeoh, E. (2024). Mapping academic perspectives on AI in education: Trends, challenges, and sentiments in educational research (2018–2024). *Educational Technology Research and Development, 72*, 449–483. DOI: 10.1007/s11423-024-10425-2

Zajko, M. (2022). Artificial intelligence, algorithms, and social inequality: Sociological contributions to contemporary debates. *Sociology Compass, 16*(3), e12962. DOI: 10.1111/soc4.12962

Zawacki-Richter, O., Marín, V. I., Bond, M., & Gouverneur, F. (2019). Systematic review of research on artificial intelligence applications in higher education – where are the educators? *International Journal of Educational Technology in Higher Education, 16*(1), 39. Advance online publication. DOI: 10.1186/s41239-019-0171-0

Zawacki-Richter, O., Marín, V. I., Bond, M., & Gouverneur, F. (2022). Systematic review of research on artificial intelligence applications in higher education: Learning, assessment, and administration. *International Journal of Educational Technology in Higher Education, 19*, 21. DOI: 10.1186/s41239-022-00326-w

Zhai, X., Chu, X., Chai, C. S., Jong, M. S. Y., Istenic, A., Spector, M., Liu, J., Yuan, J., & Li, Y. (2021). A Review of Artificial Intelligence (AI) in Education from 2010 to 2020. Complexity, 2021(1). DOI: 10.1155/2021/8812542

Zhang, L., & Xu, J. (2024). The paradox of self-efficacy and technological dependence: Unraveling generative AI's impact on university students' task completion. *The Internet and Higher Education, 65*, 100978. DOI: 10.1016/j.iheduc.2024.100978

Zhang, Y., Wang, X., & Li, H. (2023). Designing culturally grounded immersive learning for indigenous learners. *International Review of Research in Open and Distance Learning, 24*(2), 65–83. DOI: 10.19173/irrodl.v24i2.7106

Zhang, Y., & Zhou, L. (2025). Five-step ethical framework for large-language-model-based educational tools. *Education and Information Technologies, 30*(3), 567–589. DOI: 10.1007/s10639-025-13512-0

Zhou, X., Zhang, J., & Chan, C. K. Y. (2024). Unveiling students' experiences and perceptions of artificial intelligence usage in higher education. *Journal of University Teaching & Learning Practice, 21*(6), 6. Advance online publication. DOI: 10.53761/xzjprb23

Zhumazhan, B., Zhumadilova, M. B., & Abdykerimova, E. (2024). The future of artificial intelligence in inclusive education. *Yessenov Science Journal*, *48*(3), 63–70. DOI: 10.56525/AMWI6491

Zhu, X., Zhao, Y., & Li, R. (2023). Policy lag in digital education reform: A global survey of teacher readiness and institutional innovation. *Computers & Education*, *191*, 104632. DOI: 10.1016/j.compedu.2023.104632

Zong, Y., & Yang, L. (2025). How AI-Enhanced Social–Emotional Learning Framework Transforms EFL Students' Engagement and Emotional Well-Being. *European Journal of Education*, *60*(1), e12925. DOI: 10.1111/ejed.12925

# About the Contributors

**Raed Awashreh** is a seasoned academic and consultant with a distinguished career spanning academia, government, and industry across the Middle East. Since 2004, he has been engaged in teaching and educational development, serving as a faculty member, professor, director, consultant, and advisor. His areas of expertise include strategic planning, educational development, public policy, leadership, and human resource management. Dr. Awashreh has made significant contributions to curriculum design, policy formulation, and organizational development, with professional experience in Palestine, the United Arab Emirates, Oman, and Saudi Arabia. He holds a Ph.D. from Flinders University, which is ranked among the top 2% of universities worldwide.

***

**Mussa S Abubakari**, PhD, is an enthusiastic educational technology researcher and associate researcher with the Dig Connectivity Research Laboratory (DCRLab) in Kampala, Uganda, since 2024. He's an instructor in the Department of Physics and Mathematics at Kondoa Islamic Secondary School, Tanzania. He has a PhD in Educational Technology from Sultan Hassanal Bolkiah Institute of Education, Universiti Brunei Darussalam, and graduated in April 2025. Dr. Mussa obtained a Master of Education degree in Electronics and Informatics Engineering at Yogyakarta State University, Indonesia, in July 2021. He obtained his BSc. in Telecommunications Engineering at the University of Dodoma in June 2016. His academic and research interests include educational technology, technology-enhanced learning, technology acceptance, open and distance learning, generative AI, and digital competence, among others. He has over 15 journal articles published in internationally reputable journals, over seven book chapters, and papers presented at international conferences.

**Nilesh Anute** is an Associate Professor at Sri Balaji University, Pune, a prestigious institution known for its focus on academic excellence and industry-oriented education. With extensive experience in teaching and research, Dr. Anute plays a pivotal role in mentoring students and contributing to the advancement of knowledge in his field. His dedication to academic growth and professional development makes him a valuable asset to the university and the wider academic community.

**Andi Asrifan**, S.Pd., M.Pd. is a senior lecturer in the Doctoral Program in English Language Education at the Graduate School of Universitas Negeri Makassar (UNM), Indonesia. With a Doctor of Education in English Language Education, he has demonstrated a consistent commitment to advancing research in English as a Foreign Language (EFL), digital pedagogy, and the integration of artificial intelligence (AI) in language instruction. Dr. Asrifan previously served as Head of the Institute for Cooperation and International Affairs at Universitas Muhammadiyah Sidenreng Rappang and continues to collaborate across academic institutions, both nationally and internationally, actively. Over the past two years, Dr. Asrifan has led several research initiatives focused on AI-driven curriculum development, bilingual education in Southeast Asia, and digital parenting in urban Indonesia. He is frequently invited as a keynote speaker at international conferences and serves as a reviewer and editorial board member for various Scopus-indexed journals. His publications have appeared in high-impact outlets and span the disciplines of education, linguistics, and cultural studies.

**Janine Wynnona P. Cac**, born on December 24, 2002, in Bacoor, Cavite, is a BS Business Management major in Human Resource Management student at Cavite State University. She completed her basic education in Saudi Arabia and at Benedictine Institute of Learning.

**John Michael Colin M. Corpuz** is a graduate of Cavite State University, Philippines, under the Bachelor of Science in International Studies, majoring in European Studies. His research interests focus on international studies, the circular economy, maritime studies, sustainable development goals (SDGs), global governance, international trade, and other social science-related fields.

**Jaysi Tanguilan Corpuz** is a licensed professional teacher and an Associate Professor at Cavite State University, Philippines. He holds a Ph.D. in Community Development, a Master's degree in Business Administration, and a Bachelor's degree in Management. He is an active member and officer of various professional organizations focused on instruction and research. Additionally, he has published research papers in Scopus/Web of Science and other international peer-reviewed journals. His research interests include management, business administration, marine social sciences, agribusiness management, entrepreneurship, extension education, community development, and other social science-related fields.

**Rose Marian R. Cubacub**, born on March 25, 2003, in Imus, Cavite, is a BS Business Management major in Human Resource Management student at Cavite State University. She completed her basic education in Cavite, including senior high at Benedictine Institute of Learning.

**Deepak. D**, an academician of two years old, with teaching experience in the areas of taxation, accounting, and IFRS. He has expertise in academic publishing, research content writing, coaching, teaching, editing, and analytical abilities. He possesses a PhD from JAIN (Deemed To Be University) in the School of Commerce. He has participated in a number of FDPs, workshops, seminars, and conferences. He as published more than 10 research paper in different UGC Care journal, web of science, Scopus.

**Maria Cristina L. Desepida**, born on March 22, 1977, in Manila, is a faculty member at Cavite State University in Indang, Cavite, affiliated with the College of Economics, Management, and Development Studies. She obtained a PhD in Business Administration from De La Salle University-Dasmarinas, Cavite in September 2023.

**Devaki V** serves as an Assistant Professor at the Department of Education (SASHE), SASTRA Deemed to be University, Thanjavur. She holds a Master of Science in Physics from Alagappa University, Karaikudi, graduating with the distinction of second rank in the university. Additionally, she completed her Master of Education at Sri Sarada College of Education, Salem, Tamil Nadu. She qualified for the position of Assistant Professor in Physics, having successfully cleared the Tamil Nadu State Eligibility Test and also passed the Central Teacher Eligibility Test. She is currently pursuing her doctoral studies in the Department of Education at Bharathidasan University, Tiruchirappalli. Her research interests encompass metacognition, neurocognition, the pedagogy of science, and experiential learning.

**El Mehdi El Hamydy** is a faculty member in the Department of English Studies at the Faculty of Education, Boulevard Mohammed Ben Abdellah Regragui, Rabat, Morocco.

**Shyam Fardale** is affiliated with the Department of Management at DMIMS, a well-regarded institution located in Nagpur, Maharashtra. With a strong academic and professional background, he contributes to the field of management through both teaching and research. Based in the vibrant city of Nagpur, Shyam plays an active role in shaping future leaders in business and management.

**Princess M. Feliciano** is an Assistant Professor II at Cavite State University, specializing in Financial Management under the College of Economics, Management, and Development Studies. Actively engaged in an externally funded project as Project Staff II and involved in various research initiatives focused on community-related development. Passionate about entrepreneurship while embracing the dynamic and fulfilling role of teaching.

**Kiara Naomi G. Flores**, born on July 19, 2003, in Manila, is a BS Business Management major in Human Resource Management student at Cavite State University. She completed her basic education in Cavite, including senior high at Benedictine Institute of Learning.

**Purushotham H C** is an Assistant Professor in the School of Commerce at Jain (Deemed-to-be University), Bengaluru, India. He holds a Master's degree in Commerce and is pursuing a Ph.D. in the area of Marketing. His academic interests include digital marketing, branding strategies, knowledge management, and event management education. Mr. Purushotham has presented and published several research papers in national and international journals and conferences. He actively guides undergraduate research and has contributed to curriculum development and experiential learning practices. He has served as a reviewer and editorial board member for reputed academic journals. His current research focuses on the role of social media in SME brand transformation. Mr. Purushotham is also involved in academic-industry collaborations, training programs, and student development initiatives.

**Hassiba Almi** is an Associate Professor and Vice Head of the Department of Economic Sciences at Badji Mokhtar University, Annaba. She specializes in insurance economics, digital transformation, Islamic finance, and sustainable development. She holds a Ph.D. in Insurance Economics from the University of Blida 2 (2021) and has extensive teaching and research experience. Dr. Almi has taught various economics and business-related courses and has published research on fintech, insurance, corporate social responsibility, and digital marketing. She actively participates in national and international conferences, and her ongoing research focuses on economic policy, insurance, and the impact of financial technology on economic growth.

**Isumarni**, S.Pd., M.Pd., is a dedicated lecturer in the English Education Program at Universitas Muhammadiyah Sidenreng Rappang (UMS), South Sulawesi,

Indonesia. She earned her Bachelor's degree in English Education from Universitas Negeri Makassar (UNM) in 2012 and continued her academic journey by completing a Master's degree in English Education at the UNM Graduate Program in 2016. Born in Sandakan, Malaysia, Isumarni brings a cross-cultural perspective to her work in language education. With a strong commitment to advancing English language teaching, she actively engages in teaching, academic writing, and educational research. Her interests span curriculum development, instructional strategies, and educational innovation in rural and multicultural contexts. In addition to her academic career, Isumarni is also an entrepreneur, balancing her professional responsibilities with business ventures. Her work reflects a passion for empowering students and educators through thoughtful pedagogy and research-driven practices. She continues to contribute to academic discourse by writing educational books and participating in scholarly collaborations. Isumarni's multidisciplinary engagement positions her as a proactive educator and a role model for aspiring teachers in the region.

**Sowmya K.** (Krishna) has been an Assistant Professor in Electronics and Communication Engineering at ACET, Bangalore, since March 2025. Holding an MBA in Human Resource Management, she combines technical and managerial expertise with four years' industry experience. She is passionate about innovative, student-centered teaching and mentoring.

**G. Kalaiyarasan** is a Senior Professor and Head of the Department of Education at Alagappa University, Karaikudi, Tamil Nadu, India. With an extensive academic and research career spanning over 29 years in teaching and 24 years in research, he has made significant contributions to the field of education. He has supervised 15 Ph.D. scholars and 76 M.Phil. students, with more than 250 publications to his credit, including articles in Scopus and UGC CARE journals. Dr. Kalaiyarasan has played important roles in various capacities at more than 50 national and international conferences. He has been actively involved in various administrative roles, such as Dean of the Faculty of Education, Chairperson of the School of Education, and Director of the Education Campus at Alagappa University. His leadership and commitment to education have had a profound impact on the academic community.

**Asma Shahid Kazi** is an Associate Professor and Chairperson of the Department of Elementary and Teacher Education at Lahore College for Women University (LCWU), Pakistan. With over a decade of experience in teacher education, her research focuses on English language learning, blended learning, STEAM pedagogy, and teacher professional development. Dr. Kazi has presented her work at various international conferences and has numerous publications in esteemed journals. She actively contributes to enhancing teaching practices and curriculum development, aiming to foster inclusive and effective learning environments.

**Aysha Khalil** is an Assistant Professor of Education at Lahore College for Women University (LCWU), Pakistan. Her research focuses on digital education, artificial intelligence in teaching and learning, immersive technologies, and the educational metaverse. She holds a Postdoctoral Certificate in Digital Education and is actively engaged in advancing the intersection of pedagogy and emerging technologies. Dr. Khalil has presented her work at several prestigious international conferences and has published extensively in peer-reviewed, high-impact journals. Her scholarship emphasizes inclusive, equity-driven educational innovation, with a strong commitment to shaping future-ready teacher education systems. She also contributes to academic peer review and regularly collaborates with scholars across interdisciplinary fields related to educational technology and reform.

**Pothu Lavanya** is currently serving as Associate Professor and Head, Department of Education at Sri Sathya Sai Institute of Higher Learning (SSSIHL). She has been associated with the Institute for over 18 years, and has been leading the Department since 2018. She holds a Ph.D. in Education and has consistently contributed to the advancement of teacher education through academic, administrative, and research engagements. Her areas of expertise include Pedagogy of Mathematics, Knowledge and Curriculum, Assessment, Information and Communication Technology in Education, and Yoga Education. She has published research articles in UGC-CARE listed and peer-reviewed journals, contributed chapters to edited volumes, and presented papers at various national and international conferences. She is currently guiding three research scholars in the field of Education. Deeply committed to the vision of integral and value-based education, Dr. Lavanya strives to foster holistic development in future educators—balancing academic rigor with ethical and spiritual growth. Her academic pursuits are driven by a strong belief in nurturing reflective, competent, and socially responsible teachers.

**Pavendhan Madhivanan** is a faculty member in the Department of Physics at Aditya College of Engineering and Technology.

**Mahammad Ali Sunkesula** is a PGT-Physics at AP Model School and Jr. College, Amarapuram, Sri Sathya Sai District, Andhra Pradesh. He holds multiple Master's degrees in Philosophy, Physics, Telugu, and Education from various universities in Andhra Pradesh. He earned his Master of Philosophy in Education from Periyar University, Salem, Tamil Nadu, and his Doctoral research degree in Philosophy of Education from Dravidian University, Kuppam, under the expert guidance of Prof. Balaganapathi Devarakonda. Dr. Mahammad Ali has a rich and diverse experience in academic writing, teaching, translation, statistical analysis, and research. He has worked as a Junior Linguist and Project Fellow in notable projects such as ILCI and UGC. This experience has enabled him to author, co-author, and edit 17 books/reference materials and 10 research papers. He also completed Post-Doctoral research at Dr. BR Ambedkar Open University, Hyderabad, Telangana, under the guidance of Prof. MTV Nagaraju. Prior to his current role, he served as an Assistant Professor and Principal in various education colleges across five Indian states.

**Mouad Malmous** is a faculty member in the Department of English Studies, Faculty of Letters and Human Sciences, Ben M'Sik, Morocco.

**T.C. Manjunath** was born on 6th February 1967. He did his BE from RV College of Engg. in 1989, ME in Robotics & Automation from LD College of Engg. in 1992 with First Rank and PhD in Systems & Control Engg. from IIT Bombay in the year 2007. He is currently working as the Dean Research R D and as Professor in the Dept. of Computer Science & Engineering with specialization in IoT, Cyber Security & Blockchain Technology in Rajarajeswari College of Engineering, Bengaluru, Karnataka. He has completed B.E. Degree from R.V. College of Engg., M.E. Govt.'s LD College of Engg., Gujarat Univ., Ahmedabad in First Rank and Ph.D. in Systems and Control Engineering from the Indian Institute of Technology Bombay IIT Bombay He has got a teaching academic, research and administrative experience of more than 35+ years 10 years as Principal, 8 years as HoD rest as faculty and has published more than 1200+ research papers in various national & international journals and conferences, with 175+ patents, 25 book-chapters, 25 awards and also published 25 text books in various field of science, engineering and technology, completed projects worth Rs. 9 Crores till date apart from guiding 10 PhD scholars. He is a member of 30 Professional Society Chapters and is a fellow of IE, IETE, AMIEE and a chartered engineer. He got the best research scholar award in 2006 in IIT Bombay amongst all the research scholars of the institute. He has got 10 awards in academics and research activities.

**Froilan Delute Mobo** is an internationally recognized researcher, educator, and leader with over 14 years of service at the Philippine Merchant Marine Academy (PMMA), where he currently serves as a full Professor II. Rising through the ranks from Instructor 1 to his current position in March 2024, he has become a respected authority in education and public administration. Dr. Mobo holds a Ph.D. in Development Education from Central Luzon State University and a Doctorate in Public Administration from Urdaneta City University. He has also earned advanced degrees in Computer Science, Business Administration, and Social Studies

Education, with ongoing studies in Social Studies Education at Bicol University. A prolific researcher, Dr. Mobo has authored 123 publications with 282 citations in Scopus and ACI, making him the top scientist from PMMA in Education and Educational Technology. His renowned study, "The Impact of Video Conferencing Platforms in All Educational Sectors Amidst the COVID-19 Pandemic," has influenced global educational practices.

**P. Selvakumar** is currently an Associate Professor in the Department of Science and Humanities at Nehru Institute of Technology, Coimbatore, Tamil Nadu, India. Prior to joining Nehru Institute of Technology, he held positions as an Assistant Professor in the Department of Science and Humanities various engineering colleges in Coimbatore, Tamil Nadu, India, spanning from 2011 to 2023. Dr.P. Selvakumar's academic and research interests lie primarily in the field of phytochemistry. He has made significant contributions to his field, with an impressive record that includes 30 journal publications, 12 patents, and 20 conference papers. Additionally, he has organized 5 seminars and conferences, further demonstrating his commitment to academic and scientific exchange. Throughout his career, Dr. P.Selvakumar has been recognized for his dedication and excellence in teaching, having been honored with several awards, including the Best Teacher Awards. He holds a prominent position in the academic community, contributing actively to research.

**R. Arun** is an Assistant Professor in the Department of Commerce at Jain (Deemed to be University), Bengaluru. Holding a Master of Commerce (Finance) from Mangalore University, Arun has demonstrated academic excellence through prestigious qualifications, including successful clearances of the UGC NET (Commerce) thrice and KSET once. Dedicated to fostering academic excellence, Arun is passionate about teaching and research, striving to inspire students and contribute valuable insights to the field of commerce and finance.

**S. Praveenkumar** is obtained B.E Computer Science and Engineering in Raja College of Engineering and Technology, Madurai Kamaraj University. He obtained her Master of Engg in College ofEngineering, Guindy, Anna University. And he obtained his Full time Research in the Department of Computer Science and Engineering, School of Computing, SRM Institutte of Science and Technology, Kattankulathur, Chennai, Tamilnadu. His area of interest is Machine learning, Deep learning, and Big Data analytics.

**Sohel Rana Sarkar**, an accomplished educator and scholar, has cleared NET-JRF and excelled at TMB University and Ramakrishna Mission Sikshanamandira. He has authored and edited 10 books and published 25 research papers and chapters, including Scopus and UGC-CARE. Currently, he is an Assistant Professor in

Education at Hingalganj Mahavidyalaya, West Bengal State University with research interests in education, AI and sustainability.

**Chinna Suresh** is an Assistant Professor in the Department of Education at the School of Arts, Sciences, Humanities, and Education (SASHE), SASTRA Deemed to be University, Thanjavur, Tamil Nadu, India. He earned his Ph.D. in Education from Sri Venkateswara University, Tirupati, Andhra Pradesh, in 2018, and his M.Sc. in Mathematics from Sri Krishnadevaraya University, Anantapur, Andhra Pradesh, in 2010. His research interests include ICT in Education, Mathematics Pedagogy, Gender Studies, and Teaching Strategies.

**Ragupathi T** received his B.E. degree in Computer Science and Engineering from Anna University, Tamil Nadu, in the year 2009 and the M.E. Master's degree in Computer Science and Engineering from Anna University, Tamil Nadu in the year 2011. He completed his Doctor of Philosophy in Computer Science and Engineering from Annamalai University, Chidambaram, Tamil Nadu, in the year 2023.He has more than 13.5 years of teaching experience. His research area includes Deep Learning, Machine Learning, IoT and web technology. He has published papers in several International Journals, international and national conferences

**Sirajun Tahura** is a distinguished author and educator known for her outstanding achievements in the field of academics. She achieved the rare distinction of "First class first" in both her B. Sc. and M. Sc. in Mathematics from the esteemed University of Calcutta. Her academic excellence was further acknowledged with the prestigious Gold medal from the University of Calcutta. Notably, Sirajun Tahura's dedication and expertise extend to her success in various examinations, including UGC NET-JRF. She has also made a significant impact in the world of research by publishing 1 Book, 4 Edited Books and so many research papers with national and international recognition. Presently, she holds the position of an Assistant Teacher (PG) in Mathematics and is concurrently pursuing her Ph.D. in Education at Alagappa University, India.

**Ibtasam Thakur** is an Assistant Professor at Lahore College for Women University, Pakistan, specializing in Special Education. She holds a Ph.D. in Special Education from the University of the Punjab and an M.Sc. in Psychology from Government College University, Lahore. Dr. Thakur is currently on a postdoctoral fellowship in the Department of Education Studies at the University of Warwick, UK. Her research focuses on moral education, inclusive education, and intellectual disabilities. She has authored over twenty-four publications in national and international journals and is a member of the Asia Pacific Network of Moral

Education. Dr. Thakur has also served as a visiting scholar at the University of Cambridge.

**V. Vaissnave** is obtained B.Tech Information Technology in PSR Engg college, Anna University. She obtained her Master of Engg in Anand Institute of Science and Technology, Anna University. And she obtained her Full time Research in the Department of Computer Science and Engineering, School of Computing, Kalasalingam Academy of Research and Education, Krishnankoil, Tamilnadu. Her area of interest is Machine learning, Deeplearning, and Natural Language Techniques.

**Sharath Kumar Y.** is an Assistant Professor in the Department of Commerce at St. Francis College, Karnataka, India.

**Said Zaidoune** is a faculty member in the Department of English Studies, Faculty of Letters and Human Sciences, Ben M'Sik, Casablanca, Casablanca-Settat, Morocco.

# Index

## A



## B

# C



# D



# E



# F



# G

**T**

www.ingramcontent.com/pod-product-compliance
Lightning Source LLC
LaVergne TN
LVHW062215200926
848484LV00006B/1399